WHERE THE JOBS ARE

Career Survival for Canadians in the New Global Economy

Second Edition

COLIN CAMPBELL
with CAROLE HOOD

MACFARLANE WALTER & ROSS
TORONTO

Macfarlane Walter & Ross
37A Hazelton Avenue
Toronto, Canada M5R 2E3

Canadian Cataloguing in Publication Data
Campbell, Colin, 1948 –
     Where the jobs are: career survival
for Canadians in the new global economy

2nd ed.
Includes bibliographical references and index.
ISBN 0–921912–26–9

1. Employment forecasting – Canada.   2. Labor
market – Canada.   3. Vocational guidance – Canada.
4. Occupations – Canada.
I. Title.

HD5728.C26 1997   331.12'3'0971   C97–930206–4

Macfarlane Walter & Ross acknowledges the support received
for its publishing program from the Canada Council's Project Grant/
Block Grant Program and from the Ontario Arts Council.

Printed and bound in Canada

To my mother,
Hazel Jean Tomlinson

CONTENTS

FOREWORD

Increasingly we seem to caught up in a whirlwind of change that is continually breaking down barriers, boundaries, and borders between work and home life, customers and companies, companies and suppliers, and even among countries. The differences among jobs are disappearing as everyone's job description becomes to help serve the changing needs of individual customers in whatever coordinated fashion is feasible at any given moment.

Ours is a world based no longer on individualistic competition, but more on a coevolutionary process that involves cooperation as well as conflict. It requires shared and competing visions, networks, alliances, negotiated roles, and the management of complex relationships. The need for constant innovation demands that renewal or creative destruction become an intrinsic part of our daily activities. Learning to live with uncertainty and change is the only way to thrive in such an environment.

Originally this book was written in order to answer the question "If I pursue the occupation area that best fits my temperament, values, interests, and abilities, where can I find work in this field?" Answering such a question in today's world requires that we act a bit like Wayne Gretzky and anticipate where the puck is going to be rather than focusing only on where it is at the moment. I have tried to provide the reader with the kind of understanding necessary to anticipate the ways in which the job market is likely to change so that it is possible to prepare in advance for possible eventualities.

Without a strong sense of direction it is harder to commit yourself to a somewhat vague future. By developing a good sense for the way things are changing, however, you will be able to figure out what is going on as the need arises, so that you can take full advantage of the opportunities as they unfold. Much like surfers, we need to learn how to ride the waves of change. Finding a series of jobs and managing a career are very dynamic activities that require quite a balancing act. That means keeping a focus on what is looming on the horizon as well as what lies immediately before you.

The career advice everyone receives more and more is peppered with words and phrases such as "entrepreneurship," "marketing yourself," "finding your niche," and "developing leading-edge skills." Such advice presupposes that you understand the business concepts and realities underlying these phrases. The modern job seeker needs to understand the fundamentals of economics and commerce in order to acquire even the slightest grasp of how the job situation is changing. In addition, a broad understanding of business areas has become a prerequisite to entrepreneurship, empowerment, and getting hired.

Understanding technological or political change by itself does not help one develop a sense of how today's many change factors are likely to interact or unfold. We need to understand how all the forces end up both determining the big picture and influencing the cameo roles we get to choose among in life. Just as casting is vital to the success of any movie or play, so it is in finding jobs and developing successful careers. Knowing where to look for employment and knowing what kinds of jobs are emerging are as vital as having a keen sense of the kind of work you would like to pursue. Like all happy marriages, the coevolution of careers, jobs, and employment opportunities requires a common direction if you are going to avoid working at cross purposes. Indeed, it is only by identifying emerging patterns that you can plan your career strategically. This book will give you a sense of where many trends are headed so that you can decide which direction is more likely to get you where you want to go.

Chapter 2, "The Age of the Entrepreneur," new in this edition, will provide you with some advice and resources if you, like a rapidly growing number of Canadians, decide to head down that road – or down the information highway. Internet addresses are provided where available.

This book seeks to answer a number of important questions: Which industry sectors will survive and thrive – and where in the world will they operate? What business practices and organizational structures will companies adopt in order to be competitive – and how can job hunters recognize these well-positioned companies? What are Canada's strengths and weaknesses in the global playing field? And what skills are required to develop a career strategy, market oneself to prospective employers, and anticipate changes in the workplace?

Given the technological advances that are driving and accelerating the economy, an individual's employment prospects will largely depend on his or her ability to plan strategically and to prepare for the opportunities that will arise from change. Use this book as a guide to a wide variety of traditional and new career markets at the company, industry, and country levels – and as a tool for taking control of your career and future prosperity.

Carole Hood is responsible for most of the revision of Chapter 4. Her conscientious research and assistance on the updating of much additional reference information are thankfully acknowledged. I am truly grateful for all of her help and her unflagging support — both of which have taught me the meaning of true partnership and why it is hard for anyone to succeed in today's world without a helping hand. I wish to thank Jan Walter, president of Macfarlane Walter & Ross, for believing in the need for this book, and Diane Forrest and Liba Berry for their invaluable editorial contribution to the first edition. My thanks to George Brown, the Toronto regional economist, and the liaison department of Employment and Immigration Canada for allowing me to use important job-related statistics and data. And as always, I am grateful for the inspiration and advice of my mother, Hazel Jean Tomlinson.

CHAPTER ONE

THE NEW CANADIAN REALITIES

- **There's No Place Like Home**
- **The Wild, Wild Web**
- **The New Economy**
- **The Focus on Customer Service**
- **Export Markets: Canada's Lifeline to the Future**

If money is your hope for independence, you will never have it.
The only real security that a man can have in this world is a reserve
of knowledge, experience and ability.

HENRY FORD, U.S. AUTOMOBILE MANUFACTURER

Whether or not our governments take action, our employers become
enlightened, our unions and associations rise to the challenge, you and
I are required to manage ourselves, our day-to-day working lives, our
careers, our survivability.

JANIS FOORD KIRK, *SURVIVABILITY* (1996)

I n January 1995, over 26,000 people lined up and waited for hours in the freezing cold to apply for jobs at General Motors in Oshawa, Ontario. Because GM never did add a third shift, none of them ended up with a job. This dispiriting event exemplifies the bitter reality of Canada's jobless recovery.

For roughly a decade now the unemployment rate has hovered around the 10 percent mark despite periods of strong economic growth. Adding in the "discouraged" workers who have given up on finding a job, plus those part-timers who pine for full-time work, the unemployment rate would jump to 18 percent, according to the Organization for Economic Co-operation and Development (OECD). Were we to include also those who have retired prematurely following a downsizing and students who are stretching out their stay in post-secondary institutions because of poor employment prospects, the truer unemployment figure would exceed 20 percent. With governments and public-sector agencies about to begin downsizing seriously, no end to this predicament would seem to be in sight.

The obvious question would have to be: is this a permanent state of affairs in Canada? Fortunately the answer is no, as we shall see. However, this response assumes that Canadians will make the changes necessary to create and find work in an increasingly global new economy – and quickly.

What distinguishes our current period of transition to a new economic era from others in the past, such as the Industrial Revolution, is the speed at which all these changes are taking place. Downsizing, restructuring, re-engineering, automation, and outsourcing are now fashionable trends that companies engage in repeatedly, setting up a game of musical chairs for workers. After each round of change, fewer jobs remain to be had, with employees often asked to reapply for their former jobs if they still exist. No wonder many of us are already experiencing chronic change fatigue.

Fortunately every change carries in its wake new employment opportunities. The trick during periods of change is to grasp the larger patterns emerging, while trying to find where the jobs are at any specific time. It is important to understand both the overall economic playing field and the evolving employment rules as they might apply to you and your future.

There's No Place Like Home

Technology is rapidly turning the home into an office. According to Thelma Moutrie, manager of national retail operations for Xerox Canada Ltd., the home office market is expected to grow to $3 billion by the year 2000. Employers are realizing they can save money on office space if employees work out of their homes on days when it's not necessary for them to be in the office. In the U.S., roughly one-third of the entire work force already telecommutes in some way, according to Link Resources Inc., and the Business Development Bank of Canada says 40 percent of Canadian workers will be telecommuting by the end of the decade. In Toronto, Ryerson Polytechnic University researchers found that 23 percent or 2 million Canadian households run home-based businesses. Approximately one-third of these workers had either been fired or been encouraged to leave companies under early retirement plans. According to a 1994 survey by Telecommuting Consultants International, 70 percent of Canadian telecommuters feel that their quality of life has improved.

In a variation of the home telecommuting arrangement, IBM introduced a "flexiplace" program that provided 900 of its 10,000 employees with technology that allowed them to work anywhere – from their cars, homes, neighbourhood mini-offices, and, in some cases, even from the offices of customers. Consequently, IBM saved $40 million in annual real estate costs and reduced its need for such facilities as cafeterias, meeting space, and boardrooms. The company now rents two floors of the Toronto-Dominion Tower instead of the 14 floors it occupied prior to the flexiplace program. Although most of these IBM employees spend much of their time away from the office, communal offices are available in different metropolitan locations, with one work station for four employees. With videoconferencing costs likely to drop over the next few years, even the need for office work stations will disappear. Sales employees should be able to spend less time on the road, since they can deal with customers on-screen.

Companies have realized that approximately 25 percent of their assets are tied up in real estate; therefore, many are choosing to share offices with outside business people who need temporary space. According to an Industrial Development Research Foundation report, "Corporate Real Estate 2000," IBM has established such facilities for all of its British marketing and sales staff and is doing the same in 20 locations in the U.S. Andersen Consulting's 13 "just-in-time" offices shared by 70 management consultants saved the company $505,000 the first year the strategy was introduced. In 1995, Ernst & Young found that 22 percent of U.S. executives had adopted this concept of the "hoteling" of office space. Ninety percent of respondents working in this kind of environment reported that the quality of their work did not suffer.

According to Linda Russell, senior partner with Telecommuting Consultants International, Inc., switching workers to telecommuting gradually increases productivity by 10 to 35 percent, with an annual average saving of $8,000 per telecommuter. Workers don't miss the inconvenience, expense, and stress of traffic jams, parking, gas, automobile maintenance, or dry cleaning bills. According to B.C. Systems Corporation, the average telecommuter saves $1,700 in expenses and reduces travel by 3,000 kilometres. Many companies are realizing that they benefit as well and will often hire only those individuals who agree to work from home, at least part-time.

For the increasing number of men and women who are concerned about combining active careers with raising a family, working out of the home can be an extremely attractive option. The shift from manufacturing and goods-producing to a service-based economy generates many more opportunities to offer services from the home. And a more educated labour force will likely be amenable to accepting the responsibility, decision-making, and working-alone aspects of such arrangements.

For some jobs, "home" can be anywhere in the world. One can imagine many people choosing pleasant, even exotic surroundings. Real estate agents in Ontario's cottage country, for example, are already seeing increased sales to people who plan to live and work full-time at home in the country for companies in urban centres. With long-distance costs decreasing and companies going global, companies will be attracted by those workers skilled enough or willing to work for low wages out of their homes wherever they are located. Unless individuals are trained to work in the high-skill end of this market, they may find worldwide competition, even among home workers, intensifying. Indeed, Japanese companies are already planning to have 40 percent of their workers telecommuting from home by 2000. Overall, telecommuting is growing by 20 percent a year in the U.S., but by only 5 percent in Canada, according to George Karidis, chief researcher of the Yankee Group in Canada.

The Wild, Wild Web

One of the reasons working from home is becoming more of an option is the growth of "intranets," which are company-run Internet servers. Workers just log on to their company via the Internet from anywhere. Eventually this revolution in "total connectivity" – Microsoft's new rallying cry – will transform every aspect of our lives, including the job market. Although 50 percent of all the jobs that will exist 10 years from now do not exist at the moment, you can be sure that most jobs will emerge somewhere in this brave new interactive, multimedia world.

The Internet was originally constructed in the late 1960s. The U.S. Defence Department wanted a communications system that would remain operational even if part of it were destroyed by a nuclear attack. A message being sent through the system looks for all possible routes that are available, then picks the first series of connections that appears, no matter how byzantine the route might be. If a direct route is knocked out, the Internet just goes around it. In other words, if you are sending a message to someone on the Internet somewhere in Canada, the message might bounce around North America looking for any available telephone cable space not being fully utilized at the moment. It is this uncontrollability of the Internet plus its inexpensive means of transmission that has led to its rapid expansion and unlimited global reach. Once it became possible to quickly find Internet sites, using browser software that removed the need to understand arcane Unix commands, nothing stood in the way of making the Web easily accessible to everyone with a PC and a modem.

But where is it headed – and how fast? Is it just going to become another version of the CB radio craze? Eventually, the Internet will become the main means by which communication of all kinds – from phone sex to philosophy – takes place. It will be so inexpensive to distribute information this way that it will simply replace most other methods of transferring information. The good news is that it gives small businesses the same access to a main distribution channel that previously could be afforded only by large companies. In other words, it will democratize access to all forms of information and communication, much the same way the printing press put an end to the monastic monopoly on books. Already 17 percent of the Canadian adult population has access to the Internet from home, work, school, or a library (or some other public facility). According to *Internet World* magazine, the Internet community will be bigger than the PC community by the year 2000.

The losers will be those businesses whose main function was to pass on information or act as a storage location for anything you might wish to buy. Anyone who plays a redundant go-between or middleperson function may find themselves out of business or out of work. Conservative estimates are that 50 percent of all current retailers will fold over the next five to ten years. To some extent, training programs are in the same vulnerable position, because almost everyone will gain access to upgrading options courtesy of the university or college that comes to you via your laptop and modem.

Access to almost unlimited services will be available even in the middle of a desert, since any kind of information can be uplinked or downlinked via satellites. So developing countries will able to jump from the 19th to the 21st century by skipping the "wire"-limited 20th century that bestowed enormous economic advantages on countries with well-developed physical infrastructure. Although the old infrastructure is still important, as the massive infrastructure improvement efforts in the developing world indicate, the new winners will be those who can take advantage of each new technological process that brings the world closer to a true global village. The number of business opportunities will grow at an exponential rate as markets become linked together with greater rapidity. The growth in entrepreneurship we are witnessing is an integral part of this emerging global economy, where geographic advantage is minimized as distribution costs of all kinds fall drastically and niche markets become easier to identify and serve around the world.

Now is a good time to become an entrepreneur, because it won't be until around 2007 that most of the electronic homesteads will be firmly established. That is, the electronic Wild West will be somewhat citified, and some standards should be taking on more definite shape; at that point the new key winners or major players in these global stakes will be declared. For now, the rapid growth in the number of mergers, acquisitions, joint ventures, partnering arrangements, alliances, and intercompany networks or integrated supply chain linkages is but preparation for the shootout in the telecommunications and information technology corral.

A lot of what we're hearing today concerning the Internet is still hype, but in five years it will definitely begin to ring true. Sun Microsystems, Silicon Graphics Inc., and Netscape Communications Corp. have joined forces to make the World Wide Web an interactive, 3-D, multimedia environment accessible to every kind of computer, in an effort to forestall Microsoft from dominating the Net. Consequently, the next year or two will see an explosion in complex desktop publishing on the Internet. In the next phase, the Internet's commercial possibilities will begin to flourish. And before too long, most of North America will have the necessary high-speed electronic modem access required for videoconferencing and full-motion video. At that point, the race will be on in dead earnest. The rate of change will then hit warp speed for roughly 10 years.

Eventually you will need to purchase only one $500 computer system, which will function much like a cable converter attached to your TV. Just as technology is eliminating other cumbersome and inefficient means of distribution, so it will eliminate the need for anyone to purchase big hard drives, lots of RAM, expensive software, CD-ROMs, and even high-powered computer chips. Instead, all of the computing ingredients you could ever want will be on large servers located on the Net. Your simple computer plugs into these powerful servers as needed, providing you with a pay-for-use system. IBM is developing its Global Netcentric Computing system, which will offer you unlimited computing power. Once systems such as these are fully operational – which is a few years away – you will never have to upgrade your software or hardware, which is usually outdated the day after you purchase it.

Simon Fraser University's Exemplary Centre for Interactive Technology in Education has invented a software called NCompass, which can run in conjunction with Netscape or Microsoft software, allowing home users to rent hourly usage of any software or videogame over the Internet. Not surprisingly, nine venture capital firms lined up to help finance the software company, which may have more potential than Netscape itself. Another software, called Telescape, allows people on the Internet to talk on phones for the same rate they're already paying for Internet service, which should give the phone companies and resellers a run for their money. Even Netscape, which recently purchased a videoconferencing technology company, has announced that it plans to establish a new standard for multimedia communications, but Intel with its ProShare software is hot on its heels. The telecommunications race is definitely on.

Canada's first interactive neighbourhood is taking shape in the Stonehaven housing development in Newmarket, Ontario. Bell Canada, Northern Telecom, IBM, Apple, Silicon Graphics, York University, Ryerson University, Seneca College, the town of Newmarket, York Board of Education, and 70 other companies, government agencies, institutions, and Crown corporations are joining together to create a fully electronically integrated pilot study community, offering almost every interactive service imaginable from shopping, banking, entertainment, health care, and education to remote and intelligent control of every household function. (For more information: 800-898-7564 or chsol@ inforamp.net.) The rest of us will have to wait to take advantage of these services.

In the meantime, information technology development will go through its normal growing pains, with the promises and expectations far outrunning the unforeseen bugs and obstacles that plague all new inventions. From a career perspective, it is important not to discount the fact that the promise eventually will become a reality, even if the timetable needs to be readjusted occasionally. In the 1980s, automation was dismissed because of its failure to deliver as promised, but it is slowly getting better every year. No doubt many will hail the arrival of the new interactive era long before it is likely to get here – but that should only serve as a reminder to prepare for the inevitable. Those who make a habit of sitting on the fence until a trend fully manifests itself may find themselves light-years behind, wondering what happened and when. The best way to prepare for the future is to pay close attention to all of the interim developments – false starts and all – and to make career adjustments accordingly.

Are there many jobs on the Net yet? According to the 1996 *Directory of Internet Providers and Services in Ontario*, electronic entrepreneurs have created 1,388 full-time and 160 part-time jobs in Ontario since 1994. The jobs are typically in sales, accounting, and technical support (internetwork engineers, security experts, mobile technicians, Internet specialists, and information librarians); however, the pay is somewhat modest given the fledgling nature of most new on-line services. (For a list of helpful Internet addresses, see the Select Bibliography.)

The New Economy

The growth in the Internet is the lastest indicator of a complete shift in the nature of our economy. The industries Canadians relied on in the past to provide jobs – natural resources industries such as mining and forestry, for example – are no longer the main engines of growth in our economy. Nuala Beck estimates that 70 percent of Canadians are already employed in the industries that make up the new economy – such as telecommunications, computer hardware and software, robotics, and pharmaceuticals – and asserts that it is these industries that will drive our economic growth.

Every economic phase presents obstacles that have to be overcome before a subsequent phase can begin. Once these barriers are overcome – by making a process more efficient, inventing an entirely new process or substance, or enhancing a service of some kind – the rules of the economic game change and new sets of winners and losers emerge. For example, improvements in methods of transportation, communication, and delivery made trade between countries easier (satellites, planes, and computers versus cable, boats, and the mail), which made greater economic development possible and ultimately improved our quality of life. During the Industrial Revolution, the forging of steel helped make the machine age possible, which in turn helped make mass manufacturing a reality. And the discovery of the transistor paved the way for the invention of the computer chip and the dawning of the new information technology age.

Each of these changes, in turn, has a major effect on the job market, as we can see by looking at the development of the Canadian work force. A century ago, the largest single group of workers outside the home was on the farm. However, starting in the late 19th century, farm equipment became mechanized and more labour-efficient, causing the agricultural work force to diminish from 40 percent to 4 percent of the overall work force by 1975. The actual number of agricultural workers declined as well, so that by 1970 the industry employed only 25 percent as many workers as it did before 1930.

The biggest percentage growth in the work force has been among white-collar workers. In 1900, they formed only 20 percent of the work force, yet by 1965, approximately 50 percent were white-collar workers. And by 2020, over 75 percent of the work force will be white-collar – partly because of growth in the service industries.

Meanwhile, blue-collar jobs will almost disappear. So far, the decline in jobs in this sector, because of improvements in manufacturing technology, has been gradual (from a peak of 46 percent in the 1940s to 38 percent in the 1980s). But the downward slide is gathering momentum. By 2020, blue-collar workers will represent only 20 percent of the work force, applying their skills to the maintenance and repair of automated machinery. Unlike the blue-collar workers of the past, these will be highly skilled college graduates trained in the use of sophisticated technology, more properly considered white-collar. Eventually, even these jobs will probably be decimated by technology. Indeed, Jean-Claude Paye, secretary-general of the Organization for Economic Co-operation and Development (OECD), predicts that eventually only 2 percent of those employed in developed nations will be working in manufacturing and just 1 percent will be employed in agriculture.

However, with the emphasis on information and technology, white-collar professionals should continue to be in demand, and a new group, "paraprofessionals," will emerge. With scientific knowledge doubling every six to ten years, professionals will have to acquire more specialized skills and delegate their routine duties to paraprofessionals – workers in the same field, but with less training. By the year 2000, it's expected that paraprofessionals and professionals will exceed 20 percent of the work force, making these knowledge workers the most prominent segment of the work force as the more traditional manufacturing and labouring jobs continue to disappear. These new technicians are more technology-oriented than machine-oriented; they include medical technologists, materials scientists, nuclear technicians, broadcast engineers, air traffic controllers, and paralegals.

Although the transition will be far from smooth or consistent, eventually all industries will be influenced by the explosion in technology. Traditional industries will incorporate new technology to become more competitive. And the various technologies have become businesses in their own right – think, for example, of the giant computer software companies that didn't even exist 20 years ago.

Risk management is another new specialty area. There is a growing need to control and monitor the effects of the newer technologies altering the world around us. Their proliferation is leading to the setting of higher industry standards. The government has introduced the principle of "reverse onus," which requires firms to prove something is safe before marketing it. More watchdog agencies have arisen to meet the public's growing demand for accountability. There are now 19 centres in North America specializing in risk research. Anyone who specializes in how newer technologies or policies are likely to influence risk in any field – medicine in particular – will be in great demand. Nowadays we track explosive chemicals, tainted blood, dangerous criminals, effects of parole policies, new drugs, nuclear power, road maintenance, or even just the difference wearing a bicycle helmet makes.

The key to understanding the future is the way in which technology is changing our expectations of what is possible. High standards, risk management, and widespread accountability would not be possible without the technology that allows us to measure and evaluate the effects of change in a cost-effective manner. Twenty years ago no one gave a thought to risk management or to holding firms accountable for the ramifications of their products for every aspect of the world around us. Technology has given us a systems perspective because, by eliminating all boundaries, borders, and barriers around the world, it has sped up the globalization process. Globalization, in turn, has quickly exposed the interdependencies that exist between and within countries, industries, regions, cities, companies, and individuals. While on the one hand technology is stretching us in so many directions and forcing us to become multiskilled and "multitasking," it is also leading the way to convergence, as the artificial barriers between all aspects of modern life rapidly dissolve.

The four pillars of the financial industry – finance, banking, insurance, and investment – are seeing any former differences among them blurring. The distinction between producers and broadcasters has begun to disappear, especially with the Walt Disney–ABC Capital Cities Inc. merger. Even Canadian producers and broadcasters are moving as fast as they can in this direction. Outsourcing is leading to a curious blending of industries; one example is the deal between Bell Canada and IBM Canada Ltd., whereby Bell Sygma took over the management and operation of IBM's internal wide-area networks and all subsidiary networks, while IBM bought all of Bell's computer equipment and leased it back to them. At the personal level, the distinction between home and work is vanishing, as companies essentially outsource their work to your home. Even white-collar and blue-collar jobs are hard to tell apart, especially now that 80 percent of all so-called blue-collar jobs require a post-secondary degree or diploma.

Aside from creating jobs in these cross-disciplinary management areas, these changes are leading customers and companies to demand one-stop-shopping solutions to all their problems in any given area. As technology makes the world a more complicated place to live in, it is also forcing industries to restructure or re-engineer in ways that simplify everything as much as possible within these expanding realms of complexity. Consumers are restructuring their lives by simplifying them in ways that increase their quality. There is some consolation in the fact that the increased need for cross-training and job rotation in a more complicated workplace has enhanced job satisfaction and reduced absenteeism and job turnover – just as families now ask everyone to pitch in, juggling and sharing responsibilities at home.

Both individuals and companies are going through a values clarification process. Individuals are reshaping their lives to focus on those things of greatest value in their lives and are demanding that companies give them the flexibility to do so. Companies, for their part, are outsourcing all of the functions peripheral to their central value-adding process (i.e., their competitive advantage). Consumers are outsourcing housecleaning and even cooking by buying take-out or eating out more. The prime focus now is on what aspects of a product's quality customers care most about – or what do they value the most. Technology has made customizing of value possible and has provided us with the flexibility to arrange our lives in ways that better reflect our values – which are the only compass we have in a highly competitive world in flux.

Thus the technological revolution we find ourselves a part of is eliminating all geographic and categorical barriers that we previously took for granted. It is the driving force increasing the demand for common higher standards, accountability, and quality even at the international level. While fostering globalization and expanding our awareness of diversity and customized possibilities, technology is also making everyone demand that everything be simplified and extraneous functions out-sourced as much as possible so that we can take on the enormous chal-lenge of "thinking globally, but acting locally." And it this outsourcing phenomenon that is responsible for the explosive growth in small businesses and self-employment.

The Focus on Customer Service

International competition has already forced corporations to put more emphasis on customer service. In the future, with the huge stakes to be won by capturing the public's heart with a particular product, and the ability to serve customers more effectively through technology, compa-nies will continue to focus on the customer. Indeed, now that most com-panies have downsized, reduced their overhead, and lowered their prices, the only thing left to focus on is sales and marketing.

In the past, focussing on the customer too often meant seducing the unsuspecting and uninformed consumer into buying something unnec-essary or inferior. Marketing continues to be haunted by the stereotype of the brash used-car salesman. More recently, many service companies have developed the more positive have-a-nice-day variety of customer service. But while efforts to create a friendlier atmosphere should be applauded, true customer service is far more sophisticated.

In successful corporations, sales and marketing has already shifted its focus from trying to sell consumers products they don't need to finding out what the customer does need and providing the goods or services cost-effectively. Increasing global competitiveness demands not only that workers come up with innovative ways of meeting a customer's needs, but also that they anticipate problems and come up with solutions. Employees become intermediaries, informing customers about the value of their company's product while also convincing the company of the validity of their customers' needs. Even those employees who don't ordi-narily deal directly with customers are encouraged to keep the customer ever in mind and constantly seek information on trends in demand. Companies that focus on customer needs find it much easier to make priorities clearer throughout the organization. The increase in out-sourcing means that customer service will be an even bigger theme than in the past, as more and more companies begin to deal with one another on a customer-supplier basis. Meanwhile, information technology makes this shift in focus possible by taking on many of the ordering, accounting, processing, and internal and external communications tasks, thereby freeing up personnel for customer relations and for marketing, which is the wealth-generating side of the business. Over the past several years, products and services (from farm tractors to financial services) have become much more complicated. A 1994 survey by *Training* magazine found that 64 percent of U.S. companies need to train their customers on how to use their organizations' products or services. No wonder the focus has now shifted to the customer's "experience" with the product or service – an experience that must be user-friendly or inviting, and certainly not frustrating, if the company is to thrive.

The emphasis on customer service is good news for people whose main strength is in marketing and who may be wondering where they fit into a high-tech future. Indeed, customer service has become so important that often the fastest means of promotion is through the demonstration of sales and marketing ability. High-tech companies are interested in hiring individuals who not only are technically competent but also have the attributes essential for selling: initiative, flexibility, good communications skills, energy, and versatility. According to recruitment coordinator Dave Uez of NCR Canada Ltd., sales is "the best route to senior management." Ken Gravelle, staff development manager for Xerox, echoes this belief: "Every one of our vice-presidents and all senior staff in every department, including personnel, have experience in the selling field." According to a 1996 survey by Korn/Ferry International, the best route to becoming a CEO was through marketing, with international experience taking second place and finance third.

At successful corporations, the importance of sales is reflected by thorough in-house sales training. Xerox sales recruits receive a minimum of six months of basic sales training before they go on to the company's international headquarters in Leesburg, Virginia, for three weeks of intensive training. According to Jo Currie, a contributing editor to *Career Options*, "IBM, NCR, and GE [General Electric] all have highly structured programs for new recruits, involving classroom time, on-the-job training supervised by experienced employees, and self-study. Salaries while training ranged from $28,000 to $32,000." The skills, education, or training that accompanies sales ability will vary according to the industry. The less technical the industry, the more likely that business graduates of various kinds will find entry-level sales positions. Since most entry-level jobs are available on small teams or in small businesses, job seekers would be well advised to develop an entrepreneurial spirit. Those who combine an entrepreneurial drive with advanced degrees in business and a technical area have an excellent chance of becoming vice-presidents of any growing smaller company within five years. Indeed, those with computer literacy and finance or marketing skills – the "gold-collar workers" – often get to write their own job ticket.

Export Markets: Canada's Lifeline to the Future

Given the weakness of our domestic market and the political uncertainty surrounding Canada's future, the only safe bet for investments and for careers is the export field. Large companies were much more profitable than smaller companies in 1995, and the degree of that profitability was directly related to the amount of exporting they did. According to Jeff Rubin, chief economist of CIBC Wood Gundy Inc., in the *Financial Post*, "The bulk of investment has been overwhelmingly skewed to export-oriented industries, particularly in resource industries where sharp increases in prices for base metals and pulp and paper products have triggered massive increases in capital spending. By contrast, capital spending in the domestic sector (government, construction, finance, insurance and real estate, as well as manufacturing, excluding autos) remains well below the increases posted during the comparable period in the last cycle. For example, contrast a 64% increase in investment in the auto industry, where roughly 90% of production is for exports, with a 23% decline in capital spending in the rest of the manufacturing industry." Nonetheless, between 1991 and 1994, industrial machinery exports rose by 58 percent, other equipment and tools by 80 percent, and office machinery and equipment by 70 percent.

In Canada only 100 firms are responsible for half of all Canadian exports, and 900 companies account for 93 percent of all our exports. Fewer than 10 percent of our small and medium-sized businesses are in the export market (only 62,000 of 921,000 such businesses in Canada actively export). By comparison, almost all the smaller firms in European countries such as the Netherlands and Sweden actively export. The good news is that things are changing. According to the Canadian Manufacturers' Association, manufacturers exported 59 percent of their output in 1996 compared with 25 percent in 1980. Overall, exports were expected to show growth of 8 percent in 1996.

The Canada-U.S. Free Trade Agreement and the North American Free Trade Agreement (NAFTA) were lifesavers for Canada, given our crippling interprovincial trade barriers. For instance, exports between provinces, which amounted to 27 percent of our GDP in 1981, fell to 21 percent in 1994. Since 1989 interprovincial trade in goods has decreased by 14 percent, yet our exports of goods to the U.S. have risen by 70 percent over that period – a growth rate 250 percent faster than that of the U.S. economy. According to a 1995 Economic Strategy Institute study, our exports to the U.S. were roughly $14 billion higher than they would have been without a trade agreement. This represents a dramatic shift in our economy from east-west to north-south. NAFTA provisions have led to some disputes over steel and lumber, but such disagreements only affect less than 5 percent of total bilateral trade.

Whereas Canadian plants used to make 10 to 20 products each for the Canadian market, they are now more likely to make three or four for the world. The shift to an export economy is so strong that in 1981 only 27 percent of our GDP came from exporting, but that figure rose to 37 percent in 1995, and 42 percent in 1996. According to economists Richard Harris and David Cox in their 1990 report "The Service Sector and Trade in the Canadian Economy," "Each dollar of exports contained about 39 cents of service sector output." So there are lots of jobs associated with providing services that many exporting firms need. On the other hand, many services are now being exported themselves, but not to the same extent as we export merchandise. According to Statistics Canada, we are the fourth-largest exporter of merchandise in the world, but only the 15th-largest exporter of services. Indeed, we run quite a deficit in imported services. This suggests that we are missing out on many service export opportunities.

One sign of the weakness of our non-export market is that up to 1980 local factories supplied 73 percent of the goods sold in Canada; by 1995, that share was down to 44 percent. These figures reflect the fact that approximately 50 percent of our manufacturing materials, components, and technologies are imported. In other words, the very same factors that encourage exporting – too small a domestic market and interprovincial trade barriers – also encourage increased importing, since domestic firms do not see the point of investing in production facilities to meet domestic demand. This suggests that our non-exporting companies are not very competitive globally and are losing ground to imports. But it must be remembered that this is a worldwide trend, since imports are growing faster than GDP in the U.S., Europe, Latin America, and the developing countries of Asia. As a result, we can expect even more of an investment shift from domestic to export production.

One problem with tying your job fate to a firm exporting solely to the U.S. is that a downturn in the American economy could alter the employment situation considerably. One of the major effects of the freer trade agreements in North America was to reduce trade with European nations. Since 1989, exports to Canada from France have decreased by 40 percent, from Britain by 30 percent, and from Germany by 25 percent. Although efforts are under way to create a trade agreement between Canada and the European Union, progress is slow; nonetheless, during 1995 Canadian exports to Europe rose by 42 percent. Despite these surprising increases, it might make more sense for a job seeker to target a firm doing business with Asia-Pacific nations, which account for 10 percent of the world demand for goods and services – a number expected to rise by 50 percent over the next five years. Already our trans-Pacific trade exceeds our trans-Atlantic trade. Developing countries in general hold good export-job-related prospects; in 1995 Canadian exports to countries outside the 25-member club of large industrialized countries grew by 31 percent. It is extremely encouraging to see that Canadian firms are finally beginning to test the export markets outside of the U.S., since there is more opportunity elsewhere and such trade has a stabilizing effect on our economy. No business or country should rely solely on one main customer.

At the time of writing, Mexico was the only developing country to have entered into a trade agreement with developed countries. But others will quickly follow. If we can widen our focus, this trend offers tremendous opportunities for Canada. Developing countries are always short of capital goods such as resource extraction technology, commuter aircraft, and electrical equipment. Infrastructure projects are always in progress in any rapidly developing country, so opportunities exist in the areas of transportation networks, housing, energy generation and distribution systems, and construction in general. According to Everett Santos

TRADE INSTEAD OF AID?

It is estimated that restricted access to world markets is costing developing nations $500 billion per year in lost income, a figure that is roughly
ten times more than what they receive in foreign aid. According to
Lewis Perinbam, Commonwealth of Learning adviser, "The poor
nations of the South transfer annually more than $50 billion (U.S.)
more to the rich countries of the North than they receive in aid and
investment. . . . The World Bank says a 50 percent cut in trade barriers
by the EC [European Community], the U.S. and Japan would raise
exports from developing countries by $50 billion a year – about equal to
the total foreign aid to the poor countries. The North, too, would gain.
Clearly, the world will not be safe or sustainable as long as it consists of
islands of affluence in a sea of poverty."

of the International Finance Corp., a division of the World Bank,
developing countries are expected to spend US$200 to $220 billion per
year on infrastructure improvements during the rest of the decade and
well into the next century. By area, $100 billion will be spent annually
on electric power systems, $70 billion for water and waste facilities,
$30 billion for telecommunications, and $20 billion for highway improvement. Environmental technology will be needed in all developing countries before too long, as will more sophisticated financial services. Were
Canada to privatize some of its infrastructure services, Canadian companies would be able to take advantage of these opportunities as British
and French privatized companies are already doing.

It is pointless to rail against free trade; these changes were inevitable
as the continentalization of trade began to emerge. The lesson here is
that economics will always dictate what changes will take place over the
long term. As Cedric Ritchie, chairman of the Bank of Nova Scotia,
asserts, "The continued growth and prosperity of Canada must be linked
to a philosophy of looking outward. Canadians must embrace globalization despite its challenges, if for no other reason than there is no alternative for a trade-dependent nation like ours with barely the economic
weight of California."

In the immediate future, virtually all developing countries will try to
challenge the rest of the world in competitiveness. If NAFTA were not in

place, the Japanese and Europeans would still invest heavily in Mexico, something they are already doing. In other words, Mexico represents a key component in a global strategy for economic development. Whichever countries develop the strongest foothold in Mexico are best positioned to expand into the rest of Latin America. Consequently, you will find the major multinational firms expanding their presence in Mexico. Meanwhile, Japan is creating the same sort of trading bloc in Asia, shifting much of its labour-intensive activity to developing countries.

The conclusion of the World Trade Organization (WTO) agreement talks may partially offset some of the undesirable aspects of the FTA or NAFTA, since most of the U.S. "country of origin" or "dumping" restrictions will have to be considerably liberalized. Indeed, in general, the WTO appears to be very good news for Canada. Much of the worry for dairy, poultry, and egg farmers has been quelled, since quotas will be replaced with tariffs that reach as high as 351 percent on butter. Although the tariffs will be reduced slightly over a six-year period, which began in 1995, marketing boards will continue until 2010, when all tariff barriers will be eliminated.

Among the key winners in Canada are fishing, electronics, construction equipment, chemicals, non-ferrous metals, and forest products. Pulp and paper tariffs are to be phased out in Japan and Europe and lumber tariffs reduced to 5 percent. Chemical tariffs will drop to 6 percent from the current 12 to 15 percent, while manufacturers of mining, industrial,

BULLETIN BOARD – *EXPORTS*

- Trade patterns are shifting to a north-south focus, with trade regionalizing according to geographic and demographic economic competitive advantage, i.e., business is moving south.
- NAFTA will not be fully phased in until 2003 and a recent WTO agreement should help minimize most of the negative features of NAFTA for Canada.
- Regions will need to develop economic focusses and actively market their advantages abroad.
- Seek work in expanding export industries located in areas with strong competitive infrastructures.

agricultural, and construction equipment will see tariffs completely eliminated. The WTO also opens up the $1 trillion market for telecommunications and urban transit companies, and opportunities for service-sector industries such as computer software, management consulting, engineering, insurance, and banking. The trade-off that developing countries accepted in exchange for access to industrialized markets was a recognition of patents and copyrights, which should help protect enter-tainment products – compact discs and videocassettes, for example – software, seed patents, and pharmaceutical companies. However, the textile industry gets no relief, since these products can be cheaply manufactured in developing countries.

Fortunately for Canada's entertainment and cultural industries, France was able to prevent an open market for the U.S.'s multimedia products, which have already successfully penetrated most foreign markets. Nonetheless, much of the growth in Canada's entertainment industries will come from marketing our talents to U.S. consumers, who are devoting an ever larger portion of their disposable income to entertainment.

Peter Passell, writing in the *New York Times*, nicely sums up the essence of the WTO agreement: "Countries ready to grow may be more inclined to gravitate toward open trade. More specifically, the cultural values that seem to underpin growth – thrift, rule of law, respect for property rights, fiscal discipline – may also create political systems that are better at defending the interests of efficient, export-minded producers against those of groups demanding a free economic ride." Since the only way to reduce unemployment is through economic growth, Canada's unemploy-ment future rests squarely on our response to this challenge. With the WTO expanding world trade by up to $5 trillion over the next ten years, Canada's expertise in importing and exporting could really pay off if we can respond to the challenge.

These forces have specific implications for job seekers, who should plan on seeking work in a growth export industry located in an area of the country that is strategically focussed on attracting and supporting such businesses. An alternative is to seek work in a company that is expanding beyond Canada, since it will have many career growth oppor-tunities worth pursuing. If Quebec separates, only the exporting firms will benefit from a lower dollar. Moreover, because worker productivity is 20 to 40 percent higher among exporting companies, export-related jobs pay 15 percent more than the average wage. And export firms expand employment 20 percent faster than non-exporting firms and are 10 percent less likely to fail. With exports now accounting for 42 percent of our economy, no job seeker can afford to overlook these opportunities.

THE AGE OF THE ENTREPRENEUR

An invasion of armies can be resisted, but not an idea whose time has come.

VICTOR HUGO

People who get on in this world are the people who get up and look for the circumstances they want, and if they can't find them they create them.

GEORGE BERNARD SHAW

Entrepreneurship no longer means just starting up a business. Increasingly it is coming to represent an "outlook," a "commitment to change and innovation," an "attitude," and a "style of living." As an outlook, being entrepreneurial means constantly scanning the environment for developing trends and opportunities. With respect to change and innovation, it represents a commitment to finding new solutions to problems and making them a reality as the final proof that the solutions are "doable." An entrepreneurial attitude is a positive attitude toward taking calculated risks and thriving on the challenge of living with uncertainty. And lastly, the entrepreneurial style of living is learning to travel lightly to the point of being willing to fold up your tent in the middle of the night and move on if necessary.

Entrepreneurs, much like surfers waiting for the right wave, are always trying to spot a key new trend whose time has arrived. Nimbleness and knowing when to go for broke are essential. In a sense, entrepreneurs are true believers – they are waiting for the golden opportunity to realize some personal dream that requires their complete devotion. Accomplishment and ambition are motivators, just as most devoted surfers are always looking for the perfect or biggest wave. Failure is not so important as giving it your best shot. Indeed, most successful entrepreneurs have failed two or three times prior to eventually winning at the game.

Why don't they give up after initial disappointments? Quite simply, their ability to continually see new opportunities always gets the best of them. In other words, they are incurable optimists. It is this attitude, plus an addiction to anything new or innovative, that keeps them fired up. Like artists stretching the boundaries of what is possible, they are on a Promethean mission to bring something new into existence. At the very least, they want to be part of something new and exciting.

So entrepreneurs are impatient. They want the future now. Fortunately, they have the dedication, vision, and energy needed to tackle new, unclimbed mountains in novel ways. And given their need to move with the times and shape the future, they are willing to travel lightly with respect to job or personal security. After all, it takes what amounts to a religious leap of faith to mortgage your home to the hilt, rope in friends and family as investors, and forget about retirement planning. And it takes the same entrepreneurial courage to move to Southeast Asia and seek your fortune in their current golden job rush.

The challenge for employers these days is to create entrepreneurial opportunities for their work force, or the innovation needed to compete will wander elsewhere. Indeed, one can no more manage entrepreneurs than one can herd cats. Instead, we need workplaces that can act as incubators for the entrepreneurial ambitions of those busily shaping the future. For without entrepreneurs, managers in a changing economy will not have businesses to manage. Welcome to the age of the entrepreneur.

As large companies downsize, new companies are starting up in record numbers. According to David Schlanger, director of the Ryerson Centre for Entrepreneurship Education and Research, "There are 2 million businesses in Canada, half of those consisting of one person working out of the home. That's a major chunk of our economy." Small businesses are responsible for almost nine out of every ten new jobs, for two-thirds of all private-sector employment, and for 60 percent of Canada's private-sector GDP. Between 1984 and 1992, the OECD found that Canada had the highest rate of new business startups, which is reflected in the fact that the number of self-employed people grew by 89 percent between 1975 and 1993, yet total employment increased by only 33 percent. In 1993–94, self-employed people accounted for 42 percent of all new jobs and represented 16 percent of all employed workers. Just recently, the number of self-employed people actually nudged ahead of the number of government workers. But even more encouraging is the fact that, according to a 1995 Canadian Federation of Small Business survey, those who have chosen to work for firms with fewer than 10 employees are much happier than others working for companies with over 300 employees. Perhaps this partially accounts for why one-third of all Canadians, according to a 1995 Angus Reid poll, expected to be in business for themselves within five years – more than doubling the number of people in small business. In fact, of the 170,000 jobs created in Canada in the first half of 1996, 120,000 were the result of people establishing their own businesses.

Home on the Range

What is sparking this incredible growth in self-employment? The home-based businesses referred to in Chapter 1, where people commute down the hall or stairs to their office. Not surprisingly, half of all new businesses begin in the home, a baby step before taking the big plunge. By the end of the decade, home businesses are expected to account for 40 percent of all employment, according to the Business Development Bank of Canada. Even the federal government is having 220,000 civil servants work out of their homes as a means of saving on office space, which can amount to 30 percent of overhead. Thus we are likely to see many home businesses remain in the home rather than make the transition to store-front or office status. Indeed, between 1990 and 1995, the number of home-based freelancers actually grew faster than the number of new businesses situating in offices or retail outlets for the first time. Municipal bylaws, a serious obstacle to the growth of home-based businesses, will need to change to reflect this new, greener approach to job creation.

To get a sense of how home-based businesses are growing in a hot high-tech region in Canada, look at the statistics in Kanata, Ontario. Business services (such as consulting, computing) account for 27.8 percent of the home businesses; other services such as legal, social, and health, 12.5 percent; telecommunications consulting, 12.1 percent; finance, insurance, real estate, 7.7 percent; and retail (network, direct marketing), 7.3 percent.

But what if you need to entertain clients in a more formal or neutral setting? As you might expect, every problem represents an opportunity to an entrepreneur. Network Offices Inc. recently opened an Hour Office location in Toronto that rents offices and boardrooms by the hour and provides full-scale administrative and office support if required. This is just one of the many business and professional support services that are flourishing at the moment. Paul Edwards, author of *Best Home Businesses for the '90s,* feels that professional practice consulting is also a growing field. Helping professionals with sales and marketing skills, customer relations, financial planning and sourcing, management training, and technology is a growing area.

The hottest home businesses in Canada, however, are computer man-agement and telecommunications consulting, according to Don Dutton, president of the Canadian Home-Based Business Association. Desktop publishing and other multimedia businesses are easily run from home locations, just as arts and crafts businesses are doing successfully. Electronic bulletin board services and back-end Internet services such as Web-page design and on-line marketing assistance fit the mould as well. Already 48 percent of Internet subscribers are business users, and

27 percent of Internet users earn over $80,000. And Andersen Consulting found that 74 percent of businesses surveyed in 1995 indicated that they planned to make commercial use of the Internet.

Mobile services are also prospering since more and more consumers want services delivered to the home as part of the cocooning trend. Dual-income families, single parents, aging boomers, and the elderly appreciate having their lives made easier. Home-care services for the sick, supply delivery services for home offices, pet food delivery services, and home-meal delivery services are beginning to grow. Other areas include home fitness, mobile auto repair, and massage therapy.

Direct-mail catalogue sales increased by 4 percent in 1995 to $1.9 billion and are expected to continue to grow at that pace over the next several years. Some U.S. home operators do $500,000 in gross annual sales. List brokers research, organize, and select current mailing lists that you can rent; call the Canadian Direct Marketing Association at 416-391-2362 for broker information. The association also offers a $235 one-day introduction to direct marketing covering catalogue design, order generation and fulfilment, and inventory maintenance.

One way of avoiding basements full of inventories, accounts receivable problems, and prohibitive startup costs is to explore multilevel marketing businesses, which are about as risk-free as it is possible to get, while still providing the opportunity to retire within five to ten years. Most of these opportunities only require initial investments of between $100 and $300, and they no longer require that you warehouse the product or retail it directly – you can succeed just by getting more people involved. Amway is by far the most successful among a growing number of companies trying to bypass the normal distribution channels as a means of passing on the savings to its own distributors.

To make multilevel marketing work, you need to have even more missionary zeal than is characteristic of the most visionary companies. This is achieved by playing upon the egalitarian notion that you can only succeed if you help the others you bring on board succeed. This communitarian form of capitalism has a strong populist or grassroots appeal to many who view it as a merging of capitalism and Christian-like values. The ability to retire after five years or so of living, breathing, and sleeping "the plan," regardless of your current state of employment, holds great attraction for those who want a sense of running their own business without the risk normally associated with any startup operation. Essentially, it is a low-budget franchising concept that is ideal for anyone with sufficient drive and willingness to become completely immersed in both its culture and its marketing approach. Bear in mind that only about 3 percent of those who try multilevel marketing end up making six-figure incomes, and most who treat it as a part-time job give up after a while. Getting out is relatively easy to do, given the low financial commitment required upfront.

Export Opportunities

Among the less obvious home business opportunities is international trade. Peter Dawes, senior partner of Import/Export Consultants in Toronto, believes working out of the house is ideal because of the time-zone shifts that allow people to keep their day jobs and do their trading after hours. The Forum for International Trade Training offers an eight-semester course in a number of Canadian colleges covering product marketing, deal financing, agents, insurance, transportation, and logistical issues. Surplus electronic and telecommunications equipment is available for export to developing countries. One liquidation company paid Consumers Distributing 3 cents on the dollar for its returned merchandise and pieced together workable products from broken ones, then sold them to the Third World along with old office equipment.

Companies with annual exports of less than $1 million now have their own team representing them at the Export Development Corporation (EDC) in Ottawa; the EDC will refer them to all other appropriate government services as well. John Hutchinson heads up the Emerging Exporters Team, which handles two-thirds of the EDC-represented companies (small and medium-sized companies make up 84 percent of their customer base). Since EDC (800-850-9626) will cover Canadian firms for 90 percent of their losses if foreign clients renege on their payments, Canadian banks are much more willing to accept export receivables as security or collateral when lending working capital. For businesses serious about developing exporting expertise, the Business Development Bank of Canada offers a $6,000 comprehensive course called the New Exporters Training and Counselling Program, which includes optional participation in brief trade missions. For those interested in importing, there is the $55 New Foreign Imported Products directory, which lists

over 1,000 products from over 60 countries (908-686-2382); QuickTel
Electronic Publishing's $225 CD-ROM directory that lists over 100,000
importing and exporting companies worldwide (212-750-7300); and
Arthur Andersen's North American Business Sourcebook (800-626-4330).

Ernst & Young's First Annual Survey (1995) of Canadian
Entrepreneurs found that 60 percent of all respondents are active inter-
nationally, while 75 percent in Pacific Canada are (versus 65 percent in
Quebec, Ontario, and Atlantic Canada, and only 44 percent in the
Prairies). Of the small entrepreneurial companies involved in exporting
(50 percent), one in five earns 75 percent of its revenue from exports.
Canadian small businesses have done extremely well competing interna-
tionally. Ten Canadian companies earned spots in the top half of *Forbes*
magazine's list of 100 best small companies in the world: Adventure
Electronics, Champion Road Machinery, Cinram, Corel, Linamar,
Maax, Skyjack, SR Telecom, Ventra Group, and Zoom Telephonics.

Where are the hot growth export areas in the eyes of most entrepreneurs in Canada? Asia garnered 90 percent of the vote in the Ernst &
Young survey; the U.S., 82 percent; Western Europe, 43 percent; Mexico,
40 percent; Australia/New Zealand, 22 percent; Eastern Europe,
22 percent; and the Middle East, 20 percent. Euromonitor's CD-ROM of
World Marketing Data and Statistics helps small businesses gain access
to cost-effective research programs and essential market and economic
condition information even in extremely remote countries (312-922-1115).
In addition, Ernst & Young's North American Business Center is dedicated to helping small businesses do business in Mexico and the U.S.
and assists with joint ventures, site selection, international tax regulations,
business protocol, and corporate finance (contact Paul Benson at
416-864-1234 or phone 1-800-MOR-TRAD).

Franchises and Hot Prospects

Generally speaking, recycling, reusing, and reselling are growing business
opportunity areas. Microplay Franchising Inc. of Toronto has 126 buy-
and-sell videogame stores in Canada and the U.S.; Play It Again Sam has
46 Canadian and 422 U.S. franchises that buy and sell sporting goods;
and Australia's Cash Converters operates 35 Canadian outlets that
exchange cameras, electronics, power tools, sports equipment, and
jewellery. The possibilities for recycling gently used items are likely to

expand as many people worry about their economic future and declining purchasing power.

Other hot business areas identified by *Entrepreneur* magazine for 1996 include bakery-cafés, soft pretzels, specialized staffing services, family entertainment centres, computer training centres, professional employer organizations, children's educational toy stores, environmental management services, day spas, and bagels. For instance, Great Canadian Bagel Ltd. of Toronto developed 45 new franchises in 1996, and St. Urbain Bagel Bakery is franchising its Montreal-style bagel concept. Innovative companies like Calgary-based TAAG International are helping over-taxed consumers regain some of their income by running a tax appeal service.

According to Ron Scott, a Calgary partner with KPMG, only 1.8 percent of those being outplaced decided to become entrepreneurs by either going into the consulting business or buying an existing business in 1984; however, by 1994, 40 percent were considering moving in this direction. Franchises offer a welcome alternative to those who are more managerial and administrative in personality since following a proven success formula is typically all that is required. Franchisors themselves are also looking for an "intrapreneur" personality profile in their applicants: the ability to be creative and a team player, but within a defined structure, unlike independent entrepreneurs who insist on creatively defining their own structure as well. The franchise concept has even expanded to include home-based businesses such as Interactive Franchise Systems Inc. of Calgary, which offers publication and travel agency franchises in the $2,500 to $10,000 range, and Universal Teleresponse Corp. of Toronto, which franchises virtual call centres for other businesses for $25,000.

If you cannot afford the franchising fee, you can still take advantage of these trends in a fairly risk-averse way, by copying a successful franchise or business that has not moved into your area, assuming the market conditions are appropriate. Copying proven success makes the most sense for those who are not capable of coming up with some completely new, innovative solution to a current consumer need or competitive business issue. As more people leave big cities thanks to the ability to work remotely, many business opportunities will arise to transplant what has worked successfully in larger cities to growing smaller towns. Before doing so, however, you will need to thoroughly research your project's feasibility. Whereas franchises have head offices that specialize in researching ideal locations for their outlets, you will have to provide this function for yourself. If the conditions are appropriate for using a cloning strategy, then you only need the venture capital to get yourself started. And venture capitalists are likely to be receptive to a concept that has proven successful elsewhere, though they are only one source of capital.

Financing Options

Financing, which is the second-biggest area of concern to small-business owners after taxes, should be considered in the following sequence. First, try to find partners who would like to be active in the business. Not only do you share the risk, but you increase your marketing reach, stand a better chance of having complementary skill sets, and have the much-needed team to bounce your ideas off and help you stay motivated. Incorporating with a legal arrangement for share disposition or "cashing out" is essential – something virtually all equity investors will want clarified. Employee share-purchase plans or "sweat equity" arrangements (free labour in exchange for profit sharing) are other ways of getting whoever might be working for you to buy into your venture. Next consider family and friends as silent investors. It is easier to negotiate with people you definitely trust. Beyond those you know are the banks, who are not usually interested in loaning less than $100,000. Although things are improving somewhat, banks find that they tend to lose money on small business loans. For instance, on a $25,000 loan, the cost of registering the loan and making loss provisions equals any interest they might make. Since administrative costs are often twice the cost of loss provision, any loan requiring extra attention or running into temporary glitches automatically loses money for the banks.

Banks are in the big loan business, in other words. If you have inventory or accounts receivable (i.e., assets) to back up loan demands of $5 million and more, American companies that have recently entered Canada such as Congress Financial Corp., GE Capital Canada Inc., and Bank of America Canada are much more generous in the amounts they will lend against these assets. Congress Financial will lend up to 90 percent of receivables and 85 percent of inventory, versus 75 percent and 50 percent for Canadian banks.

Two Canadian banks have made a very significant change in their lending practices that you may wish to investigate. The Royal Bank and the Bank of Montreal are now willing to offer equity loans to small businesses – definitely a revolutionary move in the banking industry. For instance, the Bank of Montreal, responsible for 16 percent of all small-business lending, is making $200 million available for loans where the banks will take up to a 40 percent share ownership position in a company in exchange for funds. For established, small, profitable businesses, loans from $100,000 to $1 million are available. An additional $60 million is earmarked for the bank's Technology Investment Program, for loans between $1 million and $5 million. The $20 million remaining goes to a venture capital fund. The Royal Bank has had a similar program in place since 1991. In 1994 it set up a $125 million fund for investments in technology and exporting firms.

While the banks charge roughly prime plus two percentage points for business loans (or less), the Business Development Bank of Canada (BDC, formerly the Federal Business Development Bank) charges more for its funds but is in the microloan business; it will make loans of less than $100,000. Administrative costs are reduced by requiring borrowers to pay someone in the bank's Counselling Assistance for Small Enterprises (CASE) division to coach them and ensure that the application meets minimum standards. The cost to borrowers is usually less than $500 and can be added to the loan amount.

Angel investors are the next possibility. Angels are private investors who are looking for good investment opportunities. Often lawyers are well connected and typically play a matchmaking role; sometimes they invest themselves if a lot of heavy hitters are putting up money in what seems like a great opportunity. The Community Opportunities Investment Network and Services (COINS)/LinxNet service (416-675-1421), which is enthusiastically backed by BDC, the major banks, and regional economic development groups, matches up entrepreneurs and private investors and provides introductions and post-introduction facilitation. Many colleges and municipalities are considering copying the Ottawa-Carleton Economic Development Corp., which shows potential angels how to structure deals and what to avoid, in addition to showcasing companies seeking funding.

Venture capitalists, on the other hand, tend to focus only on businesses with high ("bonanza") potential, short-term horizons, and significant returns on investments. Normally they are seeking a return of ten times the venture capital investment in five years, and often they stipulate that the company must go public by then. Unless you can show a projected cash flow with at least a 25 percent annual rate of return over five to seven years, your bargaining position, if you have one, will be considerably undermined. Old-economy industries need not apply to venture capitalists; instead, technology companies, which often grow quickly and can realistically promise to meet this return-on-investment hurdle, accounted for 60 percent of venture investments in 1994, up from 46 percent in 1993 and 50 percent in 1994. Computer companies borrowed 18 percent of venture funds and manufacturing tapped 20 percent. Expansion-stage companies ran away with 56 percent of the venture capital available, up from 39 percent in 1993.

Overall, venture capital firms had $5 billion of their holdings invested in 1994, which was an increase of 24 percent over the previous year. One advantage of venture capitalists is their invaluable knowledge about how to make a company succeed. As seasoned players, they can help you avoid most of the expensive mistakes typical of newly minted entrepreneurs. In addition, they are usually extremely well connected to marketing, distribution, and customer channels. At the moment, labour-sponsored venture capital corporations account for 30 percent of the venture capital assets in Canada, with their attractive RRSP savings to investors helping to increase the amount of money available by one-third during 1994. Quebec business secured $800 million of the $2 billion available in 1994, but British Columbia was the fastest-growing market ($45 million versus $15 million in 1993) as a result of the B.C. Focus funds. Quebec investors, however, have taken a wait-and-see attitude since the 1995 referendum.

The biggest complaint of bankers, business brokers, and venture capitalists is the lack of "quality deals" with entrepreneurs. Indeed, 69 percent of those who sought out venture capitalists ran into difficulties because of this failing, as opposed to only 20 percent of those seeking debt financing. Enterprise Development, established by Herve de Jordy, offers a brokering service called The Focused Entrepreneur in Toronto (contact Anthony Bird at 416-363-8557), which tries to blend the four types of entrepreneurs (inventors, innovators, managers, and administrators) into one focussed consortium that is likely to win over sources of venture capital more easily. Business Centurions Centres Inc. of Toronto acts as a one-stop "dating" service for banks, governments, outplacement firms, head-hunting organizations, and venture capitalists. By acting as a clearinghouse or filter for each stakeholder, it can make better deals or "marriages."

The final option is to seek public or private placements – something which requires professional advice since they are subject to complex and rigorous rules. It is interesting to note that the average number of years before a company goes public has been shrinking steadily from 4.88 years in 1974–78 to 1.71 years in 1989–93, reflecting the rapid growth of technology companies. Of those who tried to go this route, 42 percent experienced twice as many difficulties compared with raising debt financing, and 28 percent were unable to obtain equity financing. Overall, 82 percent of companies resorted to some form of personal financing, 81 percent made use of debt financing, and only 10 percent used equity capital during the past five years.

Should you incorporate or operate simply as a registered proprietorship? If there is no likelihood of lawsuits, no possibility of bankruptcy, yet a chance that it will be a while before you realize a profit, then holding off on incorporating usually makes the most sense, because you can still deduct your losses against other sources of income you may have. When you incorporate, you must show a profit to claim expenses; however, incorporation provides you with many legal safeguards against creditors or extremely unhappy clients going after you or suing your personal estate. Moreover, the tax savings on profits are extremely attractive for incorporated businesses. For instance, with the exception of Alberta, the top individual combined federal/provincial marginal tax rate exceeds 50 percent, whereas it is now less than 25 percent on the first $200,000 of corporate income.

Customer Focus

Knowing your market and your implementation strategy is absolutely essential. After all, the customer is the most important decision-maker in any business and it is how you implement your entrepreneurial strategy to serve your customers that spells the difference between success and failure. According to the Business Development Bank of Canada, only

20 percent of all Canadian businesses of any size have a strategic vision and operational strategy. Although its 50 strategic-planning facilitators located at its locations across the country charge $9,000 to $20,000 for the bank's two-to-three-month program, over 1,500 owner-managers have taken advantage of the service.

There are many ways to divide your market into categories. John Powell of Shannon Schroeder in Calgary characterizes consumers as follows. Those in their 20s are "not yet financially secure. They demand instant gratification, lasting values and tangible benefits. Purchase decisions are based on emotions." People in their 30s and 40s "have high incomes and high debt. They are individualistic, striving for self-fulfillment, concerned about social and environmental issues. They look for information before buying." In their 40s and 50s, many who are prosperous and facing retirement purchase based on "sentimentality, brand loyalty and convenience." In their 60s and 70s, "they tend to have a lot of leisure time. They seek financial security, quality and value. They rely on knowledge and experience." The aging boomer market (those in their 30s and 40s) represents one of the biggest entrepreneurial opportunities available to all Canadians regardless of funds or education. However, like today's shoppers in their 60s and 70s, they are increasingly oriented toward quality and value as well.

As Ian Morrison, president of the Institute for the Future, notes, "When consumers are older, wiser and more cynical, quality is crucial. The basic fact is you have to have a quality product. Aging baby boomers will not buy shoddy products. The other fact about boomers and their skepticism is that old loyalties no longer exist. If Honda makes a better car than an American car maker, boomers buy it." So we are now seeing a new kind of shopper begin to emerge. Eventually the quality movement is likely to include most age groupings and will be part of the North American trend toward focussing on improving your overall quality of life (see *Boom, Bust & Echo*, by David Foot and Daniel Stoffman, for an excellent analysis of the opportunities identifiable by age categories).

As it turns out, quality is essentially entrepreneurial in origin. Or as Rosabeth Moss Kanter, former editor of the *Harvard Business Review*, observes, "Quality companies have an attitude that permits experimentation. Sometimes that's connected to a continuous improvement philosophy. But they encourage a multiplicity of experiments, constantly pushing the frontier throughout the company. They're much more open to the idea of change. They have much more flexible structures in which they're not rigidly bound by what's my territory versus what's your territory." For this reason, small businesses are often outperforming larger companies because they can be nimble and are always trying new approaches. Large companies, with their many layers of approval, coveted reputations at stake, and fear of untraveled paths, are often too slow to take advantage of the many opportunities that any period of rapid change generates.

One additional aspect of understanding entrepreneurial market opportunities is to look for niches within our increasingly diverse society. As Frank Feather, author of *Future Consumer*, told the 1994 annual convention of the Canadian Council of Grocery Distributors, "Stop thinking about ethnic marketing as being peripheral and a nice little side thing to do. Start thinking of ethnic marketing as central to your product marketing strategy. It's the core business that you're in in a global village microcosm marketplace. By 2004, a decade from now, the non-white segment will double to 50 percent in Toronto. Forty per cent in Vancouver will be non-white." The same reasoning applies to many products and services that might appeal to the growing number of consumer segments of one kind or another in our multicultural society. The number of market niche opportunities should increase even more through a blending of cultures and preferences over the long run.

In a more general sense, products or services are bound to do well if they save people time and money, entertain them or make them happier, are inexpensive and easier to use, combine a number of functions (such as one-stop shopping or problem-solving), are smaller and/or lighter, solve annoying problems, provide advice or information when needed, or eliminate worry. Many existing markets have not yet been fully taken advantage of, so a lucrative future awaits whoever opens them up further. For instance, only about 15 percent of all motors sold are energy-efficient, leaving a big market to be exploited. When you consider that only 4 to 6 percent of the world's information is stored electronically at the moment, it is clear that the remainder represents an opportunity of enormous proportions. Moreover, it will take $3 trillion to $4 trillion to create an information highway that spans the world.

When trying to identify a market, remember the real estate phrase "location, location, location" (unless you are planning to sell over the Internet or by mail order). Obviously any area that is economically growing and expanding is ripe for all kinds of entrepreneurial ventures. How do you get a sense for which locations are likely to be expanding? Aside from making use of the trend advice found elsewhere in this book, a good rule of thumb is to track the price of housing in an area over the past couple of years. For instance, in 1995 the hottest markets for new homes and resales were in Kitchener and London, Ontario – two cities that have experienced better job stability and growth as a result of their large number of export-driven companies. Exports are also beginning to firm up housing prices in Trois-Rivières, Oshawa, and Windsor. Any place where housing prices are remaining relatively high, such as Vancouver, must have people who can afford to pay for them – and for other things as well. Often areas beyond city limits, where the taxes are lower, or the farther reaches of suburbs (called "edge cities" by Joel Garreau) represent fertile growing markets if a region's economy is flourishing.

Successful Entrepreneurs

Aside from having a good grasp of potential market options, entrepreneurs need to be technologically literate. According to Computer Intelligence InfoCorp., in the U.S. a professionally self-employed person with a PC earns roughly $100,000, or 42 percent more than those without a PC. Owning and using a computer for business purposes on the information highway is the modern equivalent of owning a car to make your sales calls in the past, except that most salespeople never made $100,000 a year because they spent too much time driving from appointment to appointment and passing time in waiting rooms, couldn't qualify their buyers as easily, and saw most of their potential earnings eaten up in inefficient marketing and distribution channels.

What other characteristics define a successful entrepreneur? Some people have likened entrepreneurs to the hunters of our primitive past. Psychologist Thomas Hartmann describes a hunter as someone who "constantly monitors his environment. . . . Able to throw himself into the chase at a moment's notice. . . . Tireless, capable of sustained drives, but only when hot on the trail of some goal. . . . Visual thinker, clearly seeing a goal even if there are no words for it. . . . Independent. . . . Bored by mundane tasks; enjoys new ideas, excitement. . . . Willing and able to take risks, face danger. . . . No time for niceties when there are decisions to be made."

The entrepreneurial world has room for gatherers as well as hunters, and for adventurous people of both genders. The evidence shows that women are less likely to go bankrupt than men. According to the National Association for Women Business Owners in the United States, most female entrepreneurs think things over carefully before acting, rather than acting quickly (66 to 34 percent); most male entrepreneurs are quick to act (56 to 44 percent). Clearly certain business environments, such as relatively stable ones, favour the cautious entrepreneur. However, according to *Entrepreneur* magazine, it is usually more important to act decisively than to be right all the time. The trick is to be at least half right, and not to make all your mistakes in a row. By acting quickly and monitoring the results, you have more time to make appropriate adjustments. Thus in rapidly changing business environments it seems to make sense to follow the sequence "fire, load, aim" – the reason why Sony launches four products every day.

One of the most important tasks of the entrepreneur is to develop a risk-taking style that you are comfortable with. In Gene Calvert's *High-Wire Management* (1993), Laura Henderson, a successful entrepreneur and CEO, explains: "The biggest risk I take is managing my own way. . . . Often I learned what to do only after, not before, making a risky decision. When you're truly an entrepreneur, you don't always know what you're doing. If you're willing to make mistakes doing it 'your way' and learning from them, then I say, go for it!

"Female managers are often encouraged to go against their own basic management instincts and manage in a way out of sync with who they are and what they want to achieve. I think it's a necessity, and an obligation, for all managers to go with their intuition and manage the way that works best for them. It's not easy, but it's worth it in the long term."

Finally, the most essential ingredient for successful entrepreneurship is persistence – the persistence that comes from high self-motivation and a willingness to see failures or mistakes as learning opportunities or corrective feedback. As Benjamin Disraeli said, "The secret of success is constancy of purpose." The purpose must obviously be very self-motivating to carry one through all the obstacles that naturally lie in the path of any ambitious goal – especially when it has never been done before. As Harry S. Dent asserts in his book *Job Shock*, "It is your job to nurse your vision like a newborn child until it can walk on its own.... Success is going enthusiastically from failure to failure.... Giving up too soon is perhaps the biggest single reason I have seen entrepreneurs fail, even those who had promising products or innovations." In this department, Colonel Sanders should be an inspiration to us all. He received 1,008 rejections for his well-known chicken recipe before finally striking a deal.

For many, the entrepreneurial path is a lonely one. In Canada, two out of every three companies owned by an individual are single-person companies. By early in the next century, that number is expected to grow to a three- or four-to-one ratio. According to an Information Plus Inc. study entitled "The Coming Competition in Small Business Finance," 96 to 98 percent of all small businesses are likely to be in the service industry, which does not require a significant investment in equipment or lead to the production of tangible goods for sale. Freelancing is obviously easier when there are no financial barriers to starting up a business and no warehouses are needed to store inventory. It is worth noting, however, that people who are self-employed but do not have any employees working for them typically earn less than those who work for a company. The opposite is true for those entrepreneurs who employ others – their wages are usually higher than if they were working for someone else.

Going it alone is not always a good idea for other reasons. Many small businesses that operate in isolation are performing poorly, because many larger firms are restructuring in ways that allow them to become more entrepreneurial, much like franchises – except they also have all the marketing and other cost-saving advantages associated with franchises or large companies. Those small firms that band together and subcontract among themselves are managing to acquire some of the advantages of larger firms by offering a wider range of services and by extending their marketing reach through their cumulative efforts.

Working alone by not hiring any employees is often not fruitful either. A Statistics Canada survey of 1990 census data found that self-employed men who hired other workers earned an average of $51,300, but those who did not only earned $32,000. The average employee earned $38,000. Having others work for you or joining forces with other firms ironically ends up providing more financial rewards and more independence by increasing the number of options available.

Perhaps the most daunting factor for most people contemplating starting their own business is the fact that approximately 50 percent of all Canadian businesses go bust within their first three years. But these figures may be misleading. According to David Kirchoff, author of *Entrepreneurship and Dynamic Capitalism*, only 18 percent of new ventures actually fail. Most simply go out of business without leaving behind any creditors. In other words, they are often just part of the natural process of moving elsewhere, taking a job somewhere, or starting a new company. In 1994, Dun and Bradstreet in the U.S. found that almost 70 percent of all companies started in 1985 were still in business – with smaller companies having a lower failure rate than larger companies.

The Entrepreneurial Imperative

One of the big trends that favour starting your own business is the rapid growth in outsourcing. According to the Computer Sciences Corp., 63 percent of American and 72 percent of European businesses either outsource or plan to. The trend is likely to continue since, according to a 1993 study by Coopers & Lybrand, 65 percent of the fastest-growing companies outsource. Companies that don't outsource are developing internal markets in order to gain the advantages of entrepreneurial innovation and flexibility inside their companies. By turning parts of an organization into independent profit centres, companies are avoiding the development of large, authoritarian bureaucracies that weren't that much more efficient than the former Soviet economy. But the result is that even employees inside companies are forced to become entrepreneurs of sorts.

Before long many firms will hire people only on contract and have them work out of their homes, especially when employment-related taxes continue to discourage hiring (a 1995 study by the Bank of Canada found, for instance, that payroll taxes were responsible for eliminating 130,000 jobs during this decade). Some companies are encouraging the spinning off of existing functions to employees who are asked to start companies with help from the corporation. (Northern Telecom and Bell-Northern Research can claim parentage of 55 Canadian high-tech companies started by former employees in this manner.) Many people will find themselves invited to become self-employed, even if they never originally planned to take this route. As one result, the Institute of Small Business Counsellors in Halifax is now offering training to those interested in advising entrepreneurs at most Maritime universities. There is definitely a market for training entrepreneurs, when you consider that 25 percent of all Canadian small businesses are owned by people aged 18 to 29.

Perhaps the most encouraging news for those who end up self-employed is that when Padgett Business Services surveyed Canadian entrepreneurs in 1995, they found that 75 percent said they would do it all over again. People who work in smaller companies report higher overall job satisfaction as well. Welcome to the world where small is beautiful.

Resources for Entrepreneurs

Alliance of Independent Businesses
PO Box 280, Station R,
Toronto, ON M4G 3Z9
Tel: 800-567-8867 or 416-423-2028 Fax: 416-696-7899

Barter Plus Inc.
Tel: 416-490-9599

Canadian Association for Home-Based Business
1200E Prince of Wales Dr.
Ottawa, ON K2C 1M9
Tel: 613-724-7964

Canadian Organization of Small Business Inc.
Box 11246 MPO
Edmonton, AB T5H 3J5
Tel: 403-423-2672 Fax: 403-423-2751

Canadian Professional Sales Association
145 Wellington St. West, #30
Toronto, ON M5J 1H8
Tel: 800-268-3794 or 416-408-2654
• discounts on materials; regional networking and seminars

Canadian Association of Women Executives and Entrepreneurs
595 Bay St., Suite 300
Toronto, ON M5G 2C2
Tel: 416-596-7923

CASE (small business counselling service)
Business Development Bank of Canada
Tel: 800-361-2126

Groupe québécoise des entreprises à domicile inc.
CP 1010
Victoriaville PQ G6P 8Y1

Info Entrepreneurs
Montreal Board of Trade
Tel: 514-496-INFO

Micro Business Support Group
804 Grenan Ave.
Ottawa, ON K2B 6G2
Tel: 613-596-6262 Fax: 613-596-0266

SOHO Business Group
2255-B Queen St. East
Toronto, ON
Tel: 416-693-7646
• $120 annual fee for volume discounts for small businesses

Vancouver Home-Based Business Association
4576 West 6 Ave.,
Vancouver, BC V6R 1V5
Tel: 604-224-7243 Fax: 604-224-7245

Women Who Excel
PO Box 3533, Station C,
Hamilton, ON L8H 1N5
Tel & Fax: 416-547-7135

EXPORT MARKET

Asia Access International Business Group
#613–475 Howe Street
Vancouver, BC V6C 2B3
Tel: 604-688-ASIA or 800-656-ASIA Fax: 604-688-2788

Export Development Corp.
151 O'Connor Street
Ottawa, ON K1A 1K3
Tel: 613-598-2992 Fax: 613-598-3098

Forum for International Trade Training
Heritage Place
155 Queen Street, Sixth Floor
Ottawa, ON K1P 6L1

Market Intelligence and Technology Opportunities Service
Strategic Information Branch
Industry Canada
235 Queen Street
Ottawa, ON K1A 0H5
Tel: 613-954-4970 Fax: 613-954-2340

NAFTA Export Pages
West Marketing Resources Group
1-800-331-7384

YOUNG ENTREPRENEUR PROGRAMS

The Canadian Youth Business Foundation,
595 Bay St.
Toronto, ON
Tel: 416-408-2923
• Sponsored by the Canadian Imperial Bank of Commerce, Royal Bank of Canada and the Canadian Youth Foundation. Provides loans of up to $15,000 to unemployed people between the ages of 18 and 29. Internet service on resources for entrepreneurs.

Self-Employment Assistance Program: contact a Canada Employment Centre

Atlantic Canada Opportunities Agency
644 Main St., 3rd Fl.,
PO Box 6051,
Moncton, NB E1C 9J8
Tel: 800-561-7862

British Columbia:
Young Entrepreneur Conference Series
Tel: 800-361-2126, or contact any B.C. Regional Economic
   Development office

Manitoba:
Young Entrepreneurs or Business Start program
Tel: 800-361-2126
• funding $2,000 to $10,000

Quebec:
Société d'Investissement Jeunesse
Tel: 514-875-8674
• funding $50,000 to $150,000

CANADA BUSINESS SERVICE CENTRES

Information toll-free by Touch-Tone phone and FaxBack service. The FaxBack service operates 24 hours a day, 7 days a week. You can order main catalogue items and documents at succeeding levels of specificity. All material is free.

British Columbia
601 West Cordova Street
Vancouver, BC V6B 101
Tel: 604-775-5525 or 800-667-2272
FaxBack: 604-775-5515

Alberta
9700 Jasper Avenue
Suite 122
Edmonton, AB T5J 4H7
Tel: 403-495-6800 or 800-272-9675
FaxBack: 403-495-4138 or 800-563-9926

Saskatchewan
122–3rd Avenue North
Saskatoon, SK S7K 2H6
Tel: 306-956-2323 or 800-667-4374
FaxBack: 306-956-2310 or 800-667-9433

Manitoba
330 Portage Avenue
PO Box 981
Winnipeg, MB R3C 2V2
Tel: 204-984-2272 or 800-665-2019
FaxBack: 204-984-5527 or 800-665-9386

Ontario
230 Richmond Street West
Toronto, ON M5V 3E5
Tel: 416-954-4646 or 800-567-2345
FaxBack: 416-954-8555 or 800-240-4192

Quebec
5 Place Ville Marie
Suite 12500
Montreal, PQ H3B 4Y2
Tel: 514-496-4636 or 800-322-4636
FaxBack: 514-496-4010 or 800-322-4010

New Brunswick
570 Queen Street
PO Box 578
Fredericton, NB E3B 6Z6

Tel: 506-444-6140 or 800-688-1010

Nova Scotia
1575 Brunswick Street
Halifax, NS B3J 201
Tel 902-426-8604 or 800-668-1010
FaxBack: 902-426-3201 or 800-401-3201

Prince Edward Island
232 Queen Street
PO Box 40
Charlottetown, PE C1A 7K2
Tel 902-368-0771 or 800-668-1010
Faxback: 902-368-0776 or 800-401-3201

Newfoundland
90 O'Leary Avenue
PO Box 8687
St. John's, NF A1B 3T1
Tel: 709-772-6022 or 800-668-1010
FaxBack: 709-772-6030

WEB SITES

American Demographics
http://www.marketingtools.com
• trends analyzed

ARGUS Map Viewer
http://www.argusmap.com
• software that provides a directory according to geographic area

Bank of Montreal
http://www.bmo.com
• strategic planning organized around 15 different small business
problems; on-line forum for entrepreneurs

Canadian Consulate-General in Detroit
http://BizServe.com/canadian-detroit
• tech development in U.S. Midwest and Canada

Institute of Management and Administration (U.S.)
http://starbase.ingress.com/ioma
• excellent business info hot links

Malls of Canada
http://inforamp.net/provider/index.html
• $300 per year for electronic store window

MEDIAfusion
http://mfusion.com
• 30 Maritime companies that communicate, source funding, and
create partnerships

NAFTAnet
http://www.nafta.net

Open Bidding Service (Government of Canada)
http://www.obs.ism.ca

Small Business Administration (U.S.)
http://www.sbaonline.sba.gov

BULLETIN BOARD SERVICES

Bishop Information Group
Tel: 416-364-8770
• many small business resources

CANLOC
Dalhousie University, Halifax, N.S.
Tel: 902-494-2860
• database of 750 government financial incentive programs updated daily

BOOKS

Business Plan with a Future, Business Development Bank of Canada (888-INFO-BDC or http://www.bdc.ca/site/right/financ/index.html.

De Jordy, Herve, *On Your Own: Successful Entrepreneurship in the '90s,* McGraw Hill, 1990.

Easto, Larry, *How to Succeed in Your Home Business,* Doubleday, 2nd ed., 1995.

Hagan, Louise, *Start and Run a Profitable Office Service Business from Your Home,* Self-Counsel Press, 1995.

Hall, Daryl, *1101 Businesses You Can Start From Home: The World's Most Complete Directory of Part-time and Full-time Business Ideas,* Wiley & Sons, 2nd ed., 1995.

Hawken, Paul, *Grow Your Own Business,* Simon & Schuster, 1987.

James, Jack D., *Starting a Successful Business in Canada,* Self-Counsel Press, 1995.

Legal Guide to Incorporating, Maintaining and Carrying On Your Business in Ontario, Rational Thoughts Inc., 390 Bay St., Suite 705, Toronto, ON M5H 2Y2, tel: 416-956-7753.

Leonard, Woody, *The Underground Guide to Telecommuting: Slightly Askew Advice on Leaving the Rat Race Behind,* Addison-Wesley, 1995.

McQueen, Rod, *The Last Best Hope: How to Start and Grow Your Business,* McClelland & Stewart, 1995.

1996 Franchise Annual, Info Franchise News, 9 Duke St., PO Box 670, St. Catharines, ON L2R 6W8, tel: 905-688-2665.
• 4,210 franchise listings in the U.S., Canada, and overseas

Richards, Linda, *The Canadian Business Guide to Using the Internet,* Self-Counsel Press, 1995.

Rumball, Donald, *The Entrepreneurial Edge: Canada's Top Entrepreneurs Reveal the Secrets of Their Success*, Key Porter, 1989.

The Why EDI Guide for Small and Medium-Sized Entrepreneurs, EDI World Institute in Montreal, tel: 514-288-3555.

Worzel, Richard, *From Employee to Entrepreneur: How to Turn Your Experience into a Fortune*, Key Porter, 1989.

PUBLICATIONS AND SOFTWARE

Business Access (small business newsletter)
PO Box 4850, Station E,
Ottawa, ON K1S 5J1

EarthEnterprise Tool Kit
Institute for Sustainable Development
161 Portage Ave. East, Sixth floor
Winnipeg, MB R3B OY4

Managing Your Cashflow: available at the Royal Bank

Planning for Success (CD-ROM)
Canadian Bankers Association
416-362-6092/210

Profit: The Magazine for Canadian Entrepreneurs
777 Bay St.
Toronto, ON M5W 1A7
Tel: 416-364-4760 Fax: 416-596-5111
• the summer issue lists the 100 fastest-growing small businesses
in Canada

Scotiabusiness Plan Writer: available free at any Scotiabank branch

Small Business Profiles
Statistics Canada
25 St. Clair Ave. East,
Toronto, ON M4T 1M2
Tel: 416-973-6586
• comprehensive portraits of up to 700 industries with essential regional information

CHAPTER THREE

WHERE THE JOBS ARE IN THE NEW ECONOMY

The potential for inexpensive replication meant that early "knowledge workers"
. . . like Colt or Ford could earn far more from the ideas that they created than
even the best craftsmen could [from the articles they made].

PAUL ROMER, UNIVERSITY OF CALIFORNIA AT BERKELEY

If I introduce a new technology to create a market this morning, I'd better start
working on ways to improve it this afternoon. If I don't, someone else will, and
my market share will begin eroding by sunset.

RAYMOND SMITH, CEO, BELL ATLANTIC CORPORATION

Dividing jobs into "old economy" and "new economy" jobs does not necessarily mean that the former are vanishing while the latter expand. Old economy industries will apply new technology to keep themselves and their products competitive. We'll look at the job prospects for these industries in Chapter 4. For the moment, let's consider jobs in new economy industries – the telecommunications industry; the computer and software industry; instrumentation, robotics, and research and development; medical technology, pharmaceuticals, biotechnology, and health care; and environmental industries. Approximately seven out of ten Canadians are currently employed in information-technology-based industries, which in turn support 120 different supply industries. These industries are largely in the growth phase, and all are underpinned by heavy investment in information technology and its applications. Despite their status as growth areas, these industries are extremely competitive because such potentially large global markets are up for grabs. These are knowledge-intensive areas, and require individuals proficient in science and technology. Although individual employers may rise and fall because of a high level of competition, long-term career prospects in these industries are excellent since all these industries will experience prolonged periods of economic growth and prosperity. These industries also afford opportunities for professional development and advancement and the possibility of moving elsewhere in Canada or the world, and although there is no guarantee of job security with a particular company, there will probably always be a job somewhere in the industry. Individuals employed in these new economy industries will experience only short periods of unwanted unemployment.

Where the Jobs Are in the Telecommunications Industry

According to Columbia University's Center for Telecommunications and Information Studies, the global telecommunications industry is larger than either the computer industry or the aerospace industry. It's a $700 billion business worldwide, with Canada cornering $21 billion of this market. Although it represents only 2.7 percent of our gross national product, the industry's annual growth rate is estimated to be 6 to 7 percent, and it is growing twice as fast as any other industry in Canada as a percentage of the gross domestic product. Now that Ottawa has raised the foreign ownership ceiling from 20 percent to 33.3 percent,

American investors should be further heating up the market. Not only do more people work in the communications and telecommunications industry than in the forestry industry in British Columbia, but the telecommunications industry is larger than Canada's petroleum and mining industries combined. The Department of Industry, Science and Technology reports that there are 185,000 people working in this field, the majority of whom live in Ontario and Quebec.

In 1992, the worldwide telecommunications equipment industry was worth approximately US$110 billion, with Northern Telecom Ltd. holding a 7.5 percent share of the business. This industry manufactures terminal and mobile equipment, electronic components, switching equipment, satellite and microwave systems, transmission products, PBXs, telephones, and copper and fibre optic cables, employing 50,000 workers in Canada and generating $6 billion in business annually. Northern Telecom is the largest manufacturer of telecommunications equipment, and is responsible for supplying most of the nation's telephone terminals and central office equipment. This multinational corporation employs over 20,000 Canadians, most of whom live in Ontario, and has 50 plants located worldwide. The mid-sized companies in telecommunications manufacturing include Newbridge Networks Corp., Mitel Corporation, Spar Aerospace Limited, Toshiba of Canada Ltd., Motorola, and Gandalf Data Limited. Unfortunately, because many of these companies have been automating, their work forces have been shrinking. So where are the jobs in this industry?

Many telecommunications jobs will be available in companies that make extensive use of telecommunications equipment and services. These "end users" include industries such as broadcasting, manufacturing, finance, newspaper publishing, health care, education, and retailing. A company's relationship with its suppliers, customer service, and operation management increasingly depend on a flexible communications system that is continually improving. Jobs in the telecommunications industry often vary according to what use the technology is put to within a company and the size of the company itself. While office administrators might oversee the implementation and operation of a local area network (LAN) or telephone switching system, a dispatcher for a trucking company might coordinate and monitor a fleet's whereabouts via satellite. Larger firms often hire specialists for particular aspects of the purchasing, managing, implementation, and training aspects of telecommunications voice and data systems. Canadian banks spend more than 4 percent of their revenue on telecommunications services and often hire dozens of workers to operate this technology. To appreciate the many telecommunications employment opportunities available in banking in Canada and internationally, one has only to think of the many electronic innovations pioneered by banks: electronic funds transfer, multibranch banking, home banking, automatic banking machines (ABMs), and, recently, imaging technology. The Hongkong Bank of Canada, whose parent bank is one of the ten largest financial institutions in the world, participates in six international ABM worldwide networks that provide customers access to over 100,000 machines; corporate customers can access global accounts electronically, then carry out any banking transaction worldwide; letters of credit can be created electronically by customers who can also communicate with their banks through electronic mail.

IBM is focussing on switched virtual networking (SVN), which is a desktop-to-WAN strategy meant to speed up the adoption of asynchronous transport mode (ATM) so that routers will be obsolete within three years. Switch-centric networking will play a vital role in making the information highway fully interactive and broadband. Advances in compression technology will allow the videoconferencing market to grow by 30 to 40 percent for the next several years. MPEG-2 (motion picture expert group) video compression will produce videos of near broadcast quality.

Since cellular phones were introduced in Canada in 1985, 8 percent of the Canadian population have become users. That growth rate is expected to double by the turn of the century as prices drop and more competition from PCS (personal communication services) emerges. Northern Telecom found that telephone tag cost U.S. and Canadian businesses $4 billion a year in lost time and productivity, and 38 percent of customers who couldn't reach the person they were calling took their business elsewhere. As a result, sales of wireless office phones are booming, as are sales of pagers with message-receiving capabilities.

With more than $720 million spent on telecommunications research and development in 1992, many jobs will be available in this continually expanding field. Of the researchers hired in the industry in that year, 3,100 hold bachelor's degrees; 1,250, master's degrees; and 305, doctoral

BULLETIN BOARD – *TELECOMMUNICATIONS*

- **Job demand factors:** telecommunications is the fastest-growing industry thanks to the growth of computer networks and the globalization of trade.
- **Job growth areas:** electrical engineering; communications; technical support; end-user support; database support; education; operations; administration; law; sales; client-server support; network integration; cellular phone industry; call centres; Canadian companies taking advantage of overseas booming markets; wireless market in general ("untethered communication").
- **Skills, abilities, qualities, education needed:** college diploma or university degree in electronic engineering, electronic engineering technology or computer sciences; strong logical and problem-solving abilities; systems thinking.
- **Job reduction areas:** telephone operators; switchboard operators; receptionists; information personnel; telephone order takers; telecommunications technology will also eliminate jobs in retailing and hotels relying on business travel.
- **Growth limiting factors:** adoption of common standards for data transmission; installation of optical fibre; ability to form alliances; and government regulations.
- **Issues:** the race to establish a global standard will lead to a breakneck pace of research and development. Who will win – telephone, cable, or satellite companies? Pay close attention to ongoing developments.

degrees. Jobs are also available for those with less training: 1,100 individuals provide administrative support and an additional 1,000 provide technical support. Remember, too, that there are many non-technical jobs associated with any growing industry, in such areas as finance, marketing, administration, and data entry.

Given the convergence of a number of technologies, the telecommunications industry faces a challenging future. Telephone, cable, cellular, and television boundaries will disappear and so will some of the players in an inevitable industry shake-out. Indeed, a fierce struggle for survival is taking place at the moment, with companies being forced to globalize in order to meet end users' demands for one-stop worldwide service.

Customers are increasingly demanding integrated services throughout the world. Competition has intensified now that customers are buying quality, low-cost communications equipment and materials worldwide. Since many manufacturers are having trouble generating the capital needed for research and development, many joint ventures and mergers and acquisitions are inevitable. When a competitor like AT&T has, in addition to its $15 to $16 billion equipment business, a $50 billion service business to draw upon for cash flow, the smaller companies can survive only if they band together to share resources.

With the industry globalizing its ventures, many companies like SR Telecom Inc. of Montreal are exporting telecommunications systems to developing countries. Given the worldwide push to make telephones accessible to everyone, many companies will do so. There will be plenty of opportunity for exporting to the many countries that will go directly to cellular and digital systems, skipping the copper wire telephone stage altogether. With this in mind, avoid seeking employment in companies that are largely domestic or that trade with only one other country. These companies will either go out of business or be subject to a merger or acquisition, which could mean that you get downsized out of a job. If you are about to join a telecommunications company, ask what its strategy is on joint ventures and future markets. For example, because Newbridge Networks anticipated the impending shift to multiplexors (sophisticated electronic switchers typically used by banks and other large institutions) six months ahead of its competition, it now serves 80 telephone companies in 60 countries, with exports accounting for 90 percent of its sales. It also developed its products around universal telephone company standards, making networks easier to divide among different customers, and has entered the ATM market, which is a future growth area.

Other promising firms include Calgary's Geodyssey Ltd., which makes geographic information system software for satellites, a $2 billion industry that is growing rapidly. Companies that speed up communication or facilitate global monitoring will do well. AeroAstro Inc., a U.S. firm, develops tiny satellites (microsats) that are inexpensive to design, equip, and launch – allowing businesses to multiply the number of services and networks available to them. And don't forget global hiring. Sweden's L.M. Ericson Telephone Co. Inc. was looking to recruit 2,500 engineers worldwide in 1995 for its rapidly growing mobile phone business.

BULLETIN BOARD – *TELECOMMUNICATIONS*

TIPS

➤ A certificate in telecommunications can be obtained from Ryerson
University in Toronto or by taking the program on a part-time basis at
a number of community colleges. College technology programs focus
on the operation and maintenance of systems, whereas design and
development positions require a combination of software engineering
and electrical engineering. Other combinations of courses that have
resulted from the merging of computers and telecommunications
include information management and industrial engineering for
application-related jobs, while information management and law pre-
pares the job seeker for employment in regulatory agencies such as
the Canadian Radio-television and Telecommunications Commission
(CRTC). Additional educational and training information can be
obtained by contacting the Telecommunications Department,
Ryerson Polytechnic University, 350 Victoria St., Toronto, M5B 2K3
or telephone 416-979-5000, ext. 6740.

➤ Industry journals such as *Network World* and *Computing Canada* are
good sources of information about recent developments in this
rapidly changing field.

CONTACTS

➥ Canadian Business Telecommunications Alliance
Canada Trust Tower
Box 705, No. 3650
161 Bay Street
Toronto, ON M5J 2S1
Tel. 416-865-9993 or 800-668-2282 Fax: 416-865-0859
E-mail: cbta@inforamp.net

Where the Jobs Are in the Computer and Software Industry

After the computer and software industry surpassed the chemical
industry in 1991 to become the largest in North America, with sales of
$322 billion in the U.S., the next two years were not kind to it. It experi-
enced falling profits, fierce price wars, flat sales, and the loss of thousands
of jobs. But at the same time, personal computer makers, such as Dell
Computer Corporation, saw their quarterly sales rise by 129 percent and

their profits by 77 percent. Similarly, profits for Microsoft rose by 53 percent. According to *Career Pathways*, a U.S. career magazine, "Twenty years ago, there were 50,000 computers installed worldwide. Today, more than 50,000 computers are installed every day." In 1995, they accounted for roughly 40 percent of all spending on machinery and equipment, up from 3 percent in 1981. Indeed, in 1995, 30 percent of Canadian households had a computer – a doubling within two years – suggesting that computers are not just luxuries. In fact, computers now outsell TVs.

The products of the computer industry are becoming more or less interchangeable; witness the proliferation of hardware and software companies. Soon the only differences between products will be price, profit margins, and marketing strategy. Dell is successful, for example, because the company sells its computers directly, not through a retailer or a sales force. As a result, Dell has been able to keep prices lower than its competitors, and it incorporates the latest technology into its products because it never keeps more than 11 days' worth of stock on hand. It is unusual for an innovative high-tech business to produce such a uniform product; however, once a standard has been established, all products tend to conform to the standard. In the case of the personal computer market, the architecture of IBM computers became the industry standard for the clone market. Once an operating system becomes a standard, all software firms design their application software to conform to this standard. For this reason, the products are very much alike or commodity-like.

Once the market stops growing, the focus shifts to cost-cutting as a shake-out takes place. Revenues from the sales of computers for white-collar computer workers, who are the biggest users of computers, have been level in the U.S. since 1983, have just leveled off in Europe and Asia, and will level off in developing countries within a few years. This is partly because the price of computing power – memory size plus clock speed plus operating system efficiency plus software capability – has dropped by at least 30 percent annually. As computer components became cheaper, thanks to research and development, more companies that produced clones could afford to enter the market, and profits fell with the increased competition. Although annual computer sales run at about $300 billion worldwide, most potential buyers already have a computer of some sort. IBM anticipates that the computer hardware business will not match world economic growth in general. According to a 1993 report on the industry by McKinsey and Co., a management consulting firm, "Just surviving will be a struggle and even many of today's healthy companies could become extinct." However, most hardware companies are hoping that multimedia applications requiring faster computers will continue to spur on sales.

The software and services side of the industry, however, is expected to grow by 11 to 13 percent a year worldwide from 1993 to 1997. The software industry has more room to grow because of the infinite number of possible applications. The $60 million 3-D software market is expected to increase by 30 percent annually into the late 1990s; 2-D software editing and special effects software, allowing home users to make their own movies, will be worth $450 million annually. Home-education software grew 121 percent from 1993 to 1994, making it the fastest-growing software market. Even entertainment software grew by 38 percent over that period. Canadian software products are expected to generate $4.2 billion in 1996, up from $1.2 billion in 1991, with exports accounting for 60 percent of these revenues.

Of Canada's 173,000 software workers, one-third are in-house employees – working for banks, insurance companies, real estate firms, government, the wholesale and retail trade – and two-thirds are employed in the software industry itself, with growth rates of 20 percent annually anticipated for software companies and 5 percent for in-house software workers. There are companies that manufacture and market software, such as Cognos Inc.'s PowerHouse database or Corel's draw products; approximately 12,000 individuals are currently employed in this area. Software services are often contracted out because of a lack of skills among in-house employees. According to Paul Swinwood of the Software Human Resource Council, "Our extrapolations show about 20,000 jobs that could be filled if the right person with the right background and the right training were there.... Unfilled vacancies, as reported by employers, have jumped dramatically within three years and will probably continue to climb unless aggressive methods are sought for increasing the supply of new entrants." Based on company projections, the software work force is expected to double to 325,000 software workers by the end of the decade.

Other software companies may design "embedded software" which is needed for inclusion in other products. IBM and Northern Telecom are involved in this aspect, though this software is needed in all manufacturing sectors – CAE Electronic flight simulators and Spar Aerospace CANADARM, for example. Approximately 7,000 workers are active in this part of the industry. Information technology service companies such as DMR Group Inc. and SHL Systemhouse Inc. operate as systems integrators, software developers, and project consultants, while smaller consulting firms undertake more specific application projects; there are 33,000 software workers in this field.

Even though IBM continues to lay off staff, the company is nonetheless hiring software workers. Software represents $2.8 billion in business for IBM. In Canada, 1,500 of its 10,000 employees work in the software side of the industry. The two software products IBM now specializes in are compilers and database managers, both of which are sold globally. Given that there are 140 million personal computer users worldwide and only 30 million large mainframe computer users, IBM will very likely shift its focus to the multitask work station side of the business and to the Internet server market.

The biggest growth area for software development over the next couple of years will be "intranet" software, which allows companies to set up and run private Internet servers for their own staff, eliminating most internal communications bottlenecks caused by the use of different computers and software programs. Silicon Graphics Inc., for instance, has 800 internal Web sites with 144,000 Web pages of information. Zona Research Inc. of California predicts that intranet software sales will grow from $476 million in 1995 to $4 billion in 1997 – almost a tenfold increase within two years and four times the growth rate of Internet software. Every one of IBM's business clients has asked for intranet software. As a result, the market for Web-authoring tools is expected to grow from $2 million in 1995 to $300 million by the end of the decade. Eventually even "mission-critical" applications, such as order processing and accounting, may find their way onto intranet servers. In addition, "extranets" – servers dedicated to including trading partners, suppliers, and even customers – are going beyond transactions to focus on problem-solving, collaboration, and cooperative design processes.

Individuals who hold a master's degree in computer science or computer engineering will have very little trouble finding positions in the software industry. However, in-house software users are not necessarily computer-trained, and as a result, many will be laid off unless they retrain. The federal government and many companies that use information technology plan to spend $12 million over the next three years upgrading the skills of 15,000 Canadian software workers. The knowledge and skills requirements of information service workers are similar to those of software workers, though at a lower technical level. These workers often perform a variety of functions that are not necessarily computer-related. Job titles include programmer, systems analyst, end-user support, project manager, and maintenance personnel.

Individuals interested in pursuing a career in the computer industry will need to continually upgrade their skills to keep pace with the latest developments. Two worldwide trends are significant. First, information technology companies are diverging into either technology manufacturers or technology providers, with some technology manufacturers moving over to become providers – Control Data Systems Canada and Unisys Canada Inc., for example. Second, the industry is dividing into value-added chain segments – support and maintenance, distribution channels, applications software, software tools and utilities, system software, processors, and peripherals – with intense competition in each chain segment. The increasing diversity and segmentation within the industry means individuals contemplating a career in the software industry must specialize. At the moment there is some confusion over job titles, but these are gradually being standardized. As with any growing and expanding industry, there are many spinoff job areas that do not necessarily involve programming. There are jobs for individuals who are skilled in administration, finance, law, client services, sales, and marketing. Job seekers interested in the marketing side of the industry should be wary, however; according to a report by the Information Technology Association of Canada, entitled "Doing More With Less," hundreds of marketing jobs in the computer industry have disappeared now that U.S. parent companies are often assuming this function as a cost-cutting measure.

The training side of the software industry represents a job growth area. Since a shortage of appropriately trained software workers is anticipated in the future, community colleges and private training institutes are offering crash courses in programming. The Institute of Computer

Studies in Toronto, for example, offers an immersion course that promises to condense a regular two-year college program into five months. Students are required to eat, breathe, and sleep computer training during their five months of computer boot camp. Many of the institute's graduates have been hired by companies like Bell Canada, Sun Life Assurance Company of Canada, Canadian Imperial Bank of Commerce, Air Canada, and Lotus Development Canada Ltd. Microsoft certification courses and Novell netware administration programs are doing very well also.

At the Software Development '93 conference held in Boston, John Soyring, director of software development for IBM, announced that some of the best career prospects exist in object technology (OT) and distributed client/server computing. He made this claim because new hardware architectures such as Pentium and Power PC are extending the capabilities of personal computers for use in distributed computing, as are digital signal processing (DSP) chips and asynchronous transport mode (ATM) network switching. AT&T's GlobalView 2000 ATM system, for example, runs at 20 gigabits per second, allowing one switch to handle all the data and voice, phone, and image information and all multimedia communications. Vendors are laying the groundwork for object technology and distributed computing by creating such standards as DCE (Distributed Computing Environment), DME (Distributed Management Environment), and CORBA (Common Object Request Broker Architecture). Other efforts in this direction include Open Doc and COSE (Common Operating System Environment). Programmers who begin developing software for these new industry platforms will likely find employment easily, given the head start they will have on other programmers.

With Netscape, Sun Microsystems, and Silicon Graphics joining forces to develop cross-platform, 3-D, multimedia interactive software, there will be a huge growth in virtual reality modeling language (VRML) and Javascript. But General Magic's Telescript, which can retain items in memory as they move from machine to machine, will likely prevail in the end – despite its embarrassing attempts to get off the ground – or merge with Java. Microsoft's plan to eventually merge Windows 95 with NT software points to the strong future that lies ahead for networking software. Considering that IBM paid $3.5 billion for Lotus Notes or groupware software, any software that helps get us closer to the global village will prosper. Search engines of various kinds will be needed to sort through the endless amounts of information available. Encryption technologies that ensure privacy and security and computer forensic services will do very well as well. Toronto's Certicom, an over-the-counter encryption stock, increased tenfold in value in 1996. In addition, over 10,000 Year-2000 specialists will be needed in the next few years.

According to Peter Ward, a corporate recruiter, the ideal applicant for many growth companies has five to 15 years of experience and is willing to work on contract. Eighty percent of the professionals he hires are employed on a contract basis. Computer specialists are in short supply, according to Cynthia Lucas of Total EDP Services, a Toronto job placement agency. Shortages exist for Y-2000, Powerbuilder, Oracle 7, and graphical user interface specialists, database analysts, programmer analysts, and systems analysts with two to six years' experience. Co-op program graduates are considered for these positions, but not college or university undergraduates without previous industry experience.

Training and service have become vital to companies with a desire to maximize their investment in computer technology. According to a research study conducted by Nolan, Norton, & Co., the information technology consulting arm of KPMG Peat Marwick Thorne, the actual cost of personal computing can be as high as $20,000 per machine per year, as a result of a hidden cost of $6,000 to $15,000 for the time employees spend showing one another how to get the computer to perform some task. Thus, with 55 percent of the employees in large organizations using computers, serving the information needs of companies will be a lucrative growth area. Xerox expected that by 1995, 50 percent of its revenue would accrue from offering computer services and software information. Employees would phone Xerox to have their software problems solved quickly, instead of wasting their own company's time trying to solve a computer problem on their own.

By 1993, 52 percent of all computer sites had adopted open systems, compared with 6 percent in 1989. By 1997, it is expected that over 80 percent of all computer sites will be using open systems. Using open systems translates directly into lower computer training costs. It stands to reason, then, that most companies will adopt open systems and increase spending on open systems training, thereby creating more jobs for the

BULLETIN BOARD — *COMPUTERS AND SOFTWARE*

- **Job demand factors:** falling price of computer technology; increased power of personal computers; open system architecture allowing for networks within and among companies; compatible software; facilitation of information transfer; better imaging and document management.
- **Job growth areas:** the software industry and professional services areas; the entertainment industry; technical support; help desks; Internet services; intranet software; Web-page authoring tools; Y-2000 help.
- **Skills, abilities, qualities, education needed:** individuals with advanced skills and experience are eagerly sought by companies around the world; a university degree in computer science, accompanied by co-op learning programs, is strongly recommended; creative software solutions usually require a reasonably good knowledge of the application area – accounting, for example – so expertise in both software and an application area is a plus; business skills are an advantage since most software needs to be designed for new programs, products, services, and organizational forms; ability to work in a team and to solve problems creatively; patience; persistence; logical thinking; attention to detail; flexibility.
- **Job reduction areas:** order or information processing; middle management; information services for those who have not upgraded their skills; publishing and printing other than desktop; inventory staff; computer repair due to higher quality and rapid obsolescence; work done according to spec is going overseas.
- **Growth limiting factors:** low-cost software developers in India, Israel, Ireland, Mexico, Singapore, Hungary, China, and the Philippines.
- **Issues:** open system versus proprietary system products; increasing commodity-like nature of software and hardware, making cost a critical factor; common or compatible technology with suppliers; operating system standards for personal computer and network markets; competition focussing on each segment of the value-added chain network.

computer-literate in the process. In 1991, only 3 percent of firms used client-server systems, but by 1994 60 percent did, and more are jumping on the bandwagon.

Most software applications jobs will involve solving generic business problems or making information technology friendlier. Many small software companies get their start by designing a broad-based application package that is geared to saving companies considerable sums of money over time. Since 75 percent of large software systems don't work the way they are supposed to or at all, more emphasis is shifting to clarifying frames of reference and feasibility upfront. Numetrix Ltd. developed a software program for Kraft General Foods Inc. called Schedulex; this program tells Kraft precisely how much of each product the company should produce and in what order, with the least amount of inventory, change-overs, and overtime. Manufacturers, hard hit by the recession, are also adopting this software as an industry standard so that they can stop and start production according to the competitive needs of companies, or meet the changing needs of consumers.

Other software that improves communication (such as contact, groupware) is doing well. For instance, ComShare, which reroutes calls to telephones, answering or fax machines, or computers on a single incoming line, is a great cost-saver. Benchmark Technologies, on the other hand, has devised a software program called Integrated Software Processing Workframe (ISPW), which runs IBM mainframes so as to integrate different software being used on a mainframe; ISPW makes life easier for the computer programmer, who can apply the process to solve problems arising from the use of software written in different languages. The programmer does not need to be familiar with the different computer languages in order to solve glitches. Once successful, these programs quickly become industry standards.

Internet-related software such as intranet text retrieval software is often given away free in the hope that by creating "mindshare," commercial possibilities will arise naturally. For instance, Simware Inc. of Ottawa released free demos of its Salvo software, which translates mainframe data into Web-ready format. Other companies are going after the graphics niche. Vancouver's Totally Hip Software Inc. offers Sizzler software, which allows for real-time display of moving graphics and is compatible with Visual Basic Language and Java. Peter Eddison, of Fulcrum Technologies Inc. in Ottawa, feels that Internet software will be the driving force for the foreseeable future.

Security is becoming an important concern, especially since two-thirds

BULLETIN BOARD — *COMPUTERS AND SOFTWARE*

TIPS

➤ When looking for training, opt for computer co-op programs, since graduates from these programs can usually find work much more easily than those who have only taken courses.

➤ Check the Branham Consulting Group's annual list of the top independent software companies in Canada and the top 50 Canadian IT professional services companies (address below).

CONTACTS

☛ Information Technology Association of Canada
#402, 2800 Skymark Ave.,
Mississauga, ON L4W 5A6 Tel. 905-602-8345 Fax: 905-602-8346
E-mail: info@itac.ca
URL: http://www.itac.ca/ITAC.home

☛ The Canadian Information Processing Society
#106, 430 King St. West,
Toronto, ON M5V 1L5 Tel. 416-593-4040 Fax: 416-593-5184
E-mail: info@cips.ca
URL: http://cips.ca

☛ ASM International (Association for Systems Management)
1433 West Bagley Road
Berea, OH 44017
Tel. 216-243-6900 Fax: 216-234-2930
(chapters in Montreal, Ottawa, London, Calgary, Edmonton, Vancouver)

☛ Branham Consulting Group
560 Rochester St., 4th floor
Ottawa, ON K1S 5K2 Tel. 613-235-8270

of those on the Internet were attacked by a malicious virus in 1995. According to John Kearns, national director of information systems auditing at Ernst & Young, "Eighty-seven percent of Internet users stated they would use it more for business if security were enhanced." The same concern applies to software piracy. SoftCop prevents software piracy by embedding a fingerprint of the computer the software is loaded on – a development that is paving the way for on-line software selling.

The bridging of different proprietary computer systems to make them compatible will always be a growth area. When Adobe Systems announced a new software product allowing flawless communication among Apple Macintoshes, IBM-compatibles, and UNIX-based systems, its stock jumped US$14 in one week. Java application software has this ability built into it, so learning how to code in Java will soon become mandatory.

Creativity is very often the passport to innovative software development. Fred Cohen, inventor of the phrase "computer virus," is currently working on harnessing the positive potential of these viruses to create "vampire worms." The "worms" can be used to perform difficult computations after hours by utilizing available processing powers to carry program updates to every node in a network; reduce file corruption; perform hardware diagnosis, software upgrading, and garbage removal; destroy other viruses; and even flash subliminal gentle reminders onto a debtor's system, such as, "Please pay your overdue account at Virtual Reality Inc."

Job seekers must look at the software development industry globally when considering a career in this field. According to the World Bank, companies will often select more than one country when looking for software developers, with India chosen by 53 percent of the companies; Ireland by 50 percent; and Israel, Singapore, Hungary, Mexico, China, and the Philippines by 25 percent to 32 percent. India's software exports rose from $10 million during the 1980s to $144 million in 1992, with $350 million expected by 1995 by India's National Association of Software and Services Companies. China's Electronic Industry Ministry anticipated software export growth from $12 million in 1990 to $200 million by 1995.

These overseas operations specialize in work done to spec, that is, contract work. They are rarely asked to design new commercial products or systems, which is where the real money is made. Just as Apple Computers has decided to focus on high-end multimedia and desktop publishing computers and relinquish the low end, it also makes sense for Canadian programmers to concentrate on leading-edge software since everything else will migrate elsewhere. Whereas Microsoft hired 153 of the 160 graduates from the top engineering schools in India in 1993 and brought them to the U.S., it now hires the same graduates but has them remain in India and pays them $400 per month (a UNIX programmer in North America makes an annual salary of $50,000 to $70,000). Those that are brought over by agencies often become part of "bodyshops" in North America, much like the sweatshops of the garment trade previously. Data entry and processing jobs are migrating to these countries at an even faster rate, though eventually these jobs will be automated through the use of scanners.

Where the Jobs Are in Instrumentation, Robotics, and Research and Development

The instrumentation industry is one of the most challenging job growth areas in the new economy. At the most fundamental level, it might include developing the technology used for tracking, distribution, security, and inventory control. Such automatic data collection devices – hand-held decoders used to scan retail shelves and transmit inventory information by radio frequency to a computer database, for example – are fast and efficient and constitute significant savings for a company. At the high end of the instrumentation industry lie virtual reality and the most powerful computer chips. The developments in this area have been astounding; indeed, today there is more computing power under the hood of a car than the astronauts had during the first lunar landing.

Just as machine tools formed the basis of the industrial mass manufacturing era, electronic instrumentation is transforming every aspect of manufacturing. The average home already exploits microchip technology in thermostats, security systems, VCRs, microwaves, telephones, fax and answering machines, stereos and compact disc players, and personal computers. The transition from machine tools to instrumentation devices is evident in the size of the markets. In the U.S., the machine tool market is worth $4.2 billion annually, compared with the $23 billion annual industrial control device market or the $40 billion modern instrumentation market. The high-tech world of robotics, computer controls, and laser technology has arrived.

Canadian researchers are working on developing robots with "intelligence systems" that will allow the robots to assist in such complex tasks as brain surgery or virtual reality computer animation. This is certainly a quantum leap beyond the market for all-purpose robots used to make cars or cut down trees. Japanese engineers at the Electrotechnical

Laboratory in Tsukuba are letting the electrical hardware of the computer alter its own circuitry as it adapts to the environment. The appropriate task chips are allowed to reproduce or reconfigure more chips on an ongoing basis without needing rewiring for each new task or improvement. When small glitches occur, the robot merely reconfigures its circuits to overcome it. Programmable Logic Devices (PLDs), used to test prototype circuits, will populate a single chip, effectively putting many circuit designers out of business. For example, this kind of robot could work on the ocean floor carrying out a variety of tasks without constant supervision. In the future, robots will work as porters, house cleaners, restaurant workers, educational assistants, receptionists, library assistants, hotel workers, hospital workers, hazardous waste handlers, police workers in dangerous situations, minefield sweepers, firefighters, office-mail deliverers, space-based and earth-bound construction workers, security workers, short-order cooks, babysitters, cashiers, gas station attendants, and travel guest greeters.

Robots fall into three categories: fixed machines, which perform automatic repetitive tasks; field robots, which move around in unstructured environments and often carry out dangerous tasks; and intelligent robots, which employ artificial intelligence to solve problems. Automobile plants are the largest users of fixed robots to perform repetitive, assembly-line tasks such as spot welding, metal cutting, and painting. Component assembly of computers and electronic devices lends itself to this kind of automation. Fixed robots, while perhaps the least exciting, pose the greatest immediate threat to manufacturing jobs.

Although fixed robots have been used in Japan for a long time, circumstances in North America have not been conducive to the wide-scale use of robot technology. In Japan, investment capital was very inexpensive, labour in such short supply that it threatened Japan's export boom, competition among auto manufacturers stiff, unions helpful, engineers plentiful, and top-quality design and production methods a priority. In North America, on the other hand, complications arose in the 1980s as a result of labour disputes, the high cost of investment capital, a decline in new investment in manufacturing, the expense of redesigning factory floors to accommodate robots, and an abundant labour force. The original robots were also beset by problems typical of all products in the early stages of development and use. The upshot was that after some initial enthusiasm, robots were largely discarded among North American companies, while the Japanese have continually upgraded their robot technology and captured a significant share of the auto market by reducing costs through automation. Nowadays, no manufacturing company capable of utilizing robots can afford not to. If used around the clock, a robot can pay for itself in one year. Factories increase their competitiveness enormously by automating. For example, after automating, Nissan Canada Inc. reduced the 11 months needed to retool its body assembly for model change-over to less than two months, and at one-third the cost. The further automating of the FANUC manufacturing plant in Japan in 1982 eliminated roughly half the work force and tripled productivity.

Robots are cost-effective and increase productivity for a number of reasons: they do not require worker's compensation, sick days, pension plans, vacations, overtime pay, medical plans, unemployment insurance benefits, or retraining programs, which taken together are often a company's largest uncontrolled cost. Moreover, robots do not require specific environmental conditions, they do not get tired, and they can be stringently controlled. "Because their movements are perfectly controlled, they do not waste materials – robot spray painters, for example, use up to 30 percent less paint than human workers," states Paul Kennedy, author of *Preparing for the Twenty-First Century*.

Among the more exciting projects on the leading edge of robotics these days are two in the field of medicine. Canada's Institute of Robotics and Intelligent Systems is helping MIT with the challenging design of an eye surgery "robo-doc." In the lab, a speedy robotic gene splicer called the Genomatron is expected to finish the mapping of the human genetic code by 2001 since it can perform 300,000 DNA analyses per day.

Robots are slowly gaining a foothold in all manufacturing endeavours. Countries that do not quickly adopt robotic technology will head into a long, and likely irreversible, period of manufacturing decline. But those countries that are quickest off the mark in developing and using robotic technology will see their standard of living rise and their economies prosper through export-led growth and increased foreign investment. In 1988, Japan had 176,000 of the 280,000 robots worldwide; Western Europe, 48,000; and the U.S., 33,000.

For a robotics revolution to take hold in any country, the key ingredients are a supply of knowledge workers and an abundance of investment capital. Unfortunately, Canada falls short in both respects.

The limiting factors in the development of robotics technology are computer- and software-related. Once computer chips increase in power and decrease in price – something they are rapidly doing – and artificial and neural software intelligence improves, we will see field robots and androids emerge. According to Maureen Caudill in her book *In Our Own Image: Building an Artificial Person,* "Within 20 years, we will have the knowledge and ability to build androids that look and act in a way most people will consider 'humanlike'.... [and] will redefine the measure of mankind." Already "fuzzy logic" technology – technology that can handle ambiguity in meaning and concept and make the best decision under the circumstances – is entering photography, psychological analysis, monitoring, medicine, and prediction and decision support systems. Even autonomously driven and operated armoured vehicles and flying robots have made their debut.

Before robots come to replace brain surgeons, the latter will be using virtual reality in the form of a probe that will "see" the tumour and tell the surgeon the angle of approach to excise it from the patient's brain. Moreover, medical virtual imaging will allow a doctor to actually see the three-dimensional position of a baby in the mother's womb as ultrasound images are converted to three-dimensional images. Even psychologists will use virtual reality in treating phobias and other mental illnesses. At the moment, surgical instruments are a $10 billion industry. With new developments in virtual reality applications, that number will quickly double. The medical significance of these developments is staggering.

As discussed earlier, the training possibilities and entertainment potential of virtual reality are seemingly endless. The training potential of virtual reality has made the Pentagon's Advanced Research Projects Agency (ARPA) one of the biggest investors in virtual research. Tank warfare from the Gulf War is relived for training purposes, ground crew are taught how to manage aircraft, and pilots are taught how to fly in all weather conditions over different kinds of terrain and land at any airport. Approximately 75 percent of the $50 million spent in 1992 for non-military applications by companies interested in virtual reality was invested in research and development. Most of the development capital was spent on "experiential prototyping" – a technology that simulates machine parts or architectural layouts so that both

BULLETIN BOARD — *INSTRUMENTATION AND ROBOTICS*

- **Job demand factors:** the industry has a long period of growth ahead since it is in an early stage of its growth cycle.
- **Job growth areas:** robotics; fluid power and automation; control systems; advanced CAD/CAM and mechanical engineering; any area in need of sensing, monitoring, or control will be an applications growth area – environmental monitoring of ozone, gas emissions, water purity or radiation, for example; chemistry and physics research in laser technology; semi-conductor design; portable technologies (especially wireless).
- **Skills, abilities, qualities, education needed:** creativity; problem-solving and decision-making skills; ability to understand how people interact with technology, along with the ability to translate this understanding into software; scientific curiosity; a high level of education, including, ideally, an electronic engineering degree combined with software expertise, plus an MBA; or mechanical engineering with software and electronic expertise.
- **Job reduction areas:** robots will replace workers in performing many routine functions, particularly where danger, accessibility, or great strength is a factor.
- **Growth limiting factors:** life cycle growth determined by cost, integration level, and power of computer chips; appropriate virtual, artificial, and neural software at a reasonable cost; overall cost of laser technology and robots.
- **Issues:** company policy regarding redeployment of those workers displaced; social upheaval as robots replace humans; conflicts with unions.

clients and designers can explore proposed changes before proceeding with construction. For example, parts designed in AutoCAD can be assembled using Autodesk's Cyberspace Developer Kit, which consists of a head-mounted display and an airborne or flying mouse. Virtual reality, however, is still in its infancy. As Ben Delaney, editor and publisher of *CybergEdgeJournal*, says, "Virtual reality is where personal computers were in 1979. Personal computers back then were slow. They didn't do much. They crashed a lot. But you could start to see the promise. Ten years later, everything has changed. Virtual reality

BULLETIN BOARD — *INSTRUMENTATION AND ROBOTICS*

CONTACTS

☞ Canadian Council of Professional Engineers
#401, 116 Albert St.,
Ottawa, ON K1P 5G3 Tel. 613-232-2474 Fax: 613-230-5759
E-mail: Imacdon@fox.nstn.ns.ca

☞ Canadian Council of Technicians and Technologists
(for Engineering and Applied Sciences),
285 McLeod St., 2nd Fl.,
Ottawa, ON K2R 1A1 Tel. 613-238-8123 Fax: 613-238-8822
URL: http://www.cabot.nf.ca/CCTT/index.html

☞ Robotics & Automation Society
c/o Electrical and Electronics Engineers, Inc.
PO Box 1331,
Piscataway, NJ 08855-1331 USA Tel. 908-981-0060 Fax: 908-981-0027

may have a longer gestation period, but it has the same potential."

Even further down the road lies more sophisticated development in the area of laser technology. Although laser technology has been with us for a while and has entered the home in the form of compact disc players, applications of laser technology are just beginning to emerge. According to Katsumi Tanigaki, research manager for NEC Technologies Canada, "Chemistry and physics are converging, and lasers are at the crossroads." Chemists now use lasers to excite molecules, break chemical bonds, and grow crystals. Laser technology research currently focusses on creating higher-quality thin films for semiconductors, building materials with greater strength and durability, and transforming molecules into recording devices with a thousand times as much storage density as optical discs, and into high-speed optical switches for computers. Physicists currently make use of lasers to isolate atoms, slow them down, and examine their behaviour. Eventually such research may lead to the creation of unique atom clusters that will form the basis of new materials, to compress and confine hot plasma in nuclear fusion reactions as a means of making them more efficient, and to construct high-intensity atom beams that will be essential tools in the making of micromachines or miniature devices that can be used as sensors and robots. Once these developments come to fruition, they will revolutionize robotics, pharmacology, product creation, industrial processing, and information technology. Although lasers are still too expensive and crude, manufacturing costs are falling and lasers are quickly improving in power, lifespan, and quality.

Universities and colleges now offer courses in robotics, fluid power and automation technology, control systems, computer assisted design and computer assisted manufacturing (CAD/CAM), laser technology, mechanical engineering, and electronic engineering. All these fields will grow in importance as part of the instrumentation technology revolution that goes hand in hand with the information technology revolution. Sensing, monitoring, and controlling functions everywhere are increasingly being automated, as are design processes. Thus, the customizing of applications is proving to be very affordable and the savings or convenience realized is quickly appreciated. One example of customization is the 3-D body scans developed by Calgary's Clynch Technologies Inc., which allow the company to design artificial limbs to fit each person. Careers in these fields will flourish all over the world. Individuals who combine software expertise with engineering training will easily find positions in research and development.

There will also be major opportunities in the electronics side of the field, including semiconductor design of integrated circuits, which is an enormous growth area given ever increasing memory demands. But don't overlook the technology-driven service possibilities. Toronto-based Cardiolink Inc. lets people with heart problems take their own ECG remotely and download the results to a database, which recommends either an antacid or a trip to the hospital. The U.S. Defence Department is developing mobile operating rooms located in ambulances employing virtual reality, robotics, and satellite signals. Even CT scans and teleradiology will be available. Information technology can take many forms, but remote service delivery will grow by leaps and bounds. For instance, the sale of PC modem cards grew by 319 percent from 1993 to 1994 in a trend that is destined to continue.

While today the average Canadian interacts with an average of ten computers a day via cars, entertainment, appliances, and information technology, by the year 2000, an individual will be experiencing an average of more than 1,000 interactions a day. Moreover, every

18 months, silicon chips no larger than a fingernail double the number of components they can contain, thereby opening up endless and exciting possibilities for consumer, business, or industrial use.

Where the Jobs Are in Medical Technology, Pharmaceuticals, Biotechnology, and Health Care

The world market for medical devices was roughly $81 billion in 1990, with an annual projected growth rate of 7 percent to the year 2000. Some products can expect annual growth rates of 20 percent. The instrumentation market has already entered the medical technology industry with such technology as 3-D and CT scans, radial axial tomography, arthroscopic surgery, magnetic image resonance, and laser surgery, and will eventually enter all aspects of the industry.

Despite the recession, the health care industry has been growing rapidly. Canada, which spends $66 billion annually on health care and treatment, has increased its number of diagnostic laboratories, treatment centres, walk-in medical centres, and other specialty clinics, an increase that in turn has boosted the need for diagnostic equipment, surgical instruments, pharmaceuticals, and low-tech supplies such as surgical dressings. From 1984 to 1991, the aging boomer population created more jobs in the health care sector than in any other industry. As this generation continues to age, it is expected that health care will rise from 10 percent of gross domestic product to 15 percent. Encouraged by Bill C-91, which increased patent protection on drugs from 10 years to 20, pharmaceutical companies were planning to spend $2 billion in research and development between 1992 and 1996, double the amount spent on research and development between 1987 and 1991. The demand for new diagnostic techniques, medical treatments, and new drugs is a result of the sheer size of the aging boomer population and the rapid technological advances made possible by computerization. With health care authorities trying to reduce costs by promoting greater use of ambulatory care services and shorter in-patient stays, pharmaceutical companies benefit, because such strategies tend to increase the use of drug therapy as a cost-effective means of patient treatment. The Canadian Medical Association reported that Canadians now spend over $11 billion on medication, thanks to the rising cost of drugs, which is more than the $10 billion they spend on doctor services. One private health care plan reports that drug costs are responsible for 73 percent of all its health bills.

Fortunately, the health care industry has brought together universities and pharmaceutical, biotechnological, and medical companies in order to satisfy the demand for new or improved products and treatments. According to McGill professor Peter Macklem, in Canada the link between the health industry and academia is perhaps more evident than in any other country. Professor Macklem is also president of Inspiraplex, a federally sponsored Centre of Excellence that links private business and medical research. Six of the 15 networks of Centres of Excellence focus on the health care industry. Both universities and business benefit from this arrangement, with universities getting the much-needed funds and technology transfer royalties for research, and business getting the innovative products the market is demanding. Furthermore, the presence of the networks has encouraged foreign medical companies to increase investment in Canada. For example, Merck Frosst Canada Inc. is investing $15 million to create a research and development facility in Vancouver close to one of the university Centres of Excellence. The University of Manitoba has done the same in attracting a British respirology company to set up nearby. In order to retain the benefit of research and development carried out in Canada, however, and to build a robust health care industry, Canada must create stricter technology transfer agreements. At the moment, technology initially researched in Canada is subsequently sent back to head offices in other countries where final research and development takes place.

Despite the growing demand for health care products and services, deficit-ridden provincial governments have curtailed medical expenditures. Hospitals, forced to do more with less money, are outsourcing many services to specialized clinics; professional administrators have replaced doctors in the running of hospitals, since the emphasis is on improving quality, cutting costs, and reducing the length of time a patient stays in hospital. Given that Canada ranks 18th out of 21 countries in medical cost control and 17th in system performance, health care industries will increasingly make use of information technology to improve medical productivity and efficiency. Computerization helps contain costs. Computerized inventory control can eliminate the needless waste of expired pharmaceuticals. On-line statistical information systems can measure the effectiveness of various administrative solutions, diagnostic and surgical procedures, and treatment techniques. According to John Goudey, director of Ernst & Young's Life Sciences Division, "Cost containment and improved productivity are going to be the themes in hospitals and the health care industry [throughout] the 1990s. New technologies, especially information technologies, are going to help out in a big way." One need only consider that the over-40 crowd already accounts for 65 percent of all health care costs to realize the importance of cost containment as the boomer generation ages.

To cut costs, the ways in which medical services are delivered must be changed. Since doctors' services constitute the greatest expense in delivering medical services, attempts are being made to decrease the need for doctors in the health care system. Each additional doctor adds an estimated $500,000 a year to medical costs. Even though the population has increased by only 12 percent since 1983, the number of doctors has increased by 38 percent. And today, there is one physician for every 450 Canadians, compared with one for every 860 in the early 1980s. Medical schools have been instructed to reduce enrolment. Forty-six percent of the doctors surveyed by an independent firm for the Canadian Medical Association supported reductions in medical school enrolments. It has been proposed that nurses take over some of the functions traditionally performed by doctors. Therefore, individuals interested in pursuing a nursing career would be well advised to obtain university degrees as part of their training. Nurses who specialize, become nurse practitioners, and obtain a master's degree will have very little trouble finding employment. Regular nurses in hospitals, however, are being replaced by nursing assistants in many instances. Community college nursing programs will be eliminated and the number of nurses graduating is expected to decline as a result; instead, colleges will focus on courses for registered nursing assistants (RNAs) and health care aides as demand increases for these medical workers.

In 1991 there were 3.2 million Canadians over 65 years of age; by 2001 there will be 4 million individuals older than 65. The aging of the baby boom generation will mean increased demand for geriatricians, long-term care administrators, registered nurses with management skills, dietitians, physiotherapists and occupational therapists, eldercare workers, social workers, and recreational therapists. Jobs requiring minimal post-secondary school training include health care aides and nurse's aides (who will make up 75 percent of the long-term care work force), cooks, laundry and housekeeping aides, maintenance workers, ward clerks, office coordinators, and admissions receptionists. Since roughly 30 percent of the cost of providing services to seniors – such as home nursing, homemaking, delivered meals – is devoted to administration, Price Waterhouse found that amalgamating many services into a single "multiservice" agency would reduce overhead to around 16 percent. Since this one-stop-shopping model has the support of various seniors' groups, this way of delivering services will likely prevail.

An aging population requires more medical testing, so there will be increased demand for medical laboratories, which will hire more lab technicians and assistants, radiologists, computer systems technicians, drivers, and, in the short term, data entry operators. Individuals working in this environment will need to cultivate problem-solving skills, team skills, and measuring skills. Continuous learning and academic upgrading will be essential in this field as the simpler functions become automated. MDS Health Group Ltd.'s Autolab processes 70 percent of its samples without human intervention. Health Canada, for its part, is piloting its comprehensive health organization to help hospitals run their labs more efficiently though some hospitals have outsourced this function already.

Pharmaceutical companies are also tailoring their research to meet the growing needs of aging boomers. People are expecting to live longer and are demanding products that will allow them to retain a 50-year-old lifestyle into their 70s. Since post-menopausal women constitute the fastest-growing segment of the Canadian population, many companies are developing drugs to treat the effects of menopause and osteoporosis. Research into ulcers, arthritis, endometriosis, cancer, Alzheimer's disease, and cardiovascular problems is also proceeding apace.

Normally, a new drug costs at least $250 million and takes ten years to develop. A new generation of computer software, however, is transforming the ability of researchers to visualize and design molecules. With computer-assisted molecular design (CAMD), molecules can be designed that behave in a specific way – to regulate pain or hypertension, for example. Now that biological research is revealing the detailed structures of target receptor sites that drug molecules must latch onto, it is easier to design molecules that fit properly. HyperCube Inc., a Waterloo, Ontario,

BULLETIN BOARD — *HEALTH CARE*

- **Job demand factors:** aging boomers' health concerns will dominate all aspects of the health care industry, which is in its early growth phase; over one-third of Canadians are expected to develop cancer during their lives; only 17 percent of Canadians over 15 are physically active; one-third of Canadians are obese.
- **Job growth areas:** research in medical instrumentation and pharmaceuticals; sales positions in medical instrumentation and pharmaceutical companies; registered nursing assistants; health care aides; physiotherapists; respirologists; speech pathologists; dental hygienists; occupational therapists; radiologists; home-care registered nurses; operating and emergency room registered nurses; nurse practitioners; activation coordinators; risk management.
- **Skills, abilities, qualities, education needed:** pharmaceutical sales representatives must first acquire a science degree, then complete a pharmaceutical representative course; for positions with biotech companies, math, science, and computer literacy skills; managerial positions will require expertise in program planning, finance, human resources, policy development, project management, communication skills; the best jobs in the pharmaceutical and biotechnology fields combine at least one other area of expertise with pharmacology – for example, neuropharmacology or biochemistry plus microbiology; knowledge of software applications; nurses and RNAs at the moment require Grade 12 English and math and two senior sciences; medical students must complete a two-year premedical program for admission, with the exception of McMaster University, which includes non-academic criteria; all medical schools expect applicants to have some medicine-related volunteer experience.

software company, developed a sophisticated molecule builder capable of advanced analysis called HyperChem, which may become the industry standard for desktop molecular modeling since it is compatible with existing software.

In deciding which biotechnology companies to apply to, it's important to find out how many alliances the companies have with others in the field, particularly with large pharmaceutical companies. According

BULLETIN BOARD — *HEALTH CARE*

- **Job reduction areas:** generic drug firms; doctors, except for specialties addressing the needs of the elderly – gerontology, cardiology, neurology, radiology, oncology, cosmetic surgery, urology; general nursing; middle management; dentistry.
- **Growth limiting factors:** governments' ability to pay for services; fee for service; shortage of venture capital for biotech firms; regulations; potential taxation of dental and other medical benefits; better preventive oral-health practices.
- **Issues:** patients becoming partners in the health care process; the legal implications of the cost containment or rationalization of services process; shift in emphasis to prevention of illness; effects of pollution on health; a variety of ethical issues prompted by advances in technology.

to a 1992 study by Ernst & Young, 70 percent of all Canadian biotechnology companies have formed at least one alliance. The $200 million to $250 million cost of getting products to market requires such alliances. Medium-sized companies have usually formed more than seven alliances, while the industry average is four. Alliances aimed at acquiring marketing and distribution expertise are becoming more important as competition is increasingly focussed on commercializing research and development results as quickly as possible. Cangene Corporation of Mississauga, Ontario, formed an alliance with Akzo Pharma, a Dutch pharmaceutical giant, which gave Akzo a licence to market Cangene's diagnostic technology, such as its AIDS diagnosing technology. Small research and development companies working on specialized technologies require alliances with well-established pharmaceutical companies to take advantage of the latter's capital and worldwide distribution and marketing networks. Similarly, the large pharmaceutical companies need the smaller biotechnology companies to provide them with leading-edge products in need of further development.

Although the number of biotech companies in the U.S. is decreasing because of industry consolidation, Canada lags behind the U.S. by about five years, so growth here is still likely. According to the Canadian Biotech

BULLETIN BOARD — *HEALTH CARE*

TIPS

> For more job-specific information about occupations in health care industries, consult *Health Career Job Explosion* by Dennis Damp.

> For information regarding health care restructuring refer to *Strong Medicine* by Dr. Michael Rachlis and Carol Kushner, and for biotechnology refer to *Opportunities in Biotechnology Careers* by Sheldon Brown.

CONTACTS

☛ Canadian Medical Association
1867 Alta Vista Dr.,
Ottawa, ON K1G 3Y6 Tel. 800-267-9703 Fax: 613-731-9013
URL: http://www.hwc.ca:8400/

☛ Canadian Institute of Biotechnology
130 Albert St.,
Ottawa, ON K1P 5G4 Tel. 613-563-8849 Fax: 613-563-8850
E-mail: cib@biotech.ca

☛ Canadian Nurses Association
50 The Driveway,
Ottawa, ON K2P 1E2 Tel. 613-237-2133 Fax: 613-237-3520

☛ Canadian Pharmaceutical Association
1785 Alta Vista Dr., 2nd Fl.,
Ottawa, ON K1G 3Y6 Tel. 1-800-917-9489 Fax: 613-523-0445

☛ British Columbia Society of Medical Technologists
#202, 8091 Granville Avenue
Richmond, BC V6Y 1P5 Tel. 604-231-6603 Fax: 604-231-6023

☛ Ontario Society of Medical Technologists
#600, 234 Eglinton Ave. East,
Toronto, ON M4P 1K5 Tel. 416-485-6768 Fax: 416-485-7660

'94 survey, between 1991 and 1993, biotech firms had the most growth in the western provinces and Quebec. Although the main area for biotechnology innovation is health care, agriculture and environmental protection and remediation are strong emerging markets. Even though the U.S. is the world leader in the biotech field at the moment, Japan has set the goal of becoming the dominant player by 2000.

Takeovers, restructurings, and mergers among the brand-name drug makers have resulted in 1,000 to 2,000 companies being lost between 1993 and 1995. As patents are expiring, new and innovative drugs are needed so the number of medical and research jobs is increasing. The generic drug manufacturers, on the other hand, saw their sales rise by 35 to 40 percent in 1994. Since 1987, the number of workers in the generic drug industry has doubled as a result.

There will be an increase in medical specialization with the advent of newer technologies, treatments, and procedures; for example, there will be greater demand for rehabilitation specialists and radiation oncologists to serve the needs of an aging population. At UCLA some radiologists now specialize in parts of the body and diagnose neurological images sent over fibre-optic cable or satellite to the U.S.'s first transcontinental telemedicine service.

Overall, however, the orientation of health care is likely to shift to a more family- and community-based model. Greater emphasis will be placed on health protection and disease prevention. Given the move toward patient empowerment, high-quality physical and psychological environments will be demanded by everyone everywhere. This will mean more jobs for patient rights advocates, ergonomics specialists, community home workers, psychologists, psychotherapists, and alternative medicine deliverers.

Consulting jobs for MBAs and MHScs will proliferate in connection with planning, operational reviews, mergers, organizational develop- ment, utilization reviews, total quality management (TQM), continuous service improvement, service facilitation, and internationalization. St. Michael's Hospital in Toronto reduced its $63 million debt to $13 million by using private-sector management approaches. Job seekers looking for managerial positions will require expertise in program and service plan- ning, finance, human resources, policy development, and organizational development, as well as computer literacy skills such as Larg*net and Larg*health or HealthLink community health information systems. Specialized abilities required include consensus management and project management as well as analytical, listening, and writing skills. Today, it is taken for granted that a candidate for a job in the biotechnology and medical fields has strong math, science, and computer literacy skills.

Many ethical issues are likely to arise in the future with respect to the rationalization of services – who gets what, why, when, where, and how much. These issues will also mean that the job descriptions of health care workers will need to be clarified, especially in sensitive areas.

In the short term, government debt will constrain health care growth at the expense of patients. In Ontario, a 1995 report recommended closing 12 Toronto hospitals, merging others, and closing one-third of emergency wards, affecting the jobs of 2,800 people in order to meet a 78 percent reduction in hospital grants. Saskatchewan has already converted 54 rural hospitals into clinics. Such drastic measures reflect the fact that many hospitals are operating below capacity and administrators and non-medical staff almost outnumber the doctors and nurses – accounting for one-third of hospital budgets. Should this trend continue, a two-tiered system will emerge as more deinsured services are relegated to private coverage. The number of private clinics will continue to grow as long waits for crucial testing increase the health risk to the critically ill or those needing early diagnosis for therapy to be effective. Already there is a critical shortage of radiologists, and the heart surgery backlog is at an all-time high.

Even now, 35 percent of health care funding comes from the private sector in the form of consumer purchases, drug plans, eye plans, and the cost of nursing homes – up from 28 percent in 1993. Already there is a private MRI clinic in Vancouver. In either a public or a two-tiered system, the drive for cost containment and rationalization will characterize the health care profession well into the future. The 31 companies in the Employer Committee on Health Care in Ontario have seen their health care costs rise 74 percent between 1990 and 1994, a period when consumer prices rose only 9 percent. Magna International, impatient with the costly medicare system, is opting out and offering its own system which includes focussing on preventing illness, providing mandatory health classes at work, and setting up company-run clinics and hospitals eventually.

Private firms pursuing the health care market are involved with managing facilities, financing major equipment purchases, insuring some services, and delivering services directly. Once fee-for-service becomes part of the cost-cutting equation, private-sector health care solutions will begin to appear. Given that waiting times for cancer treatment are three to four times longer than in the U.S. and far longer than radiation oncologists consider the maximum medically acceptable times, the private sector should grow rapidly. The provinces are asking the federal government to identify "a basic range of health services" as opposed to requiring them to provide all services deemed "medically necessary."

Where the Jobs Are in Environmental Industries

Canada's environmental industry, which employs 150,000 people and is the fifth-largest sector of the economy, is expected to generate approximately $12 billion in sales annually by the year 2000 in what is now a $250 billion industry worldwide. Ironically, much of this growth is a result of Canada's dubious distinction as one of the world's largest per capita users of energy and producers of garbage or waste material. Although the federal government's Green Plan, which promised to provide $3 billion in funding for research, cleanup, and public involvement programs, went the way of most political promises – indeed, Environment Canada's budget was cut by 37 percent in 1995 – environmental industries will continue to grow worldwide simply out of necessity. Within 50 years, the world's population will reach a minimum of 9 billion, regardless of efforts to curtail population growth. Economic output will likely be five times what it is today. Along with these developments will come world-wide shortages of renewable resources. Currently, environmental damage resulting from water, soil, and air pollution costs China over 15 percent of its gross national product. The World Bank estimates it would cost approximately $100 billion annually by the year 2000 just to provide developing countries with adequate water and sanitation services, or 2 to 3 percent of their gross domestic product.

Countries that postpone initiating environmental reforms will find that at some point, the savings accrued in curtailing environmental damage exceeds the cost of implementing environmental programs. Unfortunately, political will to bring about necessary reforms is sluggish, perhaps because the payback period may be lengthy or the environmental damage not yet conspicuous enough. In the meantime, many companies are selling environment-friendly products, services, or consulting advice to individual companies concerned about environmental costs or conforming to current legislation. Four out of five Canadian companies now conduct in-house environmental reviews, though they are much slower than European companies in changing their practices, according to a 1994 study by Ernst & Young Environmental Services Inc.

The environment industry is one of the fastest-growing industries in the western Canadian economy, with annual growth of 5 to 15 percent expected into the late 1990s, according to a 1993 report by Sentar Consultants of Calgary. About 2,000 "green" companies were responsible for $1.8 billion in sales in British Columbia, Alberta, Saskatchewan, and Manitoba. The 20,000 people employed in the industry work largely in the service sector – predominantly consulting – in such areas as recycling, site remediation, and air quality. Only 15 percent of these companies derived their primary income from selling environmental products, and manufacturers of environmental products reported average sales of only slightly more than $2 million. In Ontario, environmental protection is a $2.5 billion industry employing 30,000 workers; of the 15,000 who work in waste management, over 50 percent have low- or medium-skilled jobs, and in environmental manufacturing, roughly 33 percent are employed as labourers.

On the scientific end of the industry, most environmental researchers hold doctorates in chemistry, biology, physics, engineering, or meteorology. Typically, one BSc engineer and two technologists – electronic, computer, biological, or chemical – assist each researcher. In response to the demand for trained technicians to assist environmental researchers, community colleges offer two- or three-year technician and technologist programs, and many universities offer degrees in environmental studies. Hydrogeologists with a BSc, MSc, or PhD in hydrogeology are in demand in global areas where water pollution is increasing. They assess and design landfill sites, and are instrumental in environmental cleanup. The industry also employs administrative support service personnel who must be knowledgeable in scientific terms and techniques, computer literate, and prepared to supervise technical staff.

A background in biology is a prerequisite for all environmental jobs as research shifts from the physical sciences to the impact that environmental corruption has on life forms. This change of emphasis has spurred growth in jobs involving environmental audits and impact studies.

Since 1993, Ontario's educational institutions, construction and demolition companies, food service establishments, health care facilities, hotels and motels, manufacturers, multi-unit residential buildings, office buildings, and retail shopping complexes have been required to carry out waste audits and establish work plans, implement source separation of recyclables, and implement work plans so as to reduce unnecessary waste disposal. All audits and work plans must be updated annually and the work plans displayed for municipality or Ministry of Environment spot checks. Of the 10 million tons of solid waste generated annually in Ontario, 60 percent is attributable to the commercial, industrial, and institutional sectors; clearly, many job opportunities will open in the handling and reduction of waste disposal. Already Ontario residents are the country's top recyclers (94 percent of households participate).

Environmental companies are discovering that solving someone else's waste problems is a growing market. Eco-Tec Wastewater Treatment Inc., for example, recovers metals from the industrial wastewater that used to be dumped into streams, rivers, and lakes. For companies employing the Eco-Tec technology, the payback period is as short as three months. Philip Environmental Inc., which is in the business of cleaning up hazardous waste, saw its sales climb from $100 million in 1991 to $157 million in 1992. Consolidated Envirowaste Industries developed a speeded-up composting process to take advantage of rising tipping or dumping fees and the demand for fertilizer. Now that all provinces have planned to reduce landfill waste by 50 percent by the year 2000 (using 1987 as the base year), there are tremendous opportunities for companies of this kind. Bovar Engineering Products is involved in site assessment, waste disposal, medical waste disposal, and product research and development. By exporting pollution monitoring and control equipment to Latin American countries that are now in the process of developing environmental legislation, the company is anticipating a 20 percent annual growth rate.

Many corporations are also finding that they can enjoy significant cost savings by cutting energy costs. IBM now saves $200,000 annually in energy costs by using a cool storage system at one of its offices. Other companies realizing savings from similar initiatives include Xerox ($187,000), Bell ($250,000), Novacor ($200,000), and Oshawa Foods ($250,000). Inco Limited plans to save $1.6 million in annual energy costs through energy conservation, and autoglass manufacturer PPG Canada Inc. expects to save $656,000 yearly. Energy performance contracting is a $70 million business. There are 25 energy service companies that design, implement, and finance cost-saving energy technology in exchange for a percentage of the savings a company accrues. Since

BULLETIN BOARD — *ENVIRONMENTAL INDUSTRIES*

- **Job demand factors:** population explosion; stricter environmental regulations; potential for cost saving; landfill shortages; dumping fees; garbage collection costs; recyclable usages; water contamination.
- **Job growth areas:** marketing, administrative, auditing, finance, legal, public relations, technical and research jobs for business graduates who are technically conversant with a particular environmental area or who have technical diplomas in the relevant areas; cleanup jobs which do not require highly skilled workers; jobs with companies which want to find alternative uses for waste products, save energy, eliminate toxicity, monitor pollution levels, or dispose of waste products; water-related sanitation jobs (e.g., hydrogeologists) have the greatest demand worldwide.
- **Skills, abilities, qualities, education needed:** computer and technological literacy; area-specific scientific and technical comprehension; ability to work in small teams and to prepare and present reports; precise data collection skills; good knowledge of environmental regulations; ability to work within a strict budget; ability to work independently; flexibility and patience.
- **Job reduction areas:** none.
- **Growth limiting factors:** affordability; government regulations; political will; ability of technological knowledge to keep up with need.
- **Issues:** how long government action can be delayed by cutbacks; society's response to the impending results of environmental audits; continental and international pressure on Canada to improve environmental practices; determination of safe levels and potential "sunsetting" of environmental pollutants; search for safe alternatives to pollutants; waste management and prevention; success of green marketing.

TIPS

➤ For more information about environmental careers, consult *Environmental Career Guide* by Nicholas Basta, and to learn more about energy technology companies, take a look at the *Canadian Directory of Efficiency and Alternate Energy Technologies*, the *Canadian Environmental Directory 1995/96*, *Get a Life: A Green Cure for Canada's Economic Blues*, and the *Financial Post*'s Annual Environmental Management Award Winners.

building owners do not pay for anything, the energy service companies assume all the risk. Many energy contractors, such as Tescor Energy Services Inc., have seen their operations double because of the potential savings to their clients.

Land reclamation also presents many employment opportunities. In Canada, urban expansion and soil erosion has reduced farmland by 65 percent, with 54,000 hectares of farmland converted to concrete each year. Moreover, the water supply is becoming increasingly contaminated as farmers replace topsoil with chemical fertilizer. Environmental degradation will pose a serious problem for Canadians as the population continues to expand, and many jobs in the environment industry will emerge in the effort to contain damage growth rates.

Many companies have been successful because of growing export markets. Canada has a world-class reputation in certain environmental industries, such as wastewater management. American demand for green technology outstrips Canadian demand because of the stricter regulatory laws passed in the U.S. Consequently, Canadian companies such as SolarChem, which makes equipment to clean toxic chemicals from wastewater, do little business in Canada. Undoubtedly, Canadian regulations will become stricter, creating opportunities for Canadian environmental companies, particularly in the area of waste associated with primary resource extraction and processing – such as sludges, slag, mine tailings, or unremoved clear-cut timber – which accounts for 98.6 percent of our waste problems.

Many imaginative ways of recycling products have formed the basis for new businesses that range from making graffiti-proof freeway walls from plastic pop bottles and used tires, to making plastic lumber. However, recyclable waste is worth only 5 to 10 percent of its initial value, with some items prohibitively expensive to recycle – polystyrene containers and utensils common to the fast-food industry, for example. In the future, the focus will likely shift from recycling to developing non-polluting and easily reusable or disposable products. The provinces have approved a national program to curtail the amount of waste created or to put in place other methods of disposal or recycling by 2000 to achieve a 50 percent improvement over 1988 levels. Understandably, the recycling industry is now growing by 10 percent a year in Canada.

Environmental concern has also entered the investment world.

BULLETIN BOARD — *ENVIRONMENTAL INDUSTRIES*

CONTACTS

☛ Canadian Association of Recycling Industries
#502, 50 Gervais St.,
Don Mills, ON M3C 1Z3 Tel. 416-510-1244 Fax: 416-510-1248

☛ Canadian Association of Water Pollution Research & Control
Canadian Association on Water Quality
Technology Development Branch, Environment Canada
425 boul. St-Joseph, 4e étage
Hull, PQ K1A OH3 Tel. 819-953-9365 Fax: 819-953-9029

☛ Canadian Environment Network
#1004, 251 Laurier Avenue West
Ottawa, ON K1R 5J6 Tel. 613-563-2078 Fax: 613-563-7236
E-mail: cen@web.apc.org

☛ Canadian Environment Industry Association
Phase II, Room 204, 6 Antares Drive
Nepean, ON K2E 8A9 Tel. 613-723-3525 Fax: 613-723-0060
E-mail: ceiae@captialnet.com

☛ Canadian Environmental Auditing Association
6519B Mississauga Road
Mississauga, ON L5N 1A6 Tel. 905-567-4705 Fax: 905-567-7191

Approximately $14 million worth of mutual funds in Canada are directed to companies with a reputable environmental record. In North America as a whole, "green investing" represents a $600 billion market. Screening criteria include a company's air and water pollution record, its approaches to waste management, its recycling policy, and its prosecution record. Eco-Rating International, a Zurich-based firm, has developed a ten-point system for rating a company's environmental performance, which includes its environmental sustainability and the ecological standing of its technologies among its rating categories. A green magazine for executives, called *ECO*, outlines the costs that result from environmental damage, cleanup, and regulation.

Even natural resources companies, which are laying off frontline workers, have had to hire environmental personnel. Ten years ago, Inco employed between 15,000 and 18,000 individuals in Ontario; in 1993,

BULLETIN BOARD — *ENVIRONMENTAL INDUSTRIES*

- ☛ Canadian Environmental Equipment Manufacturers' Association
  #701, 116 Albert St.,
  Ottawa, ON K1P 5G3 Tel. 613-232-7213 Fax: 613-232-7381
- ☛ The Canadian Environmental Law Association
  #401, 517 College Street
  Toronto, ON M6G 4A2 Tel. 416-960-2284 Fax: 416-960-9329
- ☛ Canadian Society of Environmental Biologists
  PO Box 962, Stn F, Toronto, ON M4Y 2N9
- ☛ Canadian Water Quality Association
  #A201, 151 Frobisher Dr.,
  Waterloo, ON N2V 2C9 Tel. 519-885-3954 Fax: 519-747-9124
- ☛ Canadian Water & Wastewater Association
  #402, 45 Rideau Street
  Ottawa, ON K1N 5W8 Tel. 613-241-5692 Fax: 613-241-5193
- ☛ Pollution Probe Foundation
  12 Madison Ave.,
  Toronto, ON M5R 2S1 Tel. 416-926-1907 Fax: 416-926-1601
  E-mail: pprobe@web.apc.org

this figure dropped to 6,600. While Inco's work force was shrinking, its environmental department increased its hiring of engineers and individuals with degrees in physics, chemistry, biology, and forestry.

Other professions that will be in demand will be wildlife conservationists, administrators, secretarial staff, public relations and communications specialists, environmental planners and managers, lawyers, environmental accountants, architects, journalists, truck drivers, and pickers and sorters of garbage. Moreover, since many small companies in the industry are run by scientists and engineers who may lack expertise in marketing, human resources management, or strategic planning, many positions will open up in these areas. Already seven out of ten Canadian offices have waste reduction programs in place. Before long, every company will be hiring waste and energy management planners and consultants. Xerox has enhanced job descriptions to include environmental goals and has even reassigned territories for service representatives so they can take public transit or walk from one customer location to another.

The future of sustainable economic growth has become one of the most pressing issues facing the world, and the job market potential of sustainable development will likely expand faster than the world's population. Perhaps the most substantial job growth will occur in water sanitation, given that 80 percent of the diseases affecting the global population are attributable to contaminated or unsafe water resources, and one in five countries is suffering from a water shortage. All countries facing large population or economic growth will be in dire need of environmental monitoring, planning, and remediation. By the year 2000, India's population will exceed 1 billion despite its having one of the world's oldest population control programs. Thus, India, Asia, and Central and South America will provide employment opportunities in the environmental industry and will be insatiable export markets. For instance, by 1999, India's environmental management spending is expected to reach $2 billion per year, or four times the amount spent in 1994. As country after country tightens its environmental regulations, environment-related jobs will become an extension of every company's or institution's responsibility.

As an industry, the environment has almost limitless growth potential. By the 21st century, no country will be able to afford not to be environmentally responsible without suffering irreversible damage to its natural resources. Quality of life is at stake in a smog-filled, ozone-depleted, litter-ridden, no-swimming world. The world's population increases by 100 million people a year; moreover, the world's big cities are growing by 1 million people a week, and over the next ten years they will hold over half the world's population. Change has to occur; whether it will take place smoothly or chaotically remains to be seen. According to Norman Meyers in *Environmental Exodus*, "There are at least 25 million environmental refugees total [versus 22 million traditional refugees from war, oppression, and disaster]. The total may well double by 2000, if not before."

CHAPTER FOUR

WHERE THE JOBS ARE IN THE SERVICE, MANUFACTURING, AND NATURAL RESOURCES INDUSTRIES

- The Dynamic Service Industries
- Traditional Services
- Manufacturing and Natural Resources
- Job Survival in the Old Economy

In rich countries today, over half the workers in a typical manufacturing firm do service-type jobs – design, distribution, financial planning; only a minority make things on the factory floor.

THE ECONOMIST

The lines between the services and manufacturing industries are becoming blurred, and the notion that manufacturing is somehow more real or more productive than services is just not valid. While one cannot export a fine dining experience or a weekend at a resort, services are becoming increasingly "tradable." The fine dining experience or holiday retreat that attracts tourists amounts to importing trade. Such factors as deregulation and falling trade barriers will likely encourage trade in services, particularly to developing countries in need of finance, telecommunications, and consulting expertise. Over 60 percent of the gross domestic product of developed countries comes from their service industries, which also account for approximately 40 percent of the stock of foreign direct investment by the Big Five industrial economies – the U.S., Germany, Japan, France, and England. Manufacturing will diminish as a percentage of gross domestic product as labour-intensive industries move to countries that offer cheaper labour. Since more value is added by inventing a software program or designing a circuit than by grinding out yet another auto part, high-wage, knowledge-intensive jobs will stay in countries with the best-trained work force. In the long term, as robotics and automation increasingly replace workers on the factory floor, manufacturing will migrate to knowledge-intensive countries that are in strategic positions for the acquisition of raw materials or the distribution of finished products. When the automotive industry is completely automated, for example, companies will not have to move their factories to Mexico, with its cheaper labour and proximity to the large U.S. market; they will simply locate in the U.S., where the product is sold.

Since the early sixties, the service sector has doubled in Canada and in nine other industrialized nations. Approximately 8 million Canadians currently work in service industries such as finance, communications, real estate, transportation, community and personal services, and public administration. Of all jobs created since 1980, 93 percent have been in the service sector. By 1990, 72 percent of Canadian and U.S. workers were employed in the service industry as compared with 58 percent in 1960. On average in the service industry, 5.1 percent of workers held multiple jobs in 1991, compared with 2.2 percent in 1976. From 1976 to 1991 the growth of employment in the service sector surpassed the growth in the working-age population. While this increase is partly a result of the large numbers of women entering service-sector industries and the greater demand for social services and household workers, the shift to knowledge workers accounts for the lion's share of this growth.

Between 1978 and 1986, 32 percent of job growth in Canada occurred in service companies with 100 or more employees, and 58 percent in small service companies with fewer than 20 employees. The largest percentage of employment in small companies is in the traditional services – retailing, hospitality, amusement and recreation, and personal services. Overall, most service jobs are in medium-sized or large organizations – banks, insurance companies, and educational institutions.

The image of the service job has changed dramatically, no longer consistent with the stereotype of someone mindlessly flipping burgers or performing tedious clerical tasks. The information technology revolution is reducing – even eliminating – these mundane tasks as more and more of these jobs become automated. The most promising service-sector careers are in the knowledge sector. In fact, over half the workers in the developed countries are engaged in the production, storage, retrieval, or distribution of knowledge – all areas that offer the most promising service-sector careers.

While skills upgrading has been least significant in traditional services, large increases in retraining have been required in distributive, information, and non-market services such as government, education, health care, libraries, and other non-competitive services. The 1980s showed substantial activity in skills upgrading in the areas of finance, communications, insurance, the amusement and recreation industries, public administration, and health.

During past recessions, the service sector – except for the areas of retail and wholesale – was not severely hit by layoffs. Often there was a countercyclical trend in the non-market services as rising unemployment led to increased enrolment in education programs and the number of social service jobs increased to meet the needs of the unemployed, who had formerly been engaged in the goods-producing sector of the economy. And while consumers were buying less, the service sector did not suffer appreciably. This is no longer the case.

Like the manufacturing sector, service industries were hard hit by the recession. Corresponding to a decreased demand for manufactured goods or natural resources was a decline in demand for services. The resultant slowdown of the economy, the lowering of computer prices, and the advances in information technology provided companies of all kinds with a perfect opportunity to restructure or downsize.

Whereas the 1970s and 1980s saw substantial productivity improvements in manufacturing, the 1990s are a time of productivity improvements in the service sector on a very large scale. The heating up of global competition in the service industries – largely an outgrowth of the information technology revolution – has made it mandatory that service companies use the new technology if they are to survive. With technology altering the flow and processing of information, companies have to find more efficient organizational structures so that they can run their businesses more competitively. Many traditionally secure service jobs have begun to disappear altogether. In the U.S., automation has reduced the number of new jobs created annually by approximately 700,000. Considering that NCR's 7780 work station is capable of processing cheques, remittance slips, and other documents at 500 items per minute, this hefty reduction is not surprising.

Public service jobs have also felt the impact of information technology, especially since bureaucracies, which need to continuously process large volumes of information, are often the best candidates for productivity improvement. Cash-strapped governments have had to adopt labour- and cost-saving technology at the expense of many public service jobs. This approach has also been taken by large institutions like banks and insurance companies, which have been forced to trim their operations. The information technology revolution has changed virtually every occupation in the service industry – usually for the better as workers are relieved of the more tedious aspects of their jobs through automation. While many jobs have disappeared, many new jobs have emerged, and with them, opportunities for workers to grow professionally. To survive in these new service jobs, an individual must become a knowledge worker, comfortable with information technology and conversant with software applications relevant to the service the company provides. Employees who can use technology to process information or raw data and who can communicate the results to others in the form of business plans, newsletters, annual reports, and direct mailings to clients will be indispensable to the company.

SERVICE IS BIG BUSINESS

The decline of the industrial era has shaken the already turbulent world of business and commerce with some great moments of truth. An intense interest in service or, more specifically, an intense interest in the quality and range of services has created a powerful new wave of business opportunities. Companies that have made the shift to service through waves of restructuring and re-engineering are reaping the benefits of sustained growth and increased profitability. So the quest for quality and service is on, and the shift to a service mode involves every facet of operations. Service management makes especially good sense in any industry that deals in an intangible product or in an industry where products are relatively indistinguishable from one another. So it is with the financial services. Credit card companies extend credit, brokerage houses have chequing accounts, banks issue credit cards, and department stores sell securities. As the difference between the offerings of various financial institutions decreases, the importance of service quality increases.

The Dynamic Service Industries

The dynamic services comprise two *producer industries* – financial services and real estate; and business services – and two *distribution industries* – transportation, communications, and utilities; and the wholesale trade. These high-value-adding industries are becoming key players in international trade. Over 20 percent of employees in dynamic services industries are dependent upon exports for their jobs.

Until teleconferencing and electronic highways become universal, most high-skilled jobs in the dynamic services will be located in large urban centres, where well-trained individuals are available and where the headquarters or main divisional offices of goods-producing companies are found. Goods-producing companies, in fact, are the largest users of the dynamic services.

The interdependence between the dynamic services and the goods-producing sector is dramatized by the fact that in 1985 a $1 output in each of the goods-producing industries, when added together, produced a total demand of 96 cents for finance and real estate services and 85 cents for wholesale services. The seven service industries most dependent upon demand from the goods industries are utilities, finance, real estate, the wholesale trade, business services, transportation, and communications. In 1988, these dynamic services were responsible for 56 percent of the service sector's gross domestic product and 36 percent of the country's gross domestic product. In the past, this interdependence has led to a concentration of non-primary goods – that is, goods from industries other than agriculture, forestry, mining, and fishing – and dynamic services in urban centres, particularly the finance, insurance, and real estate industries. This was also the case for management consultants, architects, and urban designers, personnel and executive-search services, computer services, and engineering and scientific services, and to a lesser extent for legal and accounting services.

Once teleconferencing and telecommunications become universal, companies that traditionally locate their offices in urban centres will consider other options. The trend toward home businesses means that service industries can be located anywhere. Indeed, a knowledge worker could develop software on a sailboat crossing the Atlantic as expeditiously as in an office downtown. The migration of work to off-site locations has had the greatest impact in the knowledge-based service industries, which do not have to be on-site to produce a result in the same way as, for example, a cleaning service has to be.

In the past, routine information transfer could be easily handled electronically, but complex decision-making required face-to-face contact. With the restructuring of companies into teams and the wider use of teleconferencing, all players can now meet face to face electronically. Thus, a worker's ability to operate both independently and as a team member is becoming a greater asset in the dynamic services. Moreover, as education, skills, and knowledge increase worldwide, and employers are in the position to hire globally, individuals will have job security only if they have more education, knowledge, experience, or skills than other workers in other parts of the world. Job seekers must keep this in mind when researching companies they may wish to work for, and must choose only those firms that offer them opportunities to increase their skills and knowledge. Upgrading continuously is essential for career survival in a global economy.

PRODUCER INDUSTRIES: FINANCIAL SERVICES AND REAL ESTATE; BUSINESS SERVICES

Where the Jobs Are in Financial Services

• **Finance Companies** • **Banks and Trusts** • **Insurance** • **Investment**

The four pillars of the financial services industry – banks, trust companies, investment brokerages, and insurance businesses – are mutating into more convenient one-stop-shopping locales serving a wider range of client needs. Management and customer-service skills are critical in this industry, and a solid educational background is a hiring prerequisite. Marketing and service-oriented personnel who are knowledgeable about financial services and products will be selected for their potential to move into many different areas of the banking world. The niche markets will require value-added skill sets such as knowledge of international markets, languages, cultures, and specialty sales.

BULLETIN BOARD – *FINANCE COMPANIES*

- **Job demand factors:** businesses need loans to grow and compete globally.
- **Job growth areas:** marketing, financial planners, loan experts.
- **Skills, abilities, qualities, education needed:** decision-making, problem-solving, financial, marketing, analytical; college diploma or university degree in business is essential.
- **Growth limiting factors:** competition from banks and other lending institutions.

CONTACTS

- ☛ Association of Canadian Financial Corporations
  Sussex Centre, #401, 50 Burnhamthorpe Rd. West,
  Mississauga, ON L4B 3C2 Tel. 416-949-4820 Fax: 416-896-9380
- ☛ Canadian Council of Financial Analysts
  #1702, 390 Bay Street
  Toronto, ON M5H 2Y2 Tel. 416-366-5755 Fax: 416-366-6716
- ☛ Trust Companies Association of Canada
  #205, 335 Bay Street
  Toronto, ON M5H 2R3 Tel. 416-866-8842 Fax: 416-364-1993

Finance Companies

Finance companies have entered almost every arena of bank lending, including credit cards, mortgages, and real estate and commercial loans. Generally, these companies have been more successful than banks even though they lend to companies that banks would probably turn down, especially during tough economic times.

Since lending is the primary business of finance companies, they will lend money even during a recession. With banks reluctant to lend to small businesses, there is more opportunity for finance companies to step in with business loans. Banks, conservative by nature, will not lend money without loan guarantees in the form of personal or business assets. Thus, Canadian banks would never have lent money to Bill Gates, president of Microsoft, because software is not considered an asset by the banks. Canada has had a long-standing tradition of not supporting local entrepreneurship, a deficit which it now seems to be trying to address.

Individuals interested in the world of business and finance would learn far more working for a finance company than for a bank. Since

---

PACT TO OPEN WORLD TRADE IN FINANCIAL SERVICES

Twenty-nine members of the World Trade Organization, the new global commerce watchdog, agreed to an accord which will open up global trade in financial services. The pact covering the booming multibillion-dollar trade in banking, insurance, and securities involves a total of 43 countries. Among major backers of the deal – apart from the European Union, its major promoter – are Japan, Canada, and Australia from the established economies; India, Malaysia, South Korea, Indonesia, and Singapore in Asia; and Brazil, Chile, and Venezuela in Latin America. For the finance industry in developed countries, it will bring guaranteed access, although at varying levels, to the fiercely protected domestic markets of the emerging and transition economies, including Poland and Hungary. Additionally, under most-favoured-nation rules the accord will be extended to about 50 other present and pending World Trade Organization members with commitments in the sector, including the United States, which argues that the pact does not go far enough. The accord officially runs to the end of 1997, when it will likely be extended and improved for a further period.

---

most new businesses in the future will be small businesses, finance companies will likely grow to meet a demand for small business loans. And since marketing plays a vital role in the industry, marketing graduates with an interest in finance and financial products are frequently recruited.

Banks and Trusts

If you're like many Canadians, you probably don't go into your bank branch more than a handful of times during the year. Experts say that 1995 was the year debit cards and telephone banking really caught on. According to the Canadian Bankers Association, 802 million electronic transactions worth $443 billion were handled by Canadian banks during fiscal 1995. As many as 1,000 Bank of Montreal employees telecommuted from their homes the same year. With home computer banking and smart cards expected to make their debut in 1996, the march toward the cashless society is speeding forward. This is good news for shareholders

BULLETIN BOARD – *BANKS AND TRUSTS*

- **Job demand factors:** the move to the cashless society; boomer retirement planning; growth of small business and foreign banking opportunities.
- **Job growth areas:** financial experts and planners as well as insurance-knowledgeable staff; marketing and customer-service-oriented positions; software and hardware maintenance staff.
- **Skills, abilities, qualities, education needed:** computer literacy; communication skills; creativity; problem-solving and decision-making skills; diploma or degree in business is essential.
- **Job reduction areas:** all teller, paper handling, or account reconciliation functions.

CONTACTS:
☛ Institute of Canadian Bankers
  Tour Scotia, #1000
  1002 rue Sherbrooke Ouest
  10e étage
  Montreal, PQ H3A 3M5
  Tel. 514-282-9480 Fax: 514-282-8881

and consumers who can access services 24 hours a day, but it's bad news for many bank employees. A 1995 Deloitte and Touche study said that within 10 years, half of the 8,000 Canadian bank branches may be closed and up to 35,000 jobs could vanish.

Technological changes in the way people conduct their finances and restructuring in the Canadian banking industry are responsible for these events. They will reverse a trend which saw the number of bank branches increase from about 7,000 in 1985 to 8,000 ten years later. The size of bank branches will tend to become smaller, and a much larger proportion of their space will be devoted to electronic processing with ABMs (automated banking machines). "Digital money," telephone banking, ABMs, and smart cards will probably make bank teller jobs as we currently know them obsolete. The demise of bank branches as transaction-processing centres will occur as many move to value-added customer-service functions and to these new forms of banking. This will open opportunities for people who can be retrained to sell a wider range of services, including mutual funds, insurance, and other investment products.

As the number of very large banks grows as a result of mergers south of the border, Canadian banks can expect to face more intense competition in Europe and Japan. In 1994, for example, foreign borrowing by

---

INSURANCE AND CAR LEASING AT THE BANK

The Canadian Bankers Association has been lobbying for measures that would enable banks to enter the lucrative insurance market. Canadian banks feel they are losing ground to foreign banks that already have full insurance powers at home and with which they must compete for investors' attention in international capital markets. Banks are promising reduced costs and better access for clients.

At the same time, auto dealers and vehicle manufacturers are urging the federal government to keep the Big Six banks out of car leasing, another area targeted by the banks for expansion. The Canadian Bankers Association is viewing with interest figures that show that leasing grew to 39 percent of the value of Canadian car sales in 1994, up from 21 percent in 1989. That represents a jump to 245,000 leases from 44,000.

provincial governments exceeded domestic borrowing for the first time, accounting for 54 percent of the total. Globalization and the resulting increase in both international trade and investment are pushing banks to provide support and service wherever domestic corporate customers require it. The Royal Bank, for example, led its five Canadian competitors in providing more than $3 billion in 1995 in financing for Latin American trade. CIBC actively pursues trade finance with Chile and Peru, where economic growth in 1995 was expected to top 7 percent, and the Bank of Nova Scotia has bought equity in banks in Chile, Mexico, and Argentina. The Bank of Montreal has announced its intention to buy a 15 percent stake in Grupo Financiero Bancomer SA, Mexico's second-biggest financial services group. The Bank of Nova Scotia says it will boost its shares of Mexico's Grupo Financiero Inverlat SA to 51 percent from an initial holding of 8 percent.

The fact that financial services players in the global market require a large capital base and a large domestic base is fueling mergers and acquisitions in the banking industry. A 1995 report on banking by CS First Boston of New York stated that the banking industry "may be on the verge of some of the most dramatic structural changes in its history, led by enormous technological advances, accelerating industry consolidation, more progressive regulatory reforms and an increasingly competitive (and integrated) financial services environment.... Technology will be a key strategic element in virtually every aspect of banking including significantly altering retail delivery systems, achieving scale advantages in commodity-like business areas, gathering detailed customer information, and maintaining strong internal risk management systems."

The banks are in a fine position to finance these moves through self-funding, having had in 1995 another record year of profits; the total was $5.2 billion for the Big Six banks, up 21 percent from the previous year. Annual salaries (including bonuses and other perquisites), such as the $2.52 million paid to the Bank of Montreal's vice-chairman, add to the attractiveness of the top jobs in the industry. Canada's second-biggest bank, the CIBC, posted a record profit of $890 million in 1995 and is taking steps to train its senior managers and even some clients in its new derivatives school, where they learn about these exotic securities.

During 1995 a confluence of factors – the healthy dollar, a strong bond market, and growing interest from U.S. investors – put the Big Six

---

SMART CARDS

As the move to a cashless society accelerates early in 1997, the city of Guelph, Ontario, will be the first locale in North America to try out the Mondex smart card, a credit card with a computer chip implant, which can be used to buy goods and services. Royal Bank, CIBC, and Bell Canada are shareholders in Mondex; with a combined, aggressive marketing approach many other communities will join rapidly. The system will deliver the equivalent of an in-home, in-car, and even in-pocket automatic banking machine, enabling consumers to download "electronic cash" from their bank accounts – via automated teller machines, telephones, or computer modems – to smart cards.

It is expected that smart cards requiring the use of a PIN (personal identification number) will bring more security to credit transaction. Paul Facciol, director of card services security at the Canadian Bankers Association, estimates that credit card fraud accounted for $73 million in losses in 1994 alone for Canada's banks, and worldwide, Visa, MasterCard, and American Express were taken for something like $1.4 billion in the same year.

Canadian banks at the top of the Toronto Stock Exchange. Mutual fund manager Altamira Management Ltd. has placed fairly large bets on the banks, in particular CIBC and Royal Bank, with a $3.9 and $2.85 million share respectively. Canadian banking institutions are also catching the eye of American investors, who consider Canadian bank stocks undervalued; shares of U.S. banks such as Wells Fargo and Bank of Boston rose more than 50 percent in 1995. Aggressive growth strategies are being followed by banks such as the CIBC, which in 1994 planned to spend about $500 million over three to five years on its U.S. division's ventures into the international derivatives and investment banking business.

Criticisms about lack of willingness to serve the financing needs of small business have encouraged the banks to look more closely at this market. A 1995 Financial Post/Arthur Andersen survey of entrepreneurs indicated that many were seeking financing outside the banking system, with 65 percent turning to leasing and 51 percent drawing on personal or family finances. In contrast, in 1994, 47 percent used their own money, and in 1993, only 25 percent reported doing so. Forty-five percent of the

BANKING ON THE NET

Banks are in hot competition with trust companies such as Canada Trust and Bayshore Trust (which launched an Internet instant loan service in 1995) to offer transactions and secure market share via the Internet. U.S.-based Forrester Research Inc. predicts that secure Internet transactions will be available earlier than most people think – making the Net a safe place for interactive banking. Purchasing and funds transfer were expected to be available on the Net in 1996, while bill payment and securities trades will be ready in 1997. While the encryption and security issues are being worked on, most banks are setting up information sites on the World Wide Web. Late in 1995, many were offering extensive Web pages of information on bank products and services, running small businesses, economic conditions, and interest rates, as well as executive speeches and press releases. In 1996 the Bank of Montreal introduced Mbanx, which allows customers to bank by phone, ABM, fax, PC, or Internet, for a lower service charge than branch banking. Similar "virtual banks" are planned by Vancouver City Savings Credit Union and the Dutch multinational ING GroepNV. Eventually the telecommunications companies – or even Microsoft – may change the banking landscape by allowing any electronic media player into the game as a partner in the banking process.

entrepreneurs surveyed in 1995 said they planned to invest in capital equipment during the year, and 54 percent said they would expand their exports during 1996. Financing is going to be necessary for many such businesses, and there will be competition to provide it.

There will be banking jobs in research, assessing the risk factors tied to various investments such as the junk bonds issued by the banks. In 1995 the U.S. high-yield market on junk bonds generated a return of 17 percent, with a 3.1 percent default rate. Canadian banks are viewing this American business with interest, TD and CIBC in particular. These and other developments may offset shrinking corporate demand: traditional areas of banking such as converting deposits to loans are slowing as corporate treasurers in large companies lend to other companies, bypassing banks entirely. In fact, the volume of commercial paper issued in Canada has tripled to $30 billion over the past decade, and the volume of bonds has soared 50 percent to almost $1 trillion in only half this time.

Asset-based lenders such as Newcourt and GE Capital are gaining market share at the expense of banks, and mutual funds now siphon off a large portion of savings that used to sit in customers' accounts.

As Canada's banking institutions mutate from transaction-processing centres into sales offices, we're likely to see a structure where sales, planning, and advice are handled to some extent through commissioned employees. In 1995, for example, Laurentian Bank of Canada had a mobile sales force selling investment products such as GICs, term deposits, and mutual funds, and arranging car loans with compensation consisting entirely of commissions. While these employees are linked to a branch, they're usually on the road conducting business on location, which may well include the kitchen tables or coffee tables of their clients. At the Royal Bank about 200 retirees form a team of commissioned retirement planners who offer advice to recently retired clients and those approaching 71 who must start converting their RRSPs into retirement income.

In addition to the Royal Bank, the Bank of Montreal and the Canadian Imperial Bank of Commerce also have product sellers and mortgage specialists who work on commissions. These mobile commissioned salespeople tend to concentrate on new business, while salaried employees in the branches spend their time looking after existing customers. In late 1995 the Royal Bank was creating in-branch positions called "investment specialists," who work with a combination of salary and bonus based on performance. At CIBC, investment specialists have been expanded across the country to about 115 advisers who serve five or six branches each, usually dealing with clients who have more than $50,000 invested.

Toronto-Dominion Bank is also making an incursion into private banking, with specialty services for high-income-earners with $50,000 to $60,000 to invest. This is substantially less than the $250,000 minimum many institutions have required in the past. As the product mix in banks shifts to more closely resemble brokerage products, however, it seems likely that this trend will continue. Aging baby boomers who are inheriting wealth estimated at $1 trillion over the next 15 years and preparing for their retirement years provide a fertile market for the customized asset allocation and long-term planning offered by these services. The realization that government cannot be relied on to provide retirement income is also driving general demand for investment products over credit. Roving specialists armed with laptop computers and high-level customer-service orientations are part of the new banking scene and are likely here to stay for the next little while.

The Bank of Montreal boosted its presence in the niche market of aboriginal banking by buying a minority share in First Phoenix Fund Co. Ltd., an investment management firm set up to tap the aboriginal market. Estimates of the settlement money on the books of various aboriginal bands across the country are in the area of $2 to $3 billion. In a similar vein, Canada's big domestic banks compete with the Hong Kong Bank of Canada (now the seventh-largest bank in the country) in Toronto's Chinatown for the business of Asian Canadians, using Chinese lettering and Chinese-speaking staff. The Bank of Montreal has 60 branches specifically geared to servicing the Chinese community in Canada.

In a bold move early in 1996, the Canadian Imperial Bank of Commerce announced a deal with the Used Car Dealers Association of Canada which will enable UCDA's 3,000 members to arrange customer loans and leases simply by phoning CIBC Finance. Canada's used-car business is estimated to be worth at least $22 billion a year, with about 16 percent of the market in the hands of used-car dealers.

In 1995 the TD Bank blazed a new trail in financial services and further expanded the role of a bank by offering sales of brand-name mutual funds through its branch network. TD's Asset Accumulation

---

BANKERS – AT YOUR SERVICE

A Cambridge Reports study of 1,500 consumers found that 44 percent agreed that "ease of doing business with" was the principal reason for choosing a financial institution. Second was "quality of personal service" (named by 28 percent) and third was "range of financial services available" (at 22 percent). It's interesting to note that finding an institution easy to do business with, being well treated, and having a choice of services outranked other more traditional factors such as location, interest rates, and other non-service items. With increased competition, the financial institutions are attempting to get consumers to consolidate all their financial services in one place – chequing, savings, financing, investing, and the rest.

TECHNOLOGY ON THE BANKING SCENE

Canadians are among the world's most prolific users of automated banking machines. At the end of 1993, there were about 55 ABMs for every 100,000 Canadians, a rate exceeded globally only by the Japanese, who had 94. In contrast, the Americans had 38, the British had 32, and the Germans had 31.

Increasingly companies are using direct deposits of employees' pay, and many consumers have arranged for the automatic payment of their mortgages and utility bills directly to their creditors. In 1994 there were almost 600 million electronic transactions – a figure more than double that of 1990 – worth $208 billion. Surveys show that use of automated teller machines will continue to climb, forming about 37 percent of retail transactions in 1997, versus 19 percent in 1994. Transactions performed in bank branches will decline from 70 percent to a projected 51 percent in 1997.

A survey of Canadian banks' use of technology suggests banking using Touch-Tone telephone service will increase sixfold in 1997, when it will account for about 4 percent of all retail transactions. Banking through telephone service centres – where customers talk to human operators at a centralized facility – will grow to 7 percent of transactions in 1997 from 1 percent in 1994. The impact of technology is reducing jobs as expected. In 1994 the Big Six banks in Canada employed about 165,000 people, down from 173,000 in 1991.

Account will be able to hold other investments (such as GICs) besides mutual funds, and when used for RRSPs, it will facilitate the calculation of the foreign content allowance of 20 percent. The TD, with more than 900 branches and a sales force of 5,000 across the country, is the first to offer other mutual funds at discount brokerage rates.

Insurance

A distribution revolution under way in the insurance industry may be the most profound change experienced in its 200-year history. Industry analyst Ted Belton, director of research for RBC Underwriting Management Services Inc., predicts that within five years, direct insurers operating phone centres using the latest technology will capture one-third of the home and car insurance market and enjoy expense ratios under 20 percent, down substantially from current levels. With about $16 billion of premiums sold by property and casualty insurers in 1994, the new direct sales market could easily top $5 billion.

It will, however, be expensive to implement. Because a full computer and telephone system to sell insurance directly can cost tens of millions of dollars, the shift will lead to further consolidation in the Canadian industry, which in 1995 had more than 225 active insurance companies. Insurers are being forced to find cheaper ways of doing business because their core underwriting operations have been extremely unprofitable. Expenses in the industry are about 33 cents of every premium dollar and have been worsening over the past 10 years. As recently as 1991, 82 percent of property and casualty insurers had losses on their core underwriting operations that had to be offset by profits from investment activities.

In 1994 property and casualty insurers (including house, auto, and commercial property coverage, but not life insurance) saw profits fall by 32 percent, to $683 million, the lowest in 10 years. The poor results leave insurers with a disappointing 5.7 percent return on equity for 1994, down from 9.1 percent in 1993. Investment income fell by more than $400 million to $2.27 billion, from $2.68 billion in 1993. Realized capital gains (profits on selling an investment) fell by 80 percent to $106 million.

Canada's 30,000 independent insurance brokers are bracing for the severe threat from banks competing for the insurance industry. In 1995 about 75 percent of Canadians bought their automobile and property insurance through brokers, a practice now under a critical threat. In the same year life insurance sales fell 7 percent while annualized premiums were off 4 percent. Sales of whole-life policies with fixed annual premiums fell 30 percent in 1995, and all other permanent insurance sales dipped 2 percent. Universal-life sales declined 9 percent in 1994 as the upswing in interest made bank savings more competitive in the marketplace. The sales drop is a reflection of the economy in Canada and the aging population. There are fewer younger people, and this group has less disposable income to buy insurance than earlier generations. Aging baby boomers are demanding combination products giving insurance coverage and provision for retirement.

Property and casualty insurance companies are bracing for a tidal wave of consolidation that has already wiped out 104 companies in the

---

RISK MANAGEMENT

The field of risk management has generally become much less of an insurance function and much more of a financing task over the past two decades. Thirty years ago most risk managers came out of the insurance industry. Now companies are looking for risk managers with stronger knowledge of the world of finance along with specialized education in risk management. Canadian risk managers have degrees in various disciplines, from commerce to engineering, and may have supplemented their education with a CRM (Canadian Risk Management) diploma. The Risk and Insurance Management Society (RIMS) has a ten-course program in risk management, finance, administration, and law leading to the designation FRM, Fellow in Risk Management. Risk management, which currently does not have a large profile, may assume greater importance as corporations face added or unusual challenges in their global operations.

---

past 15 years. Record aviation claims and a series of costly shipping disasters hit world insurance markets in 1994, putting pressure on the industry's profits and casting a cloud over its 1995 prospects. Airline losses reached about US$2.2 billion in 1994 – a figure significantly higher than premiums paid to insurance companies.

The trend in all industries (financial services included) toward deregulation and one-stop shopping is being keenly felt in the insurance industry, which is girding for battle against the incursion of the banks into sales of insurance. Royal Bank of Canada, CIBC, TD Bank, Bank of Nova Scotia, Hong Kong Bank of Canada, and National Bank of Canada are either in the insurance business now or planning to enter. More than 80 foreign insurance companies now have offices in China, waiting for much greater foreign access to that market. They include such industry giants as Prudential Insurance, Aetna Life and Casualty, Zurich Insurance, and Chubb. While in 1994–95 average per capita spending on insurance in China was equivalent to just $8, compared with world averages ranging as high as $2,500, insurers are looking to the future. In 1994 an estimated 350 million Chinese bought some form of insurance, and premium income is increasing by more than 20 percent a year.

At the moment, Canada has 150 life insurers fighting for business in a near-stagnant market. The betting is that this number will come down as competitive pressures and technology advances force consolidation in the industry.

Following the large increases in liability insurance premiums and the setting of very restricted coverage limits coupled with larger deductibles, 30 percent of those seeking liability insurance abandoned the traditional insurance market and developed other approaches. Reciprocal pooling is used by school boards, which insure one another rather than buy insurance in the market. Captive corporate-owned insurance companies, typically located in Bermuda for tax reasons, are used by large firms for self-insurance.

Financially, insurers are not in good shape, with many liquidating higher-interest bonds in order to cover current losses. Dividends to participating policyholders have diminished; operating costs have been cut, often meaning staff layoffs; and new information technology must be purchased so as to compete with banks, which were faster off the mark in adopting new technology. To make matters worse, fraudulent claims, which account for 10 to 20 percent of the $12 billion that insurers annually pay out, are rising at an annual rate of 12 percent.

Losses suffered by big insurance companies will diminish worldwide reinsurance capacity and force up prices in order to compensate. To achieve solvency, there will be mergers, acquisitions, and strategic alliances, a broader-risk capital base, and greater market efficiency. As the market becomes more complex, with additional risks and outside competition, insurance companies are beginning to specialize – travel, life, accident, property, for example – as part of a survival strategy.

Banks will either try to bypass the brokerage function and sell their own insurance or try to replace the brokers. Technology can help banks achieve this goal. For example, banks may wish to take advantage of Compulife Software. A computerized quote system used by many insurance agents, it surveys over 50 Canadian companies and displays the highest and lowest premiums based on the client's sex, age, and smoking habits. Banks could also use this software to fulfill the brokerage function for the more straightforward types of insurance: travel, accident, life, property, and casualty. Insurance companies may have to work harder at offering the consumer the more complicated products that banks are less likely to pursue, such as insurance against software theft and other proprietary aspects of information abuse or loss. And, as consumers become more litigation-happy, there will be a conspicuous market for various liability products, such as insurance for corporate directors. Many insurance companies are trying to help clients avoid taxes by offering universal-life policies that combine term life insurance and a savings program. Given the shrinking under-45 market – the prime market for life insurance – and the declining growth in the life insurance market, insurance companies are exploiting the older boomer market's interest in investment and retirement products; this market is already growing faster than the life insurance market. Banks are also in hot pursuit of this market, though they have yet to consolidate the life, casualty, savings, and insurance markets.

Federal legislation allowing other financial service companies to become more like banks and investment companies will result in a huge battle between banks and insurance companies for both insurance and investment business. Banks have already taken up a business opportunity by taking over trust company and investment dealer functions. They will likely pursue the life, auto, and home insurance markets as well. In the short term, banks are forbidden from using their vast branch system and customer information to sell insurance, but this will likely change eventually.

The insurance industry is plagued by a worldwide overabundance of suppliers. Many companies – even medium-sized ones – are too small to effectively compete. To compete, insurance companies will have to join multinationals similar to those already dominating the property and casualty markets in Canada. Even multinationals are demanding one-stop multinational insurance to simplify their insurance needs. Since insurance companies are already earning lower rates of return than other financial sectors, a series of mergers and acquisitions will occur so as to gain the economies of scale and greater access to a larger capital base. Zurich Canada purchased the Travelers Insurance Company, and General Accident Assurance Company of Canada became the largest company in the general insurance market after acquiring the Prudential Life Assurance Company of England (Canada)'s property and casualty operations; the Manufacturers Life Assurance Company may convert its trust company subsidiaries into a Schedule 2 bank; Imperial Life Assurance Company of Canada has issued redeemable preferreds and

Confederation Life Insurance Company offered subordinated debentures – both attempting to add to their capital base. Mutual life insurers, which are owned by their policyholders, may demutualize into public

BULLETIN BOARD – *INSURANCE*

- **Job demand factors:** growing need for new forms of insurance such as environmental or corporate responsibility insurance; bigger companies needed for reinsurance loss coverage; multinationals wanting worldwide coverage, necessitating the emergence of multinational insurance companies.
- **Job growth areas:** actuaries specializing in new areas of risk; opportunities for women selling insurance to other women; insurance jobs in banks.
- **Skills, abilities, qualities, education needed:** a firm grasp of more complicated products and knowledge in financial planning; a diploma in insurance; courses offered by professional organizations and institutes.
- **Job reduction factors:** downsizing as result of mergers and acquisitions.

CONTACTS

☛ Canadian Institute of Actuaries
  #820, 360 Albert Street
  Ottawa, ON K1R 7X7 Tel. 613-236-8196
  URL: http://www.actuaries.ca/CIA/CIA.html
☛ Canadian Institute of Chartered Life Underwriters
      & Chartered Financial Consultants
  41 Lesmill Rd.,
  Don Mills, ON M3B 2T3 Tel. 416-444-5251 Fax: 416-444-8031
☛ Canadian Life & Health Insurance Association
  #1700, 1 Queen St. East,
  Toronto, ON M5C 2X9 Tel. 416-777-2221 Fax: 416-777-1895
  Info line: 416-777-2344 Toll-free: 1-800-268-8099
☛ Insurance Brokers Association of Canada
  #1902, 181 University Avenue
  Toronto, ON M5H 3M7 Tel. 416-367-1831 Fax: 416-367-3687
☛ The Insurance Institute of Canada
  18 King St. East, 6th Fl.,
  Toronto, ON M5C 1C4 Tel. 416-362-8586 Fax: 416-362-1126

shareholding stock companies in order to take advantage of the capital markets.

What job prospects does the insurance industry offer? Not yet fully exploited are insurance sales to women, a group that represents 52 percent of the market. Women often want more information than men and are happier dealing with female insurance representatives than with their male counterparts. This represents a significant opportunity for women who wish to enter the sales or marketing side of the industry. With the financial product side of the insurance business growing, there will be a greater demand for financial planners. Mutual Life of Canada pays 30 financial planners to provide financial information to its sales agents and clients. New products – environmental insurance, for example – will require extensive risk assessment, which means more actuaries will be needed. Since actuaries frequently command annual salaries in excess of $100,000, this field is definitely worth considering.

Insurance sellers will hire people with strong teamwork skills. In an attempt to reduce the distribution costs of premiums from 35 percent to 20 percent over the next few years, the Canadian Surety Company and Canada West Insurance Company, for example, have put employees in self-managed teams, which eventually will be recruiting their own members, setting their own priorities, and providing one-stop shopping for their clients' needs. Individuals interested in pursuing a career in the insurance industry are strongly advised to develop these skills. As the industry makes new incursions into global markets, languages and an understanding of different cultures will become considerably more important.

Bear in mind that skills are escalating, since almost half of the students with BAs hired in 1995 by London Life were given clerical jobs. And the 14 finalists for their risk-analysis area all possessed PhDs. However, London Life picks its sales force from competitive intercollegiate sports teams – unlike Sunlife Assurance Co. of Canada, which hires mostly MBAs.

Investment

Among investment choices, the mutual fund industry is one of the most competitive arms of the financial services industry, with companies fighting vigorously for market share. There are career opportunities for extensively trained registered financial services representatives who are capable of working within the complexities of the global marketplace, and advising on investment opportunities in the various regions of the world.

In January 1996, sales of Canadian and foreign money market funds reached a staggering total of $146.2 billion. One market study projects that the total fund assets of mutual funds will rise to $400 billion by 2000. With 29.7 percent of Canadian households owning shares in a mutual fund, Canada has almost caught up with the U.S. level of 31 percent, although the dollar amount of the average U.S. holding (C$97,000/US$71,500) is more than double the Canadian household figure of $42,000. Indeed, at US$2.6 trillion, total U.S. fund assets under management are about 20 times the Canadian figure. Mutual funds account for $75 billion, or more than a quarter of the $240 billion Canadians have salted away in retirement savings plans.

Equities were the flavour of 1995, with Canadian stock market funds posting sales of $3.1 billion while foreign stock funds grabbed $2.4 billion. Since the end of 1992, IFIC members (Investment Funds Institute of Canada, the industry trade group) have seen their assets soar 118 percent from $67 billion. The big growth was in companies that sell their funds only through brokers and dealers. Trimark Investment Management Inc. saw its assets jump 49 percent to $13.8 billion, Templeton Management Ltd. grew 38 percent to $6.3 billion, and Dynamic Mutual Funds grew 41 percent to $3.4 billion. The top ten members ranked by assets were Investors Group, Trimark, Royal Mutual Funds, Mackenzie Financial Corp., AGF Management, Templeton, CIBC Securities, Fidelity Investments, TD Asset Management, and Altamira Investment Services.

Efficiency and competitiveness issues in the Canadian market have led to some standardization practices and a call for a harmonizing of the securities industry. Harmonization would mean a common standard among provincial securities commissions for reporting insider trading in all Canadian jurisdictions. In addition, a financial advisor could apply for recognition in one jurisdiction and have it apply to other jurisdictions as well.

With the emphasis on customer service, it is understandable that the financial services companies are intensely interested in the large and lucrative financial planning market for pre-retirement baby boomers. An interesting series of findings in a Royal Trust poll conducted by Decima Research shows that nearly half of Canadians in the top 25 percent earnings bracket are expecting an inheritance, making them part of what has been called the Trillion Dollar Generation. Most of the survey group define themselves as middle class, with average household income at $86,000. Ninety percent of those polled said they considered properly passing on their estate to their heirs a priority, and 88 percent cited minimizing taxes on their estate as a priority. A full 95 percent said preserving the value of their assets after retirement was a significant goal. This will be a fertile field for financial planners, estate planners, and legal services. Ninety-three percent said they would seek as much information as possible before making financial decisions, but nearly a third did not know where to get good advice. Only 41 percent said they had an estate plan drawn up, but nearly 60 percent said they intended to do so over the next five years. When the group was asked what steps they would take in the event of inheriting a considerable estate, 84 percent said they would place most of the inheritance in investments, while only 39 percent said they would make an immediate major purchase.

It is demographics as well that is driving the upward trend in RRSP savings. Current projections estimate that almost a quarter of the population will be 65 years or older by 2031. Canadians socked away a record $20.9 billion in registered retirement savings plans during 1994. Women constituted 43 percent of RRSP contributors and put in a third of the total $7.2 billion. People aged 55 and over were the biggest contributors, averaging $5,910. While this may sound somewhat rosy, the 1994 total was just 16.6 percent of the $126.3 billion in tax-deductible contributions people could have made. According to Ray Leu of Investor Economics Inc., a Toronto firm that advises financial companies, most RRSP investments are made by people at the high end of disposable incomes who make maximum contributions. He feels that brokers and financial planners have to do a better job of marketing to people with lower and middle-level incomes.

The industry is quickly realizing that customizing products and services for women makes a great deal of sense. Nearly 90 percent of women will be responsible for their own financial needs and those of their children. One-quarter of small businesses are currently headed by women. Women are well represented in higher education programs as well. Fifty-three percent of undergraduate university students are women; 27 percent are in master's degree programs, and 10 percent are earning doctoral degrees.

Since women often appreciate a relational approach to doing business, sales opportunities for women to market products to other women are vast. Industry research shows that female clients want information, a long-term relationship with an institution or financial manager, and a convenient location. Karen Hughes, a sociologist at the University of Alberta, dug into occupations which were almost the exclusive preserve of men for the past quarter-century. She found that financial management was the area in which women made the third-biggest gains between 1986 and 1991, following optometry and services management in a list of twenty-two occupations.

In one-quarter of all families, a figure more than double the number in the late 1960s, women earn more than their spouses. This does not take into consideration the unpaid work that women continue to perform in the majority of households, which Statscan estimates to be worth at least $234 billion. Women occupy 40 percent of all managerial and administrative positions in the Canadian work force and account for nearly 30 per cent of doctors and dentists. Women now own a third of U.S. businesses and have become a major force in the economy. In Canada, women are opening businesses at three times the rate of men. The average income for women working full-time in 1991 was $26,842, up 2 percent from 1990. The average for men remained steady at $38,567.

It is estimated that between 80 and 90 percent of women, regardless of marital status, will have to handle their own finances at some point in their lives. While they are still earning less than men, they have to save more because they tend to live longer. Between 1981 and 1991 the proportion of female contributors to RRSPs rose to 42 percent from 31 percent. About 40 percent of women own common or preferred stocks and 50 percent own mutual funds. The old stereotype that the head of the household is a male who makes all the financial decisions is out of date.

From 1989 to 1994, Canadian mutual fund assets grew by 30.5 percent, almost twice the U.S. growth rate of 17.1 percent, according to a report

by Colin Deane, a partner with Ernst and Young, a Toronto-based
management consulting firm. Total fund assets are expected to rise
to $400 billion by 2000. In 1995 mutual fund sales in Canada totalled
$5.2 billion.

Banks and trust companies have been aggressively promoting the
benefits of investing in mutual funds, thereby enhancing consumer
education and awareness. Growing consumer understanding about the
professional management and risk diversification available to small
investors through mutual fund management has contributed to steady
growth in this field.

In addition, the aging Canadian population is becoming more
concerned about investments for retirement. A 1995 study by Goldfarb
Consultants for Scotiabank indicated that few Canadians have faith in the
Canada Pension Plan. Four out of five respondents in the 30-to-49 age
group said they are not very confident or not at all confident about the
capacity of the CPP to provide them with income when they retire. Most
people apparently put most faith in their RRSPs, with the CPP ranked
second and company pension plans third. At the same time, 40 percent
of those surveyed said they had less than $10,000 worth of savings and
investment. Among those who have saved, Scotiabank points out that
most have taken advice and drawn up financial plans. According to
Peter Cook of the *Globe and Mail*, Canadians have become the industrialized world's worst savers. They also have the industrialized world's
most-expensive-to-service debt, which undermines faith in the CPP and
fosters more investment for retirement.

Financial planning is becoming an intensely competitive arena, with
market segmentation and customization becoming the norm. Mutual
funds with a global perspective designed specifically for Canadians are
being offered by a number of investment services, for example. The
Canadian market is growing by about 15 percent a year and over the
next few years, there will be greater interest worldwide in value items,
such as no-load mutual funds.

Canadian investors are beginning to view the global market with great
interest. This means not only investing in companies around the world,
but also viewing North American companies from a global investment
perspective. Double-digit growth in booming markets such as Asia and
Latin America is characteristic of the huge pool of capital moved around

the globe by investors and money managers. Four trends have contributed to increased globalization of money markets: the increase in
the mobility of money; the growth of cross-border trade; the spread
of capitalism, especially in rapidly growing countries; and a growing
movement to put investment assets into easily tradeable securities.

As global barriers continue to topple, many more mutual funds sponsored by foreigners will set up shop on Canadian soil. A considerable
amount of American money is flowing into emerging stock markets;
foreign institutional investment in these is now at $50 billion, up from
$500 million just five years ago. According to Robert Hain, executive
vice-president of marketing at Investors Group, the largest Canadian
mutual fund company, the mutual fund industry is becoming a worldwide industry and as such, will be led by a few big and powerful global
brand leaders. Canadian investors will in the future have their choice of
the top global funds. There will also be more joint ventures and alliances
between Canadian companies and newcomers looking for an entrance
to the market and added clout in it.

According to the Washington-based Institute of International Finance
(an organization which includes several Canadian banks), in 1996 some
US$175.3 billion of savings was expected to end up in private or public
projects in Brazil, Mexico, China, India, the Philippines, South Africa,
Russia, or Poland. That's almost C$242 billion at exchange rates in
early 1996. This level of investment is driven not just by high growth in
demand, but also by the depth of the financial sector in these emerging-
country economies, the openness to international trade, the level of
human skills or capital, and the level of political stability and debt
burdens. Of the estimated investment of US$175.3 billion, the Institute
of International Finance expects that almost half, or US$86.9 billion,
will go to the Asia-Pacific region, US$51.7 billion to Latin America,
and US$12.8 billion to Central and Eastern Europe. Asia's economy
was expected to grow about 8.5 percent in 1996, Latin America by
2 percent, and Central and Eastern Europe by 3 percent. By investing
in these emerging markets, we are building up a 3-billion-person
customer base for Canadian industries. The challenge for Canadians
will be to create products and services for these markets and to pursue
them effectively.

Where are the jobs in this industry? Most are in the growing mutual

fund and RRSP markets. In fact, many individuals have struck out on
their own as financial planners who offer to guide confused investors
through the maze of RRIFs, RRSPs, estate planning, and life insurance
packages. There are many success stories: one MBA, unable to get a job
after graduation, decided to sell mutual funds to teachers and netted
$1 million in his first year!

The future looks bleak for traditional stockbroker jobs. These positions are very market-sensitive, and with the increase in computerized
trading, individual investors will be able to carry out their own transactions before too long. The increasing sophistication of the boomer
investor coupled with greater access to ever-expanding on-line information sources will change the standard stock-market way of doing business.
The banks already offer no-frills trading through the Toronto-Dominion's
"Greenline" and other discount trading services that provide on-line
service to investors through their personal computers. Investors can view
quotes from all North American stock exchanges, U.S. options, and
indexes. These services can be customized to provide complete bid/ask
prices, offer sizes, day's opening, high/low, last trade and data, spread-
sheets, and real-time or historical graphs.

No-load mutual funds will also contribute to the continuing erosion
of brokerage commissions over time. Currently, pension funds are keeping the stockbrokers in business. The proportion of shares in the U.S.
held by institutions rose from 20 percent in 1970 to over 50 percent in
1992, and will continue to climb – though more slowly – as baby boomers
pour more money into their pension funds over the next 20 years.

Career opportunities will be available in mutual fund organizations
and in on-line information services, which update investors on relevant
developments. Banks and insurance companies will seek financial planning experts as they make more aggressive moves into these areas.
Accountants and stockbrokers would be well advised to earn a Certified
Financial Analyst (CFA) designation to take advantage of the opportunities in mutual funds and other financial planning services – stocks,
bonds, and annuities.

In a world of round-the-clock trading, factors like access to information, investor psychology, and timing will be decisive. Thus the market
for investor and financial planning advice books and specialized trading
services will flourish. Moreover, increased interest in financial matters

will mean more jobs in financial journalism. In fact, all media will likely offer more financial advice and information.

Another job growth area is in the "middle office" – the new structural aspect of the securities business. The middle office handles the increasingly risky but lucrative trade in derivatives – futures, options, swaps – which technology is helping companies create. Derivatives are used both to hedge the risk of changes in exchange rates, interest rates, and equities, and to speculate on those changes. Middle offices provide data entry, trade processing and authorization, compliance control, risk management, revaluation of portfolios, and calculation of profit and loss for the derivative markets, much the same way as the back office does for bonds and equities. With middle offices reporting directly to the derivatives department, hedging, risk management, and global positioning can be built into products and trading operations right from the beginning.

The trend toward the development of middle offices is part of a broader re-engineering aimed at streamlining operations and bringing the back and front offices closer together. Technology such as the UNIX operating system allows for work stations which are capable of running several programs simultaneously, thereby connecting many different aspects of the business. The middle office is a growth area because banks and securities houses usually avoid such high-risk areas. To offer such services, however, one must account to regulators who want to see that the risk is being appropriately managed by a middle office. The major players adopting middle offices include Merrill Lynch Canada Inc., Goldman Sachs Canada, the Chase Manhattan Bank of Canada, and Japan's Nomura, Sumitomo, and Mitsubishi.

According to the Bank of International Settlements, trade in derivatives rose by 35 percent in 1992, with $4.5 trillion in outstanding contracts at the end of 1992. America's Federal Reserve monitored about $7 trillion in derivatives in the first quarter of 1993 alone. Tax and hedging strategies are encouraging the growth in derivatives. Thanks to outdated tax laws, investors enjoy many tax loopholes in this market. In addition, currency and interest-rate hedging accounts for the marked growth in this area, particularly in Europe, where trading soared 66 percent in 1992 in response to concerns over Europe's Exchange Rate Mechanism – currency equalization among European Community countries. Uncertain economic times will continue to make the

BULLETIN BOARD – *INVESTMENT*

- **Job demand factors:** aging boomers preparing for retirement and wanting diverse financial planning services; growing mutual funds and RRSP markets.
- **Job growth areas:** financial planners; mutual fund investors; media experts; middle office personnel specializing in derivative trading; and mergers and acquisitions.
- **Skills, abilities, qualities, education needed:** creativity; problem-solving, decision-making, risk assessment, and analytical skills; a diploma in finance essential.
- **Job reduction factors:** sophisticated investors demanding specialized information and trading services; investors able to trade stocks from any location; banks and insurance companies taking over many of the functions now delivered by stockbrokers and individual financial planners or small companies; the mutual fund market is extremely vulnerable to downturns which will scare many investors out of the equity markets and into the money markets.

CONTACTS

☞ Investment Dealers' Association of Canada
121 King St. W., Suite 1600
Toronto, ON M5H 3T9 Tel. 416-354-6133 Fax: 416-364-0753

derivatives market an employment growth area.

Broker investment expertise will prevail in the mergers and acquisitions and the bond and share-offering markets. Government debt and the privatization of many government services will keep many dealers in business, as will the record merger and acquisition activity that began in 1993, with $19.3 billion in deals that had to be put together by security dealers and lawyers.

Although the Canadian brokerage industry's revenues increased 45 percent in the first half of 1993 over the same period in 1992, the recent volume has strongly affected the processing side of the business. According to Ian Hendry, vice-president for human resources with Richardson Greenshields of Canada Limited, "Technological enhancements and organizational streamlining have enabled us to absorb the increase in business without affecting our employment numbers. There is a good deal of caution in the market due to the economic and political uncertainty which creates hesitancy to make capital expenditures that would generate jobs." Thus, employment figures for the industry were only up to an annualized 21,193 in 1993 over 19,666 in 1992 – still significantly lower than the 27,000 employed in the brokerage industry in the pre-crash days of 1987.

Finance, however, is still perceived as holding many lucrative opportunities – especially by MBA graduates of the University of Western Ontario. Twenty-four percent of Western's grads go into investment banking, and 8 percent pursue financial services.

Where the Jobs Are in Real Estate
• Housing • Industrial and Commercial Real Estate

The real estate market will be somewhat segmented because of the influence of demographic factors and the development and exploitation of technologically advanced infrastructures in various locations. Over-building in the 1980s and low inflation in the 1990s have altered the way real estate is valued. Real estate stocks have somewhat lagged behind the key Toronto Stock Exchange 300 Index since the beginning of the decade, but in 1995 shares plummeted, and 1996 could be worse. After the boom years of the 1980s when office towers, condominiums, and shopping centres opened at a record pace, real estate stocks were especially vulnerable to the recession in the early 1990s. According to Rob McConnachie, an analyst with Canaccord Capital Corp. in Vancouver, most future growth in the real estate industry will be found not among companies that concentrate on traditional shopping centres and office towers, but more likely in hotels and resorts across Canada.

Industry analysts are expecting to see more bulk sales toward the end of the 1990s as institutions pull together several properties and sell them as a single package. In 1995, for example, Royal Bank of Canada sold a $500 million portfolio of real estate to Goldman Sachs & Co. for about $220 million.

Housing
According to a 1996 Royal Bank report by economist Carlos Leitao, the extreme weakness in the housing market was due to the combined impact of declining real disposable incomes per capita and a deep-seated

sense of job insecurity. While the housing affordability index was at the
lowest level in the decade, the big thing missing was consumer confidence. In addition, longer-term factors such as demographics will have
a lasting impact on the health of Canada's ailing housing industry. In
the 1970s baby boomers made housing sales flourish; in the 1980s they
upgraded; and in the 1990s, homes in retirement communities and near
golf courses are selling. What is missing is the driving force at the bottom
of the market: the first-time homebuyer. Bruce Clemmensen, president
of the Canadian Home Builders Association, described 1995 as the worst
year for housing starts in 35 years and estimated that 100,000 to 150,000
jobs would be lost in 1996 because of this dismal showing. It appears that
Generation X and immigrants are not forming households at a rate
comparable to older generations. Baby boomers are also passing on
real estate property to their children.

As baby boomers reach the age of reflection, indications are that
many will not follow the path of previous generations in seeking retirement havens in Florida, Arizona, or White Rock, B.C. Boomers value the
illusion of individuality and independence, and their retirement choices
will reflect complex desires for privacy, exclusivity, association with diverse
communities, and opportunities for meaningful pastimes. Many aging
empty-nesters will sell their homes and purchase condominiums or town-
houses to support their options for spending winters in warmer locales.
The cottage market will pick up as aging boomers with inheritances purchase summer residences for their extended families. Smaller towns and
acreages near deserts and oceans are attracting interest from boomers
who, as they age, seem to enjoy reflecting on time and space. On
Canada's west coast, the Gulf Islands seem destined to become virtual
suburbs of Vancouver and Victoria. Small towns in the Maritimes, rural
Ontario, and the interior of British Columbia are the best Canadian bets
for the boomers' retirement ideal. Property values in idyllic parts of
Mexico, Costa Rica, France, Spain, or Italy will rise smartly as word gets
out that they offer boomers the relaxed settings they desire. Opportunities
for profitable market-making are considerable where limits to the growth
of such places can be assured.

As Canadians relocate locally, Toronto and British Columbia are
attracting most movers, and that's putting pressure on housing. A
Canada Mortgage and Housing Corporation study in late 1995 showed

that Toronto and Vancouver were the two most popular destinations for Canadians relocating to another part of the country or moving to Canada. Housing markets were more active in these areas, with a higher number of starts and resales. Young movers were most likely to go to Canada's three largest cities and some mid-sized communities such as Ottawa, Kitchener, and Calgary. Smaller communities in British Columbia and southern Ontario were attracting people aged 45 and older. Eight of the top 15 cities were in British Columbia. In Ontario the fastest-growing areas were Barrie, Windsor, and Kitchener.

While this movement creates a flurry of activity, industry analysts feel that high unemployment rates remain a barrier to any sustained recovery in real estate. According to most forecasts, the annual total for housing construction is unlikely to go above 150,000 units through the rest of this decade, down from 170,000 in the early 1990s. According to a 1995 report by Nesbitt Burns Inc. economists David Rosenberg and Bill Johnston, homebuilders will face a shrinking market as demand from the aging baby boom generation wanes. The number of first-time buyers (generally 25-to-34-year-olds) is poised to fall by 8 percent by the end of the decade. Growth in the trade-up cohort (those between 35 and 44) is also expected to slow. The demand for renovations and shelter for the elderly will rise, but sales will be restricted by sky-high levels of consumer debt, job insecurity, and an oversupply of unsold homes.

Industrial and Commercial Real Estate

Leasing in the industrial sector (manufacturing and warehouse space) is expected to perform well across the country as a result of falling vacancy rates. The industrial vacancy rate was expected to hit 7.5 percent in 1996, down from 8.3 percent in 1995. Leasing in the office markets is regionally influenced; Toronto's vacancy rate was expected to ease to 13 percent from 16.4 percent, and Vancouver was expected to fall to 8 percent from 9.1 percent. Vacancy rates in cities like Ottawa and Edmonton will remain around 16 or 17 percent, three percentage points above the national average of 13 percent predicted for 1996. The early 1990s office-conversion-to-condominium craze has reached its peak. The value of industrial and commercial construction permits across Canada in late 1995 reached $1.2 billion, with a rate of increase not seen since 1990. In 1994 Calgary was Canada's hottest industrial market, with an industrial vacancy rate of 3.7 percent, compared with 15.3 percent in Toronto, 11.5 percent in Montreal, and 4.3 percent in Vancouver.

Competition for telecom call centres heated up as Saskatchewan joined New Brunswick, Manitoba, and Nova Scotia in rivalry to lure business from central Canada with various benefits, from tax breaks to outright financial grants. The decentralization of call centres captured much media attention in 1995, yet the overwhelming majority remain in central Canada, often as adjuncts to corporate locations. Ontario is estimated to have 1,000 call centres and Quebec 1,500, together employing 35,000 people. Vancouver is attracting high-tech companies and proving a rival as a popular corporate headquarters location, although Toronto still reigns supreme as a head office locale. Vancouver is home for the Hong Kong Bank of Canada, the country's seventh-largest bank, with $16.7 billion in assets. According to David Bond, spokesperson for the bank, it made sense when the bank started back in 1981 to be positioned for trading in finance with Asia. In the future, this will assume greater importance since China has already become the third-largest economy in the world and will be number one by 2010.

Increasingly in the global economy, connections matter; communities must open their boundaries to multinational companies and welcome foreign investment and trade. Those areas with the infrastructure, which must include a powerful network system to support these critical links, will become the most sought-after real estate locations in the world. The active come-and-do-business-with-us program of Fredericton, New Brunswick, was assisted by the province's highly sophisticated telecommunications system, which offered services at competitive costs. N.B. Tel was the first phone company in North America to go 100 percent digital; it started ten years ago to build a province-wide fibre-optics network, and both the phone and cable systems are technologically advanced. The McKenna government spread the word about lower operating costs, high-tech communications, a bilingual work force, and a welcoming atmosphere in New Brunswick. Statistics Canada says the province had the country's highest new-jobs growth rate in 1994 – 6.3 percent, compared with a national average of 2.9 percent.

Eventually these linked communities will become very widely established, so it will be interesting to watch the evolution of the electronically enabled housing development called Stonehaven West, in Newmarket,

Ontario. This is a state-of-the-art network community with huge connectivity potential. (See Chapter 1 for further information.) Futuristic communities like this will inject new life into real estate markets, and there will be a corollary demand to tackle the problem of old industrial sites now that traditional heavy industry is on the decline. This will mean continuing pressure on industrial lands for redevelopment for retail and residential purposes.

As the facts of globalization and the information technology revolution become increasingly felt in the real estate business, the skills and knowledge required of individuals in the field will escalate. No longer

BULLETIN BOARD – *REAL ESTATE*

- **Job demand factors:** emptynesters moving into condo market, and younger boomer families taking over the larger homes being vacated; pension funds will increase real estate investment from 5 percent to 8 percent of their portfolio, mostly in the already-built market.
- **Job growth areas:** long-term prospects in latter part of 1990s for property managers, home inspectors, commercial and residential appraisers, commercial and industrial sales positions, and residential sales positions in the condo, cottage, and larger home markets; service industry geared to facilitating the private home-selling market will emerge now that the technology exists to make this a cost-effective and less time-consuming way of buying and selling property.
- **Skills, abilities, qualities, education needed:** negotiating, selling, communicating, problem-solving, analytical, and multimedia skills.
- **Job reduction areas:** commercial and residential sales jobs in the short term.
- **Growth limiting factors:** real estate fees will decline over the long term; office building market is oversupplied; fewer new-home buyers following on the heels of the boomer generation.

CONTACTS
- The Canadian Real Estate Association
  Place de Ville, Tower A,
  #2100, 320 Queen St.,
  Ottawa, ON K1R 5A3 Tel. 613-237-7111 Fax: 613-234-2567
  URL: http://crea.ca/crea.htm

will the basic ability to sell, to negotiate, and to understand the basics of financing be sufficient; salespeople will have to have a good understanding of both the technology used to showcase real estate offerings, and the electronic linkages in various areas as well. Real estate specialists will require a good grasp of the dynamics associated with the development of regional areas as information "capitals" and retirement havens.

Where the Jobs Are in Business Services
• Accounting • Legal Services • Advertising and Public Relations • Architecture, Ergonomics, and Interior Design • Engineering • Consultants and Small Professional Service Companies • Employment Agencies

Accounting
In 1994 there were 53,000 professional chartered accountants (CAs) and 14,000 accounting students in Canada; 24,000 certified management accountants (CMAs); and 43,000 certified general accountants (CGAs). (CAs engage largely in auditing; CGAs and CMAs work mostly in industry.)

One of the issues that currently concern the accounting profession is the broadening of accounting responsibilities to all accounting designations. That is, accountants of some designations in one region of the country are permitted to perform functions that are not allowed of accountants of similar designations in other regions – for example, the auditing function that can be performed by CGAs, CMAs, and CAs in British Columbia can be done only by CAs in Ontario and Prince Edward Island. Ontario is now in the process of reforming the licensing system to allow CGAs and CMAs to prepare audits and validate financial statements, and the P.E.I. Supreme Court has ordered an end to restrictive licensing practices. As a result, many small firms will be able to offer a fuller range of services that will ultimately save companies money. In the past, a company might have hired a small accounting firm to handle its day-to-day finances, but engaged the services of a chartered accountant to prepare its taxes; the chartered accountant would then have to be apprised of all the company's financial dealings, something the small accounting firm had been acquainted with for some time. Companies working in more than one province will now be able to use the same small accounting firm in each province. This will simplify the accounting process for the company, saving time and money.

Accounting firms have grown in size and scope of service to meet the global accounting needs of their clients. Many large full-service firms merged and consolidated in the 1980s to create six large firms that dominate the accounting profession: Price Waterhouse, KPMG Peat Marwick Thorne, Coopers & Lybrand Limited, Arthur Andersen & Co., Ernst & Young, and Deloitte & Touche. As capital becomes more global – that is, people now invest around the clock worldwide – companies are trying to raise money in various countries. However, with accounting rules and procedures differing from country to country, complications in doing business globally arise. Establishing an international standard has become one of the accounting profession's abiding concerns.

Many companies have gone under as a result of the recession, and many unhappy shareholders are now suing the accounting firms that gave ailing companies a clean fiscal bill of health. Even though errors made by auditors may have been small, the judgments against the accounting firms have been stiff simply because the firms have insurance and there may be no one else to sue. Insurance premiums are rising substantially, especially as accounting firms handle more global business, exposing them to billions of dollars in potential damages. Coopers & Lybrand was looking at over $500 million in lawsuits in 1993 in Canada; in the same year Ernst & Young agreed to pay a U.S. government agency US$400 million over its audits of defunct savings and loans companies. The Big Six now pay about 12 percent of their accounting and auditing revenues for practice protection insurance.

Although the accounting profession is trying to limit liability to a proportional blame level, partners in accounting firms face unlimited liability, standing to lose not only their jobs but their investments and personal assets as well. According to Bill Broadhurst, the former chair of Price Waterhouse, "The coverage available in the insurance market is really limited. Deductibles have been increasing, coverage has been decreasing, and premiums going up tenfold." As a result of these changes, accounting firms assess their potential clients more carefully, educate clients on the limits of the accounting function, and have industry audit experts review the work of juniors as well as partners. And, to spread out the risk factor, there have been more mergers and

BULLETIN BOARD – *ACCOUNTING*

- **Job demand factors:** growing need for financial information and financial management; environmental auditing; collection of accounts receivable; bankruptcies and receiverships; business fraud; globalization of competition.
- **Job growth areas:** environmental accounting; health and social services accounting; credit and collection accounting; budget analysis and financial management accounting; forensic accounting; bankruptcy and receivership accounting; activity-based accounting; small business consulting; estate planning; ISO 9000 consulting and registration.
- **Skills, abilities, qualities, education needed:** consultancy, planning, computer, and system design skills in addition to traditional accounting skills; degree, diploma, certificate in accounting.
- **Growth limiting factors:** need for common accounting standards; economic growth; global competition; government regulations.

TIPS

> The official federal government forecast for 100,000 new jobs in accounting being created between 1989 and 1995 was revised downward in 1993 to 60,000.

CONTACTS

- Canadian Institute of Chartered Accountants
  277 Wellington St. West,
  Toronto, ON M5V 3H2 Tel. 416-977-3222 Fax: 416-977-8585
  URL: http://www.cica.ca/
- The Society of Management Accountants of Canada
  #850, 120 King St. West,
  PO Box 176
  Hamilton ON L8N 3C3 Tel. 1-800-520-4262 Fax: 905-525-4533
- Certified General Accountants Association of Canada
  700-1188 Georgia St. West
  Vancouver, BC V6E 4A2 Tel. 604-669-3555 Fax: 604-689-5845
  URL: http://www.cga-canada.org

consolidations among Canada's 20 major auditing firms. This has led to a 10 percent reduction in staffing, especially among support staff and trainees as technology takes over their functions. Such reductions are encouraging many accountants to go directly into industry; whereas 4,823 students sat for their chartered accounting exams in 1991, only 3,700 did so in 1993. Overall, the hiring of accountants in 1995 was down about 30 percent from pre-recession days.

Business fraud – some of the fallout of the recession and staff cutbacks – has resulted in more than $100 billion in business losses in North America. According to Lloyd Posno, forensic and litigation accounting specialist for Ernst & Young, forensic accounting "has grown extremely quickly in the past ten years ... helped by the recession in the past three or four years." And downsizing has both reduced corporate loyalty and eliminated the jobs of those who acted as checks and balances in the spending and financial monitoring process. A 1995 KPMG fraud survey found that 55 percent of Canadian firms had been victimized within the past year, and most expected the trend to increase. The recession also increased demand for accounting managers who specialize in credit and collections. Obviously, accountants specializing in bankruptcies and receiverships do well during times of economic hardship and industry shake-outs. Money shortages are also increasing the need for financial managers and strategic planners in the areas of health and social services.

In 1993, 44 percent of Canadian annual reports contained information related to environmental issues, according to the Canadian Institute of Chartered Accountants. As public concerns over the environment mount, companies increasingly use the services of valuation experts, environmental damage assessment specialists, and accountants with regulatory experience. Large investors – pension funds, for example – will want to assess a company's environmental record before allocating equity funds. To meet these needs, accountants are showing companies how to integrate environmental procedures and reporting systems with their products. Many accounting firms also provide environmental audits.

Advances in technology, coupled with the broadening of accounting responsibilities to all accounting designations, are creating a greater trend toward in-house accounting. This is affecting many mid-size and small accounting firms, which are trying to meet these changes by specializing in more areas and playing a greater consultancy role. Activity-based accounting, which helps a company break out its cost structure according to how much value each activity adds to customers, is also a growing trend.

Although accounting is already a large field, it will likely grow even larger as the demand for financial information increases. New technology notwithstanding, there will always be a need for budget analysts, auditors, and credit/collection specialists, since these positions are necessary regardless of economic circumstances. The bigger firms offer the best opportunities and highest salaries, while smaller firms will likely merge in the long run to become full-service, consulting-oriented concerns in order to offset the shift to in-house accounting. For instance, accountability is shifting to ISO 9000 quality management standards, which can apply to all organizations. KPMG has set up a separate division to handle ISO consulting and another one, Quality Registrar, to act as a registrar and auditor for those companies seeking certification.

Legal Services

Statistics Canada reports that there was one lawyer for every 3,214 Canadians in 1967, but one for every 1,115 in 1992. Whereas there were 7,000 lawyers in Canada in the 1960s, there are now approximately 53,000, with over 3,000 new graduates each year. At the University of British Columbia, approximately 30 of the 230 law graduates were without articling positions – triple the usual number. With many small and medium-sized law firms still hurting from the recession, some graduates have had to accept unpaid positions instead of the usual $30,000 to $50,000 plus benefits. In order to deal with the current situation, some firms are coming up with novel arrangements such as sharing articling students or allowing articling outside the province, as Quebec is proposing.

The Law Society of Upper Canada found that 40 percent of graduates completing the bar admission course in 1994 had not obtained jobs, up from 25 percent in 1989. Increasingly, law firms are contracting out work to lawyers, especially since overhead takes up 52.5 percent of revenues nationally. A partner in a downtown Toronto firm costs between $150,000 and $250,000 for secretarial help, rent, and other overhead. Firms are also hiring fewer students because of the time, money, and energy required to train them. Instead, these firms are using law clerks or first-year lawyers who can do the work of several students. Working from the home has become a major cost saver for firms such as McInnis, Cooper & Robertson in Halifax. Those firms heavily invested in offices are hiring professional managers to keep costs under control. Temp or placement agencies for lawyers, such as Advocate Placement in Toronto or Counsel International in Vancouver, have gained credibility and exposure so they are doing a brisk business. At Advocate Placement Ltd., 49 percent of the placement hours logged by lawyers have resulted in permanent work.

Lawyers now face competition from independent paralegals – 70 percent of whom are women – who offer routine services to the public at lower fees than those of traditional law firms. Stiffer competition has meant that law firms now concentrate on aspects of the business that contribute most to the bottom line. Compensation is increasingly performance-based and includes a lawyer's bringing in new clients and training staff on the latest technology. Law firms are even using the services of market research companies to find out how better to serve current and potential clients. Clients – more sophisticated legal consumers than their predecessors – often require that their lawyers furnish them with a cost/benefit analysis of various courses of action, along with a budget, and ongoing documentation and reassessment of the benefits or options during the litigation process.

Alternative dispute resolution is gaining ground in many areas – aboriginal land claims, international trade agreements, and environmental disputes, for example. The average cost of suing someone is $30,000, but using alternative dispute resolution has saved 74 percent of clients between $1,000 and $10,000 in legal costs; 26 percent have saved $10,000 or more.

There is a trend toward "boutique firms" in which a network of specializations is created within a firm, each responsible for its own profitability. Some legal specialties are growing, while others are in a serious slump. International law has become a growth area, with the globalization of trade and increased demand from multinationals for legal representation. Outsourcing has encouraged the growth of contract law. Family law (the divorce rate doubled from 18.6 percent in 1970 to 38.3 percent in 1990), intellectual property, estate planning, wrongful dismissal litigation, and criminal law are other growth areas. Personal injury lawyers are suffering, with the advent of no-fault insurance, and the real estate market is slowing owing to a slowdown in the economy and job insecurity fears. But environmental and public relations law will become increasingly important as companies try to manage

BULLETIN BOARD – *LEGAL SERVICES*

- **Job demand factors:** globalization of trade; increasing rates of crime and divorce; rates of wrongful dismissal allegations.
- **Job growth areas:** international law; mergers and acquisitions law; criminal law; family law; labour law; bankruptcy law; environmental law; information and telecommunications law; public relations law; entertainment law; immigration law; medical, corporate, and accounting malpractice law; paralegal work; legal assistants; estate planning and disposition; wills.
- **Skills, abilities, qualities, education needed:** computer literacy; analytical, endurance, problem-solving, communication, and stress management skills; two years university, four years law school, one year articling, six months to bar exam.
- **Job reduction areas:** legal secretaries; court reporters; in-house corporate lawyers.
- **Growth limiting factors:** market oversaturated with lawyers; alternative dispute resolution mechanisms; excessive costs.

CONTACTS

☛ Canadian Bar Association
#902, 50 O'Connor St.,
Ottawa, ON K1P 6L2 Tel. 613-237-2925 Fax: 613-237-0185
Toll free: 1-800-267-8860
URL: http://www.algonquinc.on.ca/cba.engmenu.html
gopher: //inforamp.net:70/11/society/law/cba

☛ Canadian Association of Legal Assistants
PO Box 967, Stn B,
Montreal, PQ H3B 3K5

☛ Canadian Association of Legal Support Staff
PO Box 3186,
Winnipeg, MB R3C 4E7

risk and damage control more effectively.

With performance, hiring, and purchasing contracts becoming more complicated in the entertainment field – residual rights in connection with media merging and complicated marketing agreements, as well as product endorsements and television appearances, for example – celebrities will need lawyers as much as they need agents. Also in demand are lawyers who are conversant with the complexities of the high-tech computer world, as software piracy, telecommunications, joint ventures, alliances, and information theft and copyright infringement increase. Immigration law will continue to grow, given the internationalization of trade, the presence of multinational firms, the refugee claimant hearing process, and increasing worldwide migration of individuals from less developed countries to developed ones. Since malpractice is a growing area of concern, with doctors, accountants, corporate officers, and even lawyers themselves being sued, there will be more activity in this area of the law. And the long-term trend toward consolidation and mergers and acquisitions as part of a global competitive strategy, or as a consequence of industry shake-out, promises to make mergers and acquisitions law a job growth area.

The contracting-out of government civil law practice is imminent in many provinces. Legal aid provisions are being seriously reduced, and more clients once covered by legal aid now pay user fees or contingency fees; in some cases legal aid is allocated according to the likelihood of prosecution. Ontario's move toward contingency fees will largely legitimize unofficial practices, and will affect only about 3 percent or less of a lawyer's total billings, as in B.C. Legal aid cases are auctioned off in blocks of 50 cases to the lowest bidder in Manitoba.

Job security is in doubt as 64 percent of firms surveyed in 1993 by *Canadian Lawyer* – particularly the large firms – indicated that they planned to lay off lawyers or staff that year. Most CEOs were contemplating outsourcing all legal work; however, corporate lawyers with an MBA are faring well since they are able to combine legal knowledge with strategic business thinking. Figures provided by the Law Society of Upper Canada indicated that 41 percent of the articling students in 1992 were retained, 17 percent found work elsewhere, and 42 percent were without work. In better times, 80 percent of the articling students are usually retained by the articling firms.

While it is difficult to get summer articling jobs, often with 500 to 600 law students vying for five or six positions, those who are hired can make up to $15,000 in a summer. According to *Canadian Lawyer*'s 1992 national compensation survey, entry-level salary upon call to the bar fetches $38,000 nationally on average, and $50,000 for large firms.

The time required to become a partner has increased by a couple of years, to seven to ten years in many instances – or indefinitely in some cases. The top ten Canadian law firms with respect to training, guidance, and partner feedback, according to *Canadian Lawyer*, are Hicks Morley (Toronto), Scott & Aylen (Ottawa), Heenan Blaikie (Vancouver), Nelligan Power (Ottawa), Harrison Elwood (London), Swinton & Co. (Vancouver), Duncan Craig (Alberta), Owen Bird (Vancouver), Lapointe Rosenstein (Quebec), and Bennett Jones (Alberta).

The technology revolution has taken its toll on jobs for legal support staff. Software such as the Dragon-Dictate system used with Word Dancer allows lawyers to produce all correspondence, court documents, and memos without ever having to touch a keyboard or enlist the help of a secretary. Thus, it is now possible for four or five lawyers to share one secretary. Ontario will soon make a dent in the number of court reporters it hires by replacing many of them with video cameras and voice-recognition computers. The high-tech world is even entering the court appearance procedure, with many arraignments or meetings with public defenders or probation officers being conducted via videoconferencing. Clearly, these developments threaten employment for legal secretaries and court reporters.

On-line researching and communication is skyrocketing. The Supreme Court of Canada is fully on-line, and judgments are available within hours of decisions being released. Do-it-yourself legal software such as Desktop Lawyer is becoming available to the general public and may reduce the need for lawyers in areas where matters are relatively straightforward, such as incorporation, real estate, partnership and distribution agreements, termination notices, and employment contracts.

Advertising and Public Relations

In the future, advertising and marketing will take a different approach to reaching its public as a response to the growth of the multimedia information age. The proliferation of television channels will lead to narrowcasting or niche marketing – special channels devoted to particular interests or markets so that target markets can be reached more efficiently. Database marketing will become common: when a consumer purchases items electronically, a computer profile of that household's viewing and buying patterns will be generated and sold to interested manufacturers and retailers. Manufacturers will then contact the consumer directly about products that might interest him or her. And the consumer will be able to access product information electronically. The product can then be ordered by using a simple voice command. Already alternative media, such as the Internet and direct marketing, are stealing business from traditional advertising media.

Some consumers will hire purchasing agents who will carry out product analysis for them and document the consumer's past purchases and preferences. Products that may interest consumers will be brought to their attention so that they are not besieged by electronic junk mail. Purchasing agents will be paid by the consumer on a fee-for-service basis and agents will be forbidden from accepting any compensation from manufacturers. While advertisers will still be in the business of gathering and providing product information by selling an image, it will become harder to fool sophisticated consumers who have more ways of determining the quality or usefulness of a product through, for example, the purchasing agent.

An information-gathering function now in place is Compusearch, a leading micromarketer – that is, a company that engages in direct marketing to a focussed group in society. Compusearch has classified Canada's 644,000 postal codes according to 70 "lifestyle clusters." Each cluster is then coupled with spending estimates for 1,000 goods and

---

BUYING A BICYCLE ELECTRONICALLY

You wish to purchase a bicycle with certain features and in a specific price range. Once you enter this information into your computer, all available products meeting the specifications you have set out will be listed on the screen. A local showroom will feature a wide array of bicycles for you to examine and test. The showroom will arrange for the bicycle you have chosen to be delivered to you within a short time. You will have a chance to examine the bicycle again and test-ride it. If you are not satisfied with the product, you will be allowed to return it as long as it is in pristine condition. If you are satisfied and purchase the bicycle, the customer relations department and your purchasing agent will contact you from time to time to determine your level of satisfaction. All recommendations will be noted and product improvements will be brought to your attention electronically.

service categories. These are examples of Compusearch's "wealthstyle" clusters: Canadian establishment (1.2 percent), aging urban sophisticates (2.3 percent), lifetime savers (2.7 percent), the materialists (6.5 percent), armchair seniors (2.4 percent), country comfort (15.1 percent), middle Canada (15.4 percent), starting out (5.6 percent), mortgage slaves (16.1 percent), urban blue-collar (18.2 percent), rural working poor (9.6 percent), beyond their means (1.5 percent), and rough times (1.4 percent). The company produces a CD-ROM that provides on-screen access to a city intersection along with the number and type of businesses with the number of their employees, and a breakdown of the households in that neighbourhood – all within any radius requested. Its "do-it-yourself" data are based on the 125,000 consumers who purchase saws and hammers; similarly, exact incomes, ages, and languages of the 500,000 bargain hunters, 750,000 investors, and 185,000 cottage owners are available. Another such company, Target Mail of Toronto, sells information to the packaged goods industry on the products and brand names that each household purchases.

With superior manufacturing accessible even to smaller companies, the differences between brands of the same product have decreased. The recession helped make consumers aware of this, since many consumers, more conscious of their personal bottom lines, began to purchase no-frills or store-label products and found that there was little difference between these products and the better-known brands. This has focussed consumers on the price or value of items. Ironically, as products are becoming more similar, they are also becoming more numerous. In 1992, 16,800 new products were introduced – a third more than in 1987. Retailers took advantage of this increase by auctioning off shelf space and diverting advertising budgets into promotions, which focussed consumer attention on price. Currently, branding has shifted to the retailer, as Loblaws Supermarket Limited's President's Choice products illustrate. In the U.S., the country's biggest retailer, Wal-Mart Stores Inc., has launched its second own-label line called Great Value and carries President's Choice products under a Wal-Mart label. Once entrenched in consumers' perceptions and purchasing outlook, the focus on price and value will be hard to dislodge, especially among aging boomers. As price becomes a crucial purchasing factor, advertising revenues will fall as advertising costs are sacrificed in order to reduce prices.

BULLETIN BOARD – *ADVERTISING AND PUBLIC RELATIONS*

- **Job demand factors:** fragmentation of media into narrowcasting or niches; crisis management; new technology lowering imaging and printing costs.
- **Job growth areas:** freelancing; public relations; corporate communications; market research; specialty advertising.
- **Skills, abilities, qualities, education needed:** multimedia and computer literacy; problem-solving; creativity; negotiation skills; image awareness; communications skills; college or university degree in advertising, corporate communications, or marketing; MBA highly desirable, and essential for public relations work.
- **Job reduction areas:** advertising generalists; permanent positions.
- **Growth limiting factors:** high advertising costs; shift to product promotion based on price or value; size of market niche.

CONTACTS

☞ Association of Canadian Advertisers, Inc.
South Tower, #307, 175 Bloor Street East
Toronto, ON M4W 3R8 Tel. 416-964-3805 Fax: 416-964-0771
Toll free: 1-800-564-0109

☞ Canadian Association of Marketing Research Organizations
#1105, 191 The West Mall
Etobicoke, ON M9C 5K8 Tel. 416-620-7420 Fax: 416-620-5392

☞ Canadian Automatic Merchandising Association
PO Box 778, Stn. Q
Toronto, ON M4T 2N7 Tel. 416-932-2262 Fax: 416-932-3732

☞ The Canadian Public Relations Society
#720, 220 Laurier Avenue West,
Ottawa, ON K1P 5Z9 Tel. 613-232-1222 Fax: 613-232-0565

Price begins to play a major role when quality becomes a commodity common to all products offered. At that point, products become market driven in the sense of creating a market through interactive developmental education of the consumer and manufacturer and through continuous improvement. Transaction-based marketing, which is tied to raw sales, market share tactics, and one-time promotions or sales, no longer applies. The new focus is on relationship marketing – the knowledge that computers are capable of tracking in massive detail. It's a database version of the relationship you once had with the local small-business owner who knows you well. Customer retention has taken the place of conquering the customer in a single transaction. Loyalty and product gap identification programs that allow companies to cross-sell or up-sell are proliferating as a result.

As the focus shifts to customizing products to the individual customer, many markets are suddenly emerging in a multicultural society, creating jobs for marketers of every ethnic and cultural background. Perhaps the most obvious new category of marketing involves focussing on women, who will be responsible for nearly 90 percent of their own financial needs at some point in their life. With the majority of women working and accounting for 53 percent of the university undergraduate student population, they are an undeniably powerful, informed sector of the economy. The mother-daughter suds ads just won't impress them any more.

Indeed, one of the prime purposes of setting up a Web page is so that customers can provide feedback on a product; companies, in turn, can better shape a customer's "experience" with their products or services and make continual improvements. In other words, advertising and marketing are turning into a mutually beneficial interactive process. However, in an age of customization, it is not possible to serve all customers equally well, so expect to see both advertisers and companies focussing on those market segments to whom they can provide first-class interactive service.

New technology such as full-colour digital copiers – which provide colour proofs for $2.50 – and 3-D software is facilitating in-house advertising and allowing the boutique or specialty advertising firms to better exploit the small-business market. The trend toward narrowcasting also enhances the boutique or specialty advertising market. Small advertising companies are thus specializing in particular markets, such as the over-50 market or the foreign-language programming market.

The 1980s saw many mergers in the advertising industry as agencies responded to the needs of national or multinational companies. Currently, medium-sized companies that lack a specific market focus or specialty are struggling for survival. These companies will have to develop niche markets or join networks of specialized agencies if they expect to succeed.

Hiring freelancers has become a common practice in general advertising agencies as well as in direct-mail agencies, particularly to pitch new accounts. The best places to get a start in the advertising industry – and perhaps the most exciting places to work – are the smaller agencies. What these lack in job security, they make up for in challenges and learning opportunities. Since individuals working in small advertising agencies may be called upon to perform a number of diverse jobs, this environment offers the opportunity to learn many different aspects of the business.

Market research jobs will grow as collecting consumer information electronically increases in scope. Until some form of artificial intelligence is used, someone will have to process and analyze all that information. As the cost of launching a new product increases in a marketplace already crowded with new products, market research will become more essential in determining the risks involved in introducing a new product. With the need to increase communication within an organization in order to stay focussed on pleasing the customer, anticipating market changes, and developing appropriate new products, corporate communications positions are a job growth area, as are public relations jobs. Crisis management – in such areas as environmental damage, product scandals, political blunders, questionable practices – the disappearance of the mass market, and the high cost of advertising all favour public relations as a means of reaching a target audience more cheaply and, in many instances, more effectively.

A 1995 survey conducted by MacDonald & Co. Communications Inc. found that over the past five years public relations responsibilities had grown in 71 percent of the companies surveyed. The importance of external communications to organizations increased from 57 to 75 percent, and internal communications from 42 to 62 percent. The one-press-release-fits-all approach has given way to customized targeting of information. The extra workload has caused 90 percent of PR departments to use outside suppliers. Given the rash of downsizings and layoffs, those core employees remaining are required to do more and therefore must develop more skills, including public speaking, according to Roger Davies, president and managing partner of McLuhan & Davies Communications Inc. With responsibilities often including government relations, charitable and sponsorship policy, development, trade shows,

database tracking of press references, and relations with industry partners, more people in the field are forced to become generalists. Most in
the industry view the Internet and multimedia as offering significant
public relations potential.

In an industry where clients are often more loyal to the public relations individual who represents them in public than to the company,
there has been a significant shift in market share lately from large multinationals to smaller agencies. At the moment in Canada, there are more
than ten boutique PR operations billing in excess of $1 million.

Architecture, Ergonomics, and Interior Design

Architects have not fully recovered since the recession, nor has architectural drafting design, where only about one-third of the graduates are
finding jobs and many programs are being eliminated owing to the
automation of such functions. The building era that the baby boomers
spawned is drawing to a close, and employment insecurity and underemployment are preventing the tail end of the baby boom from purchasing homes. Instead, many are still living at home and hoping to inherit or
buy their parents' homes when the older generation seeks out retirement
residences. What remains is largely renovation of existing homes, especially kitchens and bathrooms. Indeed, renovation outpaces the building
of new homes nowadays.

Architects specializing in industrial design, however, are beginning
to feel more optimistic about the future. Many older buildings located
in urban settings need modernization, and now that land values have
dropped substantially, and the cost of money has declined, constructing a
new building is becoming as cost-effective as renting an existing building.
In addition, construction costs are down; suppliers have trimmed their
profit margins to the point that materials are now 30 percent cheaper,
despite the rise in the cost of lumber and the cost of hiring unionized
labour. With the supply of preferred developed space diminishing, there
is often no shortage of serviced land, with many municipalities having an
eight-year reserve supply of unserviced land and potentially a 20-year
reserve of unserviced land. Moreover, land prices may fall even further
and many manufacturing companies are moving outside large cities to
avoid punishing property taxes.

Typically, design-build projects are custom-built by a landowner or developer to specification for a future tenant at a prearranged price. Prospective tenants may include retailing operations such as discount retailers and medical, pharmaceutical, and high-tech companies that often need modern buildings with a combination of office, laboratory, testing, and shipping facilities. The oversupply in the office building market will persist for some time, particularly given the trend to office sharing and working at home or in work stations. Therefore, many units in office buildings may be converted to condominiums. Malls will be in for a shock, when the full potential of home shopping is realized. Once the economy recovers somewhat, there may be growth in the construction of monster malls that combine entertainment, shopping, and dining in innovative ways, such as the West Edmonton Mall.

Eventually, office and home design that incorporates the latest technology with emerging work, entertainment, landscaping, or recreation concepts will flourish. Furthermore, the trend toward working at home will encourage growth in the home renovation market. Since spending 50 to 100 percent more on construction and design can pay for itself in three to five years through increased productivity, any company in which salaries account for a substantial part of the company's cost is a prime candidate for this kind of renovation or construction. Moreover, the trend toward growth in smaller companies will create a demand for the construction of smaller, more flexible office space.

While the residential market will likely remain relatively soft now that most boomers already own homes, the renovation industry will pick up as people customize their houses in response to the cocooning trend of the 1990s. As retiring boomers leave cities, more design opportunities will present themselves in both rural and urban areas. Eventually, more luxury condominiums will be built for snowbirds and retiring boomers no longer willing or able to bother with home maintenance.

The prefabricated or modular homes market has become a worldwide growth area. In the case of Ibor Canada, an architect designs and markets the homes but contracts out construction to factories in Ontario, Quebec, and the U.S. The units are assembled – except for brick and masonry – in the factory and transported to the location. The homes do not look any different than regular homes, but are better constructed in ideal factory conditions and are approximately 15 percent cheaper. Clearly, this will be an excellent area for architects to take advantage of.

An employment growth area for architects and builders is the home inspection business. Although only 10 to 20 percent of Canadian home buyers have a property inspected by an independent home inspector, the trend is growing, with an estimated 50 percent of the homes sold in Toronto inspected prior to sale for a fee of $300 to $400.

The imagination reels at the many architectural possibilities of the future. There will be many freelance, project-based opportunities with companies aggressively pursuing business in the Far East and Pacific Rim, where construction of all kinds is planned on a mammoth scale. For example, the proposed Australian-Japanese joint venture for building Multifunction Polis (MFP) is planned as a $10-billion urban development prototype that will set the standard for quality for the 21st century by combining elaborate resort facilities, telecommunications services, and high-tech programs designed to attract major companies worldwide. The City of Shanghai and the Chinese government are planning a massive redevelopment project involving an airport, container docks, tunnels, and bridges, which will cost $10 billion and require the relocation of over a million people; the Phoenix World City is a cruise ship that will hold 5,000 passengers in its multistorey apartment buildings, along with a 2,500-seat theatre, a 100,000-volume library, nightclubs, cabaret, discos, a casino, a conference centre, a marina for smaller craft within its hull, and a television and broadcast centre; Aeropolis 2001 is a 500-storey highrise approximately five times as high as the World Trade Center in New York and costing an estimated $326 billion.

Now that new technology is capable of providing lighter fabric domes at lower costs, many projects that were formerly too costly are being reconsidered. The agribusiness is anticipating the construction of "bubble farms" in which thousands of acres are covered by dome units that protect seedlings and genetically engineered crops. The Japanese are proposing to alter the weather patterns of low-lying islands by enclosing them in tentlike structures, thereby making these islands more habitable. They plan to use this approach on the ocean floor to redirect currents and create new fishing zones.

Architectural and interior design firms now seldom hire full-time employees. In the late 1980s and early 1990s, most people employed in the design industries worked for large companies; now, however, the majority are self-employed since firms cannot afford to retain staff when

BULLETIN BOARD – *ARCHITECTURE AND INTERIOR DESIGN*

- **Job demand factors:** industrial design-build opportunities represent a better solution than renting older buildings; large multipurpose malls; ergonomic redesign of work and home environments to meet technological innovations; retiring boomers moving out of cities; renovation, landscaping, and in-fill market – building new structure where older building was torn down – in existing residential locations of cocooners; retiring boomers' desire for condo lifestyle.
- **Job growth areas:** industrial design; prefabricated or modular home market; home inspection; luxury condo market.
- **Skills, abilities, qualities, education needed:** proficiency in math, sciences, art, urban planning, ergonomics; five-year university program
- **Job reduction areas:** new-home market; office building market except for condo conversion; conventional malls.
- **Growth limiting factors:** the economy as a whole; saturated housing market; construction costs.

CONTACTS

- Interior Designers of Canada
  Ontario Design Centre,
  #506, 260 King St. East,
  Toronto, ON M5A 1K3 Tel. 416-594-9310 Fax: 416-594-9313
- Royal Architectural Institute of Canada
  #330, 55 Murray St.
  Ottawa, ON K1N 5M3 Tel. 613-241-3600 Fax: 613-241-5750
  URL: http://www.aecinfo.com/raic/index.html

business is slow. Everyone in these industries has had to develop entrepreneurial and co-venturing skills, so as to successfully seek out projects. Indeed, it is essential that those interested in these fields expand their skills. Even interior designers are expected to have a thorough knowledge of computer-assisted design since it can greatly reduce the time they spend on a project.

Jobs are not widely available in these industries. Only 33 percent of University of Waterloo's architecture students obtained summer work in architectural companies in 1993, compared with 85 percent in 1987.

According to a University of Waterloo co-op coordinator, "The graduating classes are not only looking at private firms, but at facilities management in institutions and corporations [and in] design fields like graphic design. They are branching [out] into urban planning and pursuing home-building companies."

Since 1993, the International Ergonomics Association has increased its membership by 45 percent, and overall membership has doubled since 1980. Ford, General Motors, Chrysler, and many hospitals and government departments have hired full-time ergonomists. Many unions are demanding that ergonomic provisions be put in contracts. Of the $4 billion in Canadian lost-time injuries in 1991, roughly 60 percent were from repetitive strain disorders. Sheldon Robinson, a psychologist and information officer at KRG Management Inc. in Toronto, says the combination of improved technology, software, and ergonomics has improved productivity by 120 percent since 1991. The importance of integrating all aspects of design has even led Steelcase Canada Ltd. to alter its focus from simple furniture sales to a consultative process. According to Howard Cohen, president of the Design Exchange in Toronto, "One reason Canada seems to be falling behind is only 2% of the goods manufactured in Canada are designed in Canada" – thereby limiting the opportunities for ergonomists.

Engineering Services

While technology such as computer-assisted design and computer-assisted manufacturing has reduced the need for engineers in some areas, there are critical shortages in many specialized areas. The Canadian Council of Professional Engineers (CCPE) projects a shortage of as many as 15,000 engineers in Canada by the year 2000. The CCPE reports that the demand for chemical engineers is expected to grow by 42 percent between 1990 and 2000, with most growth occurring during the latter half of the 1990s. The number of chemical engineers is expected to grow by only 22 percent during this period, causing a significant shortage. Similarly, the demand for electrical engineers, who often go into the computing and systems development field, is expected to grow by 44 percent, with supply increasing by only 18 percent. For mechanical engineers, 70 percent of whom enter manufacturing while 30 percent work in mechanical engineering, a 45 percent increase in demand is anticipated versus an increase in supply of a scant 6 percent. For civil engineers, a 42 percent rise in demand will be accompanied by a supply increase of only 11 percent. Clearly, economic circumstances will play an important role in demand fluctuations, as will the immigration and emigration of engineers. Historically, the growth in the demand for engineers has closely corresponded with growth in the Canadian economy. However, since 1971 there has been a gradual reduction in the relative percentage of engineers in relation to the growth in gross domestic product, as a result of productivity improvements achieved by engineers already in the field. One factor undermining the growth in engineering positions has been the replacement of engineers with engineering technologists and technicians in many cases.

The increase in demand for engineers will also vary according to industrial group, with agriculture and mining demand growing at a rate one-third less than that of most other groups. The demand for petroleum engineers is expected to show the highest growth rate – 58 percent – thanks to projected energy investments. Proposed northern gas development – $4 billion – and environment and infrastructure improvement projects – $10 billion per year – will also generate a demand for more engineers. Recent areas of job growth for engineers have been the automotive industry (which has tripled since 1993), printing and publishing, communications, plastic products, industrial construction, engineering surveying services, and machine shops. To a lesser extent, some hiring has taken place in plastic and synthetic resin manufacturing, quarries and sandpits, and non-ferrous smelting and refining.

According to Bob Leek, general manager of Hamilton Executive Consultants, which places engineers in auto, chemical, telecommunications, and sales positions, "Generally, these jobs require three to five years' experience, a track record of achievement on specific projects, good communication skills, and the ability to wear many hats. Manufacturers are asking for multi-tasking from engineers, which could include engineering design and implementing ISO 9000 quality standards." With all auto suppliers needing to be QS9000 compliant by 1997, there is a rush to meet these exceptionally rigorous standards, especially since contracts for 1998 and beyond are now being awarded.

Salaries for engineers typically plateau at the $65,000 level, beyond which engineers interested in higher salaries must move into management positions – a phenomenon which accounts for the significant representation of engineers in MBA programs. The average life cycle of most engineering disciplines is less than 20 years, as a result of engineers being promoted to management. In fact, many engineers become managers within ten years of entering the profession. The trend toward outsourcing, however, may decrease the need for engineer-managers, except where managerial positions are consultative.

In Ontario, 2.5 percent of the province's 52,000 engineers were unemployed in 1994; many of those were civil engineers who will benefit from infrastructure improvement projects, which are badly needed but have been delayed because of government deficits. Wayne Roth, director of Employment and Immigration Canada's Labour Market Outlook, reports that Ontario has a shortage of design and development engineers, and electrical and electronic engineers. Gennum, a Burlington-based company that designs and manufactures silicon-integrated circuits, plans to increase its staff from 245 to 350 by 2000 with recruits who are able to work with analog circuits using bipolar transistor technology. But will Gennum be able to find engineers who are appropriately trained to take on this specialized work? Siemens Electric Ltd., the fifth-largest electronics company in Canada, plans to expand its work force from 3,000 to 12,000 workers by the end of the 1990s. Although the company advertised 18 positions in its London, Ontario, automotive operation, only four of the 270 applicants were hired. The company has yet to find cooling systems engineers, development engineers, and product application engineers. Since companies such as these are not prepared to put years into training personnel, many are recruiting overseas, particularly in Asia.

The trend toward outsourcing, along with the growth of small businesses, will put engineers to work in smaller engineering firms specializing in outsource design work for many small manufacturing companies that cannot afford to retain full-time engineers. Even bigger companies such as General Motors are outsourcing auto parts design to suppliers who, in turn, seem to prefer to outsource on a contract basis. The brightest employment opportunities for engineers lie in the telecommunications, information technology, and instrumentation industries. Com-Dev of Cambridge, Ontario, Canada's largest exporter of communications satellite equipment, hopes to increase its work force from 530 to 800 by

BULLETIN BOARD – *ENGINEERING*

- **Job demand factors:** growth in telecommunications, information technology, and instrumentation engineering.
- **Job growth areas:** design, development, and electronic engineering.
- **Skills, abilities, qualities, education needed:** integrated manufacturing engineering program offered at University of Toronto is highly recommended.
- **Job reduction areas:** civil engineering – temporarily, until infrastructure improvements can be delayed no longer; possibly chemical engineering.
- **Growth limiting factors:** slow recovery of manufacturing industry; high cost of capital undermining expenditure in competitive high-tech industries.

CONTACTS

☞ Association of Consulting Engineers of Canada
#616, 130 Albert St.,
Ottawa, ON K1P 5G4 Tel. 613-236-0569 Fax: 613-236-6193

☞ Canadian Council of Professional Engineers
#410, 116 Albert St.,
Ottawa, ON K1P 5G3 Tel. 613-232-2474 Fax: 613-230-5759
E-mail: Imacdon@fox.nstn.ns.ca

☞ Federation of Engineering and Scientific Associations
#206, 3199 Bathurst St.
Toronto, ON M6A 2B2 Tel. 416-784-1284 Fax: 416-784-1366

☞ Canadian Council of Technicians and Technologists
285 McLeod Street, 2nd Floor
Ottawa, ON K2R 1A1 Tel: 613-238-8123 Fax: 613-238-8822

the year 2000. And Northern Telecom said it needed to hire 150 researchers in 1996.

Consultants and Small Professional Service Companies

Many executives have accepted early retirement in order to start up consulting careers, and many middle managers, especially those who are casualties of downsizing or re-engineering, have struck out on their own as consultants. This trend corresponds with companies moving toward project-based employment. There are abundant opportunities abroad for consultants who were formerly employed by a multinational and who are willing to relocate. Consultants thrive in the engineering and computing fields, as well as in toxic and hazardous waste control, geotechnical engineering, and bridge design and rehabilitation.

In the past, consulting services focussed on large and medium-sized companies; now, they will have to find innovative ways of serving smaller clients since most new businesses in the future will likely be small businesses. Since small businesses cannot afford to hire consultants, consultants may experience difficulty finding clients. They can get around this by setting charges on a contingency-fee basis. Expense Reduction Services, for example, does not charge a fee unless savings to the client company are forthcoming. The company's fee is 50 percent of the savings realized in the first year of implementing the consultant's recommendations. Consulting services will likely specialize in various aspects of small-business growth and development – how the company can raise venture capital, for example. Consultants usually focus on savings areas that small businesses tend to overlook – computer supplies, office supplies, courier services, maintenance and cleaning supplies, overhead, and materials costs.

Larger companies often need consultants to implement new technologies, solve specific technology bottlenecks, help companies reorganize or re-engineer, and provide training in working in teams, as well as helping companies save money in specific areas. With the widespread use of new information technology accompanied by corporate restructuring, many companies require advice in the design, implementation, readjustment, and staff training fields. Previous job descriptions no longer apply, and managers, supervisors, and team members must learn leadership skills such as coaching, mentoring, and delegating. For employees who are used to exercising authority or, by contrast, being told what to do, such a change can be particularly painful, especially so for older employees.

Now that more companies are outsourcing, small professional service firms that are geared to solving particular business, manufacturing, or technology problems find themselves very much in demand. Many companies realize that their new technology often requires modification, since their hardware and software may be incompatible or inadequate.

BULLETIN BOARD – *CONSULTANTS*

- **Job demand factors:** new technology; incompatible technology; special applications; re-engineering; lack of team skills; outsourcing; growth in number of small businesses.
- **Job growth areas:** small service or consulting companies specializing in solving problems that are common to an industry; professional and operational services better outsourced.
- **Skills, abilities, qualities, education needed:** communications, creative problem-solving, analytical, and business-specific skills; professional training and experience in area-specific fields.
- **Job reduction areas:** fields in which technology makes it easier to perform functions in-house – printing or publishing on a small scale, for example.
- **Growth limiting factors:** the economy in general; the number of companies entering the business; standardizing of technology; expert systems and artificial intelligence that have built-in professional expertise.

CONTACTS

☛ Association of Independent Consultants
#110, 2175 Sheppard Ave. East,
Willowdale, ON M2J 1W8 Tel. 416-491-3556 Fax: 416-491-1670

Small engineering and computer consulting companies can often provide quick-fix solutions or offer a total-service retainership. Larger companies are increasingly outsourcing infrastructure management functions. Typically, two kinds of infrastructure management functions are now outsourced. One is the management of real estate assets – lease administration, negotiation, and management – and of building operations – catering, landscaping, repairs and management, snow removal, cleaning and security. The second commonly outsourced function comprises business and facilities services – general services such as mail, courier, distribution, reprographics or photocopying, fleet management, environmental control, daycare, health services, clerical administration, and inventory administration. IBM's joint venture company, Triax Infrastructure Management Corp., for example, handles all of IBM's non-computer operations.

Competition will intensify in the consulting field, since there are few barriers to market entry. Today, there are consultants in almost every field – telecommunications, taxation, engineering, food services, broadcasting, and so on. Developing alliances with other professional and consulting agencies which offer complementary services as well as specializing in services most in demand or in areas where the cost savings of the services are immediately visible will assure success and survival in this business.

Employment Agencies

The largest private-sector employer in the U.S. is a company called Manpower, which employs twice as many people as General Motors. Indeed, one out of every 15 new companies started in the U.S. is an employment agency. Temp agencies have grown by 240 percent over the last decade. Most companies cannot afford to make a hiring mistake in the globally competitive marketplace, so the "try-before-you-buy" approach to hiring is beginning to take over. Moreover, many companies are unsure of their hiring or skill set needs in the near future, so they want to keep their options open. As a result, hiring on contract or on a temporary basis is one of the fastest-growing developments in business. Two out of every three companies hiring in Canada are contemplating using an employment agency as a hiring source, according to *Canadian HR Reporter*. Welcome to the just-in-time work force of the 1990s.

Temporary help services that provide receptionists, word processors, bookkeepers, and data entry personnel will be in great demand in the future. Since 50 to 75 percent of all employees will either be working on contract or be hired on a more casual basis – just-in-time workers hired temporarily and let go as soon as their services are no longer needed – the demand for matching employers with employees will increase. (Actually, half of the professionals hired temporarily get full-time employment at the end of their contracts.) While Canada Employment will continue to perform this function – perhaps on an on-line basis in the future – private agencies with more extensive screening facilities will be needed to service companies looking for individuals who can perform very specific tasks. KPMG Peat Marwick Stevenson & Kellogg, for example, has created a temporary executive agency as a response to the surplus of redundant middle managers looking for work. For the most part, its

BULLETIN BOARD – *EMPLOYMENT AGENCIES*

- **Job demand factors:** increasing trend toward hiring on a contract or casual basis; eventual shortages in high-tech areas; boomers retiring.
- **Job growth areas:** private agencies that can screen or recruit candidates cost-effectively.
- **Skills, abilities, qualities, education needed:** a solid understanding of the business environment; university degree in psychology, preferably at the master's level.
- **Job reduction areas:** traditional temporary employment services, since eventually office and clerical workers will use electronic bulletin boards to advertise their services and will be working at home.
- **Growth limiting factors:** low barrier to market entry; government may try to assume the screening role to some extent; limited numbers of qualified people.

CONTACTS

☛ Association of Professional Placement Agencies & Consultants
#L-109, 114 Richmond St. East,
Toronto, ON M5C 1P1 Tel. 416-362-0983 Fax: 416-360-5478

☛ Canadian Association of Career Educators and Employers
#205, 1209 King St. West,
Toronto, ON M6K 1G2 Tel. 416-535-8126 Fax: 416-532-0934
URL: http://www.cacee.com/workweb

☛ Federation of Temporary Help Services
#1105, 191 The West Mall
Etobicoke, ON M9C 5K8 Tel. 416-626-7130 Fax: 416-630-5392

clients are mid-range companies with annual sales of $200 million or more. Many of these companies found that they cut back too far when they downsized, and want to "try out" a new position before making it permanent. Given the growth of small businesses, which may not have the time or expertise to hire optimally, agencies that reliably and cost-effectively screen prospective employees will do well. Eventually, screening will go on-line, but individuals will still conduct preliminary interviews and reference checks as part of the screening process. As hiring becomes more scientific, companies will need to develop special areas of hiring expertise and will have to become more globally connected. Thus, to succeed in this area, small or medium-sized companies will have to specialize, and large firms will have to include international headhunting as part of their mandate.

Headhunting firms will be vigorously seeking highly qualified candidates, who are expected to be in short supply by the turn of the century. Since this shortage will be worldwide, headhunters will find themselves acting on behalf of foreign companies recruiting in Canada. Already the Japanese raid the University of Waterloo for its computer science graduates at the master's level. Hospitals in the U.S. often send recruiters to Canada to lure doctors and nurses to warmer climates; given the wage changes likely to occur as a result of cost containment strategies in the health care field, these recruiters may be very successful in their efforts. As technology becomes universally adopted, those countries expanding the most will experience shortages in high-tech personnel. Poorer countries, whose populations always expand the fastest, will lack suitably trained personnel even if they are able to import the technology. These shortages will become more acute as aging boomers begin to retire around 2001. Multinational headhunting firms will be the only ones remaining in the mature phase of this industry. Smaller companies will likely be out of business, merged, or acquired by the year 2000, except for the very specialized players. Medium-sized companies will have to specialize and cultivate international connections in order to survive.

DISTRIBUTION INDUSTRIES: TRANSPORTATION, COMMUNICATIONS, UTILITIES, AND THE WHOLESALE TRADE
Where the Jobs Are in Transportation
• Trucking • Railways • Shipping • Air Transport
• Postal and Courier Transportation • Road Infrastructure

In 1994, transportation accounted for 3.5 percent of Canada's gross domestic product; 450,000 people, or 3.6 percent of the work force, were employed in the transportation sector. Transportation workers enjoyed an average weekly salary of $650, which compared favourably with the national average of $550. In terms of domestic tonnes transported, trucking accounted for 36.5 percent; rail, 48.8 percent; and marine, 14.7 percent. Exports constituted 30 percent of Canada's gross domestic product, which put the country seventh in the world in exporting, despite ranking 31st in population. With the increasing continentalization of trade as a result of the North American Free Trade Agreement (NAFTA), Canada is becoming one of three major players in a marketplace of 370 million people. The growing globalization of trade is increasing the amount of export business and thus shifting the traditional east-west movement of goods to a north-south, transborder orientation in competition with U.S. and Mexican transportation deliverers. The outcome of resulting competition in the transportation industry will in many ways determine the future of transportation in Canada.

In response to the need to streamline Canada's transportation system within the country and across borders, Advantage Canada was formed in 1992, its mandate to create a completely integrated transportation system. Its goals are to establish industry standards of quality; to foster alliances among intermodal carriers – for example, when cargo moves from ship to train to truck in one container which is transferred from one mode of transport to the next – so as to provide an efficient seamless flow of cargo; to reduce shipping costs by raising the volume of cargo shipped on Canadian routes; to implement a common standard for the electronic data exchange between the various carriers; and to work toward changing the taxation system so as to establish a level playing field with foreign competitors.

A logistics revolution is taking place in the way transportation is delivered. Because it no longer makes sense to have one plant in Mexico, another plant in Canada, and a third plant in the U.S., production is being rationalized and transportation centralized. For example, it makes more sense to have one plant in the U.S. and transport the product to Canada and Mexico. Canada is at a particular disadvantage when it comes to logistics planning, owing to our sparser population densities. Canadian companies pay 5 to 10 percent more in distribution costs than American companies, reports James Ecker, a transportation consultant with KPMG Peat Marwick Stevenson & Kellogg. George Weston Limited finds that the logistics component for its bakery chain constitutes 45 percent of its products' selling price, while Northern Telecom pays only a 5 percent premium in logistics costs. As might be expected, Canadian export companies are demanding lower transportation costs in order to survive in global markets. A multinational company whose Canadian transportation costs represented 11 percent of the plant's product cost strongly suggested to Canadian National (CN) that it reduce

BULLETIN BOARD – *TRANSPORTATION*

CONTACTS
- Chartered Institute of Transport in Canada
  #600, 99 Bank Street
  Ottawa, ON K1P 6B9 Tel. 613-566-7033 Fax: 613-233-9656
- Transportation Association of Canada
  2323 St. Laurent Blvd.,
  Ottawa, ON K1G 4K6 Tel. 613-736-1350 Fax: 613-736-1395

its transportation costs to 8 percent, or it would leave Canada. This demand and others like it have forced CN to cut 11,000 jobs from its North American operation.

Warehouse facilities, plant facilities, and distribution centres are being phased out in order to facilitate the just-in-time demands of customers. IBM Canada Ltd. closed 14 warehouses in Toronto and now stores its supplies in one warehouse in Markham, Ontario. As you might expect, all inventory is controlled by a local area network, and extensive use is made of carousels and automated guided vehicles in its Sandrail high-density storage system. IBM has reduced its product-moving times to better meet just-in-time manufacturing and retailing deadlines. And since paperwork has been eliminated as a result of the company's use of electronic data interchange (EDI) to communicate with Canada Customs, border-crossing delays have been reduced by three days on average.

One way of reducing logistics problems is to outsource them to a company that specializes in logistics. Hewlett Packard (Canada) Ltd., for example, saved over $1 million in handling inventories by hiring J. D. Smith and Sons, which also provides a just-in-time delivery service for 3M. Unfortunately, according to a 1992 study by A. T. Kearney and the Canada Association of Logistics Management, Canadian companies are behind in warehousing, transportation, or inventory management, with less than 15 percent of Canadian companies using the distribution requirement planning system, which is essential for reducing inventories.

Transportation management positions now require a university degree since individuals in this profession must have a sophisticated understanding of technology as well as knowledge in such areas as logistics and total quality control. Currently working with six Canadian universities to build educational programs that meet the new high-tech requirements of the transportation industry, the Chartered Institute of Transport, an international organization with 20,000 members, continues to work at upgrading educational standards in the field.

Trucking

The overall expenditures of the trucking industry – the total amount spent annually for trucks, gas, employees – add up to approximately $20 billion; it employs 200,000 individuals across Canada. This mature industry is in the midst of a trend toward deregulation. Twenty years ago, regulation guaranteed a profit to any carrier; but now that interprovincial authorizations are easy to obtain, common carriers are competing across the country. As a result of deregulation and the continentalization of trade, large operators have put small companies out of business or bought them up. The Private Motor Truck Council of Canada has lost 120 companies – one-third of its members since 1990.

Despite the move to larger trucking companies, the three largest Canadian companies are only one-quarter the size of American companies in fleet size or revenue. U.S. carriers in the southern states enjoy

BULLETIN BOARD – *TRUCKING*

- **Job demand factors:** cost and efficiency in being able to provide just-in-time delivery; deregulation; international trade agreements.
- **Job growth areas:** information technology; quality control and logistics.
- **Job reduction areas:** fewer drivers will be needed, particularly of the private for-hire sort; warehousing jobs, which are becoming increasingly automated.
- **Growth limiting factors:** competition in the U.S.; cabotage rights; customs duties and tariffs.

CONTACTS

☞ Canadian Trucking Association
#1025, 130 Slater Street
Ottawa, ON K1P 6E2 Tel. 613-236-9426 Fax: 613-563-2701

lower costs than Canadian carriers and have cabotage rights advantages over their Canadian counterparts, given that customs rules favour their American competitors. Both U.S. and Canadian companies have been gearing up to compete for the enhanced opportunities that came into effect in 1996, allowing Canadian and U.S. trucks to pick up and deliver in Mexico. After six years, they will be able to operate anywhere in Mexico.

Technology has entered the truck-driving field in the form of truck-top satellite dishes that can locate a truck within 100 yards anywhere in North America and enter this information into a central processing system for integration with other data. Instead of waiting for drivers to call in from checkpoints, messages are relayed instantly, and last-minute schedule changes can be made to improve delivery efficiency.

Despite the many changes that will increase the competitiveness of the trucking industry in Canada, there will likely be an industry shake-out, combined with many mergers and acquisitions. Job prospects are rather dismal for all except individuals involved in the information technology, quality control, and logistics side of the industry.

Railways

The Canadian railway industry is the third largest in the world. Over $6 billion in annual revenue was generated by Canadian railways in 1994. It employed more than 60,000 people and purchased $3 billion worth of goods and services annually. Unfortunately, Canada's large expanses of sparsely populated land do not provide the tax base necessary to support railways on a competitive basis with the U.S.; Canadian railways pay 54 percent more tax than American railways. According to the *Financial Post*, "A train going from New York to Seattle pays $10,000 less in fuel taxes than one moving from Montreal to Vancouver." In terms of the overall cost of moving freight containers, Canadian railways pay 75 percent higher taxes per container-mile than American railways. Were market value assessment to proceed in Toronto, taxes would increase by $40 million.

This competitive disadvantage accruing from heavy taxes, as well as competition from truckers and a slowdown in the east, has resulted in countless layoffs in the industry and strong efforts to improve productivity. Labour productivity on Canadian railways is only 60 percent of that in the U.S., according to the University of Manitoba's Transport Institute in

Winnipeg. Even with new labour agreements signed in 1995, Merrill Lynch estimates that Canadian railways are still about five years behind U.S. railways in terms of labour costs and productivity.

A massive restructuring of the railway led to the elimination of 11,000 jobs, or close to one-third of the work force, between 1993 and 1995 at CN. CN plans to eliminate 1,000 jobs a year between 1996 and the end of the century. CP announced in late 1995 that it would trim 1,450 administrative jobs, resulting in annual savings of $100 million. CN's eastern operations now break even after losing $200 million annually as recently as 1993, but CP Rail's eastern operations still lose money, prompting the establishment of a special-purpose unit to address the problem. Talks on joint ventures in the east by CP and CN began in earnest in 1996. CN now moves three times as much freight as it did 30 years ago with 43,000 fewer freight cars, one-half the number of locomotives, and about one-third fewer employees.

As CN proceeded toward a $2 billion privatization and CP Rail reorganized in late 1995, both companies moved dramatically to reduce operating costs, with CP slashing $120 million from its total administrative operating budget. Not only were thousands of positions abolished, but tough battles with the unions were fought to obtain more flexible, less costly labour contracts. In addition, thousands of kilometres of track were abandoned or sold. Even with major restructuring, both railways still face a major challenge in competition from their U.S. counterparts, which are far more aggressive in economic efficiency. In the interests of competitiveness, there may be some pressure to merge CN and CP in the face of a proposed US$5.4 billion merger of Union Pacific Corp and Southern Pacific Rail Corp. Such a merger would create the largest railway in North America, with an estimated annual revenue of $9.5 billion, more than double CN's revenue of about C$4.3 billion.

The container industry, which dominates how freight is carried by rail and ship, is growing, with 5.8 million 20-foot containers in the world fleet. Intermodal transportation now allows containers to be carried by ship, truck, or rail as required. For 1995 CN's intermodal revenue was $680 million to $700 million, while CP Rail's was about $630 million. This has become the rail industry's fastest-growing segment, based on the number of units carried. CP wants to take some of the 1.2 million to 1.5 million truck movements annually in the Toronto-Montreal corridor

BULLETIN BOARD — *RAILWAYS*

- **Job demand factors:** an increasing export market.
- **Job growth areas:** information technology; finance and marketing.
- **Job reduction areas:** everywhere except in the information technology and quality control aspects of the industry.
- **Growth limiting factors:** uncompetitive cost structure in connection with taxes, wages, and geographical markets; automation.

CONTACTS

☛ Railway Association of Canada
#1105, 800 René-Lévesque Blvd. West,
Montreal, PQ H3B 1X9 Tel. 514-879-8555 Fax: 514-879-1522

off the highway. The intermodal business, which accounts for about 13 percent of revenue at both railways, grew in 1994 by 19 percent at CP Rail and 10 percent at CN, but showed slower growth in 1995 because of price cuts from the trucking companies. CP Rail's RoadRailer uses hybrid freight-carrying trailers which have both rubber tires and steel wheels, so that the entire trailer can be switched from a highway to a train or vice versa. To enhance the freight handling capacities of cargo trains, steel containers are now stacked on top of one another, thereby doubling the amount of freight a train can carry.

The trend toward using high-speed trains may shift more business to the railway industry. While Bombardier Inc. has acquired the North American rights to France's TGV railway system, it is more likely that we will see Sweden's slightly slower X-2000 adopted in Canada, since it does not require an entirely new track infrastructure and is only half the price.

The Canadian railway industry has taken some tough steps in a process of rationalization and revitalization of its operations toward economic efficiency. Labour negotiations have weakened employment security arrangements and lower-skill jobs have been eliminated with technology improvements. Middle management positions will continue to be lost, and if a merger does take place it is likely that the dovetailing of operations will result in additional trimming of the work force.

Shipping

Half of Canada's total waterborne trade and approximately 60 percent of our international seaborne trade passes through the Canada Ports Corporation's 14 ports. Including the Harbour Commissions and the Public Harbours and Ports Group, Canada's ports collectively handled 324 million tonnes of cargo in 1993. Vancouver's new general cargo and cruise ship terminal and container terminal are expected to go from a throughput level (moving a container from one place to another) of 73.5 million containers to a worldwide level of 110.6 million containers by the year 2000. The new projects double Vancouver's container handling capacity. And as the Pacific Rim becomes a greater focus of trade, Vancouver's business should increase accordingly.

The government is moving on a new national marine transport policy which will deal with commercializing the St. Lawrence Seaway system and will develop a new ports policy that will give the ports more authority to determine their own development while being overseen by local authorities. The St. Lawrence Seaway is facing serious competitive difficulties. Although Montreal has spent $37 million over the past decade building container terminals, it must work harder to reduce Seaway charges. With shipping facing transportation challenges from Canadian and American rail networks, some ports may have to close and fleet sizes will diminish. With the Seaway not realizing a profit over the last decade, 15 percent of the staff have been laid off since 1990 and another 25 percent reduction is expected by the year 2000, leaving only 600 employees. Although dredging has increased load passage – that is, the weight a boat can carry before its hull hits the bottom in shallow waters – by up to an extra thousand tonnes for every foot dredged, or $150,000 worth of extra cargo business on every voyage, Seaway charges cannot be reduced, and the Western Grain Transportation Act provides subsidies for shipping grain from western ports which the east cannot compete against. Since the Seaway cannot survive much longer if present circumstances prevail, it is likely that the west coast will increase its capacity at the expense of the east, and grain will be shipped to the rest of the world from Vancouver instead of from eastern ports.

Many of Canada's natural resources are shipped because of the bulk nature of the cargo. Thus, the shipping industry is very dependent on how well Canada's natural resources are selling abroad. While Canadian

---

BULLETIN BOARD— *SHIPPING*

- **Job demand factors:** increasing Pacific Rim trade; increase in inter-modal transport.
- **Job growth areas:** the west coast.
- **Job reduction areas:** St. Lawrence Seaway.
- **Growth limiting factors:** competition from Canadian and U.S. railways and U.S. ports.

CONTACTS

☛ Canadian Port and Harbour Association
8 Parmalea Crescent
Toronto, ON M9R 2X7 Tel. 416-245-1742 Fax: 416-245-1250

☛ Canadian Shippers' Council
48 Balsam Drive
Baie-D'Urfé, PQ H9X 3K5 Tel. 514-457-7268 Fax: 514-457-7269

☛ Shipping Federation of Canada
#326, 300 St-Sacrement St.,
Montreal, PQ H2Y 1X4 Tel. 514-849-2325 Fax: 514-849-6992

---

fruit, frozen meat, and seafood are sought after in the Far East, the grain market is more vulnerable to worldwide weather conditions, political subsidies, and protective tariffs.

Overall, the Ports Canada system has created more than 50,000 direct and spinoff jobs. Total revenues collected in 1991 were $5.7 billion. Any employment in the shipping industry will likely be on the west coast, primarily in Vancouver.

Air Transport

The Canada-U.S. Open Skies Agreement has expanded the air travel market dramatically. Canada's main airports expect more passengers and additional flights under the Open Skies bilateral air agreement signed in February 1995. The agreement permits Canadian air carriers to serve any transborder routes immediately, without constraints on aircraft size or frequency. U.S. carriers obtained the same rights, subject to a two-to-three-year transition period for new services at Montreal, Toronto, and Vancouver. Forecasts call for 1.4 million additional transborder seats a year in the Montreal market, a 40 percent increase. The

1995 transborder forecast for Vancouver, before adding the impact of Open Skies, was about 2.5 million passengers, or 23 percent of Vancouver's total traffic. It is expected that the number of medium- to long-haul flights will increase by almost 90 percent, resulting in an additional 400,000 passengers and $4 million to $5 million in additional revenue.

Airfares have effectively been deregulated, and Open Skies will bene- fit many Canadian companies now spending more of their corporate budgets on travel. According to an Amex Canada survey, Canadian com- panies almost doubled their spending on travel between 1987 and 1994, from $6.2 billion to nearly $11 billion. Open Skies will also deliver increased business to travel agencies because travelers will require more information. This will spur agencies to make greater investments in technology to speed up administrative processes and reduce costs, while maintaining personal service.

A cooperative services agreement between Canadian Airlines and its partner American Airlines involves code-sharing to make the best use of the equipment of both airlines. According to Don Casey at Canadian Airlines, the code-sharing arrangment (the use of identical flight num- bers for aircraft of either airline) is the largest of its kind in the world. By code-sharing, Canadian says it has increased its cross-border flight frequencies to 833 from 105 a week. The airline says it now serves 19 new U.S. markets as a result of Open Skies, which provided a much larger customer base in a market that is worth $1 billion a year in gross sales for scheduled passenger airlines. Technology is making additional inroads in the industry with the concept of ticketless air travel, an electronic system which enables travelers to book a seat by telephone and check in at the airport without ever seeing or touching a physical ticket.

The agreement has affected employment for pilots as well. Before the agreement Air Canada had laid off 243 pilots, and many had been on furlough for up to three years. All of those pilots were recalled. In April 1995 Air Canada also hired an additional hundred pilots and was discussing taking on another 600 in the future. Canadian Airlines Inter- national has also reinstated large numbers of its previously laid-off pilots.

The fact that more people are flying, combined with the effect of vigorous cost-cutting, has resulted in the general revival of Canada's major airlines. Air Canada achieved savings by modernizing its fleet, replacing aging planes with modern fuel-efficient Airbus A320s and Boeing 767s. In addition, both airlines have been able to squeeze more capacity out of their fleets with tight crew scheduling and faster turn-around times. The carriers also attempted to cut costs by farming out the management of many of their information systems – the computer systems that manage seat inventory, flight and crew scheduling, and a variety of management functions.

Open Skies has created new markets for non-hubbed direct flights and for makers of smaller airliners. Bombardier is betting on the economics of small commercial jets; a company spokesperson says its US$17 million plane can break even with only about half the seats filled.

The transition to Open Skies coincides with the federal government's push to divest itself of airports and put them in the hands of local airport authorities. It has also struck a $1.5 billion deal to privatize the vast air traffic control network, marking another large-scale transfer of government services to the private sector. The transfer to Nav Canada, a not-for-profit corporation controlled by the major airlines, business aircraft owners, pilots, and air traffic employees, in 1996 is part of Transport Canada's aggressive plan to get out of the subsidy business. This privatization is likely to lead to a major rationalization of the extensive air traffic control network since sophisticated computers and new satellite technology will allow controllers to monitor flights from fewer locations. The system now costs about $850 million a year to operate, a sum funded partly through airport taxes and airline levies, but with an annual shortfall of about $250 million.

Canada Post is the country's largest distribution company and the airlines' biggest freight customer. Electronic mail, fax machines, interactive computer networks, and teleconferencing may decrease the need for travel but at the same time spur international business. As home shopping becomes popular through the Internet, there will be a greater demand for fast delivery from manufacturers around the world. Social travel is likely to be stimulated by the emptynesters and retired baby boomers.

One by one air travel markets are being opened up to competition, and around the world airlines are integrating their reservation systems and expanding their networks. There is a worldwide trend for privatization of national carriers and a loosening of protective walls around them, so that smaller airlines are being allowed to spring up.

BULLETIN BOARD— *AIR TRANSPORT*

- **Job demand factors:** emptynesters stimulating the air travel market; Canadian companies getting more involved in exporting.
- **Job growth areas:** the air cargo market, particularly to Asia; increased business travel.
- **Job reduction areas:** industry sectors scheduled for privatization.
- **Growth limiting factors:** teleconferencing; oversupply of competitors; geographic and demographic considerations; larger, more cost-efficient U.S. airlines and carriers; declining importance of Canada Post; taxes and fees which can amount to 35 percent of the cost of an airplane trip.

CONTACTS

☛ Air Transport Association of Canada
#747, 99 Bank St.,
Ottawa, ON K1P 6B9 Tel. 613-233-7727 Fax: 613-230-8648

Postal and Courier Transportation

Although many people predicted that electronic mail and the fax machine would mean decreasing business for Canada Post and courier services, the opposite has been true. Faxes and e-mail have brought expanded opportunities for commerce, which has led to an increased need for courier service. Canada Post now moves 44 million pieces of mail daily and is forecasting a profit of $26 to $30 million for fiscal 1995–96, following two years of losses. In its 150-year history, Canada Post has built up a collection and delivery network that includes 18,500 retail outlets, 884,000 mailboxes, 22 mail processing plants, and 12 million addresses.

With its $55 million purchase of a 75 percent stake in Purolator Courier Ltd., the nation's largest express company, in 1993, Canada Post captured a market share at that time of 32 percent. In 1994 Purolator signed a five-year deal with Kelowna Flightcraft Air Charter Ltd. to take over its linehaul requirements; in 1995 it had the largest chartered air cargo fleet in the country, with 44 planes. Competitors peg the post office's share of the courier business at between 40 and 60 percent; it handled about 95 million documents and parcels in 1995. Annual sales of $637.6 million in 1994 represented an 11 percent increase over the previous year. In 1995 the industry filed an official complaint with the federal Bureau of Competition over what it maintains is Canada Post's lowball courier pricing. The post office denies that its letter mail business subsidizes the courier activities.

In 1990 the Canadian courier business was worth $1.9 billion; in 1995 it totaled $2.5 billion, and the world market was worth more than $30 billion. The Canadian market included $1 billion in domestic deferred service; $1.3 billion in domestic overnight service; and $200 million in international packages, 70 percent of which went to or from the U.S. While there are no precise numbers on market share, Canada Post and Purolator are believed to hold about 45 percent of the market. United Parcel Service and Federal Express Canada Ltd., Purolator's main competitors, each have about 12 to 15 percent of the market. Another 4 or 5 percent of the Canadian market is held by each of Loomis Courier Service, CanPar, and DHL International Express Ltd., and the remainder is divided among a number of small regional carriers. Sixty percent of Canada's courier users are in the service industries, 20 percent are manufacturers, 14 percent are in government, and 5 percent in the agri-resource industry; consumer users contribute only 1 percent of the total business.

The large courier companies, facing decreasing profits on express

---

ELECTRONIC DATA INTERCHANGE SERVICES AT CANADA POST

Canada Post Corp. is offering to bridge the gap between early adopters of EDI (electronic data interchange), a fast, reliable information transfer protocol, with its new HDI hybrid data interchange (HDI). The system accepts electronic-based information from EDI-enabled companies and then outputs it in more traditional forms, including fax, e-mail, and even letters in envelopes. Non-EDI companies can have paper-based information translated to electronic format and transmitted by Canada Post. Roger McCune, director of electronic products and services at Canada Post, says that physical distribution will be the mainstay for a while, but this service enables small and medium-sized businesses to keep those key customers who are demanding EDI.

deliveries, are turning to business logistics – such as maximizing the speed versus cost trade-offs – and other value-added services like preprinted mailing labels and small computer terminals that print way-bills and simplify customs problems for small clients. Each of these courier companies is investing large sums in new technology with the hope of outdistancing its competition through improvements in efficiency. DHL International Express of Mississauga, Ontario, manages 100 global accounts of multinationals that require comprehensive logistics services for warehousing and freight consolidation, air and road transportation, parts banking, and just-in-time deliveries. According to Ken Sternad of UPS, "Be it mail order, catalogue or TV merchandising, just-in-time retailing is already an important part of our business and should grow substantially in future years." With the price of overnight delivery dropping, thanks to lower airfares, more catalogue retailers are opting for this service.

Internationally, the world's largest courier, UPS (United Parcel Service of America Inc.), had total 1994 revenue of US$19.6 billion. UPS Canada registered more than C$346 million in revenue in 1994, a gain of $63 million from the previous year. With Canadian exporters on the move and using more air cargo, growth in the next five years is expected to soar worldwide. One study indicated that the volume of goods shipped by air by Canadian companies has increased by an average of 6.8 percent annually over the past five years, ahead of worldwide growth of 5.5 percent. Using tonnage figures, the International Air Transport Association says air cargo worldwide is expected to increase by 9 percent a year to 1998, a rate that will increase volumes by more than 50 percent in five years.

The air cargo industry looks set to boom. Growth in the total industry over the next five years is expected to be 6.5 percent a year, but according to Merge Global, the Canadian industry will surpass that. A survey of small Canadian exporters conducted by Federal Express showed that one in four exporters expected volumes to increase in the next five years, three in four expect their export business to increase this year, and nearly one in three expects a dramatic increase. According to Jon Slangerup, general manager of Federal Express Canada, "People with experience in exporting understand that speed and reliability are critical to their long-term success in overseas markets. It's a learning curve. The more you ship, the more you realize that the mode of transportation is often as valuable as the product itself." Also contributing to the boom in shipping by air is the trend to world sourcing, in which transnational companies choose their most efficient plant to manufacture a product line for all world markets. Cabotage and route co-terminalizing (which allows foreign carriers to pick up and deliver packages within Canada) was not part of the Open Skies negotiation, but could be when the agreement is reviewed in three years. According to Kal Tobias, president of DHL International Express Ltd. and president of the Canadian Courier Association, business to all of North America, including Mexico, is up because of the free trade agreement.

Air cargo is still an important part of the operations of airlines. According to Stephen Davis, vice-president of Airline Marketing Inc. of Toronto, which represents a number of overseas airlines, "cargo is the fastest-growing side of the business." For British Airways World Cargo, business is up 12 percent over 1994, with Vancouver being up 18 percent above target. Cargo represents 8 percent of Air Canada's revenues. In 1994, Canadian Airlines registered $242.4 million in cargo and mail revenue, roughly 10 percent of the airline's overall sales. FB On Board Courier Service Inc. is a Canadian firm in this niche of the international courier business. The company buys passenger tickets on flights to London, Hong Kong, Japan, and Miami, and a passenger accompanies each courier shipment, cutting clearance times.

The air cargo market in Asia is expanding strongly, spurred by the region's buoyant economic growth and its rising role as the manufacturing base for the rest of the world. In the first half of 1995 the amount of cargo carried by Asian carriers grew 17 percent, compared with a 14 percent increase for the industry as a whole. It is believed that Asia will be the strongest growth market for cargo in the years ahead; a 14 percent increase in air freight tonnage in the region (excluding Japan) is expected in the years to 1998, compared with growth of 11 percent in Europe and 7 percent in North America. The market's growth has both airlines and specialized cargo transportation companies, like Federal Express of the U.S. and Nippon Cargo Airlines (NCA) of Japan, scrambling for market share. NCA, Japan's only airline that specializes in cargo, saw its revenue grow by 40 percent in 1995. Malaysian Airline System saw a 42 percent increase in freight carried in the first

BULLETIN BOARD — *POSTAL AND COURIER TRANSPORTATION*

- **Job demand factors:** increasing importance of mail order; eventual revolution of television home shopping direct from the factory; just-in-time delivery; outsourcing of distribution logistics; global contracts; value-added services.
- **Job growth areas:** drivers involved in the pickup and delivery of mail order or home shopping items; intercompany delivery of parts and components.
- **Job reduction areas:** mail sorting and delivery; post office positions dealing with the public.
- **Growth limiting factors:** willingness of public to accept home shopping as alternative to shopping in person; fax machines and other forms of electronic communication; cost of air transportation; price of gas; potential for cross-subsidization between Purolator and Canada Post and preferred air rates.

CONTACTS

☛ Canadian Courier Association
555 Dixon Road
Etobicoke, ON M9W 1H8 Tel. 905-242-2570 Fax: 905-242-9874

---

quarter of 1995. During this period, Cathay Pacific, a Hong Kong–based carrier, enjoyed a 23 percent increase, and Singapore Airlines saw an 11 percent increase.

The major impetus behind these increases is intra-regional trade and the shift of Asian industry to higher-value-added production, such as electronic goods, components, and car parts. A pattern has emerged in which Japanese manufacturers send key components to assembly plants in Malaysia, Thailand, or China, which export finished products back to Japan and from there to the U.S. The U.S. computer industry is also a growing source of cargo traffic involving Asia, where many computer components, PCs, and periperals are produced. In summary, Asia's air cargo market is beginning to take off, although there is some worry about a coming overcapacity and drop in profits as competition heats up.

Road Infrastructure

Although automobiles account for approximately 90 percent of passenger travel in Canada and the bulk of freight travel is conveyed by trucks, four out of every ten kilometres of Canada's highways are below minimum standards. A federal study released in 1993 indicated that approximately 800 of the 3,534 bridges were below grade, 160 deaths were attributable annually to poor roads, and $20 million in property damage resulted from these accidents.

Roads have deteriorated because Ottawa has underfunded road infrastructure improvement projects. Whereas Washington assumes 23 percent of highway expenditures in the U.S., in the past Ottawa has pitched in only 5 percent for improvements to its highways. The federal Liberal government's infrastructure program, including road improvements, has been extended from the original three years to five years, but promised spending has been cut back and is scheduled to decline further. To bring back Canada's highways to minimum standard would require $14 billion over a ten-year period.

The Canadian highway system is worth $200 billion; however, it will likely cost three to five times the maintenance costs to replace it. The Fraser Institute estimates that repairing the roads would net the federal and provincial governments $350 million a year in savings from operating savings – the costs associated with clearing up accidents, plus the wear and tear on vehicles used to patrol highways, for example – reduced

---

INTERCITY BUS INDUSTRY

The intercity bus industry provides the most extensive route structure of all the public modes of intercity passenger transport in Canada. Altogether the industry employed 3,034 people in 1993. Intercity bus service ranks third in popularity after motor and air travel as a mode of transport. Since scheduled service bus passengers provide two-thirds of revenues, attempts to increase the industry's share will continue to focus on satisfying the public demand for comfort and convenience with renovated or new terminals and vehicles. Voyageur and Greyhound have experimented with luxury coaches, and new types of services are planned to promote market appeal.

BULLETIN BOARD — *ROAD INFRASTRUCTURE*

- **Job demand factors:** 40 percent of Canadian highways are below minimum standards.
- **Job growth areas:** civil engineers; road construction crew and jobs in road supply companies.
- **Growth limiting factors:** some governments' refusal to pay a fair share of highway improvement; limited provincial funds.

CONTACTS

☞ Canadian Society of Civil Engineering
Tour Guy, #840
2155 rue Guy
Montreal, PQ H3H 2R9 Tel. 514-933-2634 Fax: 514-933-3504
E-mail: csc@musica.mcgill.ca

accident-related property damage, travel time savings, job creation, and reduced unemployment insurance payouts. The province suffering the most is New Brunswick, which requires at least $2.2 billion to restore its 961 kilometres of highway. Ottawa signed a $300 million highway deal to improve that area of the Trans-Canada, with the province chipping in an additional $300,000.

Much the same kinds of problems also exist in other public works. According to the Federation of Canadian Municipalities, $15 billion is needed to restore our public works to current standards. Thirty-year-old methods of maintenance are still being employed. A 1995 National Research Council study claims that new technologies for roads, sewers, and bridges could save millions and form the basis for exporting expertise on infrastructure standards.

Canada's competitiveness depends, to a very great extent, on having an adequate infrastructure. Should Ottawa or the provinces not work hard to restore the country's highways, there will be costly long-term effects on all sectors of society. If, on the other hand, funds are made available for road restoration, there will be considerable employment opportunities for civil engineers and others involved in the various aspects of road repair and construction. Since most provincial budgets are slim, governments may well institute user fees that would help raise money for the recovery process. Unfortunately, this would only add to Canada's already prohibitive transportation costs.

Where the Jobs Are in the Communications Industries
• Telecommunications • Radio and Television
• Writing and Journalism

Telecommunications

Apple Computer predicts that a decade from now, the global business in multimedia will be worth $3.5 trillion. With this in mind, delivery companies for various modes of media are intent upon grabbing as big a piece of the market as possible. Time Warner, the second-largest U.S. cable television company and the world's largest media company, is one of the companies racing to control various media services. Even Canadian investors have placed their money on Time Warner as the potential winner of this big-stakes contest: the Bronfmans bought a 5.7 percent share for $702 million, and Paul Desmarais's Power Corporation has also taken a major share position in the company. Microsoft is providing the hardware and software necessary for television reception. Phone and cable companies will depend upon one another well into the 21st century because cable companies – until they incorporate switching technology – will be the largest deliverers of video transmission, but the phone companies are necessary for the delivery of video-on-demand to subscribers. Phone and cable companies are teaming up to compete against the new "deathstar" satellites capable of delivering 150 channels to subscribers. Even Maclean Hunter Limited was purchased by Rogers Communications Inc. in what was perhaps Canada's first foray into the merging multimedia field. Although Bell Canada is eliminating 10,000 jobs as its share of the long-distance market stabilizes at 70 percent and many information services are automated, the telephone giant is still hiring people in marketing, especially as it aggressively pursues the Internet market and fends off the long-distance resellers.

Computerized switching, controlled by phone companies, allows viewers to watch a program whenever they wish by simply pushing telephone buttons. Since it takes only five seconds to download a movie from an information warehouse, viewers can use their VCRs to control all aspects of watching the video, including rewinding, fast forwarding, or freeze framing. With digitization becoming the standard, all information from any medium can be translated and manipulated. The digitization of the transmitted signal will allow viewers to manipulate, edit, or store the video signals in any manner desired. Digitization also allows for compression of the signal, with the result that more channels can be broadcast in a given frequency range. Moreover, it improves channel reception.

The multimedia convergence war will be a clash of the titans. U.S. West, a Baby Bell phone company, invested $2.5 billion in Time Warner's multimedia unit in an effort to build a 28-city interactive cable television network, which would then compete with local telephone companies to provide enhanced telecommunications services such as computer databases. In Canada, Videotron of Montreal has teamed up with BCE Inc., Bell's parent company; and CUC Broadcasting, an Ontario cable company, has formed a partnership with Telus Corp., owner of Alberta Government Telephones. In the U.S., AT&T is approaching Tele-Communications, the largest U.S. cable company, in order to take on Time Warner. In Canada, Rogers is likely to join forces with AT&T to take on Bell. AT&T has a global long-distance network, owns a computer company, makes customer terminals and computer chips, and has the world's largest privately owned research and development facilities. AT&T's new equipment division spinoff will be spending over $200 billion over the next ten years on switching and wireless technology and software. Recently Stentor, an alliance of 11 major Canadian telecommunications companies, joined forces with MCI Communication Corp. in Washington to provide an intelligent network platform that extends across the continent to integrate all services available – a precursor to their global telecommunications market ambitions.

Even without optical fibre, which would allow telephone companies to supplant cable companies, telephone companies can deliver two or three video-on-demand channels to the consumer's home over copper wire, thanks to frequency-boosting techniques. The British government has already granted licences to companies to send television signals over telephone lines experimentally. To ensure its eventual dominance in the delivery aspect of the multimedia format, Bell Canada is spending $93 million to convert from copper to fibre-optic wires and from analog

BULLETIN BOARD — *TELECOMMUNICATIONS*

- **Job demand factors:** telephone companies control the switching technology for video-on-demand and the enhanced telecommunications services.
- **Job growth areas:** telecommunications research and development; optical fibre installation.
- **Job reduction areas:** cable industry jobs in the long term.
- **Growth limiting factors:** rate of optical fibre installation; government regulation of the industry; ability of cable companies to entrench their share of the video and network market.

CONTACTS

☛ Canadian Independent Telephone Association
#107, 2442 St. Joseph Blvd.,
Orleans, ON K1C 1G1 Tel. 514-834-1177 Fax: 514-834-8806

☛ Canadian Communication Consortium
1234 Bowser Avenue
North Vancouver, BC V7P 3H1 Tel. 604-222-4444 Fax: 604-222-1222

to digital technology. Worldwide 18 million kilometres of new optical cable was laid in 1994 alone.

The CRTC has yet to give telephone companies broadcast licences. However, since cable companies are providing some telephone services and holding shares in long-distance carriers, Bell is pushing for its share of the video transmission market. While it is unlikely that the issue will be resolved before the turn of the century, competition will likely emerge in the short term between telephone and cable companies for alarm services, database access, voice messages, and electronic mail. In the long run, the multinational linkages and alliances are likely to play havoc with the attempts of individual governments to regulate electronic media effectively.

In the meantime, Bell and Rogers are going toe-to-toe in broadcasting, phone, Internet server, and fast-speed cable or ADSL (asynchronous digital subscriber lines) modem markets to establish or consolidate their footholds in these industries. Already Bell is planning to pilot cable TV, video-on-demand, and educational services in London, Ontario, and Repentigny, Quebec. And B.C. Tel and Quebec Telephone are demanding exemptions from ownership restrictions under the Broadcasting Act. Cable companies are expected to invest $1.2 billion by 2000 to try to capture 6 percent of the local telephone market, while telephone companies will likely spend $600 million in an effort to win 15 percent of the cable market, according to Phil Armstrong of Northern Business Information. Northern Telecom's Cornerstone Data will allow cable subscribers access rates of 27 megabits per second (mps) and output rates of 2 mps (versus 28.8 kilobit regular high-speed modem rate), so the cable companies are likely to win the first battle in the multimedia wars – at least until Bell can put ADSL in place. By 1997 ADSL will be capable of delivering high-definition TV over phone lines.

Jobs in the telecommunications industry will definitely get a boost from these developments. In the long run, telephone companies are likely to win. The computer and software industry will hire staff to develop this side of the technology. Despite eventual consolidation through mergers and acquisitions, most high-tech employees will be hired in this global growth industry for at least the next 20 years. The telephone companies are likely to win the overall struggle in the end, considering that their annual revenues are seven times greater than all cable operations combined. Indeed, according to the OECD, in 1995, the top 25 public telephone operators in the world were more profitable than the world's largest 100 banks.

Radio and Television

Every aspect of the broadcasting industry, from recording to editing and transmission, is being digitized. It will soon be possible, using "suitcase studios," to perform such functions as sound and video recording, editing, and transmission from the field using D-CART or laptop radio. A documentary about Antarctica could be put together on location and the footage could be broadcast by satellite from the location over a network. This innovation will require field staff to develop the appropriate skills to perform these functions, if necessary, from a remote location.

Digital transmission reduces sound signal reception breakup, and it can also reduce station operating costs by 50 percent, because of the low levels of energy needed for transmission (200 watts versus 50,000 watts). Broadcasters can offer other services that generate money, such as mapping systems that lead car drivers to their destinations via car radio;

systems that display information regarding artists, songs, and CDs; and a program that lets listeners pay to have a CD or song downloaded into their music collections.

Since digital signals can be compressed to create more room in a frequency bandwidth, digital transmission will alter the number of channels or stations that can broadcast. It is now possible to have eight television channels in the frequency band used at the moment by a single channel. This will allow cable companies to increase the number of channels offered to subscribers before the introduction of optical fibre puts more stations on an individual's radio dial. The additional channels or stations will increase competition between stations for audience, advertising dollars, and program material. The outcome is expected to be more narrowcasting – broadcasting to select audiences – such as jazz, rock, comedy, country, fashion, finance, age-specific programming, 24-hour news, nostalgia, real estate, sport-specific channels, classical music, and so on. More local coverage will appear, as stations attempt to come up with new material to fill additional air time. This will create more jobs for roving reporters, sportscasters, commentators, program producers, talk-show hosts, and newscasters. Video or sound recording technicians will be needed to accompany broadcast journalists on their field trips, as well as technicians who can do on-site editing.

Many radio stations have chosen syndicated musical formatting, which narrows the role of the program director and the disc jockey to that of coordination and the bridging of material and information – that is, the commentary between songs. AM radio will likely make more aggressive moves into non-music narrowcasting with business news, consumer affairs shows, children's programming, religious programming, and seniors programming. Advertisers are insisting on narrowcasting to better reach the 25-to-54-year-old market.

The focus on community affairs will increase the importance of news reporting and sports coverage for both television and radio, especially for local cable companies. And since the greater number of channels will increase competition for advertising dollars, more advertising sales and promotion representatives will have to be hired. In order to reduce expenses, stations will share more resources and services with one another, including promotions, contests, and advertising options. There will be a conspicuous trend toward group ownership of or alliances between stations or channels so as to save on costs by sharing functions, equipment, and other resources. Toronto's City TV, which owns MuchMusic and CHUM FM, illustrates such an alliance.

To reduce costs, stations are using the services of videojournalists rather than expensive television crews, both locally and abroad. Instead of sending out the unwieldy and costly unionized crews that most network stations employ, New York 1, a cable station that delivers local news 24 hours a day, employs 20 videojournalists – or veejays – equipped with compact HI8 cameras to film and report local events. According to Michael Rosenblum, a videojournalism consultant and lecturer at Columbia University in New York, "The traditional television crew is dying. The HI8 camera puts more people into the field and takes the news to places you can't afford to go with regular television crews." Once optical fibre is installed universally, veejays will be able to feed live from anywhere. A Canadian company, Patterson-Partington International TV Productions, already covers events live using satellite dishes mounted on trucks to send information to another truck for editing and graphic work; costs are thereby reduced by 80 percent. The British Broadcasting Corporation (BBC) is using software written in-house to create a "virtual" studio that appears to be four times bigger than it actually is, and has replaced the need for three studios. The 13 camera operators that a traditional studio would have had to employ have been replaced by robotic cameras.

Competition between in-house production – broadcasters who do their own production rather than contracting it out – and syndicators will mean more jobs for producers and technicians in in-house production for the various networks and cable companies as each tries to develop its own profile or "branding." Independent production companies will form joint venture alliances with the networks as a way of outsourcing production functions which are not performed on a regular basis. There will be demand for more documentaries and news-based programming, two areas that appeal to aging boomers.

Competition will intensify everywhere in the industry. Cable companies have to worry about competition not only from other cable companies, but also from telephone companies entering the multimedia field. They are also competing with satellite dish companies, which offer consumers small-dish satellites that can send over 150 channels into

BULLETIN BOARD — *RADIO, TELEVISION, AND CABLE*

- **Job demand factors:** proliferation of number of services, channels, or stations; need for original programming; globalization of information; Canada's lower production costs compared with those in the U.S.
- **Job growth areas:** newscasters; sportscasters; talk-show hosts; community information and documentary hosts; on-the-scene reporters; producers; technical support staff; advertising and promotion representatives; videojournalists.
- **Skills, abilities, qualities, education needed:** creativity; versatility; technical or area-specific expertise; flexibility; ability to use the various portable technologies; college diploma is minimum requirement.
- **Job reduction areas:** potentially all areas depending on how the multimedia competition unfolds; television crews.
- **Growth limiting factors:** intense competition from other broadcasters and from other broadcast, information, and entertainment media.

their homes. In addition, cable companies must now provide third-party non-programming access for cable and Internet services, paving the way for on-line classifieds and newspapers.

A temporary arrangement worked out with the CRTC regarding increased channel delivery requires that cable companies contribute $300 million to the Canadian production community in order to promote Canadian content in the face of competition from the many channels coming on stream. Rogers Communications is the first North American cable company to use digital compression, transmitting up to 500 channels via cable. In anticipation of future alliances with phone companies, Rogers has designed its network for future connection with telephone services. The purchase of Maclean Hunter by Rogers represents another step in Rogers's emerging multimedia ambitions. Rogers is also involved in SchoolLink, which is a plan to allow most schools free access to SchoolNet for three years using high-speed modems.

Since the repeal of laws governing financial syndication in the U.S. gives networks more control over in-house production, networks will want to retain financial control over program ownership once a program is aired. The shift to in-house productions means more network-

BULLETIN BOARD — *RADIO, TELEVISION, AND CABLE*

CONTACTS

☞ Alliance of Canadian Cinema, Television & Radio Artists
2239 Yonge St.,
Toronto, ON M4S 2B5 Tel. 416-489-1311 Fax: 416-489-1435

☞ Association for the Study of Canadian Radio & Television
c/o Centre for Broadcasting Studies, Concordia University,
1455 de Maisonneuve Blvd. West,
Montreal, PQ H3G 1M8 Tel. 514-848-2385 Fax: 514-848-4501

☞ Canadian Animation Producers' Association
c/o Nelvana Limited
32 Atlantic Avenue
Toronto, ON M6K 1X9 Tel. 416-588-5571 Fax: 416-588-3371

☞ Canadian Association of Broadcasters
#306, 350 Sparks Street, PO Box 627, Station B
Ottawa, ON K1P 5S2 Tel. 613-233-4035 Fax: 613-233-6961

☞ Canadian Association of Broadcast Consultants
500 Van Buren Street, PO Box 550
Kemptville, ON K0G 1J0 Tel. 613-258-5928 Fax: 613-258-7418

☞ Canadian Association of Broadcast Representatives Inc.
c/o Western Broadcast Sales
#1600, 55 Bloor Street West
Toronto, ON M4W 1A5 Tel. 416-960-9205 Fax: 416-960-9795

☞ Canadian Film & Television Production Association
#806, 175 Bloor Street East, North Tower
Toronto, ON M4W 3R8 Tel. 416-927-8942 Fax: 416-922-4038

produced newsmagazine shows, more cheap-to-produce and easy-to-syndicate sitcoms, and less serious drama, which is too expensive and ambitious for in-house production. News and information shows expanded 2 percent in 1993 to 15 percent of prime-time scheduling, and comedies expanded to 37 percent of prime-time scheduling. In the future, networks will bring advertisers in early in the development phase, in order to reduce the financial risk of launching new programs.

According to J. Max Robins, TV editor of *Variety* magazine, there will be more family programming and closer financial and creative ties between commercial networks and advertisers. Speaking at the 1993 Broadcast Research Council Annual Fall TV Preview, Robins noted that because of their fear of losing advertising dollars, networks are becoming more conservative and are emphasizing family programming. With little or no advertising revenue growth projected, experimentation in programming has become too risky. Reduced advertising revenues in 1995 led to industry consolidation and restructuring such as CanWest Global Communications Corp.'s bid for WIC Western International Communication Inc. Another example was the asset swap proposed by Videotron Ltée and CFCF. There is also a tendency toward cross-ownership between broadcasters and producers. Although the "self-dealing" that results risks eliminating vital subsidies, many are pushing for looser regulation that stays within the spirit of the subsidy rules. Should this trend prevail, more jobs for producing big dramas will migrate to the broadcasters. Considerable restructuring of the industry is likely to speed up, especially now that recent deregulation in the U.S. would in effect allow AT&T to deliver broadcast television in addition to phone and cable service.

Europe and Eastern Europe with its 400 million potential viewers is a growing market. Southeast Asia and Japan combined are even bigger markets and growing just as quickly as the European and Eastern European markets. By the year 2000, approximately 900 million households worldwide will own television sets and will want specialized programming. In the short term, satellite delivery will have a more impressive effect on programming once home viewers are receiving 150 to 200 channels. Alliance Communications Corporation, which distributes television and feature films domestically and internationally and holds exclusive distribution rights to many foreign films, is proof that even Canadian independents can survive in these international markets. Ultimately, however, the very concept of the channel is being undermined by video-on-demand. Eventually consumers will pay only for shows watched and there will be only one channel, which delivers whatever is desired.

Writing and Journalism

Individuals contemplating a writing career must look at this field in the context of the information and multimedia revolution. The best-paid writing jobs will be in speechwriting, public relations writing, and

BULLETIN BOARD — *WRITING AND JOURNALISM*

- **Job demand factors:** an electronically wired world makes multimedia communication inevitable; declining literacy rates at the high end; need to consume large amounts of information of all kinds easily; importance of image in a high-profile world.
- **Job growth areas:** technical writers; public relations writers; speech-writers; TV journalists.
- **Job reduction areas:** all forms of print journalism.
- **Growth limiting factors:** size of narrowcast market and its purchasing power.

technical writing. The market for copywriters and freelancers will become increasingly fragmented and unpredictable. Technical writers will prosper since documentation for computers, software, instrumentation, home entertainment, and other gadgetry must be written. Eventually, all technical material will be presented and explained interactively, with video demonstrations built in as required.

With the broadening of news and business coverage putting corporate and government leaders in the media spotlight more often, there is a move toward presenting carefully crafted policy position statements. Public relations writers will be hired to present the growing number of corporate and public positions on issues that are publicly scrutinized and debated. As the world becomes more complicated, the need for specialization within this field increases – public relations experts in the areas of law and the environment, for example.

Speechwriters often train in corporate or government public relations before taking up this rather risky profession – risky because if the speech fails, the speechwriter may lose credibility and opportunities for future employment. Speechwriters are responsible for writing "scripts" for executives and politicians, and editorials for others, as well as helping the speech givers with their delivery style. In order to control the message going out from Ottawa, the federal government spends about $2 million a month hiring speechwriters.

Copywriters are very often hired on a freelance basis, given the variability in advertising revenues and accounts. This field encompasses

BULLETIN BOARD — *WRITING AND JOURNALISM*

CONTACTS

☛ Canadian Association of Journalists
St. Patrick's Building, Carleton University,
1125 Colonel By Dr.,
Ottawa ON K1S 5B6 Tel. 613-526-8061 Fax: 613-521-3904
E-mail: cf208@freenet.carleton.ca
URL: http://freenet.carleton.ca/freeport/prof.assoc/caj/menu
URL: http://www.ncf.carleton.ca/freeport/prof.assoc/caj/menu

☛ Editors' Association of Canada
35 Spadina Rd.,
Toronto, ON M5R 2S9 Tel. 416-975-1379 Fax: 416-975-1839

☛ Interactive Multimedia Arts & Technologies Association
PO Box 1139, Station Q
Toronto, ON M4T 2N5 Tel. 416-233-2227 Fax: 416-256-4391
Info Line: 416-636-9684

☛ Media Club of Canada
PO Box 204, Stn B,
Ottawa, ON K1P 6C4 Tel. 613-236-3325

☛ Periodical Writers Association of Canada
The Writers Centre,
24 Ryerson Ave., 2nd Fl.
Toronto, ON M5T 2P3 Tel. 416-868-6913 Fax: 416-860-0826

☛ Radio Television News Directors' Association
#110, 2175 Sheppard Ave. East,
Willowdale, ON M2J 1W8 Tel. 416-756-2213 Fax: 416-491-1670

☛ The Writers Union of Canada
24 Ryerson Ave.,
Toronto, ON M5T 2P3 Tel. 416-703-8982 Fax: 416-703-0826
E-mail: twuc@the_wire.com
URL: http://www.swifty.com/twuc/index/html

direct mail, magazines, newspapers, and radio and television. In the past, the best-paid copywriters worked in television because of the medium's market reach. With the advent of multimedia home shopping and narrowcasting, copywriters will have to focus on the objective details of a product – price, for example – and be less concerned about promoting a product's image or the image a product will give the consumer. And as more consumer shopping agents and product reviewers appear on the scene, copywriting will become less relevant, as consumers demand straightforward information for comparative purposes.

Freelance writing is an extremely competitive field which is most lucratively taken up by individuals who have previously written full-time for a print medium. Freelance writers cannot survive in this field unless their articles are frequently published in magazines. In the long run, however, magazines will be replaced by specialty television channels that provide the same information as a magazine but in a context that gives viewers greater control over the message. For example, viewers will be able to pursue information to their desired level of interest and in a preferred format. This approach to presenting information will require the talents of freelance writers who can adapt to the multimedia demands of a project.

Competition for writing jobs will continue to be stiff since the print medium as a whole is suffering staff cutbacks. With television becoming the primary delivery mode of all information, the most lucrative writing jobs will be in television journalism. To be effective in this field, performance skills and familiarity with the workings of a newsroom are important, as is expertise in a variety of information-related areas. Although news and sports broadcasts are becoming more popular, the syndication of many information, sports, and news functions may result in networks keeping a small core of staff and hiring freelancers on a demand basis in an effort to reduce costs.

Where the Jobs Are in Utilities

The recession has taken its toll on these extremely mature industries. Consequently, the utilities have suffered staff cutbacks and hiring freezes. This is expected to be the case for some time to come. Ironically, the utilities which were so aggressively promoting energy conservation have become victims of their own success in this endeavour. Now that consumers – both companies and individuals – are more conscious of ways to save their utilities dollars, the demand for utilities such as hydro has diminished. Even once the demand for utilities increases, automation of many of the management information systems will curtail employment. Before long, for example, meter readers will go on the endangered jobs

BULLETIN BOARD — *UTILITIES*

- **Job demand factors:** high price of electrical energy; public's desire for environment-friendly energy sources.
- **Job growth areas:** electrical engineers and lawyers; water purification and sewage treatment jobs for engineers in the long term; foreign ventures; data transmission experts.
- **Job reduction areas:** hydro employees in Ontario, New Brunswick, Saskatchewan, and possibly B.C.
- **Growth limiting factors:** government intervention on behalf of hydro.

CONTACTS

- Canadian Council of Electrical Leagues
  #1000, 2 Lansing Sq.,
  North York, ON M2J 4P8 Tel. 416-495-0052 Fax: 416-495-1804
- Canadian Public Works Association (Inc.)
  3370 South Service Road, Garden Level
  Burlington, ON L7N 3M6 Tel. 905-634-7736 Fax: 905-634-1304

list as the kind of information they collect goes on-line, along with other information such as water usage and sewage levels. For the moment, however, electric power is a $35 billion industry in Canada, employing 200,000 people in electric power generation, distribution, and control.

Ontario Hydro is trying to make itself more accountable by providing various services, including energy management, and becoming more market-oriented by incorporating activities that add value and produce profit, such as selling its expertise to foreign markets and developing green, industrial-technology-related opportunities. In addition, Ontario Hydro spends $300 million annually on research and development in such areas as fuel cells and power systems. Ontario Hydro's joint projects with battery manufacturers and the auto industry may lead to the development of a commercially viable vehicle which would recharge itself at night when Ontario Hydro's capacity is underused. This innovation would open up many employment opportunities at Ontario Hydro for individuals with the appropriate expertise. Bear in mind, however, that privatization or a merger may be in store for Ontario Hydro and Atomic Energy of Canada Ltd. in the near future.

The latest area of interest is co-generation – a process that uses industrially produced steam to generate electricity in an environment-friendly way and at a significantly lower cost than what Ontario Hydro offers. Provincially, hydro companies have resisted the move toward privately owned and operated co-generation because it effectively steals their business. This attitude may be changing, however, now that utilities are about to spend $110 million on renewable energy technologies – a $300 billion industry which the World Bank expects to triple by 2000. Nonetheless, with the many legal issues surrounding energy and the environment, along with the eventual privatization of some energy sources, this is an area to get into, if you are a lawyer or engineer interested in the electrical energy field. Indeed, with all nuclear generating station plans on hold, and most utilities not hiring, co-generation presents a potential growth area for employment, as long as government regulation does not impede its growth.

Improvements in electrical cars and battery technology are proceeding steadily, but it will be some time before research creates a viable alternative to traditional modes of transportation. Concerns about water purification and sewage treatment will lead to employment in these and other environment-related areas when governments and municipalities eventually address these issues, budget constraints notwithstanding.

There are rather large dark clouds forming on the deregulation horizon for Ontario Hydro, New Brunswick Power, and Saskatchewan Power. The debt loads of the first two are so great that they may drag down the credit ratings of their respective provinces. In addition, Ontario Hydro is vulnerable to competition from Manitoba Hydro and Hydro-Québec – which also poses a serious threat to New Brunswick Power by selling inexpensive power to New Brunswick's forest industry. B.C. Hydro, because of its high taxes and dividends paid to the province, is vulnerable to competition from Alberta and Washington suppliers. Hydro-Québec is in the best position of all Canada's utilities because of a 65-year contract with the hydro station at Churchill Falls, Labrador, which sells power to Quebec at only 0.25 cents per kilowatt.

Because North American utilities can produce roughly 20 percent more power than they are selling, serious price competition will soon become a reality. According to a 1996 study by the Dominion Bond Rating Service Ltd., "There will be a very difficult five-to-fifteen-year transition period as electric deregulation occurs. . . . We foresee great instability in the industry until the excess supply disappears. The problem somewhat resembles that of the airline industry, with excess capacity and heavy fixed cost structure." Although competition from the U.S. is limited by transmission line capacities and its own deregulation problems, if municipal electricity distributors were to start producing their own power using natural gas and small power plants, the provinces would be stuck with "stranded high-cost plants" and a mountain of debt. For instance, Ontario Hydro is up in arms over London Hydro's proposing to join forces with U.S. power company Trigen Energy Corp. to establish a small co-generation power plant to serve parts of London. According to a 1995 report by Moody's Investor Services Ltd., Canadian utilities can probably compete against most U.S. suppliers, but are highly vulnerable to competition from other provinces. Eventually, however, competition may come from resellers locally once electric energy is deregulated the way the telephone and natural gas utilities have been. As Richard Caarryer, vice-president of the Canadian arm of Asea Brown Boveri Inc., claims, "New technologies are going to make it possible for consumers to produce their own electric power through fuel cells powered by hydrogen or natural gas." Industry Canada believes that superconductors will make it possible to buy energy from a variety of sources in the next century.

On the innovative side, utilities such as Hydro-Québec and B.C. Hydro are experimenting with entering the telecommunications market, since fibre-optic lines have already been installed on many existing electrical poles and towers. Foreign ventures are also in the works with Ontario Hydro and others in Peru, Chile, China, India, Sri Lanka, Philippines, and Mexico. The E7 Network of Expertise for the Global Environment, based in Montreal, brings together the world's biggest electric utilities to help transfer environmental technologies to developing countries. We have a lot of expertise we can export, for as Graham Williams, senior vice-president of Moneco Agra Inc., notes, "Canada has a technological lead in coal-fired thermal power, turning low cost coal reserves into power."

Where the Jobs Are in the Wholesale Trade

Can you imagine a world in which "I can get it for you wholesale" falls on deaf ears? Although wholesaling will not disappear entirely since

BULLETIN BOARD — *WHOLESALING*

- **Job demand factors:** disappearing with home shopping and just-in-time inventory replenishment information technology replacing the need for wholesaling, except for one-stop home shopping for products lacking strong branding; small business will still need some warehousing.

CONTACTS

☛ Canadian Association of Wholesale Sales Representatives
#336, 370 King St. West, PO Box 2,
Toronto, ON M5V 1J9 Tel. 416-782-8961 Fax: 416-593-5145

small businesses will continue to require some warehousing, it will shrink in importance and the jobs associated with it will disappear. The wholesale trade will be replaced by information technology – just-in-time inventory replenishment – designed to integrate all raw material suppliers, manufacturers, and sellers. Direct delivery of goods from factory to consumer as home shopping becomes more popular will also obviate the need for wholesalers, except perhaps as order fulfilment operations for Internet and home-based businesses. The outsourcing of warehousing will likely be a growth area. But even wholesalers are trying to cut back on their warehousing inventory costs by using EDI ordering systems.

Where wholesalers are likely to prosper is in acting as one-stop-shopping brokers for a number of home-shopping-oriented manufacturers unable to create their own brand presence by other means. In retail, the category-killers and the warehouse discounters will eventually lose some market share to wholesalers or warehousers who can ship directly to purchasers from geographically appropriate areas. This function will eventually be replaced by centralized information brokers who will connect with a wide variety of manufacturers willing to ship directly to customers.

Ironically, the wholesale trade has helped keep the prices of goods higher in Canada than in the U.S., where there are far fewer wholesalers because most manufacturers ship directly to retailers. In a cost crunch, the middleperson always disappears. In an age of global competition,

Canada will not be able to afford a wholesale trade that effectively adds no value other than for unnecessary warehousing.

Traditional Services: Retail Trade, Hospitality, Culture and Recreation, Personal Services

Because traditional services are usually directed toward meeting the local or national needs of consumers, they are often not subject to as much global competition as the dynamic services industries. The lower-value-added nature of traditional service products also makes them less vulnerable to the kinds of productivity growth and technological change that characterize the dynamic services.

There is a growing need for everyone in the traditional and other services to take into account the "ethnic" market, the fastest-growing consumer segment. By the year 2001, visible minorities will account for over $300 billion in combined purchasing power. The Canadian Advertising Foundation in a 1995 report noted that 46 percent of visible-minority consumers are more likely to make purchases if members of visible minorities are included in ads. By 2000, Chinese Canadians will be our largest visible minority, totalling 1.3 million people. One company building on this trend is Balmoral Communications, which offers a specialized Chinese-language advertising campaign service. This growth is leading to greater market specialization that allows for new events such as the annual cross-marketing Expo International and the creation of Black Pages Network Inc.'s listings of black business, social, and cultural organizations in Ottawa, Hamilton, Toronto, and Montreal. New innovative approaches for reaching these target markets include such strategies as the setting up of a legal immigration clinic inside Ed Mirvish's Honest Ed's discount store in Toronto.

Where the Jobs Are in the Retail Trade
• Discounters • Department Stores • Malls • Furniture • Food • Clothing • Cosmetics • Pharmacy • Car Dealerships

In 1992, in an industry that sells Canadians $425 billion in consumer goods, 3,200 retailers went bankrupt owing $1 billion. Changes in consumer spending are revealing. Since 1991, spending per person represented 39 percent of after-tax income, compared with 45 percent in the late 1980s, 50 percent in the early 1970s, and 41 percent during the 1981 recession. From 1981 to 1992, total after-tax income doubled, prices rose by 78 percent, and the economy grew by 90 percent. Thus, although the population grew, personal spending after taxes did increase by $7,500 per person, but of that amount, retail spending accounted for only $2,500. The increase in personal spending, coupled with a decline in retail sales, reflects a tendency on the part of consumers to purchase services such as investments, health care, and RRSPs.

Overall, services accounted for 52 percent of consumer spending in 1992, compared with 44 percent in 1981. Non-retail spending rose twice as fast between 1981 and 1992 as retail spending did during the same period. Along with increased taxation reducing the purchasing power of Canadians, these trends have hurt the retail industry as a whole.

Perhaps the biggest overall challenge to the industry comes from consumers who are now heavily in debt. In 1995, personal savings reached a 25-year low as consumers saw their debt levels reach 92 percent of their take-home pay and personal bankruptcies reach an all-time high. With 25 percent of the consumer market directly employed in the public sector, which is undergoing radical downsizing coupled with wage and unemployment payment rollbacks, the decline in purchasing dollars is bound to affect all retailers to some extent.

Since loyal customers spend 500 to 600 percent more than average customers over a five-year period, watch for the proliferation of loyalty reward programs such as free air-mile points for purchases and a heavy emphasis placed on customized services, as everyone fights over the few remaining consumer dollars. Children are also playing a large role in retail purchasing. In the U.S., they are exerting growing influence in the purchase of food, clothing, vacations, furniture, computers, and automobiles, affecting $157 billion in sales in 1993, up from $50 billion in 1984.

With retailers losing 1 to 4.5 percent of their revenues to theft, there is bound to be a severe crackdown in this area during these times of narrow profit margins.

According to retail analyst Joe Williams, the recession is over as far as retailing is concerned, and factors that are influencing shoppers today will continue to the end of the 1990s. Aging boomers traditionally spend less in retail stores and shop at fewer stores. The 24-to-34-year-old age group is typically the biggest retail spending group, since they are engaged in setting up a home and having children. Unfortunately, their numbers will drop by 20 percent between 1991 and 2001.

Even if we ignore the likely devastating effects of the information highway on retailing over the next five to 15 years, Canadian retailers are in big trouble. According to a 1995 study by the Ontario Retail Sector Advisory Board, 50 percent of our retailers could be out of business by 2000 unless they become more competitive with U.S. retailers. Canadian retailers on the whole are less competitive, don't respond to new competitive pressures, have more bureaucratic structures, do less market and location research, lack advanced skills in data and software use, and are less innovative – relying heavily instead on new U.S. products, formats, and fashion trends. The Dominion Bond Rating Service is putting most large Canadian retailers under review and is predicting that one-third of Canada's homegrown retailers will be out of business by the end of the decade. These predictions are supported by a 1994 study by American Research, which found that over 70 percent of Canadians are willing to buy at a new competitively priced store instead of staying with their current one. Coupled with the fact that, according to Thom Blishcock, vice-president and chief business scientist for AT&T Global Information Solutions, 45 percent of all retail sales by the year 2010 will be made over interactive televisions, retailers are in for the ride of their lives.

Who will survive? Probably those who invest more in computers to track customer buying habits. According to Blishcock, between $4 and $6 of profit is made for each dollar spent on information creation. Wal-Mart is the world leader in this department; its EDI distribution system helped it grow from a $1.2 billion operation in 1980 to $94 billion in sales in 1995. Make sure any retail stores you are interested in working for are heavily invested in this strategy.

How are customer buying habits evolving? The 1995 National Retail Report, a Canadian first of its kind, indicated that a growing number of consumers are at opposite ends of the buying spectrum. Those lacking time and willing to pay for convenience represent 38 percent of purchasers (especially now that more women have entered the work force, making shopping more of a functional and less of a social activity); and those short on funds, but with ample time for bargain hunting, accounted for 34 percent (discounters now take in 55 percent of total sales). Wal-Mart, having largely conquered the discount market, has already moved upscale in many areas in an attempt to attract the value-conscious high-income shoppers. The Jim Patterson Group created fully automated stores in lower-class areas in B.C. to attract price-sensitive customers willing to do their own grocery checkout; just to remind purchasers of how much they are saving, the grocery bill compares the price of each item with prices in other grocery stores. Obviously those consumers with jobs and putting in extra hours (particularly the growing number of dual-income households) are attracted to the former and the increasingly cash-strapped low- and middle-income earners to the latter.

Discount store prices have fallen 20 percent since Wal-Mart's entry into Canada, seriously affecting Zellers, whose profits were cut in half in 1995. Wal-Mart with its 133 Canadian stores had sales of $2.7 billion, versus Zellers' $3.5 billion, and greater sales per square foot. K-Mart has also been stung and may fold its doors in the next couple of years as a result. Look for stores with a sensible high-tech strategy. By using their information database, stores can identify and target the 20 to 35 percent of the customers who typically generate 70 to 80 percent of company profits.

Another key trend affecting the retail trade is the growing use of EDI (electronic data interchange) equipment, which has the tendency to make retailers rely on fewer, larger suppliers. Retailers are downloading labeling, warehousing, and shipping functions to suppliers so as to create faster inventory turnaround times, but this is increasing the cost structures of suppliers and manufacturers at the moment as they scramble to meet two-day order-filling targets. T. Eaton Co. Ltd. now uses 40 percent less warehousing than four years ago – despite expanding the number of its stores – by deploying an automatic replenishment system. Expect a shake-out and consolidation among supplier companies as a result.

Discounters

Shoppers demanding better value have given rise to the category-killing discounters or low-price, high-volume companies such as Toys "R" Us (Canada), Costco Wholesale Corporation, Price Club Canada Inc., Business Depot, and Aikenhead's Home Improvement Warehouse Inc. In 1993, discounters and warehouse clubs rang up $9.5 billion in sales in general merchandise, not including food, in contrast with traditional department stores, which had $9.1 billion in sales in the same year. The category-killers succeed because they offer a large selection of items which they sell at reduced profit margins – 11 percent on average versus 40 percent for a full-line department store. Unlike traditional stores, they are not burdened by high overheads and inventory investments that constrain their ability to reduce their profit margins or prices. Warehouse chains have their goods shipped directly from the manufacturer to the store, thereby sidestepping wholesale and inventory warehousing costs. Fast turnover of merchandise because of low prices and just-in-time inventory systems eliminates the need for separate warehousing.

The formidable presence of category-killers is best illustrated by the recently merged Price/Costco, which will operate 195 warehouse stores in Canada, the U.S., and Mexico, with annual sales of approximately US$16 billion. According to Doug Tigert, retail and marketing professor at Babson College in Massachusetts, "Virtually every city in Canada that has 100,000 people in the trading radius will get a warehouse club." He forecasts that approximately 75 to 100 "warehouse clubs" will be operating in Canada by the end of the 1990s, with the invasion coming largely from the U.S. Tigert predicts that market penetration will reach 45 to 50 percent in Toronto and other major cities. Vancouver and Montreal warehouse clubs have already reached penetration levels of 22 percent and 21 percent, though Toronto is still only at the 5 percent level.

The last upsurge in spending on homes and the accompanying purchase of high-ticket items like washers, dryers, refrigerators, stoves, televisions, and furniture occurred during the 1980s as the last baby boomers reached their peak family-forming years. Demographic trends indicate reduced consumer spending in the 1990s on footwear, clothing, and household items by 15 percent as a percentage of disposable income. Consumers are currently more conservative and pragmatic in their spending since they can no longer count on a growth in personal income. A drop in real income is one of the reasons for the current low inflation rate.

The retailers who will likely succeed in the immediate future will be the Aikenhead Home Improvement Warehouse or Toys "R" Us style of discount store, since they focus on a specialty market and offer a wide selection of goods. In the future, the only viable alternative to home shopping will be to visit an outlet that allows a consumer to view merchandise in a particular category, and choose and purchase an item at a cost slightly above the home shopping price. Retail outlets will act as convenience stores when consumers need a product immediately. Lower-priced items will fare best in this purchasing environment since, in most cases, the savings from home shopping for more expensive items will outweigh the premium the consumer would have to pay for convenience. For example, the consumer in the market for a refrigerator would visit an outlet that displays a selection of these items. The consumer would then order the appliance electronically from the manufacturer. Since on any given day the manufacturer would have a large number of orders from the city in which the consumer lives, shipments of manufactured items would be delivered to that city daily. Purchasing directly from the factory allows the factory to get a sense of what is selling and in what quantity. With everyone in the supply, production, and delivery chain interconnected electronically, no one in the value-adding process is carrying much in the way of inventory, which means prices can be kept low.

One of the weaknesses of the category-killer strategy is their often-remote locations. In order to stock and display a wide selection of products, discounters must use large tracts of land. To avoid the exorbitant taxes that they would have to pay if their outlets were in large cities, most discounters locate their stores in industrial areas or just outside the city limits where taxes are lower. So it is often inconvenient for consumers to get to a discount location. Savings-conscious consumers will make the long trek to a discount warehouse or mall but once they can have a product delivered to them straight from the factory, the tide will shift to the home shopping market for all major purchases.

Although in the future consumers will be able to rotate or zoom in on any product and have all questions answered interactively on their television screens, the desire to personally examine products will not disappear, and will create a demand for display outlets that feature a sample of each product from a number of manufacturers who rent space at the display outlet. The consumer will come to the display outlet – which will be conveniently located – and examine the product he or she is interested in and will order the item from the manufacturer represented at the outlet. In every large urban centre, this kind of ongoing trade show will exist for each category of items. Large discounters will have to narrow their market to lower-priced, low-involvement products requiring minimal floor staff, so as to keep prices competitive with the home shopping market. However, there will always be a demand for face-to-face customer service, since not all consumers are sophisticated enough to trust their own judgment. Moreover, just as not everyone subscribes to or takes the advice of consumer report magazines, some individuals will balk at the idea of hiring a consumer purchasing agent for assistance.

How close are we to shoppers' nirvana? Although it's still a few years off, the fact that Wal-Mart is now offering its entire 200,000 product inventory for sale on the Internet should tell you that it is definitely becoming a reality.

Department Stores

Department stores such as Eaton's, Sears, Woodwards, and The Bay will run into serious trouble trying to hold onto their customers. In the long run, these stores will not survive, at least not in their present form. Already significant changes are in progress at the major department stores. Downtown anchor stores are disappearing as shoppers stay in the suburbs. For instance, Toronto's Eaton Centre attracted 25 percent of consumers when it was built, which was much below the 50 percent who shopped downtown in the 1950s. By 1994, only 5 percent of shoppers were spending their money downtown. Eaton's has shifted to a boutique style modeled on J.C. Penney in the U.S., coupled with a three-pronged strategy that includes well-known brands (for immediate recognition and quick shopping), private-label brands (to give Eaton's its own identity), and lower-priced products (to attract the price-sensitive). Knowledgeable staff are used to distinguish it from the discounters. Re-engineering of its warehousing using EDI has already lowered inventory wage costs by 23 percent, with more savings to come. Sears has shifted more to fashion, a weak area for Wal-Mart, and from its command-and-control model – which required a 29,000-page manual of rules and procedures – to one of salesclerk empowerment. Sears managers now spend 80 to 90 percent of their time on the sales floor, as opposed to 20 percent before. Employees' pay, including even that of upper managers, now depends on customer satisfaction and subjective employee ratings. With profit margins being squeezed by falling prices, staff at all levels are rewarded by profit sharing if they help reduce costs. Even part-time employees at Zellers can earn up to $1,000 annually through profit sharing.

In 1992, Japan's department store sales were down by 5.7 percent –

the first fall in their sales since 1965. Although the Japanese are not used to discount stores, big discount companies such as Bic Camera are growing so rapidly that, for some of Bic's specials, up to 6,000 shoppers line up to get in to the stores. Using the same point-of-sale inventory control technology as the Price Club, Japanese discount retailers are willing to give up the right to return merchandise to suppliers in favour of lower prices. The regular retailers have had to resort to bypassing wholesalers altogether by buying directly from the manufacturers so as to keep prices down. The bigger companies like Bic grow, the more cost-cutting measures they can demand from manufacturers and wholesalers. As in North America, the shift in power from suppliers to discount retailers is reducing prices dramatically. When interactive shopping arrives, however, discounters will be out of business once items can be bought directly from the manufacturer via a consumer's television screen. In the U.S., department stores have begun to offer shopping channels for their stores – Macy's and Lindstrom's, for example – so that customers can browse at home first. Department store CD-ROMs are also replacing catalogues in the first step toward interactive shopping. This device allows consumers to roam the aisles visually and choose and order items electronically.

Malls

To succeed in the future, malls will have to come up with a compelling mix of retail stores and services. Some malls will focus on a common theme, such as kitchen and bathroom items. The most successful malls will carry select specialty merchandise. Besides staying on top of trends and providing excellent customer service, an innovative approach will be crucial to survival. For example, more and more malls are growing up around large discounters in order to take advantage of complementary shopping potential. Eventually, large related specialty discounters will locate their stores close to one another in order to increase their consumer drawing power. These coordinated discounter developments will become the true discount malls of the future. But no matter how a mall is configured, all Canadian mall retailers will have to deal with fierce competition from the large U.S. retail chains following in the wake of The Gap, Toys "R" Us, and Price Co., which have huge supplier networks in place in the U.S. Since these U.S. chains are typically better managed and financed, they will use price and aggressive advertising as a means of stealing market share and driving competitors out of business.

According to Daniel Sweeney, vice-chairman of retail consulting at Price Waterhouse, "You will see more superstores in malls." Independent mall stores accounted for roughly 58 percent of the retail market in 1991; however, by 1995 they constituted only 42 percent. "Big-box" retailers, in contrast, doubled their retail space from 1991 to 1995 and increased their sales 8.7 percent. Over the next ten years they plan on moving into the electronics and soft goods (for instance, women's fashion) markets. On the truly deep discount end, Liquidation World, whose stock doubled in the last half of 1995, plies its fire-sale trade through 30 Canadian warehouse stores. Other retail formats prospering in Canada over the same four-year period were catalogue stores (up 10.7 percent), specialty food stores (up 10.5 percent), specialty clothing stores (up 9.7 percent), and computer stores (up 9.7 percent).

Furniture

Between 1989 and 1995, 50 percent of the industry's 60,000 workers lost their jobs. Furniture store sales dropped 1 percent in 1995. The furniture market has been beset by a record number of bankruptcies, and will likely continue to suffer since demographics do not favour this market. There are fewer first-time homebuyers needing to furnish a home and prepare for a family. The furniture market has shifted to the home-office market, which is expected to account for 40 percent of all work done by the year 2000. While many furniture stores are going under, the Business Depot is expanding in the office supply market thanks to the boom in home offices.

Job growth will keep pace with the growth in the home office market, either in furniture or in equipment. Corporate cost-cutting and the recession have opened the markets for rented or leased furniture and recycled furniture. In addition, new technology makes it possible to remanufacture and reassemble used furniture at a fraction of its original cost. And don't overlook the office equipment export market, which flourished in 1995, nor the furniture rental market. All told, Canadian manufacturers shipped $1.69 billion worth of dressers, beds, tables, and desks down to the U.S. in the first 11 months of 1995, up 7.6 percent from the previous year. The lower Canadian dollar and the growing consumer preference for solid wood furniture as opposed to composites have helped about

50 manufacturers such as Shermag Inc. and Durham Furniture Inc. who send Colonial-style furniture south.

Food

In food retailing, discounters such as the Price Club succeed because 92 percent of their shoppers buy bulk food at discount prices, and there is a smorgasbord of items selling at a discount that browsers buy on impulse since they know the price will be reasonable. Floor staff is kept to a minimum to reduce costs. As grocery stores begin to offer bulk discount food at prices close to those found at the Price Club, as Loblaws has already begun to do, the reason for making a long trip to a warehouse – 20 kilometres on average as opposed to two to three kilometres to traditional supermarkets – will diminish, given the limited selection in the non-food categories. As other retailers move to the warehouse approach, consumers will head to the appropriate specialty discounter's warehouse.

Further intense competition in food retailing is expected to force at

---

THE ELECTRONIC SUPERMARKET

It has been predicted that by the year 2001, 20 percent of American households spending $24 billion annually will do their food shopping electronically. Demographics indicate that electronic shopping will be adopted in Canada once it can be done interactively. In Quebec, Videotron's customer services are added to the cost of cable services. Computer software marketed by Chicago's Peapod Delivery Systems allow IBM or Mac users to access an electronic supermarket stocked with 15,000 grocery items. Payment of the purchasing fee – the cost of buying goods electronically – representing 5 percent of the grocery tab plus a $4.95 delivery fee can be made electronically or on delivery. U.S. Order permits shoppers in the Washington and Detroit areas to order from a catalogue of 6,500 items using a ScanFone equipped with a credit card scanner and a light wand for scanning bar codes. Consumers have the option of avoiding delivery fees by picking up the food themselves. For those who prefer to shop in person, Anderson Consulting and Videocart have devised a shopping cart that allows shoppers to scan their groceries and pay with a debit or credit card without having to go through a checkout counter.

least one major supermarket chain out of business. A 1993 report by Ernst & Young suggests that North American supermarket chains will have dwindled from 30 to ten by the year 2000. The food retailing industry has seen more changes in the past three years than in the past 30. Consumers spend less on staples than they did 20 or 30 years ago, and most consumers are purchasing fewer higher-priced or impulse items. As a result, stores have cut prices on all items. Not surprisingly, then, Coca-Cola Beverages Ltd. share prices have dropped by over 25 percent below their 1989 high, while Cott Beverages Inc. and its house-brand soft drinks beat its 1989 high by 2000 percent. The shift has been to running low-cost, low-price operations with everyday low prices. These changes will have a profound effect on suppliers who will have to cut prices even more. This will not be a good job growth area.

According to Glen Terbeek, director of Smart Store, "Consumers have more demands on their time than ever before. They have little time to shop and prepare meals. If it makes sense for consumers to buy staples at home, retailers are going to have to be offering more specialty goods and services to attract people to their stores." This trend, along with an increase in the number of meals eaten at home but prepared elsewhere, should take hold in 1997, as emptynesters in record numbers begin to embrace such conveniences. Already many grocery stores in the U.S. are going out of business as this trend away from home cooking gathers momentum.

Clothing

Clothing stores have been hit hard not only by the recession but also by a preference on the part of the consumer to purchase casual clothes. Since these are far less expensive than the more traditional office "uniform," clothing retailers are feeling the crunch in no small measure. During 1995, men's clothing store sales fell by 6.4 percent. Ironically, with the fashion industry suggesting that women develop their own personal style, women now buy clothes less frequently. As a result, the overall 3 percent increase in clothing retail sales experienced in 1995 was at family clothing stores and department stores, suggesting that children's clothing is responsible for the increase in sales.

Demographics – such factors as the aging population, the growing wealthy retiree market, two-income families, and the increase in the

---

DRESSING FOR SUCCESS...?

Companies like General Motors and IBM are questioning their dress codes as well as their corporate structures. The president of General Motors now allows executives to dress casually if they are planning to work in their offices. Likewise, IBM – originally called Big Blue after its former blue-suited executives – is trying to alter its stiff image and mindset. Even its Canadian president has been known to wear sports shirts and casual slacks to work. Between 1985 and 1992, the number of suits sold in the U.S. fell by 34 percent, and in Canada, suit sales fell by 25 percent from 1990 to 1991. A Mediamark Research report shows that during 1992, 41 percent of men in the U.S. purchased jeans, 14 percent bought suits, and 13 percent acquired sports jackets.

---

number of children – will dictate future areas of job growth in the clothing industry. Less expensive designer lines aimed at the affluent baby boomers have done well. Similarly, the mini baby boom will lead to more designing for the upscale children's market and the maternity outfit market. Greater emphasis will be placed on meeting the clothing demands of emptynesters and the growing number of retirees. The increase in weddings has sparked more interest in this area of retail clothing as well. Even upscale designers are successfully segmenting their lines to reach different markets. In Canada, for example, six Ralph Lauren marketing salespersons earn over $600,000 each annually by marketing the various lines to different target markets.

The clothing retail market is undergoing a change structurally. Increasingly, designers and manufacturers are bypassing traditional retailers by setting up shop themselves, particularly in the high end, where there is a narrower market and where they can avoid the shake-out taking place among the department stores. Outlets operated by manufacturers and designers are replacing jobbers or discount stores. Even with department stores, the trend is toward boutiques run by manufacturers and designers who are responsible for staffing and displays. In the stores themselves, a computerized point-of-sale network called Quick Response links manufacturers, suppliers, and retailers so as to prevent overruns and to reduce order delivery time of goods. Benetton takes the guesswork out of consumer purchasing habits by using Pinpoint Retail

Systems, which identifies what customers are buying, including size, colour, and style of item. These strategies help designers and manufacturers determine what is selling and what is not, thereby allowing them to test-market merchandise and avoid costly overruns.

Another smaller but growing market is the knockoff fashion market. Within three weeks or less of the haute couture or expensive ready-to-wear lines hitting the runways, companies specializing in credible imitations at deeply reduced prices have copied the big-name designers. This market has done exceptionally well. Many designers have tried to pre-empt this business by offering their own less expensive ready-to-wear lines.

If you are interested in pursuing a career in this field, your safest bet is to stick with the demographics-oriented markets. The trend toward centralized – head-office-controlled – marketing in the U.S. has created a demand for product managers employed by apparel companies to help retailers decide their clothing design needs and then arrange for producers – typically foreign – to provide the requested items.

Where is it all headed? Itami Knitware in Japan has a software-driven machine that allows customers to design their own clothing with an automatic loom that weaves the desired material to measure. Perhaps the personal fashion statement will become the final frontier.

Cosmetics

The US$16.8 billion American cosmetics industry weathered the recession well as it experienced a 5 percent annual increase in sales. Sales for specialty products that protect the skin from sun damage have grown by 7 percent a year; men account for 27 percent of the sales from skin care products; and makeup sales are expected to increase by 10 percent annually, given an increase in demand from the aging boomer population. Job prospects in this industry are good.

Pharmacy

Currently, the pharmacy market is trying to cut costs in any way it can. Mail-order drugstores such as Meditrust Pharmacy Inc. take orders by phone, fax, and mail, then ship drugs by courier or Priority Post within 24 hours. By paying $5 per prescription as opposed to the usual $9 to $12, and ordering three months' supplies at once, individuals and companies can cut their drug plan bills by 25 percent. In the U.S., mail order has become widely accepted, with the biggest supplier, Medco Containment Services Inc., enjoying a revenue of $2 billion annually. Similar services have captured 6 percent of the pharmacy market. With drug prices often jumping 15 to 20 percent a year and the boomer population aging, an increased use of expensive pharmaceuticals will force company drug plans and governments subsidizing drugs for seniors to shift their business to the mail-order market. With drug plans expected to cost employers as much as pension plans by the year 2000, mail-order delivery is expected to grow from 17 percent to 20 percent of the market. Long-term drugs such as those for allergies, birth control, diabetes, and heart disease will end up in the mail-order market.

Fortunately for local pharmacies, the aging boomer market will likely ensure a dependable cash flow well into the future. The trend toward

BULLETIN BOARD – *RETAIL TRADE*

- **Job demand factors:** value for consumer's money; wide selection; lowest price; customer service; convenience; low inflation which lowers savings levels; low interest rates which lower household mortgage payments and other debt payments.
- **Job growth areas:** large discount stores; specialty stores offering wide selection; mail-order pharmacies; home office businesses; aging boomer fashion market; casual wear; high-tech car mechanics.
- **Skills, abilities, qualities, education needed:** computer literacy; marketing and communications skills.
- **Job reduction areas:** department stores; supermarkets; furniture stores; clothing stores; car dealerships.
- **Growth limiting factors:** the economy; home shopping technology; competition; demographics; inflation; high interest rates.

CONTACTS
- Retail Council of Canada
  #600, 210 Dundas St. West,
  Toronto, ON M4G 2E8 Tel. 416-598-4684 Fax: 416-598-3707
- Retail Merchants Association of Canada
  1780 Birchmount Rd.,
  Scarborough, ON M1P 2H8 Tel. 416-291-7903 Fax: 416-291-5635

ambulatory out-patient care favours the increased use of pharmaceuticals, which will benefit all pharmacies. With an already saturated market,
the pharmacy industry does not offer many future employment opportunities except in the mail-order area. Mass merchandisers are also beginning to steal market share, with a 32 percent growth rate in 1995, forcing
pharmacies higher up the value-added chain by offering better customer
service or a more focussed approach. Pharma Plus Drugmarts Ltd.
recently opened a 24-hour hotline and hired 10 pharmacists to answer
the calls.

Medicine Shoppe is a franchise that avoids the traditional drugstore
approach of selling everything from diapers to perfume; it uses a highly
computerized system that maximizes prescription sales. By focussing 94
percent of sales on prescriptions, pharmacists are able to earn six-figure
salaries by minimizing costs and restricting employees to one or two staff.
The biggest losers of all are the local, independent, traditional pharmacies whose market share dropped by 50 percent in the U.S. over the last
decade; the same is expected to happen in Canada. All told, aside from
the pharmacy chains with 60 percent market share in patented drug
sales, independents accounted for 17 percent of sales in 1995; food
stores and mass merchandisers, including Wal-Mart, for 6 percent.

By the end of 1995, all drugstore sales were down by 1.6 percent – the
ban on the sale of cigarettes adding an extra challenge to the industry.

Car Dealerships

According to automobile industry analyst Dennis DesRosiers, the industry has twice as many dealerships as it needs and will consequently suffer
an unavoidable shake-out and change in management style. The industry
will place greater emphasis on lowering inventories, attracting more
repair and service work, and keeping overheads low. The casualties will
likely be the big dealerships with their bloated inventories and large lots.
In Canada, the average after-tax price of a car rose to 49 percent of the
average family's annual income in 1993, compared with 37 percent in the
early 1980s. Inflation, more sophisticated automotive components, taxes,
the move from small cars to minivans and four-wheel-drive vehicles, and
the desire for more loaded vehicles account for the lag in sales as consumers cannot afford the more expensive transportation they now prefer.
In 1995, average car prices broke the $20,000 psychological barrier,

compared with $18,000 in 1993 and $16,000 in 1988. In 1991, it took 24 weeks of average salary to purchase a new car; in 1996, 32 weeks of income was required. Buyer resistance has set in to the point where used-car selling and leasing is booming.

Leasing has become a vital part of the car selling business, accounting for about 30 percent of retail sales. The latest innovation is used-car leasing. Now that cars are of higher quality, they are lasting longer, and leasing an older car makes sense since it is possible to walk away once the lease expires. The used-car market grew by 10 percent in 1995, while new vehicle sales declined by 7.6 percent. Ford has introduced Program Plus, which is geared to the leasing of older cars. In 1994, it accounted for 10 percent of the car leasing market; in 1995, 17 percent; and in January of 1996, 20 percent. By 1997, 51 percent of potential purchasers are expected to buy or lease a used car or truck. CIBC is actively pursuing the used-car loan business as a result. Most of the industry's 3.3 percent gain in sales in 1995 came from used-car dealers, gas stations, and parts and service centres.

The new-car industry and dealerships are headed for a definite crisis. New-vehicle sales fell to a 12-year low in 1995. With many car and light truck prices expected to rise by 20 percent by the year 2000 (not counting inflation) and another 20 percent in the following five years, affordability will become the dominant issue (except in the sport utility vehicle market, where the more expensive ones sell the best). Electronics will account for 20 percent of the cost in 2005, up from 15 percent in 1994 as a result of improved safety technology and other conveniences such as self-diagnostic systems. In Canada, taxes can account for 16 percent of the cost of the vehicle, compared with 5 percent in the U.S. As price becomes the main focus, buyers will buy cars over the Internet in much larger numbers through the expanding list of Web site vendors.

Superstores which sell cars, offer money-back guarantees, and have largely automated the selling process are springing up in the U.S., and even third-party selling channels such as the Price Club are entering the market. Samsung and Daewoo, which are about to enter the car market, plan on using only discount retailers such as these to sell their vehicles. When you realize that $6,700 out of the price of a $20,000 car is spent by manufacturers and dealers to distribute, market, and sell a car, there are considerable savings to be realized by a more direct means of selling.

Something has to give – especially since North American automakers have lost $100 billion over the past decade on the passenger side of the business, with only the truck market keeping them afloat. Even the replacement market, if fully exploited, is still expected to leave carmakers with 15 percent excess capacity by 2000. A shake-out of sorts is clearly inevitable. According to industry consultant J.D. Power, "Car dealers may go the way of other local retailers in groceries, home appliances, travel, and a host of other businesses."

Small reputable specialty garages will survive, since economic uncertainty makes consumers hang onto their cars longer. Now that people are driving their cars longer before trade-in, and do-it-yourselfers are having trouble fixing cars that are equipped with modern technology, the automotive repair business is bound to improve for dealers who can afford all the required technology. It is predicted that the repair market will grow from 25 percent to 27 percent of dealership business by 1997, translating into a $200 million increase. The cost of repairing old vehicles has improved slightly as a result of the free trade deal, which has kept auto parts prices competitively low, as has the selling of parts through such outlets as Price/Costco warehouses. Mechanics specializing in the newer technologies as they relate to luxury cars will be in demand as the luxury car market improves later in the decade. One factor dampening demand, however, is the increased quality of cars. Whereas ten years ago a seven-year-old car would be in the garage every couple of months, now it needs service only once or twice a year, if that.

Where the Jobs Are in the Hospitality Industry
• **Travel** • **Accommodation** • **Restaurants, Food Shops, and Catering**

Travel
The Canadian travel industry is a $29 billion business, which employs 615,000 people and attracts $8 billion a year from foreigners. It is Canada's fifth-largest export after motor vehicles and trucks, auto parts, business services, and lumber. The decline in the dollar's value has curtailed travel plans by Canadians outside Canada, but has definitely made Canada more attractive to foreigners looking for travel bargains. The exception might be visitors from the Pacific Rim who do not come for Canada's lower dollar since travel has always been inexpensive for them;

however, annual overseas travel from Taiwan jumped 121 percent and from Korea, 101 percent between 1983 and 1993. The staggering growth in the size of the middle class in Asia coupled with the globalization of trade is causing many people in emerging nations to discover the advantages of traveling. Indeed, trips by travelers from nations other than the U.S. rose by 14.6 percent in 1995, helping the industry reach an all-time high. According to the World Tourism Organization, the number of worldwide tourists is expected to double by the year 2010. Already 10 to 15 million Chinese and 80 to 85 million East Indians can afford to travel. Within five years, India's middle class should reach 400 million, given their 7 percent annual growth rate. Asian travelers now spend $15 billion per year in North America. Even domestic travel in Canada rose by 5 percent in 1995, helping to boost car rental prices by 25 percent and hotel rates by 3, 5, and 8 percent in Montreal, Toronto, and Vancouver.

Tourism is a fundamental part of many provincial and regional economies. Climate often plays a large role in determining where the vacationer will choose to go. For example, the west coast with its milder weather was favoured in 1992–93; this hurt travel to the east coast during that period. Provinces that are aiming at the 45-plus age group, such as Prince Edward Island, will likely experience substantial growth in travel. Overall, travel undertaken by aging emptynesters should pick up considerably. Vacations aboard one of the many cruise ships that sail the Inside Passage to Alaska will likely find favour with this crowd, as will adventure trips, health-related tourism, cross-border shopping trips, and ecotourism or low-environmental-impact travel. A key area that Canada can exploit is the adventure travel industry (the active exploration of a landscape, wildlife, or culture), which is one of the fastest-growing sectors of tourism, worth over $200 billion annually in the U.S. According to Jerry Mallet, president of the Adventure Travel Society, "Adventure travel includes any participatory human-powered activity such as river rafting, hiking, biking, fishing, hunting, bird-watching or wildlife viewing."

In Ontario in 1991, travel generated $17 billion, which was more revenue than forestry, agriculture, and mining combined, and accounted for 6.6 percent of Ontario's work force. Losing 7 percent of the U.S. and overseas market between 1986 and 1991 was cause for concern, considering the travel industry is the fourth-biggest industry in Ontario and represents the fourth-biggest area of exporting.

Canada's poor road infrastructure, with 40 percent of its roads sub-standard, will take its toll on tourism, because Americans traveling by car make up 78 percent of Canada's foreign tourism market. Since 1986, 17 percent fewer Americans have traveled to Canada, yet the number of Canadians traveling to the U.S. during that period doubled. The demographic shift of Americans to the South hasn't done the Canadian travel industry any good, either. Aggressive marketing is necessary to impress upon Americans that travel bargains are to be had in Canada. Hopefully the Canadian Tourism Commission, created in 1995 as a public-private partnership devoted to promoting Canada as a tourist destination, will be more effective in getting the message out now that more of the marketing and promotional activities will be delivered by the private sector.

"Canada has become the world leader in taxes on air travel," according to Brian Symic, president of the Canadian Travel Associates. Taxes and fees now amount to 35 percent of an airplane trip. The Canadian Tourism Research Institute found that the GST alone cost the travel industry $1 billion in 1993. Unless this situation is addressed, no amount of tourism advertising can overcome a lack of competitive pricing, especially if the Canadian dollar ever appreciates in value. Unless the cost structure is reformed Canada may miss out on a potentially larger share of a world growth industry.

Canadian business travelers are definitely returning to the skies and staying away longer as well. According to the Canadian Tourism Research Institute, international travel rose by 11 percent, with trips to the U.S. increasing by 8 percent and domestic travel by 2 percent. Since business in South America and the Far East requires several trips in order to clinch deals, we can expect this travel segment to grow.

Cruise lines, airlines, resorts, and hotels will compete with one another in selling travel services themselves to avoid paying travel commissions to agencies. On-line services such as the American Sabre reservation system make this easy since consumers can use their home computers to reserve directly. Ameritech and Random House jointly acquired the virtual company Worldview Systems, which publishes an electronic current-event travel database on over 170 travel destinations around the world; it could be used to deliver travel information directly to customer homes. TravelWeb gives individuals booking access to over 6,000 hotels with photos, room rates, weather forecasts, local area maps, and complete descriptions of all amenities information as well. At some airlines, such as United Airlines, roughly 15 percent of reservations are already being made by electronic means, which allow remote ticketless booking and automated-boarding-pass pickup. Air Canada's similar system helps curb distribution costs, which constitute 20 percent of operating expenses. Airlines are even experimenting with on-line auctions as a kind of Internet last-minute club. Microsoft is joining with United Airlines "to lead travelers into the 21st century" by combining air, hotel, and car reservations into a single consumer computer access system that completely bypasses travel agents. Microsoft, which is building its travel services into its Windows operating system, proposes to charge only $5 versus the 25 percent of a hotel room's revenue that a travel agent normally earns in commission. GTS Global Travel Services in Mississauga, Ontario, offers its do-it-yourself booking system called ResAssist to corporate clients so that they can completely manage and monitor all aspects of their corporate travel arrangements.

As a consequence of all this interactivity, there is a shift away from agency commissions, which were being capped anyway, to fee-for-service, commission splitting, rebates, or direct negotiation, as recommended by the Business Travel Contractors Corporation in the U.S. The BTCC will negotiate airfares directly with airlines on behalf of a number of large corporations, thereby reducing fares by up to 20 percent. Already the American Society of Travel Agents is anticipating that one-third of its members could go under as a result. As if these problems weren't enough, in France supermarket chains are now selling travel services. Thus there will have to be a consolidation of travel agencies in the upcoming shake-out. According to *Travel Weekly*, the small or medium-sized agencies which survive will do so by targeting small and medium-sized corporations, often in the sales incentive market, which rewards top sales staff by giving them trips. Specialization and niche marketing will become the key to survival, especially for small travel companies, and consortiums of independent, non-chain agencies will have to form networks to match the purchasing and marketing power of chains and franchise operations. Some travel agents are proposing to charge customers directly – a strategy that will require innovative value-added solutions.

Automation is expected to increase in the industry as more agencies

BULLETIN BOARD – *TRAVEL*

- **Job demand factors:** low dollar; aging boomer market; eventual economic growth; globalization of trade; growing number of middle-class travelers in Asia and South America; Open Skies.
- **Job growth areas:** companies focussing on the 45-plus boomer market; ecotourism; adventure trips; corporate incentive travel; computer travel systems experts; B.C.'s Golden Triangle (Vancouver, Victoria, and Whistler).
- **Skills, abilities, qualities, education needed:** computer literacy; communications, problem-solving, and marketing skills.
- **Job reduction areas:** companies restructuring, merging, or going out of business.
- **Growth limiting factors:** teleconferencing and fax machines; disappearance of middle management; the weather; road infrastructure; the Canadian dollar; international competition for tourists; travel taxes, fees, and duties.

CONTACTS
- Alliance of Canadian Travel Associations
  #201, 1729 Bank Street
  Ottawa, ON K1V 7Z5 Tel. 613-521-0474 Fax: 613-521-0805
- Tourism Industry Association of Canada
  #1016, 130 Albert Street,
  Ottawa, ON K1P 5G4 Tel. 613-238-3883 Fax: 613-238-3878
  E-mail: tiac@achilles.net
  URL: http://www.achilles.net/~tiac/homepage.htm

complement their on-line reservation systems with computerized management systems that track suppliers and customers. Worldwide travel computer standardization is slowly taking shape and will require the hiring of corporate travel professionals or managers with appropriate computer skills for multinational companies.

According to the report "Travel & Tourism: The World's Largest Industry," gross sales of travel and tourism accounted for $3.5 trillion of gross domestic product in 1993 (6 percent of world total, 7 percent of global capital spending, 13 percent of worldwide consumer spending, and 200 million jobs, or 10 percent of the global work force). Expenditures on travel and tourism are expected to rise from $1.8 trillion in 1990 to $5.8 trillion in 2005, a compounded growth rate of 3.9 percent annually, adding another 150 million jobs. Despite further worldwide political fragmentation and tension in such countries as Germany, Russia, and the former Yugoslavia, the 1990s are viewed as more promising than the 1980s with respect to the travel industry.

Accommodation

The hotel business will be adversely affected by the decline in business travel. The construction boom of the 1980s led to an oversupply of hotel rooms similar to the overbuilding that characterized the commercial real estate. The ensuing intense competition in the 1990s is likely to bring about industry segmentation with two types of hotels emerging: the high-quality luxury hotels catering to the older, affluent traveler, and the limited-service hotel geared to the economy market. As with the travel agency market, consolidation of hotels is likely to continue, given that

---

BULLETIN BOARD – *ACCOMMODATION*

- **Job demand factors:** aging boomer market; globalization of trade; hotel rooms need to substitute for offices; growing market of economizers who cannot afford luxury travel.
- **Job growth areas:** multilingual staff for international hotels; marketing personnel; luxury hotels aimed at older wealthy patrons; market-focussed budget accommodation.
- **Skills needed:** communications; knowledge of foreign languages; computer, problem-solving, and marketing skills.
- **Job reduction areas:** medium-level hotels which are neither budget- nor luxury-oriented; hotel jobs which are being automated.
- **Growth limiting factors:** telecommunications technology replacing business travel and eventually personal travel to some extent; international competition.

CONTACTS

☛ Hotel Association of Canada
  #1016, 130 Albert St.,
  Ottawa, ON K1P 5G4 Tel. 613-238-3878 Fax: 613-238-3978

half of the rooms worldwide are already controlled by the top 25 chains. If independent hotels are to survive, they will have to join chains, or form consortiums to gain the financial and marketing competitiveness of the larger chains.

To capture the business travel market, hotels will have to offer guests rooms that include fax and answering machines, computers, modems, and other office equipment, as CP Hotels & Resorts, Hyatt Hotels, and Delta Hotels & Resorts now do. Other services – meeting rooms, sports and health facilities – will need to be first-rate. The economy business travel market will likely offer business facilities centrally located, and the rooms will operate on a self-serve basis, with food vending machines and built-in bars.

Hotels are becoming internationalized as trade becomes more global. They must now offer foreign guests the services and cuisine they are accustomed to in their own countries. Hotels interested in capturing this end of the market must hire multilingual staff, offer cosmopolitan menus, and provide multilingual directories, brochures, and pamphlets. Moreover, staff must be willing and able to offer a variety of information and assistance to foreigners confused by Canadian customs.

The hotel industry is shifting from operations-based management to a marketing focus. Hotels are working harder to bring in business by catering to the particular needs of a market segment. Hotels will, for example, begin to offer special services directed to an aging population, such as nursing care and geriatric health care while the individual is a guest of the hotel. Eventually, the hotel industry may even enter the senior citizen housing market by renting rooms to seniors on a monthly or yearly basis, and by providing appropriate support services such as health care.

Technology and automation are facilitating the reservation and service aspects of operating a hotel – remote check-in, in-room checkout, robotic cleaning, and smart cards that serve as keys – but will reduce the numbers of check-in, cleaning, and reservations staff.

Motels, resorts, and bed and breakfast accommodation geared to the needs of aging boomers will grow in those areas or locations most likely to appeal to the travel and sightseeing wishes of this market segment. The accommodation market improved enough in 1995 that many providers were able to raise their fees back to more profitable operating levels.

Restaurants, Food Shops, and Catering

Restaurants must keep a close eye on their bottom lines, or they will very quickly go out of business, especially since in 1995 there were twice as many restaurants per capita in Canada as in the U.S., according to the Canadian Restaurant and Foodservices Association. The average restaurant had an after-tax return on sales of only 2.1 percent in 1994, with seafood and steak theme restaurants being the least profitable. To a great extent, the prima donna chefs and extravagant restaurants of the 1980s have been replaced by restaurants serving simpler foods in generous portions. The emphasis has shifted to value and comfort foods.

The risk associated with seeking employment in trend-oriented restaurants lies in the restaurant's timing in taking up one trend or moving on to the next. Following trends usually implies frequent renovations, expensive chefs, fickle public tastes, and lots of competition. Complicating matters further, consumers are increasingly patronizing take-out gourmet shops, the precooked-food departments of supermarkets, delis, drive-throughs, and food delivery companies. As a result, the restaurant market is shrinking and will continue to do so, at least until emptynesters grow in numbers and begin to go out to restaurants again. Since many older people often prefer blander, healthier foods, it is likely the neighbourhood restaurant that offers excellent customer service, a healthier menu, value for money, and take-out and delivery will do well.

The shift to cocooning and the emphasis on family values has also created a shift to convenience foods. Parents who would prefer to spend quality time with their children rather than hours preparing meals from scratch are opting for convenience foods. A survey conducted by the Canadian Restaurant and Foodservice Association indicated that consumers were moving away from better-quality food, which saw an 8 percent drop from 1991 to 1992, toward better value, which increased by 11 percent over the same period.

As the closing of a number of Olive Garden restaurants and 13 of Red Lobster's 70 full-service, sit-down restaurants indicates, Canadians do not like the concept of dining uniformity in the medium-priced restaurant market. In contrast to the U.S., where Red Lobster had more than US$1.5 billion in sales in 1992 and over a 25 percent share of this particular food market, the cost of doing business in Canada – high

overhead, the Goods and Services Tax (GST), other taxes, minimum
wage – precludes success unless the volume is extremely high. In the
U.S., Olive Garden and Red Lobster restaurants account for 33 percent
of sales for General Mills Inc., which plans to open 50 more restaurants
there. Taco Bell Corp., on the other hand, is enjoying a phenomenal success in Canada. Pursuing a no-frills fast-food approach, the chain was able
to drop its prices by 25 percent over the past five years. Half the items on
its menu sell for under a dollar. Its expansion into the public gathering-
place market – airports, schools, and movie theatres – via portable carts
and kiosks has been a stunning success. Taco Bell opened 30 new outlets
in 1996, a 36 percent increase, by teaming up with its KFC franchises.
The convenience and value that are the winning combination here will
also boost sales in the food vending machine business. Customers are
now able to purchase a cappuccino from a machine for as little as 70 cents.
Items such as pizza, piroshki, and french fries are also available in vending machines.

According to Dun & Bradstreet, the most profitable restaurants are
franchises, with the best money makers offering baked goods (such as
doughnut, coffee, and bagel shops). Slightly less profitable were pizza
and soup-and-sandwich restaurants. Although there has been growth in
coffee bars serving espresso and cappuccino, Americans (and presum-
ably Canadians) only drink about half as much coffee as they did in the
early 1960s. According to industry analyst John Maxwell, "People have
been moving away from hot and acrid drinks for decades."

Where are restaurants doing the best? The most profitable restaurants
are in Manitoba and Saskatchewan, and the least profitable ones are in
Quebec. With respect to stability, however, Ontario had the least stable
market and Quebec and the Maritimes the most stable. The restaurant
industry has never fully recovered from the introduction of the GST in
1991 – as a result, Canadian restaurants' "share of the stomach" fell from
42 to 36 percent, whereas it is still 44 percent in the U.S. Profit margins
have fallen from 8 to 5 percent. The only good news is that chains have
boosted their market share from 39 to 53 percent at the expense of
independent restaurants. Those restaurant chains pursuing the emptynesters, such as Kelsey's, are doing well by blurring the differences
between fine dining and casual fast food. Chart your career course with
a chain going after this market.

BULLETIN BOARD – *RESTAURANTS, FOOD SHOPS, AND CATERING*

- **Job demand factors:** aging population wishing convenience foods and healthy light foods; weak economy reinforces value as a priority; cocooners or families preferring to eat at home.
- **Job growth areas:** take-out; delis; supermarket-prepared foods; home delivery; catering to the elderly.
- **Job reduction areas:** expensive restaurants which do not give value for money.
- **Growth limiting factors:** public tastes; economy; competition; demographics.

CONTACTS

☛ Canadian Restaurant and Foodservices Association
316 Bloor Street West
Toronto, ON M5S 1W5 Tel. 416-923-8416 Fax: 416-923-1450
Toll-free: 1-800-387-5649

Value-oriented catering companies will do well in the 1990s once the economy shows a modest improvement. Catering, chain, or contract firms that target daycare centres, nursing homes, continuing care communities, and facilities for the elderly of any other kind are likely to prosper over the long term.

Where the Jobs Are in Culture and Recreation
• Culture • Publishing • Motion Picture, Audio, and Video Production and Distribution • Sports and Recreation Clubs and Services • Hobbies and Crafts

Culture
Approximately 430,000 Canadians work in the cultural sector. Canadians spend $29 billion on the arts and cultural goods and services annually. This represents a 63 percent increase from 1982 and is surpassed only by the amount of spending on shelter, food, and transportation.

Although the federal arts policies of the 1970s and 1980s led to a cultural labour force growth rate of 122 percent over the last ten years – twice the growth rate of the labour market as a whole – total direct

BULLETIN BOARD — *CULTURE*

CONTACTS
☛ Canadian Conference of the Arts
   189 Laurier Ave. West,
   Ottawa, ON K1N 6P1 Tel. 613-238-3561 Fax: 613-238-4849
   Toll-free: 1-800-463-3561
☛ Council for Business & the Arts in Canada
   #1507, 401 Bay St.,
   Toronto, ON M5H 2Y4 Tel. 416-869-3016 Fax: 416-869-0435

and indirect federal arts spending has declined from approximately
$2.93 billion in 1989–90 to $2.4 billion in 1995–96. The GST has reduced
magazine circulation by 5.7 percent, and newsstand sales are down
30 percent. The postal subsidy to book and magazine publishers has
been reduced by 50 percent, with further cuts pending. Canadian film
production capital cost allowances have dropped from 100 percent to
30 percent, and legislation to give Canada more control over film
distribution was abandoned in the wake of the Free Trade Agreement.
These reductions have lowered employment in many areas and short-
ened the season for performing arts groups. Thus, although "the cultural
industries . . . in the 1980s ranked fifth in employment, fourth in wages
and salaries, and ninth in revenues among Canada's manufacturing sectors," according to a Film and Television Council of Canada report, those
looking for jobs in the cultural sectors should be aware of government
cutbacks in funding and their likely impact on the future of employment
in this sector.

NAFTA, which militates against Canada's strengthening its cultural
sectors, will pose a serious challenge to Canadian cultural industries.
Consider the following statistics: Canadian books account for only
20 percent of the Canadian market; Canadian sound recordings,
11 percent; Canadian magazines, 10 percent; Canadian-made English-
language television drama, 8 percent; and Canadian films, 4 percent
of the movie market and 5 percent of the home video market. One
happy exception was the 30 percent jump in the sale of recordings with
Canadian content in 1993–94. Perhaps the Liberal government's job

creation programs will boost the cultural sector in a way that does not breach NAFTA, since it takes only $20,000 to create a job in this sector, versus $100,000 in light industry and $200,000 in heavy industry. Indeed, spinoff industries create 490,000 jobs and generate an additional $22 billion for the Canadian economy.

A 1995 study by Ekos Research found that most Canadians are not very concerned about the fate of CBC newscasts or theatre and dance companies. According to Revenue Canada, charitable donations to the arts from individuals have declined since 1990, and corporate donations fell $30 million between 1990 and 1994. In contrast to the U.S., our tax deductions for charitable donations do not make giving to the arts very attractive – but do favour donations to hospitals and universities, which benefit from Crown corporation status.

Although 60 percent of the people working in cultural industries are men, women dominate dance and choreography (69 percent), visual art (60 percent), arts-related clerical and sales positions (63 percent), and arts-related teaching positions (53 percent). Cultural workers are often self-employed (43 percent), with half holding two jobs (though the second job is not necessarily in the arts). A second job is often necessary because the average fine arts graduate earns only $15,800, with painters and sculptors receiving only $8,800 annually in 1993. Ironically, despite low salaries, 90 percent of fine arts graduates say they would choose the same field again, compared with 15 to 25 percent for most other occupations.

Although only 15 percent of the Canadian labour force has a university degree, 51 percent in the arts do. Most cultural workers (77 percent) are found in Ontario, Quebec, and British Columbia.

Publishing

The publishing industry serves a $1.5 billion market which is headed for difficult times. Costs are killing the industry as the GST and shipping, mailing, and paper and production costs reduce profit margins to less than 1 percent in some cases. In addition, in 1995 publishing subsidies were reduced by $24 million, newsprint and paper prices soared 40 to 70 percent, recycled paper costs jumped 400 percent, and advertisers began exploring other media such as on-line advertising. Consequently, 24 to 50 Canadian publishers (22 percent) may disappear between 1995 and 1997, eliminating 8 percent of the jobs in this sector. The 18 percent further reduction in postal subsidies as part of the 29 percent cut in the Department of Heritage's spending between 1994 and 1999 will hurt Canadian books and magazines.

Competition in the form of electronic books will pose a new challenge to the industry. At the 1993 American Booksellers Association conference in Miami, the Voyageur Co. showed a compact disc that provides both text and a video performance of *Macbeth* on the same monitor. By the 1995 ABA conference, CD-ROMs, floppy discs, and game cartridges, which are carried by 24 percent of ABA members, accounted for 15 percent of total revenues, and their product displays took up twice as much floor space as in 1994. At the 1993 Frankfurt Book Fair, 170 companies filled a hall under a banner that read "Frankfurt Goes Electronic" and displayed electronic gadgetry that sang, spoke, and moved. Klaus Sauer of the German Booksellers and Publishers Association tried to put these changes in perspective by saying, "The function of the publisher does not consist of trading paper. [It is] the task of communicating the intellectual product of the author to the end-user by the best means possible." Some industry experts predict that by the year 2000, roughly 40 percent of the publishing business will be electronically based. Will this new technology kill the printed book? Florian Langenscheidt, whose family owns one of Europe's biggest language and reference publishers, answered the question cryptically: "Neither the bicycle nor walking were killed off by the car."

The Canadian book market has been growing by only 3 or 4 percent annually over the past couple of years, compared with 10 percent growth in the U.S. once superstores made their presence felt. Mass merchandisers in Canada such as Price Club/Costco or Wal-Mart, which carry only a limited selection, are capable of selling up to 20,000 copies of a bestseller in one weekend by discounting them by 25 to 40 percent off retail price. Only stores selling in excess of $1 million of a publisher's product get a 45 percent discount off retail price when purchasing wholesale; everyone else pays closer to 40 percent, so independent booksellers are seriously threatened by the advent of large megastores such as Chapters, the mass merchandisers, and on-line bookstores such as Amazon.com. As the 31 percent growth in book sales in the U.S. between 1991 and 1994 demonstrates, consumers end up reading more when prices are lowered and when they can buy books from more kinds of outlets, such as drugstores and supermarkets. However, the independent sellers cannot keep pace; their market share fell from 32.5 percent in 1991 to 19 percent in 1994 in the U.S. Since consumers always dictate who will win in the end, job seekers should avoid independent booksellers, except those specializing in niche markets that are doing well, such as business and computer books.

Which Canadian book publishers are likely to survive? Those publishers who exported saw their sales triple between 1989–90 and 1993–94, while domestic sales rose by only 7.6 percent during that period. Library sales fell by 22 percent and schools made do with older textbooks (spending on books and other such classroom resources fell by 8.5 percent between 1991 and 1995, yet education spending increased by 38 percent, according to the Canadian Book Publishers' Council).

Textbook publishers are not immune to the impact of new technology, either. McMaster University is the first Canadian institution to use "demand-print" technology: it uses Xerox's Docutech machine to print books and course materials on demand, allowing revision on an ongoing basis. These custom textbooks can be produced for $12, including royalties, as opposed to the $35 price for the average publisher-produced university textbook. This technology now makes it possible for any book to be published wherever the system is located (perhaps in a bookstore), bypassing publishers entirely and eliminating distribution, inventory, and warehousing costs – and with no unsold copies left over. Docutech can reproduce an entire book, including binding and cover, within a minute.

According to Statistics Canada, 162 Canadian magazines have folded since 1989, and those remaining have seen their circulation and revenues decline, causing salaries to fall by 4 percent and full-time employment by 8.5 percent. General interest magazines such as *Maclean's*, which are the biggest sellers, saw their circulation fall by 1 million in 1993–94 alone. The full brunt of the decline in postal subsidies will be felt in 1996–97, reducing circulation figures further. The dramatic rise in newsprint cost has had the newspaper industry reeling as well and caused Southam Inc. to lay off another 750 workers in 1996 on top of the 1,400 let go over the previous three years. Although the industry is relieved that split-run publications which combine foreign content with Canadian advertising, such as *Sports Illustrated*, are now effectively cost prohibitive, it is likely only a temporary victory since the U.S. has appealed to the World Trade

BULLETIN BOARD – *PUBLISHING*

- **Job growth areas:** researchers; scriptwriters for broadcast journalism.
- **Growth limiting factors:** electronic books; other media; trend toward multimedia presentation of information and fiction; U.S. split-run magazine publications.

CONTACTS

☛ Association of Canadian Publishers
#301, 2 Gloucester Street
Toronto, ON M4Y 1L5 Tel. 416-413-4929 Fax: 416-413-4920
URL: http://www.can.net/marketplace/pub/acp/acp.htm

☛ Canadian Association of Photographers and
      Illustrators in Communications
#322, 100 Broadview Avenue
Toronto, ON M4M 2E8 Tel. 416-462-3700 Fax: 416-462-3678

☛ Canadian Book Marketing Centre
#301, 2 Gloucester Street
Toronto, ON M4Y 1L5 Tel. 416-413-4930 Fax: 416-413-4920

☛ Canadian Book Publishers' Council
#203, 250 Merton St.,
Toronto, ON M4S 1B1 Tel. 416-322-7011 Fax: 416-322-6999

☛ Canadian Booksellers Association
301 Donlands Ave.,
Toronto, ON M4J 3R8 Tel. 416-467-7883 Fax: 416-467-7886
E-mail: cba@flexnet.com

☛ Canadian Daily Newspaper Publishers Association
#1100, 890 Yonge St.,
Toronto, ON M4W 3P4 Tel. 416-923-3567 Fax: 416-923-7206

☛ Canadian Magazine Publishers Association
#202, 130 Spadina Avenue
Toronto, ON M5V 2L4 Tel. 416-504-0274 Fax: 416-504-0437

☛ The Don't Tax Reading Coalition
301 Donlands Ave.,
Toronto, ON M4J 3R8 Tel. 416-467-7904 Fax: 416-361-0643

☛ Electronic Desktop Publishing Association
258 Poole Drive
Oakville, ON L6H 3W4 Tel. 905-842-9534

Organization regarding the legitimacy of the tax sanctions recently instituted. Time Warner Inc. has plans to use the Internet as a means of reaching Canadian readers, thereby rendering government intervention meaningless. Since on-line publication allows viewers to be directly in touch with advertisers and manufacturers, this is where the advertising dollars will go. Between 1989–90 and 1993–94, advertising revenues fell by 14 percent – even the *Toronto Star*'s ad revenues declined 35 percent in 1995 from their 1988 peak.

Newer innovations include Chinese-language editions of *Toronto Life* and *Maclean's* magazines, produced by teaming up with *Ming Pao Daily* and *Sing Tao Daily* respectively. These editions are aimed at the 500,000 Canadians of Chinese origin in Canada, of whom 30 percent earn over $47,000 and 58 percent have a university degree. Of the specialty magazines prospering at the moment, the big revenue generators are the computer, sports, fishing, and hunting magazines.

In the long term, magazines and newspapers will be replaced by the multimedia format, which is where their advertisers will probably migrate. The increasing trend toward narrowcasting and information programming on television will overtake the magazine and newspaper industry once television becomes fully interactive. In the not too distant future, viewers will be able to ask their "channel box" – VCRs will disappear since VCR-type information can be computer-stored – to scan all programs that cover certain topics and anthologize the material for later viewing. Using Compuserve, a computer information service, viewers can ask their computers to search for news stories on any topic from the various wire services and store them. The Journalist program, by PED Software, will customize a consumer's on-line newspaper by gathering news items of interest from the various news services and placing them in prearranged columns. Some magazines now appear first in Compuserve, America On-line, or Prodigy before they turn up on the stands. Over 25 magazines such as *Maclean's, The New Yorker,* and *The Economist* are now available via the electronic newsstand found on the Internet. Recently *Time* magazine and Kiplinger's *Personal Finance* magazine allowed subscribers to view text, ask questions, and comment on articles through these networks, and *Newsweek* introduced a quarterly CD-ROM. Within three weeks of its introduction, *Time* found that its subscribers had used the service 126,563 times.

According to Opinion Search Inc. of Ottawa, in 1994, 40 percent of businesses and 30 percent of households indicated an interest in subscribing to electronic newspapers. Now that the CRTC has designated cable as a common carrier, newspapers will able to take advantage of cable Internet services, as can other forms of publication. Already Yahoo, a large indexing service on the Web, lists 94 commercial newspapers, including three Canadian papers. Infopike News offers news customized to your preferences in an on-line, interactive, multimedia format. It will ultimately replace regular TV and newspaper news services.

Many publishers are diversifying out of non-growth areas such as newspaper publishing into on-line companies; Thomson Corp., for example, sold off 46 North American newspapers (as well as all of its British papers) and spent $4 billion purchasing Information Access Co., a U.S. reference data service, and Medstat Group, an American medical information service. Southam has applied for a specialty TV licence and purchased an on-line job-search service along with Torstar. And Torstar has invested in a U.S. cable-television channel.

Motion Picture, Audio, and Video Production and Distribution

In 1995, films and television projects generated over $750 million in revenue for Canada, with local network programs, commercials, and in-house corporate film bringing the total to a record $1.2 billion. Between 1990 and 1994, film and video production sales increased by 12 percent per year, TV production by 31 percent per year. Exports grew by 90 percent between 1991 and 1994, with made-for-TV productions accounting for over 80 percent of total exports in 1994. Between 1983 and 1988, the independent Canadian film and television industry personnel roster grew from 6,400 to 29,000. And in 1995, the production industry generated 30,000 new jobs in Ontario. In 1995, the film industry spent $501 million in Ontario, $495 million of the total in independent productions; film and television production in B.C. brought the province $400 million in 1994. For Ontario, the centre of activity was Toronto; for B.C., it was in Vancouver. Every dollar spent in film and production in Canada generates several more in spinoff businesses, with real estate companies, car rental companies, cleaners, hotels, caterers, and restaurants among those benefitting.

Ninety-five percent of Canada's $1.2 billion film industry is concentrated in the Greater Toronto Area. More than 500 films have been shot in Toronto in the past decade. Toronto is the third-largest film-making centre in North America. Several factors contribute to the industry's growth in Toronto: high-quality, low-cost equipment, talent, and film crews are available in Toronto – $75,000 per day to film a television show in New York, $35,000 in Toronto; Toronto's post-production facilities eliminate the need to fly to Los Angeles or New York for editing; American production companies have found that Canadian unions are more flexible than their U.S. counterparts; Toronto is the broadcast capital of Canada with the head offices of the Canadian Broadcasting Corporation (CBC), CTV, and Global located there. From 1990 to 1995, the Ontario government spent $14 million annually on rebates to investors in Ontario film and television productions, stimulating $400 million in production rebates; however, the Harris government froze both Ontario Film Development Corporation investment funding (which amounted to cutting its budget by one-third) and the Ontario Film Investment Program tax rebates, which had helped stem the flow of Canadian talent to the U.S. and made Canadian movies more attractive as investments.

Vancouver is equally attractive for television and film production, with its excellent locations, a climate that allows year-round shooting, and North America's largest sound stage – the Bridge Studios. Moreover, it takes only two hours and 15 minutes to fly from L.A. to Vancouver. In 1978, B.C.'s film industry was worth only $12 million; by 1996, it was worth $400 million. B.C., however, has followed Ontario's lead and has cut back its B.C. Film Fund from $4.3 million to $3.9 million. The Alberta film industry is also worried now that the provincial government is cutting its financial ties to the industry. The federal government's Telefilm budget has experienced cutbacks as well.

In 1995 Quebec was responsible for 35 percent of all Canadian production, thanks to the 18 percent tax rebate for every new job created. Its industry grew from $120 million in 1993 to $200 million in 1994. Another fast-growing province is Nova Scotia, which offers a 15 percent tax rebate that has helped its production industry grow from $13 million in 1993 to $40 million in 1994. All the other provinces, with the exception of Manitoba, have seen their film revenues rise by roughly one-third between 1993 and 1994. Even Canadian-content production broke

BULLETIN BOARD – *MOTION PICTURE, AUDIO, AND VIDEO*

- **Job demand factors:** inexpensive production facilities and flexible unions; high-quality facilities, technical staff and talent pool; need for more programming in a 500-channel world.
- **Job growth areas:** all aspects of film and television production; post-production; special effects; video production; animation and videogame development.
- **Skills, abilities, qualities, education needed:** communications, visual, auditory, analytical, creative, and problem-solving skills.
- **Job reduction areas:** film distribution industry.
- **Growth limiting factors:** legislation surrounding distribution rights; government incentives; cost advantages of filming in Canada.

the $1 billion barrier in 1994, up from $84 million in 1983.

The recession has led some Canadian broadcasters such as CTV, the country's largest, to decrease its commitment to Canadian programming by 37 percent. Since it costs only about $65,000 per hour to air an American sitcom, versus spending 10 to 20 times that amount producing the Canadian equivalent, the difference in the profits a company can realize has created considerable tension in the industry.

The Directors Guild of Canada would like to see more of the $1.5 billion in annual film and video revenues stay in Canada instead of flowing back to Hollywood companies. But it looks as though the federal government may allow Polygram Filmed Entertainment to establish a film distribution company in Canada. In the past five years, $224 million of the $232 million in film distribution payments received by Canadian-controlled companies ended up providing over 28 percent of the production money for Canadian films.

The technological innovations leading to large-screen television and video-on-demand will likely undermine the movie theatre industry as more cocooners opt for watching movies at home. Theatres which specialize in large-screen formats for Imax-style films will continue to attract an audience, but in the long run, 3-D or virtual reality movies will supplant the spectacular effects of the larger screens. By the year 2000, all movie theatres will receive their films for projection via

BULLETIN BOARD — *MOTION PICTURE, AUDIO, AND VIDEO*

CONTACTS

- Academy of Canadian Cinema & Television
  158 Pearl St.,
  Toronto, ON M5H 1L3 Tel. 416-591-2040 Fax: 416-591-2157
- Alliance of Canadian Cinema, Television and Radio Artists
  2239 Yonge St.,
  Toronto, ON M4S 2B5 Tel. 416-489-1311 Fax: 416-489-1435
- Association of Canadian Film Craftspeople (Ind.)
  #105, 65 Heward Ave.,
  Toronto, ON M4M 2T5 Tel. 416-462-0211 Fax: 416-462-3248
- Canadian Alliance of Video Professionals
  #400, 407 St-Laurent, Montreal, PQ H2Y 2Y5
- Canadian Film and Television Production Association
  #806, 175 Bloor Street East
  Toronto, ON M4W 3R8 Tel. 416-927-8942 Fax: 416-922-4038
- Canadian Motion Picture Distributors' Association
  #1603, 22 St. Clair Ave. East,
  Toronto, ON M4T 2S3 Tel. 416-961-1888 Fax: 416-968-1016
- Directors' Guild of Canada
  #401, 387 Bloor St. East,
  Toronto, ON M4W 1H7 Tel. 416-972-0098 Fax: 416-972-6058
- Independent Film & Video Alliance
  #3000, 5505 Boul. St-Laurent
  Montreal, PQ H2T 1S6 Tel. 514-277-0328 Fax: 514-277-0419
  Toll-free: 1-800-567-0328
  E-mail: ifva@cam.org
  URL: http://www.ffa.ucalgary.ca/
- Video Production Association
  PO Box 53025, Erin Mills Post Office,
  5100 Erin Mills Pkwy.,
  Mississauga, ON L5M 5A7 Tel. 905-828-0634

satellite, eliminating many jobs in the film distribution industry.

Many special effects companies have grown up around the film industry. Animation and morphing software companies have flourished in Canada, with Alias Research producing the software for such movies as *Aliens, Terminator 2*, and *Jurassic Park*. Other fringe companies focus on small market niches. Pyrotek Special Effects, for example, specializes in creating indoor pyrotechnics as well as creating the stunning effects of devastation and destruction in movies such as *Prom Night IV* and *Blown Away*.

One area where Canada is a world leader is animation, which is now a $150 million Canadian industry. In December 1995, Walt Disney Company announced its plans to open studios in Toronto and Vancouver and hire 200 people at all levels of production. According to Lenora Hume, vice-president of production for Disney's animation division, "Next to the U.S., Canada probably has the largest talent pool globally." Aside from having a large number of digital graphics artists and com-puter animators, roughly 75 percent of the software needed for com-puter animation is designed here by firms such as Alias/Wavefront (acquired by Silicon Graphics) and Montreal's SoftImage, owned by Microsoft. Hollywood studios, TV broadcasters, and even MTV are trying to set up animation studios or hire out production. Canada's two largest animation companies, Cinar Films Inc. and Nelvana Ltd., are lobbying along with YTV and the Family Channel to have the CRTC approve an animation channel. Nelvana is the major supplier of Saturday-morning cartoons to U.S. networks, while Cinar emphasizes non-violent children's programming. Since going public a few years ago, Cinar's stock has tripled and Nelvana's has increased by 59 percent. Nelvana employs 250 people and Cinar, 50; but both hire an additional 100 during busy times. The market for animation is incredibly diverse; for instance, International Rocketship Ltd. of Vancouver, founded by Marv Newland, the creator of *Bambi Meets Godzilla*, does award-winning commercials, Gary Larson Far Side specials, and pornographic satire. Vancouver's Mainframe Entertainment Inc. makes *ReBoot* – the world's first computer-animated TV series. And don't forget that computer games are worth $13 billion per year, or $1.3 billion more than Hollywood's box office receipts.

Over 75 computer animation companies employing 1,500 people are spread out across the country but mostly in Montreal, Toronto, and Vancouver. The Greater Toronto Area is home to about half of them. When the NFB's budget was cut, everything disappeared except its pro-duction department, which has spearheaded animation development in Canada. Sheridan College in Oakville, Ontario, led the way in training animators, and programs have now sprung up at Capilano College, Centennial College, Algonquin College, Emily Carr Institute of Art and Design, the Vancouver Film Institute, and many other educational institutions. Given the huge demand for work in this area, expect to see many institutions offering one-year post-diploma programs in animation.

The video industry has grown to meet the need for training, corporate, and educational videos. On a smaller scale, freelancers will continue to find work shooting videos for special events such as conferences, bar mitzvahs, weddings, birthdays, and ribbon-cutting ceremonies. If you are in the Toronto area, consider joining the Video Production Association, which tries to help people develop their own video production skills.

Sports and Recreation Clubs and Services

The five major markets in the recreational services field are the elderly; aging boomers; boomers in their thirties; children of boomers in their thirties; and children of boomers in their forties. Recreational services that combine the interests of more than one wealthy market segment and change as the interests of that market change will survive and even do well. Many will remember how Club Med went from being a singles haven to a family-oriented holiday club; both market focuses mirrored the needs of early boomers at two different stages in life. The aging boomer market is beginning to give up vigorous sports like squash or hockey, and even tennis to some extent, in favour of swimming, golf, and fishing. For that market segment, cross-country skiing is gaining on downhill skiing, and power boating has completely bypassed sailing as an interest.

The children of the aging boomers, on the other hand, are interested in weightlifting, in-line skating, rugby, baseball, hockey, tennis, and squash, but are not yet wealthy enough to support expensive club memberships. Chances are they are students, underemployed, or unemployed at the moment.

The young to middle-aged boomers are in their early to mid-thirties and have started a family. These individuals typically join ski clubs, and go to cottages and other recreation areas that the whole family can enjoy. In about seven years or so, their children and the children of aging boomers will be interested in playing hockey, tennis, baseball, and football. In the meantime, many of these children will spend their summers at sports camps.

BULLETIN BOARD – *SPORTS AND RECREATION*

- **Job demand factors:** demographics.
- **Job growth areas:** sports facilities for affluent retirees, aging boomers, young to middle-aged boomers and their children.
- **Job reduction areas:** vigorous sports.
- **Growth limiting factors:** just as demographics is a demand factor, it is also a growth-limiting factor; the economy; competition.

CONTACTS

☛ Canadian Resort Development Association
48 Hayden St.,
Toronto, ON M4Y 1V8 Tel. 416-960-4930 Fax: 416-923-8348

☛ Canadian Sport & Fitness Administration Centre
Place R. Tait McKenzie, 1600 James Naismith Dr.,
Gloucester, ON K1B 5N4 Tel. 613-747-2900 Fax: 613-748-5706
URL: http://www.cdnsport.ca/

But expect a big boom in street hockey, given Nike's big push in this area.

As for the elderly, this market segment is taking up lawn bowling, bowling, swimming, card games, curling, and boat cruises. The sale of golf clubs and accessories rose by 7 percent in 1995, and camping has spurred on the sale of tents, canteens, and other camping gear by 8 percent.

In pursuing a career in sports and recreation, the job seeker is advised to follow the sporting interests of the aging boomers, the better-off family boomers in their thirties, or the wealthy retirees market. Sports and recreation facilities geared to a kinder, gentler, and wealthier clientele will meet with success as the emptynesters arrive in full force in 1997. But don't lose sight of newer innovative high-tech-oriented sports, such as Laser Quest Corp.'s game, which includes trying to outscore opponents in laser "tag." Cybermind of Toronto has a number of virtual reality games using live or robotic gladiators. Many of these high-tech games have broad appeal.

Hobbies and Crafts

Service industries tied to emerging boomer hobbies are flourishing and will continue to do so though competition will intensify. Crafts such as

BULLETIN BOARD – *HOBBIES AND CRAFTS*

- **Job demand factors:** the recession; trend toward quality and creative self-expression.
- **Job growth areas:** craft supplies; artisans; photography; gardening supplies and design; nature stores; historical preservation and exhibition.
- **Growth limiting factors:** increasing competition from developing countries supplying craft items.

CONTACTS

☛ Canadian Craft and Hobby Association
4404 - 12 St. NE, PO Box 44,
Calgary AB T2E 6K9 Tel. 403-291-0559 Fax: 403-291-0675

☛ Canadian Crafts Council
189 Laurier Avenue East
Ottawa, ON K1N 6P1 Tel. 613-235-8200 Fax: 613-235-7425

fabric painting, knitting, and jewelry-making have become more popular. In 1992, 82 percent of all American households had at least one person who practised crafts, a 17 percent increase over 1988. Since craft and hobby participants tend to have lower household incomes than non-participants, the recession has helped spur the industry. The trend toward an appreciation of quality and creativity has increased the appreciation of finely crafted, one-of-a-kind items. Developing countries in South America and the Pacific Rim are already taking advantage of the growing trend. Moreover, aging boomers are enjoying quieter, more introspective pastimes, which accounts for the increasing interest in bird-watching, nature walks and hiking, photography, fishing, gardening, visits to historical sites, and stamp collecting. Companies taking advantage of these trends will do well.

Where the Jobs Are in Personal Services

As the boomer population ages, there will be a greater demand for convenience services of all kinds. Such areas as hairdressing, barbering, cleaning, laundering, and burial services are included in the personal services. Franchising is growing as a means of standardizing services, cutting costs, and delivering a better standard of personal service.

BULLETIN BOARD – *PERSONAL SERVICES*

- **Job demand factors:** aging boomers seeking convenience, value, and personal attention; the recession.
- **Job growth areas:** franchises; funeral services.
- **Growth limiting factors:** population size; demographics; easy entry into personal services field increasing competition for jobs.

CONTACTS

☛ Funeral Service Association of Canada
#201, 206 Harwoood Avenue South
Ajax, ON L1S 2H6 Tel. 905-619-0982 Fax: 905-619-0983
☛ Canadian Cosmetics Careers Association Inc.
109 Daniels Crescent
Ajax, ON Tel. 905-686-3401
☛ Dry Cleaners & Launderers Institute
One Eva Rd.,
Etobicoke, ON M9C 4Z5 Tel: 416-620-5683 Fax: 416-620-5392

Since it is relatively easy to enter the personal services field, competition for jobs is heavy, which is one of the reasons that franchises will likely take over this field. Magicuts, for example, is a no-frills hair-cutting business that uses technology to cut costs and offer better customer service. Each outlet tracks inventory, total sales, sales patterns, and customer preferences on computer. As a result, inventory costs have been reduced, paperwork largely eliminated, scheduling of employees and direct marketing campaigns made more effective, customers impressed by stylists who remember preferences as well as general personal information, and customer waiting times minimized.

For most personal service companies, franchises are usually the only outlets financially equipped to take advantage of technology. Heavy competition in personal services keeps profit margins to a minimum and therefore gives the competitive edge to the business that can cut costs without reducing customer service. As Magicuts reveals, it is possible to cut costs and still improve customer service. In any business, that is a winning strategy.

Non-Market Services: Educational Services, Social Services, Police and Firefighting Services

While competition has not been a major factor in determining the survival of non-market services, the services themselves have always been vital to the country's economic competitiveness. In a global economy which demands international competitiveness and at a time when governments are burdened by debt, more is being expected from these services at a lower cost. This may well result in the deregulation and privatization of many non-market services. Productivity growth, new approaches to management, and technological change are transforming the ways in which these services are being delivered. In the case of education and social services, costs and demographics are providing the impetus for change, cost accountability, and outcome-based evaluation procedures.

Where the Jobs Are in Educational Services

• Elementary and Secondary Schools • Community Colleges • Universities • Training • Libraries, Museums, Archives, and Research

In 1995 the education industry, spanning elementary schools to universities, employed more people than automobile manufacturing and parts,

---

THE ELECTRONIC CLASSROOM

The future of teaching becomes uncertain as technology transforms both the teaching and the learning processes. Burnaby South 2000 is a secondary school which is blending state-of-the-art audio-video technology and education. All classrooms are wired with optical fibre and the school has access to laser discs, compact-disc television readers, computer cameras, high-tech slide and movie projectors, local television stations, VCRs, worldwide wire services, computers, satellite feeds, and a high-tech industrial education laboratory. IBM, B.C. Tel, MPR Teletech Ltd., Dynacom Communications, Franklin Hill & Associates, and Creative Learning International are actively involved with the school. Video monitors, modems, microwave signals, and satellites allow the school to broadcast school news and interact with people all over Canada and worldwide. Free educational broadcast packages are received from overnight feeds, and an organization of teachers in Colorado provides accompanying lesson plans.

BULLETIN BOARD – *EDUCATIONAL SERVICES*

- **Job demand factors:** unaffordability and ineffectiveness of current education system; need to address learning deficiencies of individual learners; requirements of business world; ever-increasing educational potential of technology; immigration; functional illiteracy and innumeracy; upgrading needs of unemployed and employed adults.
- **Job growth areas:** ESL; adult education at the primary and secondary levels; part-time positions at colleges and universities; private learning institutes; electronic educational broadcasting; co-op education programs; specialized business areas.
- **Job reduction areas:** jobs in public schools.
- **Growth limiting factors:** increasing government and municipal debts; tax revolts; public's and business's perception of education system; business's capacity to afford training; educational or training tax incentives; demographics; population size; immigration policies.

banking, and construction combined. The bulk of the country's education employment is located in a few provinces: Ontario with 37.7 percent, or 329,384 jobs; Quebec with 24.4 percent, 213,462 jobs; British Columbia with 12.2 percent, 106,000 jobs; and Alberta with 9.2 percent, 80,637 jobs. The rest of Canada accounts for only 16.7 percent.

According to Statistics Canada, our education costs of $33 billion in 1991 were the highest in the world because we failed to cut our army of educators to match declines in enrolment over the past two decades. That failure cost the country a whopping $7.4 billion in 1991, or more than one-fifth the total budget for elementary and secondary education. The number of educators rose by almost 20 percent from 1971 to 1991, while the number of students fell by 12 percent to about 5 million. During the tough recession years of 1989 and 1993, when layoffs were the order of the day, the education industry was actually creating jobs.

The minister of education in Ontario wants to reduce direct non-classroom expenses to less than 40 percent of the total educational budget and has invited the private sector to bid on taking over the province's educational administrative services. Among recommendations in a draft version of an Ontario education task force report are pooling commercial

BULLETIN BOARD – *EDUCATIONAL SERVICES*

CONTACTS

☛ Canadian Education Association
#8-200, 252 Bloor St. West,
Toronto, ON M5S 1V5 Tel. 416-924-7721 Fax: 416-924-3188
E-mail: acea@hookup.net

☛ Access for New Canadians
#401, 425 Adelaide Street West
Toronto, ON M5V 3C1 Tel. 416-594-6611 Fax: 416-594-6590

☛ Canadian Association for Adult Education
29 Prince Arthur Ave.,
Toronto, ON M5R 1B2 Tel. 416-964-0559 Fax: 416-964-9226

☛ Canadian Association for Co-operative Education
55 Eglinton Avenue East
Toronto, ON M4P 1G8 Tel. 416-483-3311 Fax: 416-483-3365

☛ Canadian Association for University Continuing Education
#320, 350 Albert Street
Ottawa, ON K1R 1B1 Tel. 613-563-1236 Fax: 613-563-7739
E-mail: kclements@aucc.ca
URL: http://www.tile.net/tile/listserv/caucel.html

☛ Cooperative Career & Work Education Association of Canada
2 King Street West
Hamilton, ON L8P 1A1 Tel. 905-523-6682 Fax: 905-523-7753

☛ Canadian Association of School Administrators
#1133, 160A Street
White Rock, BC V4A 7G9 Tel. 604-535-6330 Fax: 604-531-6454

☛ Professional Development Institute Inc.
79 Fentiman Avenue
Ottawa, ON K1S OT7 Tel. 613-730-7777 Fax: 613-235-1115

☛ TESL Canada Federation
PO Box 44105
Burnaby, BC V5B 4Y2 Tel. 604-298-0312 Fax: 604-298-0312
E-mail: teslcan@unixg.ubc.ca

and industrial property taxes, chopping the number of school boards from 168 to 82, cutting trustees from 2,000 to 540, and centralizing bargaining. In Manitoba there is a recommendation to create 22 school districts out of 57, and British Columbia wants to shrink its school districts from 75 to 35. Across the country, proposals like these have the potential to affect employment considerably. With a reduction of $2.5 billion in federal education funding transfers to the provinces in 1996–97 and a further $4.5 billion in 1997–98, all provincial ministries are being forced into labour adjustments and systems reviews. Bureaucracies everywhere are taking hits, and thousands of workers in education are losing their livelihoods.

With the idea of lifelong learning slowly becoming more widely accepted, training and education will take different forms, and access will be a key issue. Deregulation will no doubt become part of the solution of system reform across the country as provinces deal not only with shrinking budgets, but with the impact of technological change and upheaval in the economy.

Post-secondary education will likely see increased tuition fees, more access for business to universities and colleges, and greater diversity among institutions. This diversity will probably include the establishment of private institutions as well as privatized activities within the publicly funded bodies for higher education. Not unlike newer organizational designs in business and industry, the profit centre concept of networked organic models offers colleges and universities the benefits of a smaller, more agile subsystem which is keenly responsive to market demand. Just how much autonomy these smaller institutions will have remains to be seen. The potential for quality, value-based distance education in the new global environment is simply enormous.

Clearly, competition will be part of the education scene in the global economy. Offshore institutions, private trainers, industry-based certification programs, distance education, and collaborative ventures are emerging in response to the demands from the community. There is a call for improved apprenticeship training, work experience, and cooperative education, as well as new technology programs. As in so many other sectors, this demand will have to be met with innovative solutions, as there will be fewer people to do the work.

Elementary and Secondary Schools
Escalating costs of education and the determination of governments to fight their deficits have led to a re-examination of how educational

dollars are being spent. Public and corporate disaffection with the results produced by the system is paving the way for transformation. There has been a resounding call for a reduction of educational bureaucracies and a better use of teaching talent in schools. Virtually every province and territory has had a royal commission, new school act, government white paper, or public hearings to reassess priorities and practices. Among the recommendations from these forums are consolidation of school boards, increased province-wide testing, teacher-training reforms, the elimination of permanent teacher certification, and, in several provinces, school councils. Across the country, school curriculums are being reassessed and reshaped with a stronger focus on student-achievement results, application of learning to the world of work, and mastery of core subjects.

LEARNING AND JOBS GO TOGETHER

A new rule for the workplace is becoming evident. If you have completed some form of post-secondary education – a university degree, community college diploma, training certificate – you're going to get a job. If you have anything less, you won't. In 1994 the economy added 277,000 jobs, its best showing since 1989. For those with a high school education or less, 145,000 jobs disappeared. For those with a post-secondary education, 422,000 jobs opened up. That means 99.3 percent of people entering the labour force with a degree or diploma found work. From 1990 to 1994, the economy created about 957,000 jobs for people with that essential piece of post-secondary certification. At the same time, it destroyed 836,000 jobs for people with anything less. In a job market of 13.3 million persons, that's a massive change in a short period. In 1994 people with a post-secondary certificate of some kind held 48 percent of all jobs, up from 41 percent in 1990. The share of jobs available to those who didn't finish high school fell to 21 from 27 percent. The remaining jobs went to those with a high school diploma and some post-secondary schooling. These figures don't tell us what kind of jobs went to each group, but the odds are that even those who are underemployed are better off being in the labour market than not. Adults needing a high school diploma can take the GED (General Educational Development), an international high school equivalency test now offered in all provinces except Quebec and Ontario. In 1995–96 a pilot was run in Ontario.

The Ontario minister of education and training, John Snobelen, feels that the education system needs to be transformed into a service organization which delivers education and training to its clients on behalf of its customers. In primary and secondary education, the client is the student and the customer is the taxpayer and parent. Snobelen states that the entire education system lags behind other professions in the use of computer technology for tracking clients' progress, for communication with customers, for testing and evaluating, and for raw information distribution. There is no doubt that the technology gap will have to be breached, and quickly.

Given the fact that Canada received the top grade in the 1995 World Competitiveness Report on both higher education enrolment and human development and placed second in computers per capita, prospects look good. Over the past decade the proportion of young people aged 18 to 24 enrolled in full-time higher education has almost doubled. In 1994, the figure was 32 percent. Mature students now account for 25 percent of the student population, compared with 20 percent a decade ago.

Community Colleges

Enrolment is consistently rising at Canada's 175 community colleges, with university graduates who are seeking skills-based training now accounting for as much as 15 percent of enrolment. Between 1971 and 1994 full-time enrolment in the colleges more than doubled to 386,000, while the number of part-time students jumped 2,000 percent to 181,000.

The colleges have consistently capitalized on their ability to adapt to changing priorities and to demonstrate a sensitivity to employer demand for specialized skill sets. Ontario's Humber College, for example, opened a digital imaging training centre in 1995 to meet the need for people trained in the sophisticated computer technology used to create and manipulate graphic and digital images and sound. A partnership with Kodak Canada Inc. and Apple Canada Inc. allows the centre to keep abreast of changes in technology. Other technology partnerships include an alliance between Ontario's Centennial College with Bell Canada, Silicon Graphics, Alias Research, Sony, and the CBC, creating the Bell Centre for Creative Communication. This $13 million venture has one of the highest bandwidth networks in the country, with the ability to transfer

10 megabytes of data per second anywhere within the centre. Each of 100 work stations with Silicon Graphics high-performance computers has its own digital camera, allowing for the integration of all platforms and all media.

Partnerships among the colleges are extending also to linkages with the universities. Seneca College (a directly job-oriented institution) is building a campus at York University in Toronto which will create the largest Canadian convergence of a college and a university for mutual benefit. The $55 million affiliation, which will come on stream in 1997, will provide York students with university academic and theoretical programs, followed by practical skills-based training at the college.

A growing number of colleges are forging international links to sell education and training abroad. Lambton College in Sarnia, Ontario, signed an agreement with Universidad Polytecnica de Nicaragua for student and faculty exchanges, including links with the private sector in both countries. The colleges are exploring new entrepreneurial routes to survival. Nova Scotia's University College of Cape Breton has been in active discussion with several Ontario colleges about the delivery of uni-versity-level programs leading to a bachelor of technology degree. Along with Ontario's Durham College, UCCB is among those institutions look-ing south for business. Seneca College is also pursuing opportunities in the Pacific Rim countries with the intent of raising $2 million in new fees by 1999.

Along with everyone else, the colleges are having to continually adapt to economic, social, and technological change. Niche-oriented courses, such as the four-year entrepreneurship program at Mount Royal College in Calgary, close training gaps nicely. This is a degree-granting program, which includes two work terms where students can put a business plan they've developed into action. The idea is to prepare people to work in a small business or start their own, with preparation in legal, financial, and human resource issues. Toronto's Seneca College has introduced a similar three-year program in entrepreneurship.

Other successful niche programs include Seneca's microcomputer systems post-diploma program that students enter upon completing a two- or three-year business program. This program teaches students how to design and manage networks to meet business needs. According to the college, graduates typically get four to five job offers each. British

Columbia's Capilano College offers nine months of intensive and integrated business, language, and Asia-Pacific studies for university graduates with two to five years' work experience, a strong entrepreneurial spirit, and a commitment to spending three to five years in Asia.

Employer demands for more comprehensive training and higher-level job candidates are in evidence across the country. A 1995 Quebec government study, for example, shows low employment rates and a high number of graduates returning to school 10 months after graduating from business programs at provincial CEGEPs, government schools, and private colleges in 1992–93. Of graduates from finance programs, 52.8 percent were employed, 35.7 percent had returned to school, and 16.7 percent were unemployed. Of marketing grads, 46.2 percent were employed, 40.7 percent had returned to school, and 22.2 percent were unemployed. The poorest placement rate was for human resources students: only 22.2 percent were employed, 33.3 percent had returned to school, and 50 percent were unemployed.

EDUCATION PAYS DIVIDENDS

A survey of more than 300 employers across Canada by management consultants KPMG revealed that starting salaries for graduates from the class of 1996 would be somewhat higher than offers the previous year. MBAs can expect an average starting salary of $40,400, an 11 percent increase over 1995. Grads with an MSc or MA will get an average starting salary of $38,400, a 5 percent increase over the previous year. Salaries for various other 1996 grads were listed as follows: high school – $22,000; community college or technical institute – $28,000; bachelor's degree – $31,400; bachelor's in engineering – $34,900. Actual starting salaries would vary by geographic location and industry sector. KPMG's Martin Harts says that employers are looking more and more for skills they can use straightaway. They want a new worker to start producing from the beginning.

A Royal Trust survey showed that more than two-thirds of people with income in the top 10 percent of the population have a university degree. Since only 18 percent of Canadians have a degree, extra education clearly pays off. The average household income of those in the top 10 percent was $124,000, with an average net worth of $441,000, including real estate.

Ontario's colleges are going through a rationalization process which will see some institutions cutting programs for architectural technicians, civil engineers, fashion merchandisers, mechnical technicians and technologists, dental assistants and hygienists, and social workers. The closings are aimed at eliminating courses which are duplicated at other colleges or programs for which jobs are scarce. Across Ontario the total funding cuts amount to $689 million, 15 percent of the total budget. In 1994 Ontario colleges had expanded their enrolment by 30 percent since 1990; at the same time, operating grants were reduced by 25 percent. In 1996 they cut 1,158 full-time teaching positions, which amounts to a 15 percent reduction, in addition to the 15 percent reduction taken since 1991. While they have been granted approval to raise tuition fees by 15 percent, it was expected that at least half would run deficits in fiscal 1995–96 as they paid one-time costs associated with early-retirement packages.

Universities

Although they educate some 900,000 people every year, Canada's universities are still, for the most part, configured, guided, and governed as they were at the turn of the century. A 1995 Financial Post/Arthur Andersen survey of entrepreneurs revealed that 60 percent of respondents felt the schools were not producing the type of graduates they wanted to hire. That's up from 56 percent in 1994 and 50 percent in 1993. While in the last 33 years we have spawned that same number of new universities, it appears that there is some distance to go to adapt to new realities. Changes on the horizon precipitated by restructuring will include greater specialization and differentiation, which will be assisted by the internationalization of the disciplines and electronic delivery enhancements. The schools will focus more on selective areas where they have singular strengths and unique contributions to offer higher learning, pursuing different missions and levels of students. The focus will be on teaching over research, and whatever research is conducted will likely be applied research, in collaboration with business and other university partners. Performance measures which have focussed on output, such as graduation rates, will take into consideration the ability of grads to find a job in a field related to their studies. Tenure protection, guaranteeing university faculty a job for life, will be revised. Across the country, salaries for full professors fall between $58,896 (low end of range at University of Manitoba) and $115,000 (higher end of range at University of Toronto).

A 1995 study by Edward Renner in StatsCan's *Education Quarterly Review* of 9,000 faculty members at nine Canadian universities found that the majority of teachers are over 50 and were hired in the late 1960s and 1970s to handle the huge number of baby boomers moving on to post-secondary education. Once there, the faculty never left, and when the baby boom expansion ended, jobs dried up, leading to unemployed or underemployed new PhDs in the late 1970s or 1980s. Renner's study showed that 61 percent of university faculty are over 50, 36 percent are baby boomers themselves (born between 1945 and 1960), and only 2.8 percent are under 35. The typical professor is 51, has been at the same institution for 18 years, and isn't due to retire until 2007. According to Renner this has created a "huge gap" between faculty thinking and the needs of today's students preparing for the work force. The study concluded that 25 percent of university faculty are teaching things that are no longer relevant.

It's not surprising then that questions of efficiency, cost-effectiveness, and accountability are assuming high priority at Canadian universities, much as intellectual leadership and academic freedom did in the past. With much strategic thinking, soul-searching, and restructuring already under way, hundreds of faculty and staff positions are being eliminated. The universities are considering how to deliver programs with people who are paid less or with fewer people. Salaries constitute the greatest share of universities' budgets (about 85 percent in many cases). As the future unfolds, we will see fewer professors, larger class sizes, a lot more experimentation with technology and distance education, as well as increased services for Canadian business. Tuition hikes in the region of 20 percent for undergraduate programs and more for graduate and professional programs are planned. According to the Association of Universities and Colleges of Canada, tuition currently accounts for between 15 and 40 percent of university operating budgets, compared with 13 percent in 1980.

In a research paper released by the University of Toronto Centre for Public Management, economist Doug Auld argues that Canada's system of publicly funded universities should be deregulated to allow for private institutions, vouchers for students, and increased competition for research funds. Some universities are already taking steps in this direction. Queen's University has effectively privatized its graduate business program. Royal Roads University in British Columbia has set an ambitious goal of self-sufficiency from government in five years, largely through increased tuition fees and private-sector partnerships. In the Maritimes, students now pay about 50 percent of the cost of tuition, with no government cap on fees. The government of Alberta allows out-of-province institutions to offer degree programs. Most university officials foresee some variation of privatization, such as increased deregulation of fees and contracting-out of services. As public institutions take on some of the characteristics of private-sector enterprise, and as creative and innovative models of learning and research emerge, issues of quality and standardization will have to be worked out. Eventually, these standards will be globalized. Studies in Manitoba, New Brunswick, Nova Scotia, Ontario, and Saskatchewan argue there's a need to place more emphasis on teaching and less on research. And just as Canadian business is becoming more export-oriented and international in its focus, so too are the universities becoming more sensitive to globalization issues.

As a case in point, China's growing importance in the global economy and the increase in Canada's Asian-Canadian population are affecting university recruitment practices, curriculum, and international activities. B.C.'s Simon Fraser University has partnerships with two Hong Kong universities to exchange students and faculty on research projects. At the University of British Columbia, international students make up 4 percent of the undergraduate population and more than 20 percent of the graduate population, a situation mirrored in universities across the country. This does not include students of Asian origin who are Canadian citizens or landed immigrants. The University of Toronto, University of Western Ontario, and York University also have a variety of collaborative ventures

---

UNIVERSITIES RAKE IN ROYALTIES

Among Canadian universities, the University of Waterloo takes top marks in terms of income received from patents and royalties. In the 1994–95 fiscal year, Waterloo took in US$1.4 million from such sources. Next highest was the University of Calgary, with $1.2 million, then the University of British Columbia, with $878,500.

with an Asian emphasis. Foreign students are believed to bring an average of $30,000 a year each to the Canadian economy in tuition, room and board, books, transportation, and other living costs. In Nova Scotia, they pay $6,000 in tuition, double the Canadian rate. Australia, by comparison, estimates that by 2010, foreign students will contribute $4.5 billion a year to its economy.

Canada's post-secondary institutions are exhibiting a new sense of competitiveness and an inclination to explore ways of working more collaboratively with private enterprise. Just one of numerous examples of collaborative ventures is York University's deal with Greenlight Communications to offer and market degree and non-degree credit courses on the Internet. In Alberta, Athabasca University's electronic MBA program (three to five years) is the first of its kind in Canada and, at $14,000, is considerably less expensive than some others. For example, Western's EMBA (two years) costs $45,000, and a Queen's MBA (one year) costs $22,000. Queen's University, in partnership with EDS Canada, began offering its national executive MBA classes by interactive video in the fall of 1996. With the federal government's plans to slash cash transfers to the provinces for health, welfare, and post-secondary education by $6 billion by 1997, these developments are apropos. While in 1984 the universities received 80 percent of their operating income from the government and 16 percent from fees, in 1994 government handouts accounted for only 74 percent and funds from fee payers had risen to 23.1 percent.

In 1984 the actual fees for one year of undergraduate studies ranged from $552 in Quebec to $1,474 in Alberta. A decade later, fees had jumped to $1,779 in Quebec (still the lowest in Canada) and $3,600 in Nova Scotia. The university system is moving from being publicly supported to being publicly assisted. The University of Toronto's Faculty of Management Studies gets about 40 percent of its $15 million a year from private sources. A number of schools of business at Canadian universities have received generous donations and are using the money and aggressive fundraising campaigns to become globally competitive. In this vein, comparisons with U.S. universities are instructive about competitive challenges: Stanford University, for example, has about the same number of students and professors as the University of Western Ontario, but Stanford has twice the money. That there are other issues is illustrated by the fact that more than 1.1 million American students who received their degrees in 1993 were either unemployed (6.1 percent) or working in jobs not requiring a university degree (23 percent). The U.S. Bureau of Labor Statistics says this trend will continue for at least a decade.

The trend among provincial governments to replace block grants (the equivalent of a blank cheque) with conditional funding tied to an institution's success in meeting public policy objectives seems here to stay. Alberta plans to introduce a funding formula which supports system-wide goals of accessibility, responsiveness, affordability, and accountability. B.C.'s Royal Roads University is breaking the tradition of tenure with a different form of employment contract for faculty, who will be recruited from industry and other universities. It is offering positions for a fixed term to enable it to respond to market demand, and it is working to define a particular market niche. Unlike traditional faculty-controlled senates, the governing structure – two-thirds of it made up of non-university representatives – and an education council of faculty will advise on program and research. Hoping to become one of the top four management schools in the country, management faculty at the University of Calgary submitted a proposal to its administrative body to go private.

What we're seeing across the country is a work in progress as the education and training system progresses through various degrees of reform.

Training

Most Canadian companies still use traditional human resources management models with little emphasis on training or employee involvement. Cost-cutting and technology upgrades are often the competitive tactics of choice. These are the findings of a two-year study of 2,000 Canadian businesses by researchers at Queen's University in Kingston, Ontario. Only 30 percent of Canadian companies place a high strategic priority on offering workers broad-based training, workplace involvement, and pay incentives. The 1995 study, entitled *The Canadian Workplace in Transition*, suggested that companies with more progressive policies outperform those that rely on traditional approaches.

There are a few bright lights on the training scene, however; among them are the learning institutes sponsored by several Canadian banks.

At the Bank of Montreal, for example, more than one-third of the 35,000 employees have attended its $50 million learning institute. The bank is committed to providing an average of five days of learning per employee per year – roughly three to four times more than the national average, and costing it $63 million annually. Seventy percent takes place via distance learning, through a variety of computer and satellite programs; 30 percent takes place in a classroom.

The CIBC has a sophisticated competency modeling process which involves three competency inventories: non-technical, technical, and business. Profiles for jobs and generic proficiency levels (including technical and non-technical skills) were developed for core, specific, and personal elements. Employees initiate the competency development cycle by analyzing the requirements of their present positions as well as those they aspire to. They are then in a position to plan and schedule learning activities to meet their targets.

Ryerson Polytechnic University, in cooperation with the Eaton School of Retailing and a wide range of industry advisors, has developed the Canadian Retail Management Program. This is a Canadian first – a university-level professional program designed from the ground up for retail management. Some of the topics addressed in the program are the challenges facing all retail managers today: dramatic changes in consumer behaviour, intense international competition, and new technologies.

On the federal training scene, the Auditor General has been reviewing government-sponsored training activities through HRDC (Human Resources Development Canada). Two billion dollars was spent on training in 1994, double what was spent in 1986, but there have been fundamental questions about the benefits of that training. For example, between 1988 and 1990, the department found there were on average 300,000 vacant jobs each year, but only 5 percent of training activities were aimed at giving workers the skills needed for those jobs. Part of the problem appears to be that basic information provided through Canada Employment Centres about people looking for work is often an inaccurate reflection of realities. HRDC has been spending 70 percent of its employment dollars on training. The programs were expected to be overhauled in 1996.

An example of technology advances in training is seen in Microsoft's on-line education software, which has been tested in New Brunswick, a site selected for its extensive electronic and telecommunications infrastructure. N.B. Telephone has laid digital phone lines throughout the province and cable penetration is the highest in the country. Commercial applications of this "virtual campus" will be less expensive than traditional training sessions, so that even smaller organizations can provide access to training. Interactive on-line training is better than paper and video self-study courses because it allows students two-way dialogue with an instructor and classmates. In addition to corporate applications, 100 Microsoft technicians trained a group of educators from New Brunswick to offer kindergarten through Grade 12 courses via the service. The province provided certification of all courses. This new wave of education and training will open many opportunities for the development of interactive training materials and for individuals who can serve as on-line tutors.

One simple fact is certain: training is no longer an option. It is, in fact, very crucial to our economic success as a nation. A recent international literacy study showed that four in ten Canadian adults can't deal with most of the written material they encounter every day. More than 55 percent of Canadians fell into the top three skill levels of the five-level survey, but 40 percent were in the bottom two levels, which represent marginal performance at best. The study, designed and managed by Statistics Canada and partly sponsored by the Organization for Economic Cooperation and Development (OECD), found strong links between literacy skills, employment, job status, and income. The study showed that education is only partly responsible for skill levels. For example, while adults with more formal education are generally more literate, one in ten university graduates could deal only with very simple written material. And, conversely, 1 percent of those with only an elementary education were at the highest skill level. The highest scores of the 4,500 Canadians who participated were recorded by the baby boom group in the 36-to-45 age range. Managers and professionals dominated the high literacy levels, while machine operators and agricultural workers had the lowest literacy levels. While a greater proportion of immigrants were at the very lowest level of literacy (31.1 percent compared with 14.8 percent of native-born Canadians), they were more likely than native-born Canadians to hold the highest levels (24.3 percent compared with 18.3 percent).

PARTNERS FOR CONTINUOUS LEARNING

The Canadian Continuous Learning Initiative (CCLI) is a new partnership which proposes to create a virtual campus to deliver education and training at schools, colleges, universities, and corporate facilities across the country. CCLI's electronic resources will mimic the amenities of an academic campus and include library access, Internet access, e-mail, file transfer, discussion "rooms," private "rooms," bulletin boards, and remote testing. Partners include the computer hardware manufacturer Tandem; First Class Systems, a developer of computer-based and multimedia training; Mount Allison University, a liberal arts school engaged in developing multimedia courseware; the North York Board of Education in Toronto; Worldlinx, owned by Bell Canada and other telephone companies for national delivery of telecommunications services; and Virtual Corporation, a company that specializes in developing public-private partnerships and works with computer technology for competency assessment.

Statistics Canada has produced a followup study to draw out detailed implications of the results for Canada and various groups within the country. It's clear at the moment that a push for improvement will be needed on many fronts. Challenges include motivating regular reading habits and lifelong learning, support for libraries, and the availability of ongoing adult education, as well as good basic early preparation of youngsters in reading and writing.

Libraries, Museums, Archives, and Research

No aspect of contemporary life has escaped the dramatic impact of the information revolution, with libraries, museums, and archives no exception. Everything is moving on-line. There will soon be virtual reality versions of art galleries, museums, science centres, world expositions, zoos, encyclopedias, theme parks, instructional material and fiction, and historical events. The digital imaging of documents will replace the need for physical access to primary sources or even microfiche libraries. Already the Canadian Network for the Advancement of Research, Industry and Education, the National Research Council, and a number of museums have joined together to create robot-mounted cameras to take 3-D images of art and cultural objects in anticipation of "museums without walls."

For a minimal charge, on-line information services such as America On-Line, Prodigy, and Compuserve provide unlimited amounts of information and topic-based forum-type discussions. Computer users can conduct information searches in the on-line libraries, scour press services for specific stories, browse through electronic encyclopedias, read magazines on-line before they appear in print, and collect newspaper articles by scanning on-line or home CD-ROMs.

For individuals interested in scientific and industrial research, a new library service has emerged called Teltech Resource Network Corporation, of Minneapolis. Researchers and scientists spend a frustrating amount of time learning how to use computer commands so that they can access databases in search of published research material. Teltech offers an exciting alternative. The company hires scientific analysts under contract to provide answers to research questions within 24 hours. Each analyst is familiar with the more than 1,600 databases Teltech has at its disposal. After the expert provides clients with answers to their queries, Teltech canvasses the clients to ensure that they are satisfied. The company reports that over 90 percent of its clientele is satisfied, and for those who are not, other analysts are provided gratis. Moreover, Teltech is willing to contact agencies or suppliers of products that clients may need in the course of their research. An independent study of 20 randomly chosen Teltech customers revealed that 13 felt that the profit they accrued from using the service was approximately 16 times greater than its cost. Since this service is expected to add $6 billion annually to the U.S. economy, state subsidies are making this service available to small businesses.

The Teltech example illustrates the direction in which libraries and other information storage systems are heading. Once the portable electronic book and the CD-ROM – which will even read the book to the user – become commonplace, there will be little need for "physical" libraries. As government debt continues to mount and books get more expensive to publish, libraries will likely see their budgets cut severely. Having already eliminated the Economic Council of Canada and the Science and Technology Council, and having curtailed the CBC's budget, the

BULLETIN BOARD – *LIBRARIES*

- **Job demand factors:** need for compiled information from different sources; ability to sort through increasing volume of information rapidly; need for easy access to information worldwide.
- **Job growth areas:** services which compile and sort through a variety of databases.
- **Job reduction areas:** traditional lending libraries.
- **Growth limiting factors:** diffusion of technological innovation throughout society; government's willingness to subsidize various services; speed of technological developments.

CONTACTS

☛ Association of Canadian Archivists
PO Box 2596, Station D
Ottawa, ON K1P 5W6 Tel. 613-443-0251

☛ Canadian Association for Information Science
Faculty of Library and Information Science, University of Toronto,
140 St. George St.,
Toronto, ON M5S 1A1 Tel. 416-978-8876 Fax: 416-971-1399

☛ Canadian Association of Research Libraries
Morisset Hall, University of Ottawa
#602, 65 University St.,
Ottawa, ON K1N 9A5 Tel. 613-562-5800 ex. 3652 Fax: 613-562-5195

☛ Canadian Library Association
#602, 200 Elgin St.,
Ottawa, K2P 1L5 Tel. 613-232-9625 Fax: 613-563-9895
Toll free: 1-800-267-6566
URL: http://freenet.carleton.ca/freenet/routedir/menus/
     prof.assoc/cla/aboutcla

☛ Canadian Museums Association
280 Metcalfe Street
Ottawa, ON K2P 1R7 Tel. 613-567-0099 Fax: 613-233-5438

government is unlikely to spare libraries from the ravages of downsizing, cost rationalization, or re-engineering.

In 1882, Oliver Mowat, Farley Mowat's great-great-uncle, introduced the Library Act, mandating the right of citizens to a free library; however, reductions in provincial library subsidies and municipal transfer payments are reducing staff and making fee-for-service a possible option – especially in Ontario, where Bill 26 made such changes feasible. Free libraries are likely to go the way of free parking. The ability of modern technology to provide the same information in a more widely available format will supersede the need to have access to the hard-copy version of texts, and those who insist on using the older format will likely pay a premium for a courier-based lending library. Already libraries are more self-serve, via modem access, and user fees are being actively discussed.

Where the Jobs Are in Social Services
• Daycare • Psychologists, Psychiatrists, Social Workers, and Other Mental Health Workers

Daycare
The daycare field is expected to be an employment growth area as the number of preschool children is expected to keep rising until 2005. More parents are making use of daycare services, especially as more women enter the work force. Sixty-eight percent of women with children worked outside the home in 1991 compared with 52 percent in 1981. The province with the highest participation rate of women in the work force is Alberta, followed by Ontario and P.E.I. Newfoundland had the lowest rate, with 46 percent, in 1993. The dual-income family is now the norm rather than the exception. Women are returning to work sooner after childbirth, which also contributes to the rising labour-force participation rate among women ages 16 to 44. The tendency for women to start their families later in life once they have established some career roots and the preference for smaller families favour the use of daycare. Moreover, as daycares increasingly gain the reputation of being structured and dynamic learning environments, many parents will choose this option for their preschoolers over the non-professional services of a nanny, live-in worker, babysitter, or relative.

This field is not known for its high salaries. Job seekers who choose to pursue a career in this area are clearly committed to the non-monetary rewards of the profession. The low pay, however, encourages high turnover, which increases employment opportunities.

If the federal or provincial governments were to choose subsidized daycare as an alternative to single-parent welfare, the need for daycare workers would escalate dramatically. The supply of daycare centres is nowhere near the actual demand for such services, reports a Vanier Institute of the Family study, with one licensed daycare space for every ten working mothers in Canada. Despite an election promise to create 50,000 daycare spaces, up to a total of 150,000 for each year in which the economy grows by 3 percent, it would seem that the federal Liberal government is withdrawing from its daycare commitments. Metro Toronto will receive only $4 million of the $33 million that was originally promised. With growth likely to remain below the 3 percent mark for the next couple of years, daycare will suffer somewhat. In Ontario, the Harris government is planning to introduce a voucher system which would replace subsidized daycare and give parents the option of where to place their children. School-age daycare may be completely deregulated as well.

A Metro Toronto daycare study in 1994 found that only 10 percent of parents would leave their child in unlicensed care if cost were not a factor. Costs have been rising, however. In 1992, the average cost in Canada was $2,270, which was 38 percent higher than the previous decade; but in 1994, it cost $6,850 on average in Ontario. This may explain why licensed daycare for children under 18 months accounts for only 5.4 percent of the parental choice for care. Nannies are used by 9.3 percent, relatives by 24.7 percent, and unlicensed non-relatives outside the home by 26.3 percent, according to a 1995 Statistics Canada national child care study.

BULLETIN BOARD – *DAYCARE*

CONTACTS

- Canadian Child Care Federation
  #401, 120 Holland Ave.,
  Ottawa, ON K1Y 0X6 Tel. 613-729-5289 Fax: 613-729-3159
- Childcare Advocacy Association of Canada
  323 Chapel St.,
  Ottawa, ON K1N 7Z2 Tel. 613-594-3196 Fax: 613-594-9375

The latest demand is for adult daycare centres for disabled elderly people; there are 3,000 such centres across the country. According to the National Council on Aging, roughly 10,000 centres will be needed by 2000.

Psychologists, Psychiatrists, Social Workers, and Other Mental Health Workers

An estimated 25 percent of Canadians suffer from mild depression, which is treated by drugs or counseling, while 10 percent become dependent upon long-term anti-depressants or are hospitalized. According to one British study, mental illnesses increase during times of change. In Canada, downsizings and uncertainty about the future have caused individuals considerable anguish. In 1992, a national study of stress and depression by the Canadian Mental Health Association and the Canadian Psychiatric Association revealed that 47 percent of Canadians feel "really stressed" at least a few times a week and in some cases all the time. Work and financial pressures accounted for the highest levels of stress experienced by people 25 to 54 years old. Of those employees left after a downsizing, 52 percent claimed the potential for burnout was quite high, while 33 percent felt it was very high, according to a 1994 Accountemps survey. Roughly two-thirds of working mothers and half of working fathers experience unreasonable high stress levels. The number of workers moonlighting has grown by 50 percent over the past decade, leading to one out of every five employed patients visiting doctors to complain of chronic fatigue. With the average couple spending only 20 minutes per day sharing time together, it likely that overwork and poor communication are compounding stress and depression both at work and at home. Aside from dramatically increasing marital difficulties, these factors also help explain why 670,000 workers are on long-term disability claims at a cost of $300 million per year.

In a national health survey conducted by economist Earl Berger and Price Waterhouse, the number of individuals expecting to develop health problems as a result of work-related stress doubled between 1989 and 1994, with six out of ten workers citing on-the-job stress as having already caused them health problems. Thirty to 50 percent more women than men feel they will likely fall victim to stress-induced health problems. By profession, 28 percent of professional, administrative, and managerial employees versus 18 percent of skilled, semi-skilled, and service workers felt susceptible to health problems brought on by stress at work. The Canadian Mental Health Association estimates that employers are paying $1 billion annually in costs associated with job stress. U.S. studies estimate the cost of depression anywhere between $27 and $100 billion annually through lost productivity, higher susceptibility to illness, and loss of life through suicide. The annual U.S. market for anti-depressants alone is worth a hefty $1.1 billion. According to benefits consultant Fred Holmes at Towers Perrin, as boomers approach their 50s, "people are beginning to stop treading water and drown." He expects long-term disability premiums will triple by 2005.

It was found that the major cause of stress was reorganization of the workplace. Many also suffer from stress because they are staying in jobs they hate for fear of not being able to find jobs if they quit. As casual and contract work becomes a reality for many individuals, stress-related illnesses will become even more widespread. Not surprisingly, relaxation clinics have seen their clientele double since 1993, and business for massage therapists has increased substantially as well. Anxiety and panic disorder clinics are trying to cope with a growing clientele. In 1992, between 20 and 25 percent of Canadians suffered panic attacks. Dr. Mel Goodman, past president of the General Practice Psychotherapy Association, reports, "Fifty percent of visits to family doctors involve non-organic [mental] problems." The aging population will also increase the demand for the services of therapists, psychologists, and psychiatrists. There is and there will continue to be a shortage of psychotherapists and psychologists. In fact, most of Canada's 12,000 psychologists and 3,500 psychiatrists are fully booked. Generally speaking, if you live in a large urban centre and need to visit a psychiatrist, you have a long wait ahead of you, or more frustrating, you may find that you can't even get on a psychiatrist's waiting list.

Elder care is becoming a pressing concern. By the year 2000, almost half of all workers will have some day-to-day responsibilities for elderly patients. At the moment, 34 percent of CIBC's 38,000 employees have responsibilities for elderly parents outside the home; 5.6 percent, in their homes; and 17 percent take care of children as well as parents. Employee assistance programs (EAPs) are now addressing this growing concern.

Many companies and unions, recognizing the need for employee counseling, provide access to counseling as part of the work contract. Warren Shepell Consultants Corp. of Toronto earned $8 million in 1992 by offering counseling services to the employees of large corporations such as American Express Canada Inc., Du Pont Canada Inc., General Electric, IBM, Molson Companies Ltd., and Northern Telecom. The company makes its counselors available 24 hours a day year-round, and estimates that it saves employers $7 for every $1 invested in its employee assistance programs. Warren Shepell estimates that 70 percent of all mid-size or bigger firms now have EAP programs in place, with 5 percent employing a staff counselor or psychologist.

Studies have shown that individuals in a high income bracket are more prone to anxiety, while low-income individuals are more susceptible to depression. We might argue, therefore, that since the number of low-income earners will increase as the trend to part-time, contract, and casual hiring becomes more firmly entrenched, so will the number of people suffering from depression. Furthermore, the trend toward eradicating middle management will create a very large group of displaced managers who will likely experience bouts of anxiety. With individuals almost universally uncertain about future employment in a changing economy, there will be an increased need for psychiatric nurses and addiction or human services counselors.

The doubling of violent crimes by adolescents in the past decade will likely escalate as family stress levels continue to rise. More child-care and youth-care workers will be needed to assist families in dealing with young offenders. In Canada, 60 percent of the female-led single-parent families live below the poverty line, with 45 percent of all Canadian children likely to experience life in a single-parent family before the age of 18. The devastating effect of divorce on children, as described in an *Atlantic Monthly* article entitled "Dan Quayle Was Right," suggests that the social and psychological repercussions of life in a single-parent family will be profound and will be exacerbated by the long-term effects of unemployment. According to Dr. Paul Steinhauer, senior psychiatrist at Toronto's Hospital for Sick Children, the incidence of reported child abuse has doubled in the past five years, and one in five children or adolescents has at least one psychiatric disorder. Given that stepfathers are 40 to 100 times more likely to commit serious child abuse than biological

BULLETIN BOARD – *MENTAL HEALTH*

- **Job demand factors:** the recession; corporate reorganization; uncertainty about the economic future; staying in undesirable jobs out of fear; aging population.
- **Job growth areas:** psychologists; psychiatrists; psychotherapists; community workers; child-care and youth-care workers; massage and relaxation therapists; correctional workers; psychiatric nurses; gerontology specialists or activation coordinators; eating-disorder specialists.
- **Skills, abilities, qualities, education needed:** at least a master's degree is required of those interested in aspiring to supervisory or executive positions.
- **Growth limiting factors:** ability and willingness of governments, corporations, and individuals to pay for psychological services; the economy.

fathers, according to Dr. David Popende, University of New Brunswick, New Jersey, even remarriage is a less than ideal solution – so more specialists will be needed in this area.

With governments cutting back on welfare expenditures, many social workers and welfare workers are being let go. Some colleges have now eliminated their Social Service Worker programs as a result. More responsibility for those in need is being transferred involuntarily to community and volunteer agencies.

The trend toward integrating special needs individuals – the mentally or physically challenged – into the community will create a demand for trained social service personnel who can facilitate this transition. And the trend toward moving the elderly out of institutional settings and into the home will require the services of community-based gerontology specialists.

Psychologists have moved into all aspects of the business world as human resources, leadership, teamwork, non-monetary motivation, and user-friendliness become more vital to corporate competitiveness. Cognitive psychologists are even involved in the design of software, to make sure that programs work in a user-friendly manner and that

BULLETIN BOARD – *MENTAL HEALTH*

CONTACTS

☛ Canadian Association of Social Workers
#402, 383 Parkdale Avenue
Ottawa, ON K1Y 4R4 Tel. 613-729-6668 Fax: 613-729-9608

☛ Canadian Mental Health Association
2160 Yonge St., 3rd Fl.,
Toronto, ON M4S 2Z3 Tel. 416-484-7750 Fax: 416-484-4617
URL: http://www.ie.org/~cmhator/

☛ Canadian Psychiatric Association
#200, 237 Argyle,
Ottawa, ON K2P 1B8 Tel. 613-234-2815 Fax: 613-234-9857
Toll-free: 1-800-267-1555

☛ Canadian Psychological Association
#205, 151 Slater Street
Ottawa, ON K1P 5H3 Tel. 613-237-2144 Fax: 613-237-1674
E-mail: cpa@psychologyassoc.ca URL: http://www.phoenix.ca/cpa/

☛ Canadian Public Health Association
#400, 1565 Carling Ave.,
Ottawa, ON K1Z 8R1 Tel. 613-725-3769 Fax: 613-725-9826

☛ Family Service Canada
#600, 220 Laurier Avenue West
Ottawa, ON K1P 5Z9 Tel. 613-230-9960 Fax: 613-230-5884

☛ Social Science Federation of Canada
#415, 151 Slater St.,
Ottawa, ON K1P 5H3 Tel. 613-238-6112 Fax: 613-238-6114
E-mail: Bitnet:ssfc@uottawa

instruction manuals are easily understood. As hiring and training become more "scientific," psychologists will play a greater role in career counselling, testing, and skills and personality assessment. For instance, one industrial psychologist in Markham, Ontario, specializes in helping firms spot and prepare future leaders. Psychologists' role in industrial organizations is continually expanding, with many acting as consultants when companies restructure.

Where the Jobs Are in Police and Firefighting Services

Firefighting and police services normally enjoy substantial employment growth. In the past, these occupations would grow as the population grew. Today, however, municipalities have cut back all expenditures as a result of eroding tax bases and tax defaults and are not hiring in these areas. Taxpayers are at their limit of fiscal tolerance and are unlikely to support further increases in the mill rate – the taxation rate as a percentage of the value of their homes. However, with crime rates escalating at over double the rate of population expansion, over the long term, despite the occasional downturn, the need for increased protection has become an important civic issue.

Government and municipal cutbacks are affecting employment in the police forces. Ontario's government is looking to reduce its Ontario Provincial Police force by 20 percent, closing detachments and reducing

BULLETIN BOARD – *POLICE AND FIREFIGHTING SERVICES*

- **Job demand factors:** rising crime rates and expanding population; aging population's preoccupation with security and safety.
- **Job growth areas:** private security firms; opportunities for women and minority groups in police and firefighting professions.
- **Growth limiting factors:** municipal budgets and tax revolts.

CONTACTS

☛ Canadian Association of Fire Fighters (Ind.)
  11J Rayborn Crescent
  St. Albert, AB T8N 5C3 Tel. 403-458-2503 Fax: 403-458-2503
  Toll-free: 1-800-661-4924
☛ Canadian Guard Association (Ind.)
  #305, 2841 Riverside Dr.,
  Ottawa, ON K1V 8X7 Tel. 613-737-4417 Fax: 613-737-5248
☛ Canadian Police Association
  141 Catherine St.,
  Ottawa, ON K2P 1C3 Tel. 613-231-4168 Fax: 613-231-3254
☛ Federal Association of Security Officials
  PO Box 2384, Station D
  Ottawa, ON K1P 5W5 Tel. 613-990-2615 Fax: 613-990-9077

services. In Metro Toronto, general police patrol has disappeared and the number of cruisers available at any one time has been cut in half. Improved technology and new delivery methods (such as collision reporting centres) are now responsible for a 60 to 70 percent reduction in the workload of frontline officers. In 1994, only 34.3 percent of the calls required dispatching a police vehicle, so the remaining calls were handled by an alternative response unit. People are now being asked to go to stations to fill in reports. Neighbourhood Watch and Community Liaison Committee activities are growing to include volunteer activities in area-specific mini-stations.

Alternative security employment makes sense for those looking for work with the forces; consider the trend in the U.S. In 1970, twice as much money was spent on public policing as on private policing; however, in 1990, twice as much was spent on private policing as on public security. In the U.S., there are more people working as security guards and undercover theft preventers in malls than there are people working as sales staff.

Firefighters and police departments have quota hiring systems which will benefit minority groups, including women, who seek employment in these areas. Since hiring will not increase fast enough to meet the security needs of the population at large, there will be a rapid increase in employment among private security firms. An aging population will be very security-conscious and will be willing to pay whatever price is necessary to ensure their safety.

Although the transition to a cashless society will lower the rate of mugging, thieves will still be interested in stealing personal possessions. Eventually, everyone will be fingerprinted in some sense and will own personal alarm systems. Forensic science and satellite surveillance will improve to such an extent that criminals will find it harder to avoid getting caught. Eventually, therefore, jobs will be in the high end of police work.

In an information age, there is more money to be made stealing information rather than physical items. A 1994 Ernst & Young Information Week survey found that 50 percent of companies reported compromised information systems within the past year. Catching cyberthiefs and beefing up computer security are the new economy jobs that are going to flourish.

Manufacturing and Natural Resources

Where the Jobs Are in Manufacturing
• **Construction** • **Automobiles and Automotive Parts** • **Aerospace, Defence, and Other Transportation Manufacturing** • **Food and Beverage Processing** • **Chemicals** • **Plastics** • **Steel**

About halfway into the technological revolution we are beginning to see increased shortages of skilled labour alongside the growing surplus of unskilled labour. There is fierce competition from developing countries which are becoming increasingly powerful in economic terms. From the point of view of jobs in the industrialized nations, it is important to remember that developing countries have three times as many people of working age as do OECD countries. And they are willing to work for significantly lower wages. In 1993, for example, it cost a hefty $24.90 an hour to hire a worker in Germany; American and Japanese workers were cheaper at $16 to $17 an hour. In striking contrast, hourly labour costs were $4.90 in South Korea, $2.40 in Mexico, and less than $1 in China and Thailand. In labour-intensive industries, it's not hard to see that firms have a big incentive to move to a cheaper country.

In the past 30 years only a few developing economies, such as South Korea and Taiwan, have turned themselves into industrialized ones. Over the next decade, dozens of such tigers are likely to emerge, including huge countries such as China. On the plus side, however, in recent years developing countries have been the fastest-growing export markets for OECD nations. This makes the emergence of new economies into the global market a huge opportunity, not a threat. Generally speaking, North American industry will specialize in skill-intensive manufacturing supported by advanced technology and will import humbler goods from Mexico and other lower-wage areas. The demand for unskilled workers will continue to fall, therefore, and so will their wages relative to those of skilled workers. In Mexico, by contrast, the wages of unskilled workers will rise while the underemployment rate among educated workers stays high; it was 26 percent in 1996. Doctors, lawyers, and engineers are waiting on tables and picking crops.

Locally, the 1991–92 recession and a drop in overall competitiveness (as reflected in higher labour costs between 1980 and 1992) contributed to poor performance by the manufacturing industry and corollary job losses, particularly in southern Ontario and Quebec. Between 1980 and 1992, manufacturing cost competitiveness deteriorated by 25 percent relative to the United States. This is due in part to the fact that only 35 percent of Canada's manufacturing sector uses advanced technology, compared with 50 percent in the United States.

The high cost of Canadian capital in a capital-intensive industry makes it impossible for many mature companies to afford the newer technologies, given the rate of return on capital in industries where competition is based on low prices and thin margins. However, if these companies do not invest in technology, they will not survive. Those sectors that are more technology-intensive – such as transportation equipment, rubber and plastics, electrical and electronic products, machinery, and chemicals – performed better than total manufacturing. Investment in technology is now a critical indicator of productivity and competitiveness in virtually every industry.

From 1990 to 1993 the manufacturing sector lost about 210,000 jobs, or over 10 percent of its entire work force. In comparison with manufacturing, the service industry over this period attracted attention because of strong and persistent growth. StatsCan estimates that in 1994 there were 1,949,000 jobs in manufacturing and 4,932,000 jobs in services. According to futurist John Kettle, if the present trends continue, there will be 3.6 million goods-producing jobs and 11.9 million service jobs by 2003.

Twenty years ago, manufacturing contributed 22 percent to Canada's gross domestic product; in 1996 that figure stood at 18 percent. Over the same period, however, the value and spinoff impact of the goods and services that manufacturers bought rose from 28 percent of the GDP to 34 percent. Put in this format, Canada's manufacturing industry and the services it supports represent more than half of the GDP. Ontario gained 123,000 net new manufacturing jobs in 1995, half of all new jobs created in Canada. Manufacturing unemployment fell to 8.9 percent, half a point below the national average.

The industry employs 1.9 million Canadians; creates $350 billion in production, more than half of which is exported to world markets; and has one of the highest rates of productivity growth in the entire OECD. The OECD predicted that Canada would lead all other G-7 countries in growth in 1996. It is estimated that every dollar of industrial output in Canada generates $3.05 in total economic activity. This represents greater leverage than any other sector of the economy yields. Canada's manufacturers created 100,000 more new jobs in 1995 than in 1994. The new manufacturing jobs accounted for more than 50 percent of the total jobs created in 1995.

Manufacturers are accelerating their use of advanced technologies and robotics. For example, computer-assisted design and manufacturing systems (CAD-CAM) were used by 57 percent of firms in 1992. In 1995, that number had increased to 70 percent. This trend is part of a larger reinvestment by manufacturers in new machinery and equipment. In dollar terms, reinvestment was up 9 percent in 1995 over the previous year and was expected to rise 7 percent in 1996. Reinvestment is critical because it increases productivity (and profitability), thereby enabling strong, efficient, constantly retooling, competitive organizations.

Manufacturing Our Future, a 1995 report by the Canadian Manufacturers' Association, highlights the fact that there will be more changes in the industry worldwide in the next five or ten years than there have been in the past 50 years. For example, advances in Intelligent Manufacturing Systems include a new holonic production system that reverses and exponentially expands the flexibility of the agile cellular production systems that are rapidly evolving. This system puts the factory equipment – robots, laser cutting tools, welding devices – on computerized, individually moveable carriages that can roll around on wheels. Stephen Van Houten, president of the Canadian Manufacturers' Association, comments on the system: "This is a singular new phenomenon – the factory on wheels – where the plant layout and production system are infinitely reconfigurable on a daily basis. The result is several steps closer to one of industry's central goals: the competitive batch of one, an environment in which a plant can produce car parts one day, furniture the next and kitchen appliances the day after that." Mass customization is rapidly replacing mass production in the new economy, enabled by technology advances such as this which reduce costs and improve flexibility.

Virtual organizations (loose reconfigurable networks of individuals or firms with particular skills, production capabilities, or market access which come together temporarily to develop and manufacture a particular

TOO CLOSE TO HOME

In 1980, 75 percent of the manufactured products purchased here were made in Canada; in 1995, only 40 percent were, according to the Canadian Manufacturers' Association Year End Review and Outlook. In 1980 exports constituted 25 percent of our manufacturing output, but in 1995, they amounted to 60 percent, with 80 percent going to the U.S. The export market is now 42 percent of the GDP and is the fastest-growing area of the economy. In 1994, exports to the United States amounted to $177.9 billion; to Japan, $9.3 billion, and to the U.K., $3.1 billion. Because of this concentration in U.S. markets, Canada received the worst ranking in the 1995 World Competitiveness Report on trade diversification (48th place, at the very bottom of the 48-country list). Overall, Canada was in 12th place, compared to its 16th-place spot in 1994.

product) are fast becoming the norm in the industry. Van Houten notes that the lack of scale of Canadian plants, which was once considered a competitive weakness, is becoming a strength when the premium is on rapid production and rapid distribution. In line with this trend, he also predicts that unions will not be able to stop thousands of workers from selling their skills to employment agencies that will farm them out to companies on a continual basis.

Even the Japanese laid off 2 million workers in 1993, with workers in the manufacturing sector accounting for two out of every three laid off. During the 1980s, Southeast Asian countries, which became rapidly industrialized, increased their portion of the manufactured-goods trade from 4.2 percent to 8.5 percent, taking market share away from all the industrialized countries, including Japan. Such a transfer of manufacturing to developing countries is a normal part of economic evolution, and has been facilitated by inexpensive transportation and new manufacturing techniques.

Competitive pressures have led to the universal adoption of the ISO 9000 quality assurance programs, which are set by the International Standards Organization and recognized in 89 countries. Qualification requires that a company document its procedures and upgrade them where necessary before verification by an independent agency, which also returns periodically for partial audits. Toronto Plastics, for example, implementing ISO quality initiatives, reduced its defects from 150,000 per million parts to 15,000 with the hopes of eventually reaching the world-class level of 1,000. Northern Telecom aims to have all 55 of its worldwide plants certified in the near future. And in the U.S., General Electric's plastics division ordered its suppliers to meet ISO standards. The Big Three automobile manufacturers have ordered their suppliers to meet their industry's quality standard, QS 9000, by 1997.

Given the interdependence between the goods and services sectors, improving efficiency in the services supplied to manufacturers would strongly improve the latter's competitiveness. According to *The Economist*, "GM's biggest supplier is not a steel or glass firm, but a health-care provider, Blue Cross-Blue Shield. In terms of output, one of GM's biggest 'products' is financial and insurance services, which together with EDS, its computing-services arm, account for a fifth of total revenue.... At Sony, as much as a fifth of its revenues now come from its film and music businesses. Add in design, marketing, finance, and after-sales support, and service activities account for at least half of Sony's business." Even many manufacturing-related services such as design and engineering are now being contracted out to independent companies. How important is design? According to a study by Britain's Open University and the University of Manchester's Institute of Science and Technology, over 90 percent of design projects made money, with average increases in sales of 41 percent, while 16 percent resulted in new or expanded export markets.

Most important in determining success in the manufacturing industry is the state of the economy as a whole. As Peter Cook, economics editor of the *Globe and Mail*, asserts, "The main determinant is not whether tariffs are cut by a minor amount in a free-trade agreement. It is how successful Canada is in keeping internal costs under control. The patterns of the past show that when the business climate deteriorates – because of an overvalued currency, a bout of wage inflation or government intervention to raise taxes, impede investment or increase regulation – Canada puts its manufacturing base at risk."

Employment opportunities in manufacturing will not increase dramatically over the next ten years. Individuals with expertise in high-tech areas will make up the majority of hirees. Outsourcing will spur growth

BULLETIN BOARD – *MANUFACTURING*

- **Job demand factors:** the need to reduce costs and improve production efficiency.
- **Job growth areas:** quality assurance personnel; numerical control technologists; automation design, manufacturing, maintenance, and sales personnel; independent design and engineering services; other supplier service areas.
- **Job reduction areas:** all low-skilled and some medium-skilled jobs.
- **Growth limiting factors:** government policies; multinational manufacturing decisions; competitiveness of supplier services; wages; inflation; currency's comparative value; government debt and the resulting interest rates; rate of technological innovation and its adoption.

CONTACTS

☛ Canadian Manufacturers' Association
75 International Blvd., 4th Fl.,
Toronto, ON M9W 6L9 Tel. 416-798-8000 Fax: 416-798-8050

in many small design and engineering services. Supplier services will play an important competitive role in manufacturing, and many jobs will be created in this area as manufacturers become more global or export-oriented. Government policies will likely be most significant in determining the industry's future. With 3.3 million Canadians currently working in manufacturing, the livelihoods of scores of people will depend on how these factors play themselves out.

In 1995, the industrial machinery export market did well. Also consider firms engaged in contract manufacturing, which is becoming a hot practice in North American industry. Factories-for-hire are feeding the high-tech assembly boom, particularly in the automotive, medical, consumer electronics, telecommunications, and computer fields. Where companies once ran their own manufacturing facilities to provide their branded products, many are deciding they can outsource production in profitable ways. For example, Celestica Inc., a former subsidiary of IBM, sold almost $1 billion worth of manufacturing services to non-IBM companies in 1995. While this figure accounted for a neat 25 percent of IBM's revenue in 1995, it was expected to grow to 30 percent in 1996 and as high as 50 percent by 1997. Span Manufacturing, a contract manufacturer based in Markham, Ontario, says the business is growing too fast to track. Technology Forecasters Inc. says there are 500 large contract manufacturers in Canada and the U.S., accounting for about 15 percent of all electronics manufacturing today. The factory-for-rent industry, virtually non-existent in North America a decade ago, was worth about US$19.7 billion in 1995 and was expected to top $50 billion in 1996.

Construction

National housing starts in 1995 plunged to a 35-year low of 111,000 dwellings, in contrast to average annual starts of 158,000 in the early 1990s. The collapse in the housing market wiped out an estimated 150,000 jobs in the sector, according to the Canadian Home Builders Association. The outlook remains pessimistic. Builders polled by the association expect to start only 105,000 new homes in 1996, even below the CMHC (Canada Mortgage and Housing Corp.) forecast of 111,000 starts.

The housing industry has lobbied the federal government for tax concessions on new housing on the basis of their figures that each housing start generates 2.8 person-years of employment in either construction

---

HARD-HAT ROBOTS

In the future, robotics will have a dramatic impact on the construction industry. The Obayashi Corporation already has workers using television to monitor the progress of robots. On top of an emerging building, a box-like construction factory moves up along with the construction of the building. Inside, the components are moved by automatic lifts as giant vacuum suckers grab the floor and lift them to the appropriate places. Welding robots seal beam sections while moving on circular tracks. Only one-sixth the number of workers are required. The Tansie Corporation utilizes a covered platform resting on the building's central core, which is raised by a powerful jack. With crane operators now able to build outer sections of a building six floors below it, floors can be built in three days, as opposed to the customary five or six. In these roof-covered systems, work can continue regardless of the weather.

---

or spinoff jobs in other industries. The best stimuli for housing, of course, are a strong economy and consumer confidence, two factors which may not be with us in the short term. Analysts say that the national housing market, like the economy as a whole, is suffering from a collapse in consumer confidence caused by high unemployment, government cuts, and stagnant or declining disposable income. Other trends such as young adults turning away from buying homes, possibly because of limited job prospects, and slower population growth in the mid-1990s affect housing starts.

The monthly value of residential building permits issued by Canadian municipalities was generally declining throughout 1995, auguring cuts in construction and employment. Industrial construction permits increased slightly because of several large construction projects in the paper and allied products industry. Across Canada, construction of new homes plunged to an annual rate of 101,800 in May 1995.

It is indicative of the state of the market that shares in Canada's largest publicly traded real estate developers continue to fall, reaching record lows in some cases. In February 1996, the Dominion Bond Rating Service downgraded most of Canada's developers with exposure to office or retail space. Commercial real estate developers have been suffering the fallout from dismal retail sales, high consumer debt, and an oversupply of office space. Frank Mayer, an analyst with James Capel Canada Inc., believes Canadian real estate is lagging behind the U.S. market because of overcapacity, low consumer confidence, and government downsizing. There are a number of real estate companies going through restructurings to try to come to terms with the realities of the 1990s.

While few forecasters have been very optimistic, George Vasic, vice president for strategy and economics for Bunting Warburg Inc., highlights the fact that when markets collapse and an economic slowdown is under way, it represents only a pause between the first and second halves of the economic growth cycle. Resale activity and new construction traditionally hit their best levels during the second phase; that is the period in which prices climb and activity is most likely to accelerate. The rationale for the pattern is that it takes time after a recession for people to buy big-ticket items such as housing again. Last time around, the recession ended in 1982, but the first year of substantial price gains was 1986. Capacity utilization figures, the unemployment rate, and the prime rate

BULLETIN BOARD – *CONSTRUCTION*

- **Job demand factors:** population growth; better-designed industrial buildings which efficiently incorporate information technology and work flow.
- **Job growth areas:** public construction, particularly road infrastructure; industrial design buildings; small single-family dwellings; building and exporting prefabricated houses; renovation and repair once the economy improves; cottage winterization and construction of country estates; black-market renovation; companies with contracts abroad; condos for retirees moving to British Columbia.
- **Job reduction areas:** Office, mall, and other commercial construction in the short term and possibly in the long run.
- **Growth limiting factors:** population; government funds available; home offices; home shopping; economy; labour and raw material costs.

CONTACTS

☞ Canada Construction Skills Association
2395 Speakman Dr.,
Mississauga, ON L5K 1B3 Tel. 905-822-4111

☞ Canadian Construction Association
85 Albert St., 10th Fl.,
Ottawa, ON K1P 6A4 Tel. 613-236-9455 Fax: 613-236-9526

☞ Canadian Home Builders Association
#200, 150 Laurier Avenue West
Ottawa, ON K1P 6M7 Tel. 613-230-3060 Fax: 613-232-8214

were all at levels quite similar to where we are now. Vasic does not see a repeat of the 1980s boom and is not predicting that housing will make a dramatic move soon, but he is confident that, based on these trends, it will indeed pick up in time.

The surplus of office towers, shopping malls, and industrial parks will dampen recovery in these areas. Industrial design building, however, is on the increase. Home offices, office sharing, and home shopping may eventually have a profound dampening effect on the commercial and retail markets. In 1993, the construction of single detached homes was growing at a 15 percent rate, thanks to lower interest rates, declining

BUILDERS GET TOGETHER WITH ENVIRONMENTALISTS

With an unemployment rate of about 40 percent and 20,000 of its members out of work, construction trade representatives in Toronto looked in 1995 to profitable alliances with environmentalists via a conference featuring workshops on energy-efficient materials used in residential and commercial construction. The Toronto Building and Construction Trades Council encouraged energy-efficient construction and retrofitting. According to Toronto City Councillor Peter Tabuns, a $3 billion energy efficiency program in Toronto would provide 6,000 construction jobs annually and result in electricity savings of $400 million in each year of a 10-year program.

house prices, and demand from the tail end of the baby boom.

The building repair and renovation market will continue at a moderate rate. In Toronto in 1995, 16 office buildings totalling 1.4 million square feet were converted to residential use in the city centre. While that sounds like a lot, out of the total of 146 million square feet of office space, about 26 million square feet was empty in 1995. Vancouver is expected to have Canada's lowest commercial vacancy rate in 1996 – 8.6 percent, which will eventually translate from leasing activity to development activity. In housing, new dwelling pricing will influence decisions about whether to renovate. In mid-1995 prices in Vancouver were still about 45 percent above their 1989 values, while in Toronto, the other major Canadian housing growth location, prices languished about 25 percent below the 1989 highs. Black-market renovation makes it difficult to accurately report on residential construction activity. According to an estimate by the Canadian Home Builders Association, it is believed that 55 percent of all renovations in Canada involve non-recorded cash payments. Such a significant amount of undisclosed renovation activity represents a substantial increase over the 30 percent level of black-market renovations prior to the introduction of the GST.

Some specialty industries are doing well, such as makers of prefabricated or modular homes, offices, or cottages; they are cheaper to build, are better constructed, and can be added onto at a later date. Both the domestic and export markets have been favourable for these products and will likely continue to be, as long as the virtues of price and quality remain a competitive edge. Toronto's Royal Plastics Group Ltd., one of North America's largest extruders of PVC building products, set its sights on the international housing market with the patented invention of a plastic Lego-like house in 1992. CEO Vic De Zen, 1995 entrepreneur of the year, says that "one day you and I will be living in plastic houses." With subsidiaries throughout Canada, the U.S., and Mexico, Royal Plastics' sales for its building products (windows, doors, blinds, etc.) totalled $453 million in 1994. On the west coast, Viceroy Homes, manufacturers of modular wood homes, saw sales in the millions climb dramatically with exports to Japan.

Automobiles and Automotive Parts

The auto boom began in 1965 when Canada signed the Auto Pact, a pioneering free trade agreement, with the United States. About 150,000 Canadians, the vast majority of them in Ontario, depend for their livelihood on the carmakers and parts companies that supply them. So tied is Ontario to automotive manufacturing that during the first six months of 1995, when car production fell 5.7 percent, Ontario's economy shrank by 1.5 percent. Auto assemblers and auto parts account for 4.3 percent of Ontario's GDP.

As a result of long-term foreign investment, Canadian auto-related companies have become world market leaders, and in turn, investors in other countries' auto industries. In 1994 2.3 million vehicles were produced in Canada, with 85 percent exported to the U.S. Canada's auto industry is worth $60 billion. Total sales in 1994 were 1.23 million vehicles, up 5.1 percent from 1993. In 1995 vehicle assembly and auto parts industries reported record shipments of $74.4 billion on a combined basis. Industry predictions were that production would rise to 2.5 or 2.6 million vehicles in 1996. Shipments from Canadian auto plants increased 18.1 percent in 1995 to $53.1 billion.

The auto industry is increasingly becoming a knowledge-based industry where much of the value is in the research and development, design, and engineering processes, in addition to the technology and jobs of traditional production. A study by BIS Strategic Decisions of Norwell, Mass., predicts the market for automotive electronics in the U.S., Japan, and Europe will grow to US$16.1 billion in 1999 from US$11.3 billion in 1994. This market research firm believes the fastest-growing segment in

BULLETIN BOARD – *AUTOMOTIVE INDUSTRY*

- **Job demand factors:** the low Canadian dollar and lower health care costs; outsourcing of parts design, engineering, and manufacturing.
- **Job growth areas:** large auto parts suppliers; automation and quality control specialists; parts design and engineering.
- **Job reduction areas:** all low-skilled areas.
- **Growth limiting factors:** taxes; worker's compensation; cost of electricity; social legislation such as pay equity and unemployment benefits; trainability of employees; trade agreements; origin-of-content rules; popularity of types of vehicles made in Canada; government's willingness to assist in training or financing.

CONTACTS

☞ Canadian Automobile Association
1775 Courtwood Cres.
Ottawa, ON K2C 3J2 Tel. 613-226-7631 Fax: 613-225-7383
☞ Automobile Industries Association of Canada
1272 Wellington St.,
Ottawa, ON K1Y 3A7 Tel. 613-728-5821 Fax: 613-728-6021
☞ Automotive Parts Manufacturers' Association
#516, 195 The West Mall.,
Etobicoke, ON M9C 5K1 Tel. 416-620-4220 Fax: 416-620-9730
☞ Automotive Parts Sectoral Training Council
#203, 140 Renfrew Dr.,
Markham, ON L3R 6B3

the industry will be that of driver information. High technology will be used for navigation and collision warning systems. Keyless entry and systems that sound alarms and immobilize the vehicle are also on the drawing boards. Consumers, politicians, and competitors are putting pressure on carmakers to come up with new ways to make cars safer and less harmful to the environment. Along with this trend, the industry is being very selective about new hires. Toyota job candidates, for example, experience up to 18 hours of interviews and written and physical tests for jobs that pay more than $20 an hour plus benefits. The jobs can be anything from driving a forklift truck to operating a crane that lifts dies weighing thousands of kilograms into a multimillion-dollar stamping press.

SPINNING WHEELS

As primary manufacturers, automakers generate enormous spinoff. Every dollar they spend generates almost $2 in derivative-sector growth and more than $3 in overall economic activity in the country. This multiplier effect is seen in the case of Honda Canada Inc.'s decision in December 1995 to invest $300 million in Alliston, Ontario, to build minivans. That will create about 1,200 high-paying plant jobs with a ripple effect on the Ontario economy that could mushroom to 8,000 jobs as the money spent generates another $300 million in economic activity. According to Nick Staines, an economist with the WEFA Group in Toronto, Honda's investment will have added another $117 million of activity into the economy by 1998, most of that in Ontario, for a total of $417 million. The forecasting model predicts that in 1999, with assumed full production of 120,000 vehicles, the overall impact will rise to $605 million, double the original amount. By 1999, a cumulative 6,800 jobs and by 2000, 8,800 jobs will have been created.

Ford, General Motors, Chrysler, Honda, Cami, and Toyota employ about 70,000 people, and in 1993 the plants contributed $4.6 billion to the economy. With the addition of new manufacturers, this figure has likely since increased. In 1994, the auto sector made up 17.37 percent of Ontario manufacturing and created 134,000 jobs – 81,000 in auto parts and 53,000 in auto assembly. This represented a steady climb from totals in 1993 of 130,600 (77,000 parts jobs, 53,600 auto jobs) and 1992 totals of 120,300 (70,000 parts jobs, 50,300 auto jobs). A booming U.S. auto market helped lift Canadian vehicle production in 1995 to a record high of 2.32 million units. GM was the country's top vehicle producer, accounting for 907,833 cars and light trucks. During 1995, production of cars, trucks, and minivans hit about 2.4 million, and a robust 8 to 10 percent growth was expected for 1996. The total value of all Canadian manufacturing shipments in 1995 was expected to be about $390 billion, roughly parallel to the contribution of the forest products industry's 6 percent share of the B.C. economy.

The quality of Canadian workers, our weak dollar, and low-cost health care have helped attract a string of investments from automobile manufacturers. Industry analysts say it's about 25 percent cheaper to manufacture in Canada than in the United States. Ontario plants produce about 15 percent of the North American total, even though Ontario has only about 2 percent of the population. The amount of auto investment by assemblers and parts producers amounted to more than $11 billion during the past five years. The auto industry gives the Canadian economy a huge economic boost by making 17 percent of the vehicles for the North American market, while Canadians purchase only 10 percent of continental production.

Chief economists for the Big Three automakers predicted that U.S. vehicle sales would be flat or rise moderately in 1996. Cuts in interest rates were offset by the cautious mood of debt-burdened buyers. The U.S. vehicle sales forecast for 1996 ranged from 14.7 million (Chrysler) to 15.3 million (General Motors).

Several companies are working on vehicles that respond to spoken commands. Ford has unveiled a prototype called the Synergy 2010. Using technology similar to hands-free cellular phones, the concept model will deliver voice-actuated control of traditional things like the audio and heating/cooling systems. GM is leading the drive to the alternative-energy vehicle and has promised to start selling battery-powered pickup trucks if Canadian fleet owners show enough interest. In the U.S. there has been interest by the utilities, and ten had requested some 900 vehicles as of early 1996. Upfront cost is a factor; the trucks will sell for about $46,000, and owners will need to replace the battery after about 50,000 kilometres or three years, whichever comes first. The battery price is not yet determined, but could range between $1,000 and $10,000.

By their own estimates, General Motors, Ford, and Chrysler buy parts from approximately 13,000 Canadian companies, 75 percent of which are small businesses. These small auto parts companies will continue to be threatened or absorbed by larger rivals in the next few years as the big automakers consolidate their lists of suppliers. The Automotive Parts Manufacturers' Association estimates that about 90 percent of its 200 members have annual revenues of less than $100 million, which means they may not have the critical mass required to make it on their own in an increasingly global market. Firms that emerge intact from the consolidation will have to be well capitalized for growth and expansion. Among those lining up as winners are Magna International Inc., the country's biggest auto parts supplier, with expected revenue of $6 billion in 1996. Magna won a six-year contract to build space frames for the European smart car, which will give it an annual revenue injection of $200 million beginning in 1998. Others include Linamar Corp,. Stackpole Ltd., A.G. Simpson Co. Ltd., Hayes-Dana Inc., Meridian Technologies Inc., Woodbridge Group, and Ventra Group Inc., which has annual revenues of about $280 million. These tier one suppliers get directly involved with R&D of new models and provide entire sections of a vehicle, such as the seats, safety systems, or drivetrain. Billions of dollars will be saved by designing cars which share 40 to 70 percent of their parts. Not long ago suppliers had up to 27 departments to sell parts to at GM; in 1995 that was down to just two.

Thanks to new management systems and big investments in new machinery, the parts markers now match the productivity of their American counterparts. Sales by parts manufacturers in the area of

---

CARS OF THE FUTURE

Super-efficient cars called hypercars are lightweight, have sleek stream-lining, and enjoy superior fuel efficiency. In 1991, 50 GM experts built an encouraging example of ultralight composite construction and equipped it with a hybrid-electric drive which increases efficiency by about 30 to 50 percent. Crash tests proved it to be at least as safe as today's steel cars in a head-on collision because the composites are extraordinarily strong and bouncy and can absorb far more energy than metal can. The biggest advantages of composites emerge in manu-facturing. Only 15 percent of the cost of a typical steel car part is for the steel; the other 85 percent pays for pounding, welding, and smoothing it. Composites are formed to the desired shape not by multiple strikes with tool-steel stamping dies but in single moulding dies made of coated epoxy. In September 1993, after decades of adversarial positioning, the Big Three automakers agreed to commit their best efforts to developing this hypercar – a tripled-efficiency clean car – within a decade. The hypercar's key technologies already exist; major firms around the world are starting to build prototypes. When these cars start to be mass pro-duced, there will be some major changes in the industry, including some harmful effects on other industries such as steel.

$18.1 billion in 1994 translated into about 85,000 jobs. The 1995 figures were on track to top $21 billion. In the early 1990s, however, 54 automotive parts makers closed, taking 20,000 jobs with them. Over 20 percent of the Canadian parts manufacturers have four employees or fewer, and 60 percent have fewer than 50 workers. As the automakers go global and insist that their suppliers go with them, the challenge for suppliers is to have the financial resources to follow. These smaller companies will be threatened if they are not able to go global.

According to Maryann Keller, a leading U.S. expert on the auto industry, much of the future growth in auto sales and production will occur in developing countries such as China, India, and Brazil, rather than in North America, Europe, or Japan. Demand in North America will be weakened due to an aging population which is less inclined to buy new cars at higher prices. Better quality will also continue to contribute to less frequent replacement of cars. Developing countries are building more capacity than their own markets can consume and they will become aggressive exporters. North America will therefore have to deal with surplus capacity, which could mean more plant closings. At the same time, Mexico is becoming more of a production force for North America. It will be the auto parts companies that bear much of the burden of this adjustment. They will be forced to do more R&D, to lower costs and margins, and to decide how to be players in the club of global suppliers. According to Pete Mateja, president of the Automotive Parts Manufacturers' Association, offshore companies currently buy 8 percent of their parts, or about $2 billion worth, from Canadian suppliers. As U.S. and Canadian markets mature, suppliers must be ready to move overseas to chase new business.

Aerospace, Defence, and Other Transportation Manufacturing

The Canadian aerospace and defence sector is a $10.9 billion production industry, the sixth-largest in the world, after those of the United States, Britain, France, Germany, and Japan. The industry is a vital source of foreign currency for Canada, generating a trade surplus of $2.3 billion. The aerospace industry is Canada's second-largest spender on R&D, with 1995 research and development expenditures totaling $902 million. Seventy percent of Canadian product – amounting to $8 billion of sales – is exported, with 50 percent going to the U.S.

BULLETIN BOARD – *AEROSPACE, DEFENCE, AND OTHER TRANSPORTATION*

- **Job demand factors:** small high-tech specialized aerospace firms; small regional airline planes; subway and railcar replacement or refurbishing; watercraft market.
- **Job growth areas:** subway and railcar plants; aerospace generally.
- **Growth limiting factors:** willingness of governments to subsidize various transportation markets; peace; troubles in the airline industry; decisions to refurbish as opposed to replace; popularity of water and winter sports which are demographically determined; decline of business travel.

CONTACTS

☛ Aerospace Industries Association of Canada
#1200, 60 Queen St.,
Ottawa, ON K1P 5Y7 Tel. 613-232-4297 Fax: 613-232-1142
E-mail: aiac@fox.nstn.ca

☛ Canadian Industrial Transportation League
#602, 1090 Don Mills Rd.
Don Mills, ON M3C 3R6 Tel. 416-447-7766 Fax: 416-447-7312

As in most other countries, the industry dwindled through the recession, but it managed to avoid the mergers, bankruptcies, and layoffs seen in the United States. Peter Smith, chairman of the Aerospace Industries Association, said Canada stayed afloat because it is less dependent on defence business than the United States and more adept at seeking other venues for its knowledge and expertise. Only 25 percent of Canadian aerospace production is destined for military markets. Thanks to this flexibility, Canadian aerospace manufacturers still employ 53,000 workers – largely in skilled and professional jobs – and several times this number among suppliers. Employment is expected to increase, with a growth rate of 15 percent expected for 1996 and industry sales expectations of $15.5 billion by the end of the century. About 60 percent of Canada's aerospace companies are foreign owned, however, and their manufacturing activities are highly mobile.

In export markets, Canadian companies supply a surprisingly wide array of sophisticated products to the largest aerospace manufacturers in the world, including wings, fuselages, jet engines, landing gear, rockets, satellites, and electronic equipment and instrumentation. Canadian manufacturers made a conscious decision to cut their reliance on government and military contracts, which has proven fortuitous as Western governments continue to trim defence spending. As a case in point, the Defence Industry Productivity Program (DIPP), a key source of R&D funds, will slash business subsidies from $3.4 billion in 1994–95 to $1.5 billion by 1997–98.

While hundreds of U.S. and European defence manufacturers have gone under or merged, most Canadian companies have survived because less than 30 percent of their revenue comes from military contracts. To cite several examples, Spar Aerospace cut 700 defence jobs and transformed itself into a provider of satellite communications. Software and communications now account for 50 percent of revenue for Spar. In 1996 Spar won a $30 million contract to build robotic work stations for the International Space Station program. Montreal-based Canadian Marconi Co. is adapting radar equipment to warn school bus drivers of any child standing in front of the bus. Rolls-Royce Industries Canada Inc. of Montreal has developed a special pincer that will cut through hydro or telephone cable lines, reducing the potential for catastrophe for low-flying helicopters.

Diversification into new technologies and the development of strategic alliances are enabling this industry to compete strategically. ComDev Ltd. of Cambridge, Ontario, has captured a commanding share of the global market (70 percent in 1994) for satellite subsystems that perform signal switching and multiplexing (the filtering and splitting of signals). The Canadian Aerospace Training Partnership sponsored by Western

---

MAJOR MERGER

In the United States, Boeing and McDonnell Douglas Corp. have merged their civil and military aerospace operations. This puts considerable pressure on European companies to form transnational groupings and is seen as a major threat to the Airbus Industrie consortium. This merger has created the world's largest aerospace and defence company, with turnover of more than US$35 billion.

Economic Diversification Canada in Winnipeg is an alliance between government and business to benefit the aeronautical industry in western Canada and market Canadian training skills across the world. In a similar vein, Prince Edward Island is attempting to attract aerospace companies to Slemon Park, a former military base at Summerside which houses aerospace companies and training facilities. With an attractive "No Tax Until the Year 2012" policy, it created about 400 direct jobs and 600 jobs in related industries in 1995.

Forecasts made in 1995 by the European Airbus Industrie consortium and Boeing Co. of Seattle indicate a slow but steady growth in the global industry over the next 20 years. Although the defence sector of the world aerospace industry is not strong, civilian travel is picking up and airlines are starting to renew their fleets. The report predicts a 5.1 percent growth in global air passenger traffic annually for the next 20 years, with

COMMERCIAL POSSIBILITIES FOR SPY SATELLITES

A handful of aerospace companies are investing as much as $1 billion in corporate earth-imaging systems. These corporate systems, using optical and digital technology that was freed by the U.S. government for private use in 1994, will offer days-old digital images of unprecedented clarity. Coldwell Banker Corp. is among those planning to offer real estate shoppers pictures from space of homes, neighbourhoods, and traffic patterns, a large value-added component over simple ground shots and maps. Excitement has been generated in other fields ranging from forensic crime research to forestry. Television networks such as ABC expect to transform the new digital images into remarkably detailed "flights" over battle zones for the evening news. Urban planners see new ways to direct growth and update property tax rolls. Pacific Bell is preparing to plot the laying of phone lines without sending costly crews to first study the terrain. Before the end of the decade consumers will also be able to summon fresh high-resolution pictures of far-flung vacation spots onto their home computer screens. Through the Internet, users will be able to draw from vast archives of global images for perhaps $100 a square mile, using technology from EarthWatch Inc. backed by Ball Aerospace and Technologies Corp., WorldView Imaging Corp., and Hitachi Ltd.

3.7 percent growth in America, 7.1 percent in the Asia-Pacific region, and as much as 10 percent in China.

If the forecasts bear out, the Asia-Pacific region will become one of the world's dominant airplane markets by the year 2014. Airbus believes this region and China will operate 25 percent of the world's jetliners, compared with 36 percent in North America and 26 percent in Europe. Boeing predicts a global need for 15,400 airplanes worth US$1 trillion over the next 20 years, or about 770 airplanes a year. That is below the 818 manufactured in 1991, but significantly higher than the 522 aircraft delivered in 1994. Airbus believes that 70 percent of new airplanes will be wide-bodied, with an average of 250 seats. By 2014 about 800 super-large airplanes capable of carrying more than 500 people will be needed to accommodate growing congestion in airports and air traffic lanes. At the other end of the spectrum, turboprops and small jets are proving popular locally for short hops and feeder routes, carrying passengers farther and faster at a fraction of the cost of a traditional airliner. The Canadair Regional Jet and de Havilland Dash 8 turboprops by Bombardier are selling well in this category.

Bombardier is a Montreal-based company that employs 37,000 world-wide. More than half its revenue of $5.9 billion is derived from aerospace activities, with transportation equipment and motorized consumer products accounting for the rest. Its new Global Express, a long-range (about 5,000 kilometres), high-speed business aircraft that seats 19 passengers, was slated for its first flight in 1996 and first deliveries in 1997. Upfront engineering will create 800 to 1,000 jobs in Canada, and the company confirms an order-book value of $1.5 billion, with more than 50 percent from outside the U.S., the traditional market. Bombardier has had extensive involvement in the Eurotunnel project, for which it manufactures the vehicles.

As of late 1996, Bombardier is looking for 200 engineers and technologists for its planned regional jet. However, Boeing Co. in Seattle is actively looking in Toronto and Montreal for 13,000 new employees. IMP Aerospace Components Ltd. in Amherst, Nova Scotia, doubled its work force from 160 to 300 in 1996 and is still recruiting people for shop floor and technical jobs. Ebco Aerospace Inc. in Delta, B.C., is having trouble finding machinists. In the Toronto area there is a shortage of program managers who coordinate the building of large components and customer service communication. According to Peter Broadhurst, chair of the Human Resources Committee of the Aerospace Industry Association, every aerospace company across Canada is faced with shortages and surpluses of workers of various kinds.

Food and Beverage Processing

According to the Canadian Restaurants and Foodservices Association, the foodservice industry generated $5.3 billion in tax revenue in 1994, contributing 25 percent more tax than the average Canadian industry. Canadians eat out on average 4.75 times per week. Quebec may have the highest concentration of restaurants per capita, but British Columbians spend the most. Thirteen percent of all bankruptcies in Canada were restaurants. Canada has twice as many restaurants per capita as the U.S.; most notably, Canadians have three times as many coffee-and-donut shops.

It's not surprising then to see that while meat and poultry processing provides the greatest number of jobs in the food industry, that is closely followed by specialty food products, bakery products, and beverage production. Dairy, flour and feed, and fish products trail these larger producers in providing employment.

In 1994 the Canadian food industry contributed 8.11 percent of total manufacturing capital expenditures, with a dollar value close to $1.3 billion. Beverage industries contributed 1.84 percent of capital expenditures, with costs of about $290.4 million.

Total shipments from the food and beverage industry in 1994 amounted to almost $49 billion. Food shipments accounted for about $43 billion, and the beverage industries shipped about $6 billion worth of production. In international trade, Canadian food and beverage exports in 1994 amounted to about $12.3 billion, with 73.4 percent going to the U.S. and 6.5 percent to the European Economic Community. Total imports amounted to about $20.5 billion, with 58.2 percent coming from the U.S. and 11.7 percent from the EEC. The beverage industry grew by 7.7 percent over the previous year, while food production grew by 4.8 percent.

The Grocery Products Manufacturers of Canada, a national association of 181 companies engaged in the manufacture and marketing of branded consumer products, regularly conducts tracking studies on the

BULLETIN BOARD – *FOOD AND BEVERAGE PROCESSING*

- **Job demand factors:** quality; value; specialty needs or preferences; health concerns of aging boomers.
- **Job growth areas:** specialty markets including ethnic markets; private label processors; bottled water; nutri-ceutical market.
- **Job reduction areas:** all other areas.
- **Growth limiting factors:** U.S. food processors; trade agreements; interprovincial trade barriers; consumer preferences.

CONTACTS

☛ Canadian Association of Specialty Foods
19 Burlingame Road
Etobicoke, ON M8W 1Y7 Tel. 416-255-7071 Fax: 416-255-6571

☛ Canadian Bottled Water Association
#203-170 East Beaver Creek Road
Richmond Hill, ON L4B 3B2 Tel. 905-886-6928 Fax: 905-886-9531

☛ Food Institute of Canada
#415, 1600 Scott St.,
Ottawa, ON K1Y 4N7 Tel. 613-722-1000 Fax: 613-722-1404
E-mail: fic@foodnet.fic.ca
URL: http://foodnet.fic.ca

☛ Grocery Products Manufacturers of Canada
#301, 885 Don Mills Rd.,
Don Mills, ON M3C 1V9 Tel. 416-510-8024 Fax: 416-510-8043

attitudes and behaviour of grocery shoppers in Canada. How Canadians think about shopping, nutrition, and value has changed considerably since the first study in 1987. Although the reported amount spent on groceries has remained steady since 1988, shoppers are increasing the number of outlets at which they shop. Almost half of all shoppers are looking for more product selection. In 1995 shoppers' (particularly those between the ages of 50 and 64) concern for nutrition was at its highest point since the studies began. These nutrition enthusiasts agree there are many facets to nutrition, but the study showed a single-minded focus on fat. Consumers in general are interested in educational information and labeling concerning nutrition.

Shoppers 65 and older have concerns, attitudes, and behaviour that distinguish them from younger shoppers, with lifestyle issues assuming greater importance. They see themselves as vital, active, and healthy and seem to be redefining the meaning of age. There are opportunities for products and services which recognize this change.

Shoppers between the ages of 35 and 49 are squeezed for time and money and juggling a large number of responsibilities, including work and families. Winning their confidence may take more time and effort, but they are the age group with the highest incomes, the largest households, and the largest expenditure on groceries.

There are a few other trends with interesting implications. Nutrition labeling, tamper-proof packaging, and factors related to the environmental impact of packaging are the priorities which shoppers have set for the grocery industry. Women account for eight out of every ten shoppers, with 38 percent of them over the age of 50. Work status appears to have the strongest influence on lunch consumption away from home, although two-thirds of all lunches eaten by shoppers working full-time were prepared at home.

With Canada's population expected to grow less than 1 percent per year over the next 20 years, total demand for food is expected to level off. A number of important demographic shifts, however, could signal new opportunities for Canadian food producers. Primary among them are Canada's changing ethnic mix and the growing popularity of ethnic foods.

According to the Canadian Association of Specialty Foods, in 1993 the total market for Chinese foods was estimated at $2.8 billion with over 650,000 Sino-Canadians, located primarily in Toronto and Vancouver. Specialty food stores focussing on Chinese customers, such as Vancouver's Yaohan and T&T, outsold mainstream supermarkets by about five to one. The South Asian and Middle Eastern foods markets were about one-tenth this size, at $228 million and $240 million respectively. Foodservices generally accounted for the largest share of ethnic food sales, except in cities with large ethnic communities, where specialty food stores take on added importance. Many products are being imported but there may be the potential to manufacture these products in Canada, both for local market and for export. Opportunities to produce both authentic and mass-appeal ethnic foods using local or imported ingredients could be realized through partnerships and alliances with established ethnic food distributors. Generally the most popular ethnic food styles outsell less popular ones by a huge margin. Foodservices represent the largest share of ethnic foods markets at 65 to 80 percent market share. Specialty food stores account for a larger share of total ethnic grocery sales than the large mainstream supermarkets such as Loblaws, Safeway, and Provigo.

The Canadian Association of Specialty Foods suggests there may be opportunities for Canadian food producers and processors to import ingredients and further process or repackage them in containers more suitable to the Canadian market. Food processors may consider easy-to-prepare version of traditional ethnic foods and mass-appeal versions for the North American marketplace. Alliances with established ethnic food distributors could assist with this process.

Chemicals

In a 1996 Canadian Chemical Producers' Association report, chairman Bernard West declares, "There's no question but that we see this as the top of what appears to be an eight-year cycle and our forecasts tell us we can look forward to sustained growth in volume in 1996. We're in a win-win situation. Our companies are doing well, and it's great news for Canada's economy." The CCPA represents 68 companies with over 200 chemical manufacturing sites across the country. These companies account for over 90 percent of the chemicals manufacturing in Canada.

Chemical producers saw sales and exports of manufactured chemicals in the last couple of years reach levels not seen since before the recession. In 1994 total sales hit $11.7 billion, up from about $10.3 billion in 1993. Total sales in 1995 climbed to $13.7 billion and in the same year, exports to the United States reached $6.2 billion, up from the previous year's $4.9 billion. Sales in Canada, which had been relatively stagnant since 1991, rose in 1995 to $5.5 billion from $5.4 billion in 1994. U.S. sales accounted for more than 82 percent of Canadian chemical exports in 1994 and 76 percent of total foreign sales in 1995. Total foreign sales grew by an estimated 31 percent over the previous year, however, with sales to other foreign destinations up by 53 percent. Total company sales for 1995 outdistanced the previous year's performance by 17 percent. For 1996, total sales were forecast at roughly $13.3 billion, with Canadian sales accounting for $5.2 billion and U.S. exports expected to amount to

BULLETIN BOARD – *CHEMICALS*

- **Job demand factors:** growing Latin American and Asian economies; need for environment-friendly product substitutes.
- **Growth limiting factors:** trade agreements or barriers; environmental regulations; overcapacity.

CONTACTS

☛ The Chemical Institute of Canada
  #550, 130 Slater St.,
  Ottawa, ON K1P 6E2 Tel. 613-232-6252 Fax: 613-232-5862
  E-mail: cscxt@acadvm1.uottawa.ca

☛ Canadian Association of Chemical Distributors
  #505, 700 Dorval Drive
  Oakville, ON L6K 3V3 Tel. 905-844-9140

☛ Canadian Chemical Producers' Association
  #805, 350 Sparks St.,
  Ottawa, ON K1R 7S8 Tel. 613-237-6215 Fax: 613-237-4061
  Toll-free: 1-800-267-6666

☛ Canadian Fertilizer Institute
  #1540, 222 Queen Street
  Ottawa, ON K1P 5V9 Tel. 613-230-2600 Fax: 613-230-5142

☛ Canadian Manufacturers of Chemical Specialities
  #702, 56 Sparks St.,
  Ottawa, ON K1P 5A9 Tel. 613-232-6616 Fax: 613-233-6350

☛ Canadian Plastics Institute
  #515, 5925 Airport Road
  Mississauga, ON L4V 1W1 Tel. 905-612-9997 Fax: 905-612-8664

☛ Society of the Plastics Industry of Canada
  #500, 5925 Airport Road
  Mississauga, ON L4V 1W1 Tel. 905-678-7748 Fax: 905-678-0774

☛ Society of the Chemical Industry - Canadian Section
  c/o Praxair Canada Inc.
  One City Centre Drive
  Mississauga, ON L58 1M2 Tel. 905-803-1600 Fax: 905-803-1690

☛ Potash and Phosphate Institute of Canada
  CN Tower, Midtown Plaza
  Saskatoon, SK S7K 1J5 Tel. 306-652-3535 Fax: 306-664-8941

approximately $6.3 billion. Other export markets account for the rest.

The majority of Canadian chemical manufacturers expect overall business conditions to remain buoyant in 1996. Prospects for major customer industries such as pulp and paper, mining, metals, and motor vehicles are seen to be favourable, and some firms are looking for a strengthening in construction activity. Because of expanded capacity and increased production capability, chemical producers are projecting a relatively large rise of nearly 5 percent in sales volumes for 1996. The increase may not show in sales revenues, however, because of moderate downward pressure on prices and margins that became evident in late 1995.

In this capital-intensive industry, fixed capital expenditures declined by 25 percent during 1995, but were forecast to rebound sharply by 70 percent in 1996. The decision to reduce the tax on machinery and equipment in Alberta was mentioned as a positive step which could lead to further capital investment. Numerous chemical firms are not taking their prosperity for granted. Many manufacturers are continuing to focus on internal cost management, productivity improvement, changes in product mix, and better customer service in an effort to enhance their competitive positions.

A CCPA survey indicated that total employment in the industry was reduced by 3.6 percent in 1995 to 28,699, with a slight further drop of 0.6 percent, to 28,540, forecast for 1996. Average wages and salaries rose by 5.4 percent in 1995 to $50,980, and were expected to advance by a further 1.7 percent in 1996 to $51,827.

The Canadian Chemical Producers' Association notes that there has been a redirection of trade toward the United States, and that as the North American market becomes more integrated, trade with Mexico will increase. Several years ago Canadian trade with Mexico in the chemicals sector was near $20 million and it has been increasing steadily since then. For many firms, the NAFTA is a done deal that has been integrated into their business plans.

Free trade has changed the way Monsanto Canada Inc. operates its manufacturing plant in LaSalle. The plant now focusses its production on a few specialty chemicals and ships about 60 to 70 percent of its products south of the border. The company specializes in niche markets from the point of view of working with a "North American mandate."

Fertilizer prices showed steady gains during 1995 and probably continued to increase in 1996 as North American producers tried to keep up with growing global demand. It appears likely that both North American and international markets will get stronger. Prospects look brightest for phosphate-based fertilizers like diammonium phosphate (DAP). Industry analysts were predicting that DAP prices would jump 10 to 15 percent in 1996, outstripping the other key fertilizer ingredients, potash and nitrogen. They say that supply/demand fundamentals for phosphate chemicals are tight and there is little new available capacity. A Canadian giant, Potash Corp. of Saskatchewan Limited, is currently the world's leading potash producer, controlling 19 percent of the phosphate market.

Plastics

Economist Faris Shammas, vice president of the Society of the Plastics Industry of Canada, sees signs of good health in the plastics industry. Employment among processors is up, machinery sales are excellent, and mould exports have been booming. Canadian mouldmakers shipped $426 million in moulds to Canadian and outside customers in 1992 and $626 million in 1993. Figures for 1995 were expected to approach or surpass the $1 billion mark. Export sales of machinery and equipment were a bright spot on the Canadian economy in 1994, with machinery sales reaching $618 million. Major manufacturers like Husky and Engel have had recent expansions and are heavily involved in international markets.

Many mouldmakers have been expanding their facilities to cope with increased demand and are seeing continuing steady growth In processed plastics, estimates are that Canada imported $4.47 billion of products in 1995 and exported $2.34 billion. Total shipments, including domestic sales, were $16.8 billion. With imports included, Canada consumed a hefty $18.9 billion in processed plastics in 1995. Consumption was expected to pass the $20 billion mark in 1996 and climb to over $25 billion by the year 2000.

Some areas of plastics processing have had a tougher time. The blown film market was hit by high commodity resin prices and is also subject to vigorous competition from high-volume, low-cost offshore producers. Only very cost-effective processors or those making specialty value-added films are doing well.

Overall employment in the plastics industry climbed steadily since 1991's low of 85,000 to reach about 98,000 during 1995. This was well below the 1989 peak of 115,000, but Shammas says there is no reason for gloom. The volatility in the markets during 1995 ensured that companies remained lean and mean, and the fact that the largest customers of the plastics industry had strong balance sheets during 1995 is an indicator of underlying health. He expected 1996 machinery sales to reach a new plateau and mould exports to continue to grow. If Ontario manages to reduce its plastics product trade deficit by 50 percent by 1999, as planned, increased exports would generate 3,600 new jobs and approximately 4,200 to 7,200 jobs in plastics-related and supporting industries.

Steel

Total world steel production grew by 2.5 percent in 1995, to 748 million tonnes, according to the International Iron and Steel Institute. Four countries, Japan, the United States, China, and Russia, produced 45 percent of the world's steel in 1995. Japan was the world leader.

After a decade of collapsing markets and bankruptcies by the dozens, mill closings throughout North America, and layoffs by the thousands, the steel industry is in pretty good shape for the next few years. Modernization programs and productivity improvements in the industry have improved both performance and profits. One of the key technological changes for steelmakers has been the installation of continuous casters, which greatly reduce manpower and energy requirements. Along with greater labour flexibility, new processes have produced sizeable reductions in costs. Industry analysts are worried, however, that mega-additions to steelmaking which are coming into production over the next three years will mean a downturn in prices and profits.

Strong steel prices in 1995, increased sales, and more efficient production meant that both Dofasco and Stelco reported improved profits for the year. Hamilton-based Dofasco Inc. showed a $195.8 million profit, up 68 percent from $116.8 million in 1994 if special items are deducted.

Stelco has made huge strides in cutting its debt load thanks to the strong upturn in steel markets in 1994, massive cost-cutting, and $364 million net proceeds from major issues of common shares and warrants. At the end of 1995, long-term debt stood at $457 million, compared with $581 million a year earlier. Between 1996 and the year 2000, Stelco plans a debt repayment schedule totaling $364 million. Stelco is intent on preparing for any possible downturns in the steel cycle, having faced a serious cash-flow crisis in 1991 because of recessionary steel markets and lengthy strikes in 1990. For 1996 Stelco showed a net income of $156 million, compared with $115 million for 1994.

Algoma Steel, Canada's third-largest steelmaker, is planning a modernization and expansion program over the next four years which will eliminate about 1,200 of its 5,350 jobs and push up long-term debt in a massive upgrade of its operations. Construction of a thin slab caster and hot strip mill will cut production costs by an estimated $32 a ton, increasing capacity and affording higher-quality production. The caster is part of a $525 million capital spending program planned for completion by the end of 1998. Algoma's business strategy calls for a 22 percent reduction in employment by 1999. In 1992 Algoma was insolvent but ended up being owned 60 percent by its employees and 40 percent by lenders in a bailout orchestrated by the Ontario government. With a new offering of common shares to help finance improvements, employee ownership will drop to between 30 and 35 percent. Algoma says its operating profits of $80 for every ton shipped in 1994 and $129 in the first quarter of 1995 were among the highest in North America.

North American steelmakers enjoyed peak cyclical earnings in the second quarter of 1995, but since then they have experienced falling steel prices and softening demand. Large inventories at the Big Three automakers in the U.S. will likely lead to temporarily reduced steel consumption.

The long-running trade skirmish between Canadian steelmakers and their U.S. counterparts continues. Despite two free trade agreements (the Canada-U.S. Free Trade Agreement and its successor, the North American Free Trade Agreement), the United States applies protectionist trade legislation rigidly to Canadian exports. When NAFTA was negotiated, no agreement was reached on how to handle anti-dumping and countervail concerns. Dumping occurs when a company sells its product in a foreign market at a price less than that charged in the home market or sells its product in another country at less than the cost of production. Countervail laws are designed to counter government subsidies that are

TRAINING AND UPGRADING FOR STEEL WORKERS

The Canadian Steel Trade and Employment Congress has initiated a joint union-industry venture with 19 community colleges in steel communities across Canada. Under the agreement signed in 1994, employed and unemployed steel workers have access to continuing education which recognizes their prior training and work experience. Those who lacked the self-confidence to return to school, or could not afford to take time off for a two- or three-year program, are afforded the opportunity to learn in non-traditional settings. The flexibility offered by this collaborative program is an example of a practical response to pressing transition and training issues facing workers and employers alike.

deemed to have assisted exports. The 1987 commitment made to negotiate common trade rules was renewed in 1993, but the dispute is far from settled.

Canadian producers are concerned about U.S. imports, which have grown steadily since the FTA was signed. At the same time, Canadian exporters are forced to comply with demanding U.S. Department of Commerce regulations which some have termed "discriminatory." According to Stelco CEO Frederick Telmer, since the FTA was proclaimed, there have been more anti-dumping disputes involving steel than any other product category. Since 1992 alone, U.S. steelmakers have initiated five anti-dumping disputes against Canadian exports, and Canadian steelmakers have filed four cases against Canadian exports. Since NAFTA was signed, Mexico has filed four anti-dumping suits against Canadian producers.

In late 1995 five Canadian rolled-steel producers – Stelco Inc., Dofasco Inc., Algoma Steel Inc., IPSCO Inc., and Sidbec-Dosco (Ispat) Inc. – were considering anti-dumping actions against offshore producers because of a surge in imports of flat-rolled steel. Canadian steel imports almost doubled in 1994 over 1993 owing to peaking North American demand. For the first eight months of 1995, imports accounted for about 31 percent of domestic consumption. At the same time, apparent domestic consumption (measured as shipments plus imports less exports) was only 4.4 percent. The industry is now documenting prices

BULLETIN BOARD – *STEEL*

- **Job growth areas:** product- or process-improvement research and development.
- **Job reduction areas:** steelworkers.
- **Growth limiting factors:** labour-saving technologies; imports from overseas; competition from substitute materials; super-efficient producers in the U.S.; high cost of capital; discriminatory U.S. anti-dumping rules.

CONTACTS

☛ Canadian Steel Construction Council
#300, 201 Consumer Rd.
Willowdale, ON M2J 4G8 Tel. 416-491-9898 Fax: 416-491-6461
E-mail: 76331.1001@compuserve.com

☛ Canadian Steel Producers Association and
Canadian Steel Industry Research Association
#1425, 50 O'Connor St.,
Ottawa, ON K1P 6L2 Tel. 613-238-6049 Fax: 613-238-1832

☛ Canadian Steel Service Centre Institute
#104, 370 York Boulevard
Hamilton, ON L8R 3L1 Tel. 905-524-1100 Fax: 905-524-5600

☛ Canadian Steel Trade & Employment Congress
#501, 234 Eglinton Ave. East
Toronto, ON M4P 1K5 Tel. 416-480-1797 Fax: 416-480-2986

☛ Reinforcing Steel Institute of Canada
70 Leek Cres.
Richmond Hill, ON L4B 1H1 Tel. 416-499-4000, ext. 28

of imported steel; in 1994 imports from the U.S. hit 30.1 million tons and accounted for 25 percent of domestic demand. Figures for 1995 were expected to decline to about 24 million tons.

With prices for hot-rolled steel declining in the wake of slumping auto production, U.S. steelmakers have been aggressively trying to sell steel in Canada. They fear that an oversupply would damage pricing in their domestic markets. Most of the electric-arc furnaces are being built in the United States and will come into production over the next two to three years. These new mega-capacity additions to steelmaking will add up to

20 million tons annually, an 18 percent increase over the current annual shipping capability of 110 million tons. Some observers feel that North American markets cannot absorb the new capacity without a long-term industry shake-out and the demise of weaker players. Low-cost steel from these new plants may also cut into market share for imports, affecting Canadian producers.

The steel industry's future in the steel pipe and tube area (natural gas pipe; castings for dental and surgical instruments, aircraft parts, and plastics) and wire (fine steel wire used to diffuse the explosive charge of car airbags) looks good. However, there is cause for concern in the areas of cold-rolled steel, hot-rolled steel, iron and steel foundries, and electro-metallurgical products.

Unless you are involved in the design, operation, and maintenance of steel labour-saving technology or a specialty application in a growing area, it would be wise to look for work in another field. Companies that solve problems for steel mills will have obvious hiring potential. Blast Cleaning Products Ltd. of Oakville, Ontario, for example, which designs, manufactures, and installs sandblast units for steel products, has prospered in such processes as eliminating scale from girders in the cooling-down process of making steel, cleaning railway cars of rust and paint, and scale- and blast-cleaning steel farm equipment. The company exports 90 percent of its products. China, for example, has purchased a dozen sandblast units at about $250,000 each for its steelmakers.

Most steel companies worldwide now spend their research and development funds on developing new materials and new products, given the growing competition from plastics, fibres, composites, and other innovative materials, as manufacturers are increasingly demanding higher quality or more specialized metals. Unless the Canadian steel industry shifts from research on how to reduce costs on commodity steel to developing higher-value-added products, it will not survive. Diversification into other areas – such as construction – will also be essential. For example, Lido Wall Systems of Mississauga, Ontario, has shown that studs, trusses, and basement beams can be replaced by steel – in a prefabricated manner – so as to deliver a house with perfectly straight walls within two weeks.

Where the Jobs Are in the Natural Resources Industries
• **Forestry** • **Mining** • **Fishing** • **Agriculture** • **Oil and Gas**

The prognosis for Canada's natural resources industries is poor, with Canada no longer very competitive in this area. Unfortunately, Canada has exhausted its supply of easily extractable resources. The forests that remain are harder to get to – further inland or on remote islands, in the case of B.C., for example – the major mineral motherlodes have been mined out, drilling for oil is no longer easy now that the large, easily drilled deposits have been fully exploited, fishing is an exercise in diminishing returns, and most hydro dams have already been built in the most practical locations. Other countries, particularly developing countries, can often extract natural resources more cheaply, because their labour costs are lower and the easy-to-extract resources have not been fully exploited. Since most purchasers are concerned with price, these are the markets they will patronize. Moreover, the Commonwealth of Independent States (CIS) has a wealth of natural resources waiting to be exploited. There is as much oil in the former Soviet states as there is in Saudi Arabia. Because of their political and economic difficulties, the former Soviet states have been unloading natural resources onto world markets in order to get their hands on as much hard currency – U.S. dollars – as they can. This has driven down the price of aluminum.

Compounding the problem is that the many improvements in efficiency mean that less material is required to construct or operate many manufactured items – fuel-efficient lightweight cars, for example. And new synthetic substances are replacing natural ones because they may be cheaper to make and more durable for functional purposes – fibreglass car bodies replacing metal, plastic replacing wood, and ceramics replacing steel.

While it is possible that modern technology could substantially improve the extraction and fabrication functions of the natural resources industries, few Canadian companies have shown interest in doing so until quite recently. In fact, 60 percent of Canada's pulp and paper industry has been using technology that dates back to the 1930s. When times were good – profits up and currency low – virtually all of Canada's competitors upgraded their production facilities. With few exceptions, however, Canadian companies passed up every opportunity of this kind. Economists have decried this fact repeatedly, but their protests were to

BULLETIN BOARD – *NATURAL RESOURCES*

- **Growth limiting factors:** Canada's resource industries have pursued a low-value-added, cost-based strategy that will prove their undoing now that developing countries can grow or extract natural resources at lower cost and in higher volumes; many countries which used to be importers of natural resources are now or will be large exporters of resources; most of the other major industrialized countries have much superior technology in their resource industries and a lower cost of capital allowing them to acquire newer technology as needed; greater efficiency and resource material substitution.

no avail. For example, our pulp and paper industry spent 0.3 percent of its 1988 revenues on research and development, as opposed to 0.8 to 1 percent spent by Sweden, Japan, and Finland. Historically, the pulp and paper industry in Ontario has not invested in technological improvements, choosing to rely on inexpensive wood and a low Canadian dollar instead. Economists have also urged companies in this sector to add value to the natural resources by processing them further into finished products, where the profits are higher and the long-range economic prospects better. These companies did not pay attention. Over 40 years of complacency are now having the anticipated effect. Canada's low-value-added strategy contrasts sharply with Sweden's pulp and paper industry which, when the kroner was devalued in 1982, used the increased profits to expand into higher-value production areas, unlike Canadian producers who did nothing to take advantage of a lowering of the Canadian dollar. The same situation obtains in Canada's chemical industry, where the country's trade deficit tripled between 1983 and 1986 as a result of our concentration on lower-value-added products instead of the growing, more profitable, higher-value-added specialty chemical markets.

Many resource companies are now changing their investment strategies after having done well over the past couple of years as commodity prices began to rise. Investment in newer technology is finally being recognized as an inescapable imperative in order to remain globally competitive. Our natural competitive advantage has always stemmed from our low energy prices and our closeness to U.S. markets. Big industries such as producing steel, chemicals, aluminum, and pulp and paper consume large amounts of energy – with pulp and paper actually using over 25 percent of our industrial energy. So long as we can maintain our lower energy cost advantage – which is being challenged – and couple it with world-class investment in technology and higher-value-added activities, the sector can continue to prosper. In addition, sensible, non-cumbersome environmental regulations are needed, or exploration and resource development will migrate elsewhere, as much of it has already.

Natural resources will play an ever-diminishing role in the Canadian economy, and only the downsized lean and technologically mean will survive. The one advantage Canada has is that, in the long term, there will be a shortage of natural resources as the developing countries continue to consume a larger share of the world's resources. With the world's population doubling every 40 years or so, there is only so much to go around.

Forestry

The forestry industry did extremely well in 1994 and 1995 after suffering $4 billion in losses between 1991 and 1993. In 1994, forestry employed 242,500 workers, up 3,500 from 1993, with new jobs coming from the lumber, logging, and government sectors. Compensation and benefits for the average employee rose to $59,348 from $55,606 in 1993. Despite this good news, some storm clouds are on the horizon.

Canada has lost much of its traditional competitive advantage now that power is no longer inexpensive and the low-cost wood supply has been depleted. Its competition comes largely from efficient operations in the southern U.S., South America, and Scandinavia. Canadian industry labour costs continue to be higher than in these competitor countries. Its debt-to-equity ratio is 70 percent – far above the 50 percent norm for the industry. Canadian taxes, fees, reduced annual cutting rights, and other restrictions have curtailed the industry's global competitiveness. B.C.'s decision to reduce available forests by 12 percent, its timber supply review, and the Forest Practices Code are expected to reduce the total annual allowable cut by 17 percent over the next five to ten years and the number of industry employees by 23,000 (and 71,000 in supporting industries) over the next five years, according to Price Waterhouse. Since the B.C. government controls the cutting on 95 percent of the forest lands, lumber companies have no choice but to look to acquire other sawmills and their surrounding timber rights in other provinces such as Quebec. Small mills are not worth renovating to comply with the government's low-emission standards, which are the toughest in the world, because of their small size and inability to get the needed logs or wood chips. Building new capacity does not make sense, except in Quebec and Ontario (where 95 percent of the forest is still available for logging), because most commercial forests have already been allocated and the previous building spree in the late 1980s was followed by the forestry industry's worst recession in 60 years. The recent flurry of sawmill acquisitions in Quebec is expected to lead to expansion and efficiency upgrading at the expense of the B.C. industry.

As many European countries move toward eco-labeling of forest products, companies that engage in clear-cut logging or whose pulp is bleached with chlorine will likely be accused of contravening sustainable forestry practices. This has encouraged forestry companies to redouble their public relations efforts by spending $2 million annually on demonstrating how they are taking "greener" approaches to forestry.

Canadian Forest Products Ltd. has become the first Canadian company to certify its pulp mills according to ISO standards and to allow independent inspectors to audit its sustainable forestry practices. Despite these efforts, lumber now faces a ban in Europe over sawyer beetle larvae found in two shipments of non-pine wood to Europe. Heat-treating the wood to eliminate the problem would add 2 to 15 percent to Canadian exporters' costs for certain grades of lumber. The untreated wood market in Europe represents about $500 million per year, with non-pine wood accounting for 40 percent. With the European market depressed at the moment, most shipments are headed to the U.S. or Asia. Many of these changes are inevitable since the British Columbia government introduced legislation requiring smaller clear-cuts, better access roads to prevent slides into fish spawning beds, and stiff fines to back up its demands.

Abitibi-Price Inc. has decided to broaden its product line into the specialty paper markets such as construction paper, file folders, index dividers, bag stock, and target paper. The company also hopes to enter the food packaging, automotive painting, and specialty bag markets. Such diversification is essential for survival in this industry. In the long run, the trend toward a paperless, electronic world will undermine newsprint sales; in the short term, the phasing out of tariffs on paper products and lumber as a result of GATT will help the forestry industry export more. The pulp and paper industry earned a record $4 billion in profit in 1995; 1996 may not be quite as good. However, the number of workers needed to make a tonne of paper is down 40 percent. In addition, demand in Asia, which was the main driving force behind price increases over the past few years, has tapered off and several large Indonesian mills started up in 1995. Slower economic growth in Europe and the U.S. may slow production somewhat as well.

In 1994, the forest industry contributed approximately $44 billion to Canada's economy and accounted for close to 1 million jobs, 350,000 of which were in the pulp and paper sector, which generates $16 billion in revenue. Forestry generates more revenue than fishing, farming, and mining combined. But since seedling replanting is below the sustainable cutting level, there will be an eventual decline in the industry, as dramatized by the shift to engineered wood – wood composites which are lighter and stronger, but more expensive and can be used only indoors – now that 90 percent of the Douglas fir has been logged in the Pacific Northwest. Ironically, as modern technology makes each logging industry worker more productive, it also accelerates the exhaustion of forest resources. Moreover, low-cost, high-quality, plantation-grown fibres produced in the Pacific Rim and Latin America, which have shorter replacement periods of seven to ten years versus Canada's 50 to 70 years, pose an additional threat to the industry.

With Indonesia emerging as one of the world's fastest-growing pulp and paper producers, Canadian companies, headed by the leading pulp mill engineering consultant, H. A. Simons of Vancouver, have managed to acquire $200 million of an estimated $800 million project in that country. With workers in Indonesia earning $2 a day and transportation costs lower than for the British Columbia interior or Alberta producers, Indonesia's hardwood plantations, which replenish themselves in seven years, are capable of producing pulp at a considerable profit for US$400 a tonne, compared with $600 for B.C. producers and $500 for low-cost producers in the southern U.S. MacMillan Bloedel now derives 10 percent of its wood from fast-growing poplar plantations in the southern U.S. The resulting restructuring of the Canadian forestry industry is likely to eliminate 20,000 jobs by the end of the decade,

BULLETIN BOARD – *FORESTRY*

- **Job demand factors:** lumber and paneling are currently needed.
- **Job growth areas:** environmental assessment; Far East, Latin America, and perhaps Russia eventually; wood-products engineering.
- **Job reduction areas:** almost everywhere, but particularly in the newsprint markets.
- **Growth limiting factors:** taxes; fees; cutting rights curtailments; labour costs; environmental concerns; outdated technology; transportation costs; replenishment rates; insupportable debt-equity ratios; interest rates; softwood lumber pact with the U.S.

CONTACTS

☞ Canadian Forestry Association
#606, 151 Slater Street
Ottawa, ON K2P 0J2 Tel. 613-232-1815 Fax: 613-232-4210

☞ Canadian Institute of Forestry
#1005, 151 Slater St.,
Ottawa, ON K1P 5H3 Tel. 613-234-2242 Fax: 613-234-6181

☞ Canadian Pulp & Paper Association
Sun Life Building,
1155 Metcalfe St.,
Montreal, PQ H3B 4T6 Tel. 514-866-6621 Fax: 514-866-3035

☞ Forest Engineering Research Institute of Canada
580 Boul. St-Jean
Pointe Claire, PQ H9R 3J9 Tel. 514-694-1140 Fax: 514-694-4351

according to a 1994 Price Waterhouse study. Job seekers interested in working in the forestry industry should consider obtaining jobs with companies working abroad, such as Sandwell of Vancouver, which has bid on a billion-dollar world-scale pulp mill proposed for Sumatra. With environmental experts, such as Hatfield Consultants of North Vancouver,handling over $1 million in environmental assessment related to the Simons project, jobs with companies assessing environmental concerns at home and abroad are another avenue worth exploring.

Without a doubt, Canadian forestry companies are eyeing the forests of the CIS, since it contains 25 percent of the world's wood reserves, almost double the Amazon's reserves. This will create many job opportunities for those wishing to work in the CIS once transportation costs are no longer prohibitive.

Employment in the industry is being further undermined by automation. Today, one harvester operator can replace an entire crew of lumberjacks with chainsaws, and labour-saving technology continues to overtake lumber mills. Wood-products engineering is a good field, however, now that the UBC course is tailor-made to industry needs.

Wood shortages were responsible for the huge rise in pulp and paper prices in 1994 and 1995. Indeed, North American and Scandinavian mills had to import pulp logs from Alaska and Chile. In 1994, a study for British Columbia's Council of Forest Industries indicated that coniferous species in Canada would likely diminish by 23 percent from the 1987 peak by 2010. The rapidly growing economies of China and India are expected to place even more pressure on lumber supplies and spur on plantations. Plantation-grown wood now accounts for 29 percent of the world's raw material supply for pulp and paper mills, and has already replaced old-growth forests, which now account for only 17 percent. New Zealand's plantation-grown wood has already doubled in volume since 1970 and will more than double again by 2010. Even inexpensive producers such as Indonesia, Haiti, and Mozambique have had their hardwood forest supplies reduced by the expansion of peasant farmland. According to Robert Hagler, a U.S. consultant, "we can define limits on available supply and recognize that, in many regions of the world, expansion of capacity will be difficult, if not impossible, for the first time in modern history." Not surprisingly, the proportion of recycled paper has risen globally from 31 percent to 42 percent in the past ten years. Even poor-quality aspen and poplar are being sought for oriented strand-board. All of this is good news to the steel and plastic industries, which are moving into building materials, not to mention those who use straw and hemp in papermaking.

In the short run an anticipated slowdown in the U.S. economy should reduce industry prices somewhat and reduce the number of new jobs created. The softwood pact signed with the U.S. will also curtail production so that, over the next five years, exports do not exceed "historic levels," which represent 26 percent of the U.S. market as opposed to the 36 percent share enjoyed at the moment. Thus in 1996 sawmills cut back on production even though paper use has been increasing by 15 percent a year in the U.S.

B.C., eastern Canada, and the U.S. forest industry were outperformed over the last ten years by Canada Savings Bonds – not a good sign for a capital-intensive industry.

Mining

Canada's research and development in mining is 0.5 percent of gross domestic product, compared with over 2 percent for Finland, Germany, France, Britain, Sweden, and the U.S. According to the Mining Association of Canada, investment in the Canadian mining sector fell by 50 percent between 1981 and 1991. "If this decline in investment continues," says Louis Gignac, chairman of the national mining association, "over 150 mining communities with a total population of one million could lose their main source of employment and economic livelihood. About 100,000 direct mining jobs and 300,000 related jobs are at stake."

Mining is a $20-billion industry where roughly 80 percent of mineral production is exported, generating 15 percent of Canada's total exports. Indeed, in 1992, mining firms accounted for 25 percent of the top 20 TSE companies according to market value. The industry's productivity is such that it requires only four people to generate $1 million in production versus 9.2 employees for the rest of the economy. Despite our poor R&D performance, $100 million is nonetheless invested by the industry. Exploration expenditures, which were averaging $800 million annually, fell to $300 million in 1995, the lowest level in 21 years. Over half of the 1994 exploration project budgets exceeding $2 million were allocated abroad – tripling the number of companies engaging in foreign mining activities in 1993.

Companies are looking elsewhere for easily accessible surface minerals in other countries, and they wish to avoid the regulatory problems that make it almost impossible to function in Canada. Much investment is going to Chile and Argentina, which actually have very strict environmental laws; but their regulations are clearly defined and consistent. In Canada, by contrast, there are differing interpretations regarding regulations within departments, even at the same level of government. Reports must be submitted to federal and provincial authorities, which operate under two completely different sets of schedules and requirements.

B.C.'s decision to turn Windy Craggy into parkland makes it the largest undeveloped copper reserve in the world. In B.C., only 22 mines are operating, compared with 30 in 1991, according to the B.C. mining association. Investors have largely abandoned companies that explore only in Canada, such as Noranda, which does 70 percent of its exploration in Canada.

Inco has a 30 percent market share in the world nickel market. The company forecasts consumption increases of 2 to 3 percent annually over the long run. Because of low inventories and possible metal shortages in Far East countries other than Japan, 1996 was expected to be a good year. The Voisey Bay nickel find in Labrador will make Diamond Fields Resources Inc. (30 percent owned by Inco) the sixth-largest nickel producer in the world when it goes into production. However, the area's natives are pushing for an environmental review, which could put things on hold until 2000. The review is being used by natives as a bargaining chip to have their land claims settled before allowing further development. Once these problems are addressed, there will be a serious long-term impact on Sudbury, where Inco and Falconbridge have nickel mines accounting for 18 percent of the global nickel supply. Voisey Bay could end up putting higher-cost production mines out of business.

Inco has announced that its future lies outside Canada. Since the company's laterite ore reserves in Indonesia, New Caledonia, and Guatemala exceed its Canadian sulphide deposits, it will expand in these countries. Clearly, Inco understands that surviving in the global market means going after the big, high-grade ore deposits.

Carmakers and beverage can manufacturers helped spur sales of aluminum in 1995, as did inventory levels falling below 1 million tons for the first time since 1992, thanks to a worldwide letter of understanding regarding production levels. In 1996, however, prices were likely dampened by large amounts of scrap material entering the market in the last half of the year. Employment will increase in this market since Alcan Aluminum Ltd., Reynolds Metals Co., and Aluminum Co. of America have together been responsible for production cutbacks accounting for 90 percent of global idle capacity. Now that inventories are largely depleted, production will be needed just to meet current demand.

Canada is the world's largest producer of natural uranium for nuclear reactors, with 27 percent of total world uranium output – largely located

BULLETIN BOARD — *MINING*

CONTACTS
- Canadian Institute of Mining, Metallurgy and Petroleum
  Xerox Tower,
  #1200, 3400 de Maisonneuve Blvd. West,
  Montreal, PQ H3Z 3B8 Tel. 514-939-2710 Fax: 514-939-2714
- Mining Association of Canada
  #1105, 350 Sparks St.,
  Ottawa, ON K1R 7S8 Tel. 613-233-9391 Fax: 613-233-8897
- MQS Executive Search,
  PO Box 824, Station B,
  Willowdale, ON M2K 2R1
  URL: http://www.inforamp.net/~ferdi/miningjobs/homepage.html
  E-mail: mqsjones@astral.magic.ca

in high-grade deposits in Saskatchewan. The use of nuclear power to generate electricity is expected to increase by 19 percent by 2010 despite public misgivings. Although former nuclear warhead uranium, reprocessed products, and inexpensive imports from the CIS, Eastern Europe, and China will be blended into commercial uranium, the process is expected to be non-disruptive to existing markets. Western nation capacity is expected to increase by up to 23 percent by 2000 as existing stockpiles are run down in the meantime, especially since output in the West in 1992 only covered 50 percent of its demand. Jobs should begin to emerge in this area over the next few years.

With worldwide production falling short of demand, employment in gold mining should increase over time as the Asian middle class increases in size and purchases more gold jewelry, investing in it as a hedge against inflation or fluctuating currency values. Now that some of the political problems preventing exploration in Peru are subsiding, Canadian gold companies are eagerly commencing exploration activities there. Gold selling by European banks trying to meet common currency deficit targets and IMF demands will dampen prices somewhat, however.

Chile's large, high-quality ore reserves, stable economy, and attempts to generate foreign investment have attracted 22 Canadian mining companies over the past few years. Inco, Falconbridge Limited, Rio Algom Ltd., Cominco Ltd., Lac Minerals Ltd., and Placer Dome Inc. have invested $2.3 billion in gold and copper projects in Chile. The country's tax and regulatory environments are friendlier to mining companies and the cost structure is such that, even were copper prices to drop 50 percent, the Chilean projects would still be profitable. Noranda Aluminum Inc. is planning to build an aluminum smelter and hydroelectric dam at a cost of $1.7 billion. Although Chile does not have any bauxite – aluminum's source material – the country can provide inexpensive electricity, which represents the largest cost in producing aluminum.

The major mining companies are planning to move into Mexico, Venezuela, and Bolivia next, and eventually Brazil, Cuba, and Argentina if conditions are favourable. In the long run, these companies will develop mines in China. At the moment, costs are so low in China that it mines and produces finished tungsten used for drill bits and incandescent light bulbs at less than the cost of just mining it anywhere else in the world. Not surprisingly, then, between 1986 and 1991, Canada didn't attract a single new mining project with a capital cost in excess of $250 million, yet Latin America had five. The decision to compete in mining on the basis of cost as opposed to non-ferrous metal product development, as in Japan, will eventually eliminate much of the mining industry in Canada, despite hiring increases in 1996.

In the long run, robots will assume all dangerous functions and the traditional miner will disappear. Job seekers are not encouraged to pursue a career in mining unless they are involved in designing or engineering advanced methods of ore extraction or refining.

Fishing

Fishing as traditionally practised is dying. Government announcements indicate that cod stocks have fallen from 323,000 tonnes in 1986 to 22,000 tonnes. Unfortunately, the future of the northern cod depends on the number of young fish spawned in 1986 and 1987, few of which have survived. In 1993, the Newfoundland fisheries minister, Walter Carter, announced that the number of fish old enough to spawn was less than 2 percent of the 1.2 million tonnes needed to sustain traditional fish catches in Newfoundland. In 1994, the number of cod dropped to

99 percent below 1989 levels, representing an 80 percent decline since 1993 despite the fishing ban in effect.

Despite the federal government's offer of $50,000 to anyone from Newfoundland willing to leave the full-time fishing profession – other Maritime cod fishers are not eligible – few have accepted the offer. Other offers include early retirement and retraining packages. By 1995, only 3,800 of the 30,000 Newfoundland fishery workers, those predominantly under 40 years of age, had signed up for training in such areas as nursing, construction, heavy-equipment operation, and diving – even though compensation payments will run out in 1999. Despite some improvement in inshore stocks in 1996, the most optimistic projections for cod fishing say a restoration is five or six years away, and there is a good chance that the cod will never return. Since sooner or later the entire fishing industry is likely to come to this pass, it does not make sense to look here for a sustainable job future. The Department of Fisheries and Oceans sent out notices to 24,600 fishermen in 1996, eliminating their licences since only full-time or "professional practitioners" will continue to be granted yearly licences, whose costs are about to skyrocket by 500 percent or more.

Even the west coast fishing industry has been asked to cut back its salmon harvest by 50 percent, although the number of salmon being caught each year is falling so fast that the cut could have no impact on the industry. The B.C. government is requiring that the fishing fleet be reduced by one-third, affecting 3,500 jobs. But Alaska has actually increased its limits rather than participate in a joint reduction effort. To make matters worse, 60 percent of the fish caught in Alaska would normally return to B.C. rivers. At the moment, 84 percent of all Canadian fish farming is devoted to raising salmon.

Canadians have always had to pay 100 percent more than the world competitive price for catching the same fish in the same location – for example, the Norwegian or Icelandic fleets fishing off the Grand Banks – because of the inherent inefficiencies in traditional fishing methods. Indeed, Iceland takes in more fish than Atlantic Canada with one-tenth the number of fishermen and uses 60 percent fewer people to process its fish. Even during the 1980s, annual government subsidies to the fishing industry totaled more than the value of the yearly catch and acted as the main driving force behind the overfishing that took place. Modern methods which would have lowered the price of fish to consumers, such

BULLETIN BOARD – *FISHING*

CONTACTS

- Canadian Aquaculture Industry Alliance
  45 O'Connor Street, 20th floor
  Ottawa, ON K1P 1A4 Tel. 613-788-6851 Fax: 613-235-7012
  E-mail: sford.caia@eworld.com
- Canadian Aquaculture Producers Council
  #506, 1200 Pender Street West
  Vancouver, BC V6E 2S9 Tel. 604-682-3077 Fax: 604-669-6974
- Canadian Centre for Fisheries Innovation
  PO Box 4920, Ridge Rd.,
  St. John's NF A1C 5R3 Tel. 709-778-0517 Fax: 709-778-0516
  E-mail: ccfi@gill.ifmt.nf.ca
- Fisheries Council of Canada
  #806, 141 Laurier Ave. West,
  Ottawa, ON K1P 5J3 Tel. 613-238-7751 Fax: 613-238-3542

as using large trawlers, were curtailed or forbidden. In the future, we will see more fish and seafood farming. The world's oceans provided 88 million tonnes of fish for the third year in a row, but there is some doubt that they will ever again reach the record 1989 peak harvest of 90 million tonnes. The UN believes that 70 percent of the world's various fish stock are likely past their sustainable level given current fishing practices.

Aquaculture or fish farming will grow in significance. Although only a $48 million industry in 1987, it represented $289 million by 1993, or 17 percent of Canada's fishing products. The Department of Fisheries and Oceans, however, spent only one percent of its budget in 1993–94 for this industry despite the claim by the former fisheries minister, Brian Tobin, that it was expected to grow to a $1.2 billion industry by the end of the decade and add 12,000 new jobs. In Norway, fish farming is already a $2 billion industry thanks to the government spending ample amounts in R&D. In Canada in 1995, roughly 2,800 people were involved in fish farming production and 2,400 in supply and services. Approximately 20 percent of all the world's fish and shellfish consumed is now produced in this way. According to the United Nations Food and Agricultural Organization, by the end of the decade over 40 percent of all international fish revenues will come from fish farming and approximately 25 percent of all worldwide fish production by weight will be through aquaculture. Job seekers interested in this industry are encouraged to look to this area for a career future.

One encouraging sign in 1995 was the exceptional shellfish harvest, which included a doubling of the number of snow crabs caught over 1994.

Agriculture

Farming as traditionally practised is slowly disappearing, though perhaps less conspicuously than the fishing industry. In the last century, agriculture accounted for 80 percent of all jobs in Canada, whereas it employs only 3 percent of workers today. In total, there are 247,000 farms in Canada with 50 percent of each farmer's income, on average, coming from government subsidization. Such a distortion of the natural economy is bound to come to an end sooner or later.

Under the GATT, Canada will not be allowed to impose its usual quotas on the import of chicken, dairy products, turkeys, and eggs. Import bans and quotas are to be gradually replaced by tariffs of up to 351 percent, ensuring that marketing boards will survive till 2010. NAFTA, however, requires the elimination of all tariffs on these products by 1998 with respect to trade with the U.S. and Mexico. Regardless of the GATT accord, the agreement with the U.S. allows for duty-free importation of processed food products into Canada as of 1998. Thus, some food production would move to the U.S. if Canadian farm product prices are not competitive by then. An Informetrica Ltd. study released in 1996 indicated that by 2000, the open border would eliminate

---

WHERE HAVE ALL THE FARMERS GONE?

Despite all efforts to sustain the current marketing board supply management approach – what is produced is not controlled by consumer demand and competitive pricing – the number of farmers continues to dwindle. In Ontario in 1983, there were 11,135 dairy farmers; now, there are about 8,500. By 2000, there will likely be fewer than 6,300. In 1991, 25 percent of all farmers were over 60, compared with 19 percent in 1981, and the percentage of farmers under 35 fell to 16 percent in 1991 from 21 percent in 1981.

BULLETIN BOARD – *AGRICULTURE*

- **Job demand factors:** organically grown produce; China's growth.
- **Job growth areas:** specialty farming for local markets; agricultural research; wheat, canola, and mushroom farming; fertilizer production
- **Job reduction areas:** all traditional farming areas.
- **Growth limiting factors:** increasing worldwide wheat production at a cheaper cost than possible in Canada; the GATT; the Free Trade Agreement (FTA); small farm inefficiency; marketing boards; interest rates; elimination of Crow Rate subsidies.

CONTACTS

☛ Agricultural Institute of Canada
#907, 151 Slater St.,
Ottawa, ON K1P 5H4 Tel. 613-232-9459 Fax: 613-594-5190

☛ Canadian Federation of Agriculture
#1101, 75 Albert St.,
Ottawa, ON K1P 5E7 Tel. 613-236-3633; -9997 Fax: 613-236-5749

☛ Canadian Organic Growers
PO Box 6408, Stn. J,
Ottawa, ON K2A 3Y6 Tel. 613-256-1848 Fax: 613-256-4453

☛ Canadian Society of Agricultural Engineering
PO Box 381, RPO University
Saskatoon, SK S7N 4J8 Tel. 306-966-5335 Fax: 306-966-5334

28,000 Canadian farming and food processing jobs. Since there are no production quota rules in the U.S. to restrict the size of farms there, most are larger and more efficient than their Canadian counterparts. Consequently U.S. farmers, for instance, receive 30 percent less for their milk than Canadian farmers do – a discrepancy which has led to the Canadian government phasing out subsidies over the next five years.

In 1995, wheat futures reached a 15-year high in Chicago. It was a banner year for the agriculture industry as a whole, as overall sales increased by 5 percent over 1994. The prairies were the main beneficiaries since Canadian crop prices rose 22 percent because of higher world prices. The winners were wheat, barley, and canola. Fertilizer prices were expected to jump by 10 to 15 percent in 1996 because of growing global demand – which should spur on sustainable farming practices capable of producing equivalent crop yields. These methods can grow twice as much yield using 60 to 70 percent less fertilizer. The Canadian Wheat Board is also pinning its hopes on the developing countries, which increased their per capita wheat consumption by 60 percent from 1970 to 1990. The GATT will also allow Canadian wheat farmers to compete more effectively against European wheat and U.S. growers, now that export subsidies are being reduced. Perhaps the biggest saviour of Canadian wheat growers will be China, which will likely become an importer of massive amounts of grain as it begins to industrialize. The same pattern happened in Japan, South Korea, and Taiwan, which were densely populated and self-sufficient in grain before they industrialized.

The Farm Credit Corporation is urging farmers to diversify out of agriculture and is willing to sponsor the process through loans. According to former agriculture minister William McKnight, "This will help encourage diversification, value-added processing, and the development of niche markets for farmers. The continued viability of family farm businesses, the agri-food sector, and rural communities depends on the ability of farmers to develop new markets." This approach has been most successful near large urban centres where organic farmers have grown to meet the demands of restaurants, chefs, and high-quality local food processors. Organic markets have become viable alternatives in a more health- and quality-conscious aging society. High-tech farms employing computers, such as mushroom farms, are prospering as well. Thanks to technology, Canadians farmers now feed 32 people each compared with three in 1941.

The agriculture industry must develop new products if it hopes to survive. There are jobs in the research end of the industry for individuals wishing to work on developing new or better growing techniques or strains of seeds. The ag-biotech industry consists of 80 companies, most located in Saskatoon. According to the Saskatchewan Economic Development Department, the provincial industry employs 700 people in companies which posted $200 million in sales in 1994. Employment is expected to double by the end of the decade, and sales should triple by then.

A career in ag-biotech has a number of advantages over farming, even though it usually takes 10 years for good ideas to get turned into commercial products. Unlike ag-biotech, farming itself can be a dangerous career, with an on-the-job death rate five times the national average –

worse than mining, firefighting, and construction. Sixty percent of farmers suffer a disabling injury every year, and 50 percent of farmers over 20 have lost more than half their hearing because of noisy equipment. Farmers have higher rates of cancer and chronic bronchitis, and their suicide rate is double the national average.

Federal and provincial ministers of agriculture are optimistic that Canada's annual food exports will increase by 50 percent to $20 billion by the year 2000. Food exports to the U.S. are expected to rise by 9 percent a year over the long term, having reached a record $5.9 billion in 1992. Exports to Japan have grown by 3 percent a year, and shipments to Latin America have been increasing by 6 percent annually. Total exports of food in 1993 were a record $13.3 billion.

Governments are proposing to loosen interprovincial trade barriers, provide easier access to government services, sponsor aggressive promotional campaigns, and transform the farm subsidy program into a national whole-farm income protection policy which would protect farmers during downturns, yet not violate trade agreements.

Oil and Gas

Canada's oil patch employs about 220,000 Canadians, 45,000 less than in 1985. Another 260,000 jobs are associated with providing goods and services to the industry. Mostly middle managers from larger firms were laid off in 1995, but many fast-growing medium-sized firms are still hiring. Hiring tends to be more volatile among the junior companies. Despite years of layoffs and corporate restructurings, we will likely see a wave of mergers and acquisitions and more north-south flows of oil and gas resources as continental integration of energy flows continues to grow.

Self-sufficiency is disappearing as a major concern. According to the International Energy Agency, the world is not likely to experience energy supply problems over the next 15 years. Even Iraq now allows future-sale-cost-recovery-based foreign investment in its energy sector. Iraq, which has the second-largest reserves of oil after Saudi Arabia and is a low-cost producer, is making 30 fields open for development once the embargo is lifted. The announcement that a new pipeline will be built from the Caspian oil fields of Azerbaijan and Kazakhstan to Turkey finally resolves a major obstacle to exporting oil out of former Soviet states and paves the way for future investment. All of this is reassuring, given that non-Middle East production is likely to peak between 2000 and 2010.

The good news for Canada is that our oilsands production is developing well enough that we can economically recover oil reserves in excess of Saudi Arabia's. By 2010, oilsands production is expected to equal conventional production in Canada, up from 21 percent currently. Approximately $2.5 billion will be invested in oilsands development over the next three or four years. Venezuela's Orinoco Belt has almost as much recoverable heavy oil as well.

When oil production from the $6.2 billion Hibernia oil project comes on stream in 1997, most of the crude will be shipped to refineries in the U.S. and elsewhere. Natural gas exports to the U.S., which have risen 400 percent since the late 1980s, will continue to grow and may double again over the next 15 years, with prices rising 2 percent each year. Ontario is bringing in more crude from the U.S. for processing. Ontario's decreasing reliance on western oil over the next three years will allow it to import up to 300,000 barrels per day from the North Sea and OPEC nations at a much cheaper cost. More pipelines between Canada and the U.S. are also in the works.

Even though oil and gas drilling is likely to fall from the historic high of 10,000 holes in 1995, exploration will continue at fairly high levels, keeping the Alberta oil and gas industry buoyant. The US$600 million ethylene plant, the world's largest, that Nova Corp. and Union Carbide were building in Alberta in 1996 will create 400 construction jobs and 130 facility jobs once completed. Hibernia's work force was trimmed by 800 (from 5,800 to 5,000) once the ice-proofing of the oil platform was completed. Most of the project was finished in late 1996, and only a few hundred workers will be needed to finish things off in 1997. Petro-Canada will be spending $2 billion to develop the Terra Nova offshore oil project near Newfoundland, which will employ 500 full-time workers on the rig in 2001, but fewer construction workers than the Hibernia project in the meantime.

Natural gas accounts for a larger share of energy consumption than oil. Its low cost, flexibility, and cleanliness have made it particularly appealing to the consumer. Although oil reached its structural peak in 1973, it is difficult to predict when gas will reach its peak, since the amount of gas available is yet to be determined and its many uses not fully exploited. Canada has a proven 20-year supply of gas reserves, as

BULLETIN BOARD – *OIL AND GAS*

- **Job demand factors:** world economy; environmental factors favouring natural gas; political developments increasing need for foreign currency; megaprojects; better technology reducing exploration and drilling costs.
- **Job growth areas:** experts in new geological software and newer drilling techniques; former Soviet republics eventually; specialty consulting areas such as tapping oil and gas in fractured rock formations.
- **Growth limiting factors:** political support for megaprojects such as Hibernia; Middle Eastern and Russian politics; world economy; alternative energy sources; cost of drilling and extraction; interest rates; $3 billion cost of upgrading refining facilities to meet proposed new environmental standards.

CONTACTS

☛ Canadian Association of Drilling Engineers
#800, 540 - 5 Ave. SW,
Calgary, AB T2P OM2 Tel. 403-264-4311 Fax: 403-263-3796

☛ Canadian Association of Petroleum Producers
First Canadian Centre,
#2100, 350 - 7 Ave. SW,
Calgary, AB T2P 3N9 Tel. 403-267-1100 Fax: 403-261-4622

☛ Canadian Gas Association
#1200, 243 Consumers Road
North York, ON M2J 5E3 Tel. 416-498-1994 Fax: 416-498-7465

☛ Canadian Society of Petroleum Geologists
#505, 206 - 7 Ave. SW,
Calgary, AB T2P 0W7 Tel. 403-264-5610 Fax: 403-264-5898

opposed to the nine-year gas reserve supply in the U.S. Some analysts claim that we have a 100-year supply of natural gas. At the moment, only 27 percent of the recoverable gas reserves in western Canada have been produced. Currently Canada is trying to extend the 200-mile Atlantic rim boundary because there is underwater territory the size of the three prairie provinces that may contain enough gas reserves, according to the Geological Survey of Canada, "to heat one million Canadian homes for about one million years." So although the National Energy Board believes the natural gas industry will likely peak in 2005 using existing technology, that time frame could be offset by offshore Nova Scotia gas going into production in 2007 and northern frontier gas development coming on line around 2010, not to mention the additional benefits of newer, more efficient technology. The underwater resources would extend the date even further.

According to Ted Eck, chief economist at Amoco Canada Petroleum Company Ltd., the demand for natural-gas-fed electrical power plants and cars will cause a 25 percent rise in U.S. gas consumption by 2000, with gas-fed co-generation plants responsible for 4 percent of gas usage as environment-unfriendly coal-burning plants are converted to this process. Legislation has committed the U.S. federal government to buy at least 50,000 gas-fed vehicles in the next five years. State and municipal governments are expected to help realize this mandate as well. In fact, by 2000, 4 percent of gas sales will likely be for such vehicles. The Big Three automakers have already begun mass-producing gas-powered vehicles.

With oil prices expected to rise only slightly by the end of the 1990s, some jobs but not many will be created in the industry in the short term. Given increasing demand in the U.S. and the developing countries, drilling, employment, and supply activity was expected to remain stable through 1996. Most growth will likely take place in the CIS, whose oil reserves rival Saudi Arabia's. Eventually, Iraq and Kuwait will be back to pre-Gulf War production levels, if not higher ones.

Technology is dramatically improving the production aspects of the industry. In the areas of oil exploration and drilling methods, for example, it is now possible to put a three-dimensional model of the potential oil field on a computer screen and drill as many "theoretical" wells as desired. The oil industry in the U.S. doubled the amount spent on gathering and processing data between 1987 and 1992 to US$3.2 billion. Since being out by as little as 65 feet can make the difference in striking enough oil to recover a company's costs or not, this new accurate imaging is proving invaluable. Innovative oil drilling methods such as horizontal drilling have recently led to the one-millionth barrel of oil being extracted by this technique in Saskatchewan.

Unfortunately, the percentage of knowledge workers in the oil and gas industry – engineers, geologists, scientists, and technicians – has fallen drastically since 1988 from 43 percent to 38 percent. As more sophisticated technology becomes available, it is likely that fewer but more specialized knowledge workers will be needed. Traditional oil- and gas-knowledge jobs should grow in the Middle East and the CIS, as these countries try to increase production.

Since the U.S. would like to develop CIS oil supplies so as to reduce Western dependence on the politically unstable Middle Eastern countries, expect many jobs to eventually emerge in Canadian or U.S. companies operating in Russia once a market economy becomes more entrenched in the republics.

Some wildcard factors that could affect the price of oil would include Moslem fundamentalists ousting the Saudi royal family, which would increase oil prices (however, when oil reaches $24 a barrel, conservation practices begin to kick in). A repeal of the UN prohibitions on Iraqi oil would lower oil prices. Since natural gas prices are set in North America, few surprises are likely to be in store in this sector.

Job Survival in the Old Economy

Job growth areas within old economy industries tend to be in the service or research aspects of a given sector. Design, research, and engineering play a major role in any industry that makes use of new technology. The "smart" products, like computers, will usually involve the customer in the design of the product. The need to anticipate and solve the problems of customers – self-diagnostic elevators or the fully automatic, self-propelled lawn mower that uses three navigation systems and a computer to tell it where to cut, turn, slow down, or stop – requires that the service or convenience component be built into the product itself. These higher-value-added functions are invariably service functions, and it is in this realm that most of the old economy industries will be hiring. Mature industries are in need of innovative products or processes so as to distinguish themselves from their competitors' more common or commodity-like products, whose sale is based on price alone or whose process methods are less efficient. Any mature industry that hopes to expand, or survive, must move into the higher-value-added end of the market, become more efficient, or diversify into other growth areas. Individuals looking for employment in the old economy are advised to apply to companies that are pursuing these strategies. Companies that are not doing so will most likely be out of business before the turn of the century.

CHAPTER FIVE

GLOBAL CAREER MARKETS

- **The World of the Multinational**
- **Career Markets Outside Canada**
- **Doing Your Homework**

No trade barrier will keep out the technological changes that are revolutionizing work in the rich world.

THE ECONOMIST

The pace of discontinuous change is staggering for most working people – they are struggling for context and for understanding of a whole new economic age.

LINDSAY MEREDITH, SIMON FRASER UNIVERSITY

I n order to plan a successful career, it is crucial that you understand the competitive strengths and weaknesses of the country where you'll be building that career. Job seekers must look at a country as if it were a stock they were planning to invest in: does it offer opportunity, prosperity, and long-term job security? For many of us, Canada may not be the best possible investment. Moving to another country, even temporarily, may be the only way you can acquire work or gain more marketable skills in your area of expertise. And even if you don't feel it's necessary to move right now, being aware of the possibilities offers you a backup strategy in case your industry or the Canadian economy as a whole experiences another downturn – as may occur if Quebec separates.

Working outside Canada will also help you understand the new global realities of business. Since the most successful businesses in the future will be export-oriented, we need to develop an international view of competition and economic development. Colleges and universities are helping students do just that by offering courses that have a global focus. For example, the University of Western Ontario offers programs in international business and cross-cultural management, and Dalhousie University teaches international transportation and banking. International exchange programs are part of the curriculum at the Universities of British Columbia, Toronto, Western Ontario, McGill, Saskatchewan, Queen's, and Montreal's École des hautes études commerciales. The student-run LEADER program at York University and Western sends Canadian MBA students to Eastern Europe to help businesses there solve problems. The Royal Bank sponsors internships for York University IMBA (International Master's of Business Administration) students in its Paris and Tokyo offices.

The World of the Multinational

If the idea of working in a foreign country appeals to you, how do you go about acquiring a job abroad? While you may be offered an opportunity to work directly for a foreign company, chances are your best strategy will be to look for a position with a multinational, even a small one, that exports to the country or region in which you may be interested.

This could be a wise move in any case – depending on your career and goals – because even though strategic alliances and joint ventures among smaller companies are increasing, the international economy is still dominated by multinationals. The top 1 percent of the world's multi-national corporations own 50 percent of the foreign-owned subsidiaries and affiliates worldwide.

The success of multinationals has made them a major source of employment for Canadians in the past. One of the business advantages of multinationals is that they have the ability to move operations any-where in the world, depending on what's most advantageous to them. As the availability of skilled, cost-effective labour has increased in devel-oping nations, this flexibility has meant job losses for Western workers. For example, Swissair Transport Co. Ltd. has sent much of its accounting function to India, and Apple, Motorola, Intel Corporation, and Texas Instruments Incorporated have located high-tech subsidiaries in India to take advantage of low costs in that country. Political instability, tough environmental or labour legislation, high interest rates – all can send a multinational packing. Which means that if you work for a multinational, you may not only find it easier to work overseas, you may be required to do so.

A job at your multinational of choice will give you the opportunity to learn more about the countries you're interested in and determine if that's really where you want to go. If the answer is yes, then once you get to know the company and the company gets to know you, you can begin to apply for postings. For example, if you have a diploma in construction technology or experience as a computer programmer/analyst, you might try to get a job with Computer Methods Corporation, a company that provides software for the construction industry worldwide. Seventy-five percent of its sales are attributable to exports, and the company is involved in many foreign contracts and international joint ventures. So, assuming that all goes well in your work at the home office, your job at Computer Methods could offer you many opportunities to transfer to other countries, particularly in the Pacific Rim.

You may have to establish yourself at a domestic company or an exporting company that offers you the training and experience that you can then use to win a job at the multinational of your choice. But remember exporting firms are now the lifeblood of Canada's economy, and they pay 15 percent more than domestic companies – because they are more productive. As a result of their extra profits, they are more likely to be hiring.

Just as you'd analyze any company you were planning to work for in Canada, you should also consider the long-term prospects for any overseas division you're planning to join. What are the signs of a healthy overseas operation? Make sure that the division is involved in one of the company's core businesses and that it has a clear advantage in its market. The division must have enough funding from head office to become established over the long term. And while it should be subject to strong financial controls by head office, the local managers should have enough power to make the decisions necessary for success.

For example, Bombardier, the highly successful Canadian company that grew out of the snowmobile business, has a reputation for making shrewd decisions in its expansion outside Canada. Among the companies it has acquired are Short Brothers PLC, an aircraft company in Belfast, and Learjet Corporation in the U.S. Both were a fit with Bombardier's core business, transportation, and in both cases Bombardier made an investment that was substantial enough to give these companies a better than average chance of succeeding. These kinds of acquisitions proved to be 88 percent more profitable than other acquisitions that were unrelated to Bombardier's core business. On the other hand, both Canadian Tire Corporation and Dylex Ltd., the fashion retail company, showed less wisdom when they ventured into U.S. markets. Neither company did sufficient research. As a result, they failed to assess the nature and strength of their competition and didn't offer their U.S. customers anything they couldn't already find elsewhere. Looking for a company that is expanding outside of Canada is not enough; you need to find one that's doing its homework and making smart strategic decisions.

As well as considering the chances for success of the overseas company, you should also examine the health of the economy where it operates. When Canadians think of working outside the country, we tend to think automatically of the U.S. It's interesting to note, therefore, that Canadian companies located in foreign countries other than the U.S. have been 50 percent more profitable than those located in the U.S. That's primarily because most of the growth in the recent past has been outside the U.S. or Canada. And most forecasters think that will hold true for the rest of the decade. Ironically, however, the vast majority of Canadian exporters have targeted only U.S. markets. Perhaps Canada's smaller companies will increase their export activity to the developing

BULLETIN BOARD — *WORKING OVERSEAS*

- Develop an international outlook by learning as much as possible about the country or countries in which you may want to pursue a career.
- Look for positions with exporting companies, especially those exporting to developing countries that are growing at the fastest rates.
- Canadian companies exporting to countries other than the U.S. are 50 percent more profitable than companies that focus strictly on exporting to the U.S.
- Keep an open mind about which countries may offer the greatest opportunities. But remember, you – and your family, if you have one – will have to live as well as work there.

TIPS
➤ For more information and advice on moving overseas with your family, see *Relocating Spouses Guide to Employment* by Frances Bastress.

countries now that the Canadian Export Development Corporation has upped its financial assistance to exporters by 50 percent, so that a company can now borrow up to 15 times its equity. EDC also now guarantees 90 percent of all sales to foreign nations and has removed the deductible portion of this insurance program.

So when you're thinking about what other parts of the world you might want to work in, don't fall victim to stereotypes. Developing countries have experienced remarkable progress in the past 25 years and now vigorously compete with industrialized countries in manufacturing and other value-added areas. In other words, they no longer simply ship out raw materials, but use knowledge and skill to transform those raw materials into a product: they've added value to the raw material. For example, one-third of Latin America's exports are manufactured items. Average per capita consumption in developing countries has risen by 70 percent, life expectancy has increased from 51 to 63 years, and elementary school enrolment is 89 percent of the eligible population. There are now 350 million middle-class people in these rapidly growing countries – a 50 percent increase over ten years ago; and another 250 million middle-class consumers are expected to emerge by the end of the decade. The economies of developing countries are anticipated to grow by 4.7 percent annually over the next ten years, up from 2.7 percent per year over the past decade.

North Americans tend to lump all developing countries together. These countries are very different from one another economically, politically, and culturally, and it is important to take these differences into account when you're thinking about where to relocate. Economically, one difference is in the growth in gross domestic product per capita since 1970. In Asia, gross domestic product grew from US$100 in 1970 to US$250 in 1992, but in Africa's developing countries, gross domestic product per capita has dropped from the original $100 in 1970. Since 1965, the gross domestic product has increased three times as fast in South Korea, Japan, Taiwan, Thailand, Indonesia, Malaysia, and Hong Kong as in Latin American countries and the U.S., and over 20 times as fast as in developing countries in Africa.

One last point before we consider the individual regions: while working overseas may sound exciting, romantic, and good for your career, it can also mean major adjustments, especially if you have a family. Before making any plans or decisions to locate in another country, you'll want to consider a wide range of issues. How comfortable will you feel living there? Will you be required to learn a new language? Is the country relatively safe and politically stable? Is there adequate health care? Can your children get a good education? Will your spouse be able to work there? What visas and work permits are required? These are key issues, and it's just as important to research them as it is to look into the career prospects of working outside Canada. Fortunately, there are numerous sources of information available that focus on living and working in a foreign country.

Career Markets Outside Canada
LATIN AMERICA AND THE CARIBBEAN

Latin America serves as an excellent reminder of how difficult it is for developing countries to become serious economic contenders unless key political, social, and economic infrastructures are firmly in place. There are no short cuts to becoming a developed nation. It took 20 years of disciplined economic reform to make Southeast Asia the economic powerhouse it has become. Latin America is only beginning to head down that road, which makes each step along the way vulnerable to many temporary setbacks until the necessary reforms are in place. Antiquated political parties that adhere to state-centric economic management systems instead of market-oriented ones still predominate. High-level corruption connected to drug trafficking is a perennial problem, as is the oligarchical hoarding of wealth and power. Education systems are very much in disarray, given the 30 percent funding drop during the 1980s. Years of high inflation have led to inefficient and poorly regulated banking systems and savings levels below 20 percent of GDP (except in Chile, with a rate over 25 percent, given its private pension system). Poor savings habits create an overreliance on foreign capital which makes for extreme volatility as soon as investors get nervous for any reason – a lesson firmly understood now by Mexico – and counterproductive high interest rates to offset the risk associated with this lack of stability.

Even a 3 percent growth every year would not begin to reduce the number of poor people in the region, which makes selling the necessary economic reforms to the public all the harder. So although voters now understand the importance of anti-inflationary policies, they may balk at accepting the tax and pension reforms vital to creating long-range price stability. Much is at stake now that economic benefits of the Brady Plan debt relief and large privatization efforts of the early 1990s are ended. Consequently, some countries, such as Mexico and Venezuela, are poised between improving slightly and slipping back into another crisis situation. Overall, the Pacific Rim countries (Chile, Colombia, El Salvador, and Peru) were expected to outperform the other Latin American countries in 1996, with Chile, whose open-economy reforms are now well entrenched, leading the pack. After growing by 4.6 percent in 1994, Latin America's GDP grew by only 0.6 percent in 1995.

Chile serves as an example of the kind of economic growth other Latin American countries can enjoy once they find the political means to become more disciplined, market-oriented economies. What they now have in their favour is the growing amount of risk capital available that can find high rates of return only by investing in emerging economies such as those found in Latin America. In addition, the trade agreements among the various Latin American nations now spur on diversification of exports and increase trade and competitiveness, thereby paving the way for future prosperity, growth, and investment. Trade among Brazil,

Argentina, Paraguay, and Uruguay – the members of Mercosur – more than doubled in the past three years, and Mexico and Chile signed their own free trade agreement in 1995. By 2005, the European Union hopes to have a trade pact with Mercosur, as European companies faced with weak demand at home look for growing markets.

Many of the Latin American countries are banking on an extension of NAFTA or another such arrangement to expand their trade horizons. However, the Americans will likely need a prolonged cooling-off period, considering the political fireworks created by the passage of NAFTA. The American public will not want to leap into another such agreement with other Latin American countries for some time, so unless they make an effort to begin exporting outside the Americas, companies will have to funnel their products through Mexico.

Moreover, according to an econometric study by the Institute of Public Policy Studies at the University of Michigan completed in 1994, the effects of a NAFTA-like deal would be minimal. The net benefit of a comprehensive agreement would spur growth in Canada by 0.3 percent; Mexico, by 1.2 percent; U.S., by 0.2 percent; Chile, by 2.1 percent; Argentina, by 0.5 percent; Colombia, by 1.5 percent; and Brazil, by 0.3 percent. The sooner any of the Latin American countries enters the agreement the greater the benefit, however. Nonetheless, it should be clear that the economic consequences of joining a broader agreement will mean little dislocation or transition for the countries involved since the gains are somewhat marginal. It will make more sense for Latin American countries to pursue trade opportunities globally, as Chile has done, particularly in the Pacific Rim. In the meantime, they have already created numerous multilateral trade pacts among themselves: Mercosur; the Group of Three (Venezuela, Colombia, and Mexico); a Mexican-Andean pact; a revived Andean pact (Bolivia, Colombia, Venezuela, Peru, Ecuador); a Central American Common Market aligned with Mexico; and Caricom, a Caribbean free trade agreement.

The Association of Caribbean States, created in 1995, is the world's fourth-largest trading bloc, including Mexico, Colombia, Venezuela, Central America, Cuba, the Dominican Republic, Haiti, and the Caribbean Community. Many of the Caribbean countries are convinced that the Lomé Convention agreement with the European Union will not be renewed in 2000, so the new association is seen as a means of finding new markets and as a preparation for a much-hoped-for eventual trade agreement that will encompass all of North and South America by 2005, with the possible exception of Cuba. Although the smaller countries stand to gain the most, they are fearful of being overwhelmed by Mexico or other large countries. Mexico, on the other hand, welcomes this opportunity to take greater advantage of its status as the bridge to NAFTA.

Should the "Free Trade Area of the Americas" proclaimed for 2005 ever come to pass, it would unite 34 countries under one trade treaty, which would bring together 850 million consumers who buy $13 trillion worth of goods and services. At the moment, Latin America accounts for 9 percent of the world's GDP and 3.5 percent of the world's exports.

Currently, the countries that have the strongest links with North America are Mexico and Chile. Both countries also have strong trading ties with their neighbours, so for the near future they will probably act as conduits of trade between Latin America and North America. If you are interested in Latin America, your best bet is to find a job with a Canadian company located in either Mexico or Chile.

Mexico

Mexico sends 74 percent of its total exports to the U.S.; the other Latin American countries send only 28 percent there.

Big exporters can also afford to be big importers of goods, technology, and services. Already, Mexico's imports exceed its exports as it brings in new technology, such as software and telecommunications, to improve its competitiveness and assure its growth. That offers opportunities not only to Canadian exporters but to Canadian companies that want to set up business in Latin America. Transnational companies have tripled their investment in Mexico and other Latin American countries to take advantage of the anticipated growth.

Many Canadian companies that are prospering in Mexico established a presence by the mid-1980s. Government, business, and consumers have been spending billions of dollars each year since 1992. Not surprisingly, Northern Telecom and SHL Systemhouse have been among the small number of Canadian companies that got into Mexico in the 1980s and so have been successful in making an early start in capturing parts of this market.

Other Canadian companies with a presence in Mexico include Magna International Inc. (auto parts), McCain Foods Limited, Royal Bank of Canada, Bank of Nova Scotia, Bombardier, Berclain Group (factory automation software), Dare Foods Limited, Connors Bros. Limited (fish and shellfish products), Laidlaw Inc. (waste management), Conestoga Rovers and Assoc. (waste-water treatment), ELI Eco Logic Inc. (pollution control), SNC-Lavalin Group Inc. (waste-water treatment, pressurized irrigation, power generation, railways, urban transit, and airports), Deloitte & Touche Consulting Group, International Business Consultants (finance), Sirtec Inc. (business strategy), Kanport International Inc. (forestry), Nifco Synergy (Mexican border-crossing software), TransCanada Pipelines Ltd., Nova Corp. (natural gas), and Westcoast Energy Inc. (natural gas transmission, generation, and storage, and independent power generation).

Mexico continues to have many business disadvantages: too many monopolies (62 vacant television frequencies were given to Televisa, a monopoly, without tender in 1993); poor infrastructure that forces up the cost of transport and energy; a slow pace of deregulation; an education system that's neither universal nor high in quality; political injustice and instability. The Mexican peso crisis in 1995 showed the vulnerability of emerging countries that rely heavily on foreign investment and debt. Because it requires roughly $35 billion over the next six years to improve its infrastructure, the Mexican government is allowing foreign participation and investment in areas such as energy, environment, transportation, and telecommunications. For instance, in 1996, Mexico was seeking private buyers for its railways and airways.

The export industries (such as mining and the companies located in the dramatically rising number of maquiladora districts) are naturally doing well, given the huge devaluation of the peso. The domestic market, however, is in complete turmoil. Half the country's credit cards were in default at the end of 1995, almost 2 million farmers had abandoned their land, wages had fallen 25 percent, inflation hit 53 percent (expected to drop to 27 percent by the end of 1996), 30 percent of bank loans were in arrears (the international average is 3 percent), and roughly 750,000 workers had lost their jobs. Although the economy was growing by an inflationary 7 percent in 1996, there is a chance that the country will slip back into crisis – something the U.S. will try to head off. Nonetheless,

Mexico faces very serious structural problems with large numbers of young people entering the work force every year (70 percent of the population is under 25). With the average education level at 4.7 years of education and an economic growth rate of 5 to 6 percent needed to absorb those entering the work force, problems loom on the horizon – especially since Mexico has not had a growth rate in excess of 4 percent in 16 years (except for 1996). In 1995, its GDP fell by 7 percent.

Chile

In the course of its struggle for greater political freedom and stability, Chile has become a successful exporting nation. Unlike other Latin American economies, which export only 5 to 10 percent of their gross domestic product, Chile exports over $15 billion worth of goods, which amounts to 50 percent of GDP. In 1991, Chile had 6,300 exporting firms producing 2,700 different items for 131 foreign markets, compared with 160 exporting firms in 1975 exporting 500 products to 50 markets.

One of the secrets of Chile's success has been a decentralization process that has evolved under the Allende, Pinochet, and Aylwin governments. In 1990, municipalities financed 60 percent of their own expenditures from money raised locally. Consequently, the number of professional and technical staff increased significantly at local levels from 8 percent to 33 percent between 1975 and 1988. The federal and local governments have tried to make the country inviting to foreign investors by privatizing public companies such as gas, electricity, telephone, airline, steel, and oil companies. Such widespread privatization has brought in well over $3 billion in foreign revenue and encouraged further investment, particularly in mining, given the strong natural resource base found there. At the same time, Chile has wisely expanded its export focus beyond North America to Europe and the Pacific Rim. Chile has forged direct links to the rest of the world, with 32 percent of its $15 billion in exports going to Europe, 30 percent to Asia-Pacific, 18 percent to North America, and 14 percent to other Latin American countries.

Chile represents the safest bet in Latin America for Canadians seeking jobs. This "Switzerland of Latin America" has experienced 13 consecutive straight years of economic expansion and was expected to grow by 6.5 percent in 1996, according to Salomon Bros. Its 8 percent growth in GDP in 1995 was part of its 41 percent rise in GDP since 1990.

The Economist has described Chile, ranked 20th in the 1995 World Competitiveness Report, as "probably the best-managed economy in Latin America, and one of the best in the world." Even though Canada is the second-biggest foreign investor in Chile, foreign investment in its stock market is roughly 18 percent as opposed to 60 percent for Mexico, making Chile much less vulnerable to foreign speculators. Its unemployment rate of 4.5 percent, inflation rate of under 10 percent, and consistent budget surpluses are envied by the rest of Latin America. Exports rose by over 25 percent in 1994. Although NAFTA arrangements are on hold, Canada has created its own free trade agreement with Chile in the meantime. Chile signed a free trade agreement with Mexico in 1995.

For Canadians, the best job prospects will lie with the companies, typically North American, that either bought or served as consultants when Chile's public industries were privatized. Canadian companies are involved in over 50 joint ventures in Chile. Canadian companies are involved in Chile's mining industry, and in its $10 billion infrastructure improvement program between now and 2000. Mining companies in Chile include Placer Dome Inc., Barrick Gold Corp., Bema Gold Corp., Noranda Inc., Falconbridge Ltd., Rio Algom Ltd., Cominco Ltd., Teck Corp., Lac Minerals Ltd., Kilborn Inc., and Canada Tungsten Inc. Other companies are Methanex Corp. (methanol), Nova Corp. (natural gas), Philip Environmental Inc. (waste management), CanWest Global Communications Corp. (purchased 50 percent of a TV station), Rimex Supply Ltd. (highway wheel and rims), and Finning Ltd. (Caterpillar heavy equipment).

Argentina

Although Argentina's economy suffered a significant setback during the 1980s, the reforms attempted since then by the government are beginning to pay off now that the government has simplified its regulations, lowered tariff barriers, privatized industries, and stabilized its currency. The country raised $7.5 billion by selling 51 companies between 1989 and 1992 and plans to completely divest itself of almost all its public sector. The privatization effort, which includes telephone, iron, and steel companies, has attracted large numbers of foreign investors who now anticipate that Argentina will join Chile as a booming South American country.

Like Mexico's, Argentina's economy has overly relied on foreign investors, who constitute 51 percent of its equity market, for its 7 percent or more annual growth. The "tequila effect" of Mexico's peso collapse in 1995 hit Argentina in several ways: prices rose by 60 percent because the currency is pegged to the U.S. dollar; GDP went down by 2.5 percent; and fixed investment and industrial production were affected. The good news was that exports rose by 33 percent.

Between 1990 and 1994, Argentina's manufacturing sector improved its productivity by 50 percent. Exports in manufactured goods, plastics, paper, and petrochemical products rose by 47 to 135 percent in the first 10 months of 1995, and privatized oil and gas by 35 percent. Although export trade accounted for only 15 percent of Argentina's GDP in 1995, trade officials were optimistically aiming for 35 percent. Brazil, which is Argentina's main trading partner, saw its currency rise, which encouraged more Argentinian exports. Should Brazil's economic boom falter, so would Argentina's economy. Unemployment is over 10 percent owing to privatization of the public sector, a rise in illegal immigration, and more women participating in the work force. At the end of 1996, Argentina's economy was growing at a rate of 2.8 percent.

Brazil

Brazil's 160 million people account for one-half of South America's population, making it one of the ten largest economies in the world, larger than the rest of the continent combined. While Brazil was plagued by debt in the 1980s, the economy grew by 4 percent in 1993, which was twice the rate of Mexico's growth.

Beginning in 1990, Brazil introduced a number of reforms such as trade liberalization and deregulation, reduced tariffs and import licensing restrictions, opened up to foreign investment and technology transfer, simplified government paperwork, introduced competitive retail pricing, eliminated the domestic wheat monopoly, and began the privatization process. The government has been eager to privatize, since public-sector companies were responsible for over half of its budget deficit. The faster Brazil is willing to privatize its public sector, the better the economy will perform; however, political forces have made this a rather slow, lengthy process so far.

Although Brazil's GDP grew by roughly 3 percent in 1995, it was expected to cool off slightly in 1996. Unless Brazil completely overhauls its gigantic public sector, its pension plans, its welfare system, and its state-owned enterprises, it will never conquer its inflationary problems. With a fiscal deficit of 5 percent of GDP, a pension payout that accounts for 42 percent of its payroll ($13 billion more than it receives in social security premiums), its privatization bills crippled by vote-getting amendments, and its telecommunications industry in need of $30 billion in repairs, the prospects are not overwhelmingly favourable. There are only nine phones per 100 people, with one call in four not getting through. Even the cellular phone system doesn't work well. The good news is that Canada's Northern Telecom Ltd. and Brascan Ltd. are trying to take advantage of some of these opportunities. Privatization of mining has been relatively successful, so prospects will grow in this area. The energy and telecom sectors should free up much more over the next two or three years. Given that Brazil is the second-largest Latin American importer of Canadian goods and services, more Canadians will be finding work there eventually.

Venezuela

Because of the current political and economic turmoil, Venezuela is best avoided as a potential job market at this time. President Rafael Caldera has set the country back 33 years by once again suspending the economic rights promised in the country's constitution. In January 1994, Venezuela's second-largest bank, Banco Latino, collapsed. Over 50 percent of government revenues are now needed just to pay the interest on the national debt. In the first two months of 1996, inflation exceeded 16 percent (and it was expected to reach 60 to 80 percent by year-end), and the devaluation of the bolivar greatly surpassed the 40 percent mark of December 1995. In 1995, the deficit reached 10 percent of GDP. Over 50 percent of the population now works in part of the informal economy. The average Venezuelan standard of living has fallen drastically: in 1995, food and drink took up 72 percent of household income, versus 28 percent in 1980. The middle class is rapidly shrinking and the bottom 10 percent of the population earns only 1 percent of overall income.

In 1995, $18 billion in exports were earned, yet the privatization of the Venezuelan oil industry may not be enough to quell mounting social unrest. Employment in the oil industry may be an option, but you are

BULLETIN BOARD — *LATIN AMERICA*

- Best job prospects for working in Latin America would be for a Canadian company located in Mexico or Chile.
- Mexico will become the springboard to trade in the other Latin American countries.
- Canadian firms that located in Mexico in the mid-1980s are best positioned to reap the benefits of growth there.
- Argentina, Peru, Colombia, and Costa Rica may also provide good opportunities in the near future.

TIPS

➤ Seneca College of Applied Arts and Technology in Toronto has agreed to train Mexican students in Mexico and will provide an introduction and orientation service for Canadian companies in Mexico. Job seekers interested in working there should contact the college (tel. 416-493-4144).

advised to find a more stable country at the moment. The electricity, steel, and telecommunications industries are also in the process of being privatized.

Peru

Peru is well on the road to success now that damage done by the 1968 military coup – which led to the expropriation and confiscation of many foreign-owned companies – is rapidly disappearing, along with the Shining Path guerrilla movement, which has effectively been defeated. At one time, 70 percent of the economic activity was state-run. Roughly 80 of the 200 state enterprises have been privatized, with 30 more becoming available shortly. Sold already are the banks, telecommunications, energy, food, and mining companies, with railways, ports, hydroelectric, and some mining and oil companies yet to come. Canada is the third-largest investor after Spain and the U.S., with Canadian mining companies about to pour $2 billion more into 75 of the 100 mining proposals Peru has received. Canadian mining firms in Peru include Barrick Gold Corp., Cambior Inc., Noranda Ltd., Cominco Resources, Placer Dome Inc., Arequipa Resources Ltd., Rio Algom Exploration Inc.,

Kilborn Inc., TVX Gold Inc., and Golder Associates (geotechnical and environmental mining services). Ontario Hydro has partnered with a Peruvian firm, and utility opportunities also will appear in power plants fired by gas and heavy fuels.

The Shining Path guerrillas caused $25 billion in economic damage and were responsible for the death of 27,000 people. With their defeat, mining exploration can proceed, 140,000 exiled farmers can return to their land, and some of the 45,000 Peruvian professionals abroad may decide to return to their homeland. Inflation has been reduced from 7,650 percent in 1990 to 10.2 percent in 1995. After growing by 12.7 percent in 1994, GDP growth settled down to 6.9 percent in 1995. Long-range plans include making tourism and food production Peru's main sources of foreign revenue generation.

Colombia

Although most Canadians are familiar with Colombia's reputation as one of the two largest coffee exporters in the world, along with Brazil, few are aware that it is the world's second-largest exporter of cut flowers. In the U.S., 80 percent of all carnations and 33 percent of all roses come from Colombia. However, Colombia exports only 10 percent of the world's flowers (Holland controls 60 percent of the market), and its share is being slowly eroded by competitive exports from Costa Rica, Ecuador, Kenya, and Turkey. Colombia will have to improve its infrastructure to remain competitive in the flower industry.

Unlike other South American countries, Colombia did not saddle itself with debt during 1970s. Its average annual growth in gross domestic product was 5.7 percent from 1965 to 1980 and 3.7 percent from 1980 to 1990. The country's economic health, coupled with the recent discovery of oil deposits there, which are expected to be worth $5 billion per year by 1997, will allow it to initiate the necessary infrastructure improvements. Moreover, the country's excellent education system and its artisan tradition will help it during the privatization process that has now begun in earnest and that hopes to attract investment and encourage trade. The country's politicians are often beset by drug-funding scandals, and the guerrilla wars cost the economy $13.5 billion, or 4 percent of the GDP, from 1990 through 1994; 17,600 lives were lost (over half were innocent victims). Rebels managed to blow up one oil pipeline 229 times during that five-year period. Pipeline attacks directly and indirectly cost Ecopetrol $550 million, and private-sector oil companies $430 million. To make matters worse, the number of guerrillas grew from 215 in 1964 to over 10,000 in 1994. Despite these difficulties, TransCanada PipeLines Ltd., Northern Telecom, and Bell Canada are investing $1.3 billion in Colombia, which has been Latin America's most stable economy over the past 30 years. Colombia is Canada's third-largest Latin American export market after Mexico and Brazil. In 1994, the economy grew by 5.7 percent, and it is expected to grow by 5.8 percent annually until 1998. Oil revenues are expected to rise considerably over the next two years.

Central America

With the exception of Costa Rica, the Central American countries are not a good bet for Canadian job seekers because of the political, social, and economic upheaval still going on there. However, there are some positive signs for the future: Guatemala, El Salvador, Honduras, and Nicaragua have started to reduce trade barriers, agreed to a common low tariff on import, and initiated free trade discussions with Mexico, Venezuela, and Colombia. Costa Rica, which enjoys political stability and relative prosperity, has an unemployment rate of 4 percent, unlike its northern neighbour, Nicaragua, with a 60 percent rate. To stem a potential flood of unemployed people from surrounding countries, Costa Rica has avoided economic integration with the other Central American countries. Instead, it has tried to establish its own bilateral treaties with the U.S. and Mexico. The country was hurt by a European quota on banana exports, which account for 40 percent of the country's exports. In 1994, tourism surpassed banana exports as the main source of revenue; tourism is expected to grow from a $600 million industry to a $1 billion enterprise over the next few years.

Many retiring Canadians have become Costa Rican snowbirds; it costs less to spend the winter there than in the U.S., especially with our devalued currency. This trend plus the interest in environmental tourism could provide jobs for Canadians.

Bahamas and the Caribbean

The best job prospects in this region will be in tourism. A good source of specific information is the latest edition of Jeffrey Maltzman's *Jobs in*

Paradise, which covers this and other notable tourist areas around the world. Pay particular attention to cruise ship tourism, which has become a mass market industry. Even though Caribbean hotels had occupancy rates of only 65 percent in 1992, ocean cruise liners were 87 percent full, up 9 percent from the previous year. The most favourable projections see 8 million cruise passengers annually by the year 2000. The Caribbean does not have any significant competition in the cruise realm thanks to its natural advantages: many attractive islands not too far apart and close to Miami.

Cuba remains the most interesting wild-card country in the area with the anticipated fall of Castro – or at least the evaporation of his influence – imminent. In expectation, foreign investment has already risen from less than $1 million in 1989 to over $35 million by 1990. Although Castro has cautiously opened up Cuba to foreign investors, Americans are implementing sanctions against any company doing business with Cuba – especially after several American planes were shot down in 1996. Nonetheless, ecotourism and inexpensive beach resorts now annually attract over 140,000 tourists from Canada and Europe.

PACIFIC RIM COUNTRIES

By now, we're all aware of the inspiring developments in the economies of the Pacific Rim. This is not just a historical inevitability, but the result of a keen entrepreneurial spirit and a lot of hard work. In most of the Pacific Rim countries, unemployment is never above 3 percent, and the work week varies from 52 hours in South Korea, 49 hours in Singapore, 48 hours in Taiwan, 47 hours in Hong Kong and the Philippines, to 41 hours in Japan. While these countries, like Canada, certainly have their problems, they also have some compelling competitive advantages, such as education systems that are in many ways superior to North America's, low national debts (with a few glaring exceptions), and a total population that's expected to reach 5 billion by 2050 – approximately five times greater than the European Community's and six times greater than North America's. Economic growth rates for 1995 were 9.7 percent for South Korea, 8.4 percent for Thailand, 8.5 percent for Malaysia, 6.9 percent for Taiwan, 11.4 percent for China, 7.5 percent for Indonesia, 5.7 percent for Hong Kong, and 9.1 percent for Singapore. The Asian Development Bank estimates that by the year 2000, the Asian economy will grow by $5 trillion. This is roughly the equivalent of adding another United States to the world economy. Small wonder that the U.S. is eager to develop formal ties between NAFTA and the ASEAN free trade area.

But the U.S. and, indeed, all Western nations have found themselves dealing with a far more confident region, less dependent on and less impressed by their Western neighbours. The nations of Southeast Asia now look to Japan for their economic prosperity. In 1988, they supplanted North America as Japan's biggest trading partner, and they now represent 41 percent of total world trade – as opposed to North America's 30 percent. Asia now buys 25 percent more than the U.S. and three times as much as Europe. In recent years investors, disenchanted with the slumping U.S. and Japanese economies, have been happy to pour funds into the Pacific Rim nations. These countries have a lot to be confident about, and they know it.

Because of the rapid growth in their economies, Pacific Rim countries need to develop their infrastructure. It's estimated that between now and the end of the century, Asia as a whole will have spent $2.5 trillion on roads, airports, railways, telecommunications systems – all the basic equipment that makes a modern economy possible. Over the next five years, Thailand alone plans to spend US$47 billion on its infrastructure with money borrowed from local banks – an indication of savings levels unparalleled by those in North America.

This represents an unprecedented growth opportunity for Canada, since we are a world-class exporter of the goods and services necessary to build infrastructure. It's good news for natural resource companies that supply lumber, steel, and oil, as well as companies that supply prefabricated housing, road, bridge, and hotel construction, telecommunications, and transportation systems. Already Northern Telecom is the largest supplier of computer network equipment to China; by 1994 it had installed 1.6 million phone lines in the country, 142 digital microwave systems, and over 140 switching systems. Since that still leaves only one phone line for every 100 people in China compared with 58 lines for every 100 Canadians, the potential for increased growth in the area of telecommunications is enormous. It will take approximately $400 billion in telecommunications expenditures to bring the Asia-Pacific region, including India and China, to a "teledensity" of 10 lines for every 100 inhabitants. The International Telecommunications Union reports that telecommunications services have already increased by 70 percent in the Pacific Rim, with 3 million cellular telephone subscribers and 11 million radio pager users throughout the region. Another company helping China solve its communications problems is CANAC/Microtel of Coquitlam, B.C., which has built and installed toll highway communications systems.

In construction, China is rapidly becoming the biggest market in the world, currently spending 6 to 8 percent of its gross national product on housing – more than any other country. A number of Toronto architecture firms have won contracts in China totaling over $500 million: Bregman and Hamann Architects, Webb Zerafa Menkes Housden Partnership, Murray Marshall Cresswell Architects and Planners, Kirkland Partnership Inc., and Petroff Architects. In the Pudong region of Shanghai, $60 to $70 billion in commercial and industrial development is expected over the next ten years. Even a small Canadian company such as TS Aluminum, with its reusable aluminum concrete forming capacity, has been contracted to build 7,000 units in Iraq, Egypt, and Malaysia, and is hoping to break into the Chinese market. These projects should provide overseas opportunities for Canadians in civil engineering, construction supervision, sales, and consulting.

Altogether, there are 210 technology-intensive projects in China worth $30 billion and yet to be assigned to interested foreign companies. Canadian companies planning to take advantage of these opportunities include Ontario Hydro, Hydro-Québec, B.C. Hydro, MacDonald Dettwiler and Associates (earth stations), Power Corporation, Westcoast Energy Inc.(co-generation plant), Simpson Power Products Ltd. (power systems), General Electric Canada Inc. ($180 million project secured), and Glenayre Electronics Ltd. (paging systems). Other firms getting involved in China include Manulife Insurance, Chai-Na-Ta Corp. and China Hua Yuan Industry and Commerce (Canada) Inc. (ginseng and pharmaceuticals), Chemetics International Co. (chemical technology), China-Link Communications Ltd. (high-tech), ITI World Investment Group Inc., China Gold Corp., C&C Marine Corp., Thiessen Equipment Ltd., Fairchild Investment Inc., Maple Oil & Gas Inc., Canadian Original Seafood Co. Ltd., Bank of Nova Scotia, Price Waterhouse, Coopers & Lybrand, Arthur Andersen & Co., BCE Inc., Canadian Transportation Technology Corp., Canadian Highways International Corp., Fuller-F.L.

Smidth Canada Ltd. (process machinery, electrical equipment), Goldpark Mines & Investment Ltd., Sydney Steel Co., CAE Inc. (aviation), Fednav Ltd. (ocean shipping), AKD International (petrochemical), Advanced Material Resources (mining), Bennett and Wright International (construction), Casco Engineering Inc., NASIA Group (highways), Spar Aerospace, Vickers and Benson (TV), and energy firms such as TransAlta Energy Corp., Northland Power, CanAlm International, Acres International Ltd., Monenco-Agra Inc., Agra Industries Ltd., and SNC Lavalin Inc.

China represents Canada's fourth-largest export market ($2.1 billion, or 10 percent of our exports). According to a World Bank study titled "The East Asian Economic Miracle," by 2002 the Greater China area (China, Hong Kong, and Taiwan) will surpass the U.S. economy and may eventually become our largest export market. In many ways it is a vast untapped market. For instance, computer sales are now running at about 1 million per year, and software sales rose 40 percent in 1995. Much opportunity exists because it will take 30 years before even the basic modern conveniences are widely available and a 20th century infrastructure is in place (for instance, roads) in China. In an attempt to gain entry into the World Trade Organization, China dropped its tariff barriers by 35 percent in 1996.

Canadian companies typically need to form strategic alliances with one another or with Asian partners in order to succeed in the Pacific Rim markets. This is partly because major lenders have stipulated that there can only be one bidder from each country for a contract, and also because of the obvious advantages of cooperation on large-scale projects in foreign countries. For example, the Asia Marketing Group located in Manila, Philippines, consists of engineering and environmental companies brought together by the British Columbia Trade Development Corporation for common marketing purposes.

Canadian companies forming partnerships with foreign companies include Endeco International Ltd. of Calgary; Wolcott Gas Processors Ltd. of Calgary; and TransCanada Pipelines Ltd., which joined British Gas PLC, Singapore, and Mitsui and Co. of Tokyo in tendering bids in Vietnam. Stanley International Group of Edmonton, has joined forces with EPS Ltd. of Victoria, Agrarund-Hydrotechnik of Essen, Germany, and Knight-Piesold of London, England, to develop a large China river-basin study which involves economic development and environmental feasibility. Ports Canada has been asked by Saigon Port to coordinate companies as part of a single bid to renovate its harbour. Needless to say, a wide variety of jobs in engineering and environmental areas will be created as these companies win lucrative bids abroad.

Job seekers interested in working for companies exporting to Asia, most of which will probably end up establishing overseas offices, would be well advised to look for them in British Columbia, since 35 percent of that province's exports are shipped to the Pacific Rim. The Pacific Rim represents a motherlode of opportunities for Canadian high-tech and environmental control and cleanup companies. While local workers will likely fill most positions in all of these industries, companies will still require a certain number of home office specialists to fulfill such functions as installation, training, sales, and ongoing monitoring.

Japan already has an excellent infrastructure, and since it continues to suffer through its worst recession in 50 years, opportunities for Canadians will be limited there in the near future. In order to recover, Japan must radically restructure its economy. The necessary changes, however, tend to go against the Japanese tradition – much the way Canada's need for budget cuts goes against its social support values. The Japanese government is propping up banks that should be allowed to go bankrupt; banks are continuing to prop up companies in which they have a vested interest but which also should be allowed to go bankrupt. In addition, workers will need to be let go in large numbers and real estate values allowed to fall much further.

Japan is excessively overregulated, which makes change difficult. Over 10,000 regulations act as barriers to competition – the ones the Americans always complain about. Unless Japan finds the willpower to make the necessary changes, many Japanese companies will simply leave Japan. Even if Japan has change forced upon it by a financial collapse, it will still remain in a superior competitive position because it enjoys leading-edge technology and research, well-established worldwide markets, and a well-trained and educated work force.

Japan's economy is only now beginning to overcome some of the economic structural problems that have kept the yen and unemployment (which is unofficially the equivalent of Canada's) high. Given the slow rate of corporate change toward an economy with flexible employment tied to performance and demand, and the unwillingness to re-engineer and restructure its society with the zeal characteristic of the U.S., the economy is likely to grow by only 2 to 3 percent over the next decade – the rate at which Toyota has planned its domestic production. Japan's economic power is immense, however, since it accounts for 70 percent of Asia's GDP. Worth noting is the fact that women now start five out of every six new businesses in Japan (2.5 million businesses altogether).

In the near future, aside from jobs teaching English, Canadians will find it difficult to get work in Japan – but not impossible. Despite its current problems, Japan is Canada's second-biggest trading partner, purchasing more of Canada's exports ($9.5 billion in 1994) in 1993 than Germany, France, and the United Kingdom combined. Not surprisingly, many Canadian companies have started to locate in Japan, and this should create overseas career opportunities in marketing. Indeed, many U.S. companies, fed up with local marketers and distributors, are setting up their own marketing operations or buying out Japanese firms. Nike International Inc. and Mattel, Inc., were successful in doing this in 1993, and many more companies – Canadian companies included – will likely follow suit. This will create employment opportunities for Canadians with marketing and management expertise, especially those who speak Japanese. A variety of Canadian companies are already active in Japan. The Molson Companies Limited owns Nippon Diversey in Japan, suppliers of commercial and industrial cleaning and sanitation equipment to airlines, hospitals, restaurants, and hotels, and from 1990 to 1992 saw its sales rise from $28 million to $40 million. Other Canadian exporters successful in penetrating Japanese markets include Pacific Edge Trade Group Japan (sporting goods), Moore Business Forms & Systems (business forms), Dylex (clothing), George Weston Limited (food products), Drummond Brewing Company Ltd., McCain Foods Limited, Maple Leaf Foods Inc., Clearly Canadian Beverage, Viceroy Homes, Dantzer International (tables and chairs), and Telesat Canada.

While working for a multinational is probably the easiest route to career opportunities in East Asia, don't rule out the possibility of working directly for a local company. One advantage North Americans have over the Japanese is that North Americans graduate three times as many college and university students as Japan, and while our high school standards suffer by comparison with those in much of East Asia, our post-graduate education is, on the whole, superior. So, for example, individuals trained at the master's level in high-tech areas will likely be able to find work in Japan. Indeed, University of Waterloo graduates with master's degrees in computer engineering or computer sciences are actively sought by Japanese companies. And if you have accounting certification, remember that China, a country with 1.2 billion people, has only 13,000 accountants. Taking advantage of these overseas opportunities will almost certainly require learning the appropriate language or dialect.

But while China, with its huge market, and Japan, with its competitive advantages, tend to dominate Canadians' thoughts of the East, it is worthwhile to note that many other East Asian countries offer career opportunities and a pleasant, intriguing way of life. Let's take a closer look at some of these.

Singapore

This English-speaking nation's economy was expected to grow by at least 7 percent in 1994, making it the growth leader among the young "dragons." Its main strengths are in electronics, computer and telecommunications equipment, chemicals, machinery, and transport equipment. Almost 50 percent of foreign investment is in manufacturing and the rest is divided between financial and business services. Singapore is emerging as the financial and marketing capital of the area, thanks to its all-round competitive strengths. Many foreign companies are using the country as a gateway to other Asian countries. Since Singapore trades mainly with India, Southeast Asia, and Indochina, it is immune from a possible downturn in the Chinese market should that country's economy overheat. Singapore is currently spending $60 million to upgrade its ports, and plans to add a third runway at Changi airport by 1997–98. By 2005, it plans to integrate all homes, companies, and the public sector on a single fibre-optic information grid, having already completed a digitalized network in 1995.

For Canadians looking for employment in the Pacific Rim, Singapore is the ideal country. For one thing, English is its main language; and the 1995 World Competitiveness Report ranked Singapore number two in the world for the second year in a row, and far and away the number-one developing country overall. It ranked first specifically in domestic economic strength, internationalization, government, finance, infrastructure, science and technology, and work force. In comparison with the other Asian dragons, Hong Kong ranks second; Taiwan, third; Malaysia, fourth; and Korea, sixth. To put these comparisons in a North American context, Mexico ranks eighth.

The high standard of living enjoyed in Singapore has provided food marketing opportunities for President's Choice products, Catelli Ltd. of Toronto, and McCain Foods. Singapore is eager to recruit skilled workers from around the globe and has even sought prospective employees in former Soviet states. Engineering graduates, international business specialists, and construction personnel should definitely explore the employment prospects available here. Singapore is shifting its emphasis to R&D in biotechnology, pharmaceuticals, microelectronics, computer software, and computer imaging. Its rising dollar was expected to trim growth to 7.5 percent in 1996. Unemployment is less than 2 percent. Over 75 Canadian companies are situated in this English-speaking country where 20 percent of the work force consists of foreigners.

South Korea

Korea's main exports are cars, electronics, and chemicals. Its rapid rise in economic strength has so increased wages that many of its manufacturing industries are now shifting production to other lower-wage countries. The ongoing reform of South Korea's political practices and financial system – including an attack on its underground economy, which is even larger than Canada's – should bring it further prosperity, to the point that it will rival Singapore in economic growth.

Continued growth will provide the funding for a $65 billion infrastructure program that will include $12 billion for upgrading and building ports and $950 million for Atomic Energy of Canada Candu reactors. Canadian companies, such as Scott Associates Architects, designer of Pearson International Airport's Terminal 3 in Toronto, have already bid on the $6 billion Kaohsiung International Airport expansion and a high-speed rail system. SHL Systemhouse has set up a joint venture in data-systems software with Samsung Co. Ltd. By 2000, South Korea expects to invest $13.4 billion to link Seoul and Pusan by high-speed train. It has earmarked $50 billion for 30 new power plants. Other Canadian companies hoping to cash in on these opportunities include

Northern Telecom Ltd., Newbridge Networks Corp., Mosaid Technologies Inc., and the Bank of Nova Scotia. Many engineers, more R&D, and considerable financial deregulation are going to be needed to help Korea advance further up the economic ladder. At the moment, Korea is aggressively charting new economic directions by chasing Japan as a maker of ships and memory chips and is exploring the consumer electronics and car market to a greater extent. Its expected 1996 growth rate is 7.7 percent.

Kim Jong Il has successfully taken over the reins of power in North Korea following the death of Kim Il Sung. South Korea's Kim Young Sam is ardently pursuing reconciliation with the North. South Korea would be able to combine cheap labour in the North with its own technology. For Canadian companies, reunification could offer further opportunities to help with infrastructure planning and construction. In many ways, Kim Young Sam's opening up of Korea's economy will attract more foreign investment even if relations with the North cool, as popular sentiment would prefer. Already, 2,500 Canadians are teaching English there.

Taiwan

To get a grasp of how big Taiwan's export activities are, consider that its foreign currency reserves of $120 billion are the largest in the world, compared with $80 billion held by Germany or Japan. Taiwan is shifting its economic focus from electronic and electrical goods and is concentrating on the technology-intensive aspects of the chemical industry and knowledge-intensive aspects of finance and insurance. These changes mark the country's economic evolution from a low-wage manufacturer to a higher-skilled, technology-based economy. Taiwan was planning to have a fully digital telecommunications network installed in 1996. Hoping to rival Hong Kong and Singapore, its high-tech industrial strategy includes offering very attractive financial incentives for firms specializing in telecommunications, semiconductors, information technology, consumer electronics, aerospace, precision machinery and automation, advanced materials, health and pollution controls, and fine chemicals and pharmaceuticals. Expatriates are actively encouraged to return to Taiwan to start up enterprises in these areas.

Taiwan's economy was expected to grow by at least 6.5 percent in 1996, much of the growth stemming from the resolution of Taiwan's peculiar love-hate relationship with its long-time enemy and natural business ally, China. Despite barriers to cooperation, Taiwan's investment in China exceeds $20 billion, and those barriers are gradually being removed. Chinese workers are already permitted to visit Taiwan for training. Nonetheless, China's recent sabre rattling forced the U.S. to declare its support for Taiwan, effectively causing China to retreat for the moment. But watch these developments closely, especially since China has replaced the U.S. as Taiwan's biggest trading partner. Many Canadian companies are taking advantage of this route into China's markets by forming strategic alliances with Taiwanese companies.

However, foreign investment and export growth are threatened by poor infrastructure, which has prompted Taiwan to launch a $400 billion infrastructure program aimed at improving its telecommunications system, highways, and power-generating facilities. Pollution is also a major problem in Taiwan – sulphur dioxide emissions in Taiwan are five times greater than those found in Los Angeles. This presents opportunities for environmental companies, such as Alberta Special Waste Management Corporation and MBB-Trecan Inc. of Mississauga, Ontario. Among other Canadian companies selling their services and equipment to Taiwan: Lovat Tunnel Equipment Inc. of Toronto sold the Taiwanese tunnel boring equipment for a light-rail transit system; Canada Post has been hired to set up five mail distribution systems there; Ebco Technologies Inc. and Nordion International are building commercial cyclotrons in Taiwan; Macdonald Dettwiler and Associates will be supplying all the hardware and software for a Taiwanese space ground station; Quadrant Development of Vancouver has built wood-frame housing in Taipei, taking advantage of the fact that Taiwan is the west coast timber industry's third-largest export market after Japan and Britain; Canadian Airlines has joined forces with Mandarin Airlines to exploit Taiwan's tourism potential; Scintrex Ltd. is providing safety shutdown systems and other similar equipment to the South Korea Power Commission Corporation, which has purchased Candu nuclear reactors; and Sentrex Cen-Comm Communications Ltd. will assist in building better cable TV services. Phone deregulation has allowed Northern Telecom to win a $100 million contract to provide digital cellular service. When more investment liberalization takes place, more Canadian firms will take the opportunity to invest more in oil and gas exploration. Taiwan is now considered to be more competitive than Canada; it occupied the 11th spot in 1995, up from 18th place in 1994.

Hong Kong

Now that its position as the sole conduit to business with China is being challenged by South Korea and Japan, which are using Shanghai and other northeastern ports, Hong Kong is beginning to concentrate on developing economic ties with South Asian countries. Nonetheless, Hong Kong entrepreneurs have started up more than 40,000 factories in southern China over the years and they will continue to exploit these opportunities even while exploring other Asian markets. The return of many former residents who had fled in fear of 1997, when Hong Kong reverts to Chinese rule, suggests that China will likely remain very much a market economy even after Deng Xiaoping dies. The rush is on to secure as much of the Chinese market as possible before other foreign investors stake their claims.

Meanwhile, the colony is spending $28 billion on port, airport, tunnel, and highway development, and private construction is also booming. Although manufacturing accounted for 24 percent of Hong Kong's GDP in 1984, it was expected to fall below 10 percent in 1996 (in contrast to Singapore, which developed high-tech manufacturing to replace low-skilled, labour-intensive manufacturing). Hong Kong's service sector, which is the tenth-largest service exporter and the second most developed in the world, is not able to absorb workers who aren't properly trained – for instance, in the banking or equity markets where Hong Kong still surpasses Singapore (85 of the world's 100 biggest banks are here). This skill gap, along with increased family-unification immigration allowed from China, caused unemployment to creep up from 1.5 percent in 1990 to 3.5 percent in 1995, causing 30 percent of the work force to worry about being laid off. As a result, the annual quota of foreign workers has been cut from 25,000 to 5,000, and it has become increasingly difficult for non-Cantonese-speaking individuals to find work. The over 150 Canadian companies in Hong Kong include all the chartered banks, Manufacturers Life Insurance Co., Northern Telecom Ltd., Mitel Corp., Alcan Aluminum Ltd., Teleglobe Canada Inc., MacMillan Bloedel Ltd., Bell Canada International Inc., SNC-Lavalin Group Inc., Agra Industries Ltd., and Asia Power Group

Inc. Hong Kong's growth rate was expected to slow to 3.5 percent in 1996.

Thailand

While Thailand has had some success in its main export industries – which include electrical appliances and chemicals – the country continues to be held back by a variety of political, social, and economic problems. Its mounting infrastructure problems and rising wages are causing many investors to shift their investments to other countries in the area, especially China and Vietnam. A low level of education and undersupply of technically trained workers, such as engineers and computer scientists, will hamper its evolution to a knowledge-based economy, leaving it more of a low-wage economy in many respects. Thailand desperately requires a large investment in its infrastructure. A $2 billion telephone installation project is under way, $2.5 billion is being spent on an elevated transit system in Bangkok, and an additional $3.5 billion is going toward the upgrading of the airport at Nong Ngu Hau. By 2001, 59 new power plants costing $27 billion are scheduled for completion. Serious water shortages in the country may present employment opportunities for foreigners in the area of water conservation.

Canadian firms (mostly environmental) in Thailand include International Environment Management Co. Ltd., Alternative Fuel Systems Inc., Bovar Inc., Dessan International Ltd., Cougar Helicopters Inc., Ocean Produce International, Hatfield Consultants, Philip Environmental Inc., Burnaby's Target Products, Beak Pacific Inc., Theratronics International Ltd. (medical), PBK Engineering, and Siam-Canadian Foods Co. Ltd. The economy was expected to grow by 8.3 percent in 1996.

Malaysia

Malaysia specializes in labour-intensive exports in the auto parts and electronic component industries as well as in the forest products, metal products, chemical, and petroleum industries.

Beginning in the early 1980s, the government began liberalizing foreign investment laws, reformed and simplified its tariff and tax system, and privatized many state enterprises. Since 1991, many more industries have been privatized, including a cement factory and a shipyard. Plans

BULLETIN BOARD — *PACIFIC RIM*

- The Asia-Pacific region will spend $2.5 trillion on infrastructure by the turn of the century, representing an unprecedented opportunity for Canadian companies and individuals specializing in these areas.
- Over $400 billion will be spent on telecommunications alone in the Pacific Rim.
- Given the high growth rates and rate of return on investment among the Pacific Rim countries, a substantial amount of investment has moved into these countries.
- Numerous Canadian companies have successfully penetrated Asian markets. Teaching English is a rapidly growing field.
- Australia and New Zealand offer many opportunities to both companies and job seekers who want to take advantage of the Asian market without the attendant culture shock.
- Asia's middle class now doubles every four or five years.

TIPS

- For more information about Canadian companies in Japan, consult Michelle Brazeau's *Directory of Canadians Doing Business in Japan.*
- For more information about opportunities in the Pacific Rim, consult the *Pacific Rim Almanac* by Alexander Besher, the magazine *Asia Inc.*, or Robert Sanborn's *How to Get a Job in the Pacific Rim.*
- Of interest if you are considering working in Japan: *Making It in Japan: Work, Life, Leisure and Beyond,* by Mark Gauthier ($18.95 from 59 Maywood Rd., Kitchener, ON N2C 2A2).
- Seneca College of Applied Arts and Technology in Toronto serves as liaison between Canadian businesses and the Chinese business market. Job seekers interested in working in China may inquire about companies located in China through Seneca (tel. 416-493-4144).
- Capilano College offers an Asia-Pacific Management Graduate Co-operative Program that includes a one-year paid work term in Asia. Tel. 604-984-4981, Fax 604-984-4992, e-mail kchute@claude. capcollege.bc.ca.

are under way to privatize both water and telecommunications, areas responsible for 15 percent of the country's gross domestic product. The government has also launched a major $9.1 billion infrastructure program, including the $1.2 billion Pergua dam, already under construction and scheduled for completion in 1996; a fibre-optic cable installation project worth $6.4 billion; and a gas pipeline that will cost $1 billion. However, the country suffers from a shortage of Malaysians capable of speaking English well enough to conduct business internationally. Anyone interested in teaching English in Malaysia will likely receive a warm reception. Canadian companies in Malaysia include the environmental firms Bovar Inc., Gartner-Lee International Inc., Keir Consultants Inc., and Waterworks Technologies; in construction, Bombardier Inc., Ellis-Don Construction Ltd., David Ellis Architect Inc., Nicholls Yallowega Belanger Architects, Top-Mech Asia Pacific Terra Engineering International, SNC-Lavalin Inc., and Adamson Associates Architects; in power, Hydro-Québec, Teshmount, and Stothert Group; and Syndel Laboratories, Dantec Electronics (agriculture), and Silvacom Industries Inc. (hydraulic engineering). Trade with Canada has increased by 12 percent per year over the past five years.

Indonesia

Indonesia shifted from a plantation-based economy in 1966 when foreign investment laws were liberalized. Between 1967 and 1985, foreign investors poured billions of dollars into the country, 70 percent of these funds going to the petroleum industry. Since 1987, there has been considerable investment in manufacturing, particularly in the textile and electrical equipment industries, which are labour-intensive and export-oriented.

Among its infrastructure projects, on which it plans to spend $11.8 billion, Indonesia is undertaking expansions in telephone cabling, switches, and buildings worth $260 million; a power transmission facility upgrade on the islands of Java and Bali worth $640 million; and the $150 million Madura Island bridge project. With growth rates averaging 6 to 7 percent over the past 10 years, investors and Canadian firms have been drawn to Indonesia. Roughly 30 junior mining companies are exploring here, Bre-X being the most notable in its success. Other Canadian firms in Indonesia include SNC-Lavalin Inc. (with over 40 development projects since 1974), Canora Asia Inc. (environment), AECL (nuclear energy), P.T. Dewata Wibawa (real estate development), Bracknell Airport Development Corp., Chinook Group (vitamin manufacturer), Sun Life Assurance Co., Golden Griddle Corp., LanSer

Technologies Corp. (telecommunications), Monenco Agra (construction), Flora Manufacturing and Distributing Ltd., Tiertasari Taman Oasis, Survival Systems Ltd., Urban Resource Technologies Inc. (recycled homes), Can-Do International Inc. (prefabricated cement houses), H. A. Simons, Sandwell Swan Wooster Inc., Chemetics International Co. Ltd., Asamera Inc., Bow Valley Energy Inc., Nova Corp., CAE Electronics Ltd., Hughes Aircraft of Canada Ltd., Trenton Works, and Inco Ltd.

Philippines

President Fidel Ramos is responsible for turning the Philippines from a backward nation into a leader in the privatization of infrastructure. Foreign companies such as Canada's Teleglobe Inc. have taken advantage of the opening up of the telephone industry to competition in 1993, and Canadian Highways International Corp. is involved in the $300 million Metro Manila Skyway. Intel Philippines Manufacturing has earmarked $200 million for the expansion of its memory chip and microprocessor plant, Procter & Gamble is building a $100 million detergent plant, and GM is planning to create a $1 billion export-oriented car assembly and parts manufacturing plant. The Japanese manufacturers trying to circumvent the high value of the yen were responsible for 58 percent of foreign investment in 1995.

The long period of sustained growth that lies in store for the Philippines is managing to attract back some of the 4.2 million Filipinos working abroad – especially managers and engineers for the real estate, construction, and consumer goods sectors, which have flourished. Subic Bay has managed to attract 80 companies from around the world, including Canada's SR Telecom Inc. and Ritchie Brothers Auctioneers Ltd. The Taiwanese, drawn by the highly skilled English-speaking work force, are planning to set up 700 companies in Subic Bay. The opening up of the country's financial sector to foreign capital should also help create more jobs. Infrastructure improvements worth $4.5 billion should help as well.

Vietnam

Since 1989, the government of Vietnam has shifted to market pricing, legalized private enterprise, reformed the tax system, lifted domestic trade controls, decreased subsidies, decentralized government control, introduced a stock exchange, and allowed its currency to float internationally.

The freeing up of the economy has led to a revival in many craft indus-tries such as tailoring, shoemaking, furniture making, silk weaving, and ceramics. Liberalization in agriculture has also helped spur growth in this large sector of the economy. Vietnam is expected to be the next big growth area as it sets out to repair the damage left by the civil war.

Despite the red tape that slows project approvals to a crawl, the lack of a viable banking system, the contradictory legal system, and widespread corruption, Japanese investors promised in 1996 to invest $1.2 billion in Vietnam. Eleven car industry giants are bumper to bumper in their pledge to invest close to $1 billion in car plants there.

Anyone interested in working in Vietnam should contact one of the Canadian consulting firms brought together by ACS Canada Group of Companies, Vancouver, to bid on Vietnamese contracts: Stanley International Group, Edmonton; Associated Engineering International Ltd., Burnaby; Klohn-Crippen Consultants Ltd., Richmond, B.C. The group hopes to use its complementary skills and experience in resource development, transportation, and water and sanitation to get an early start on opportunities in Vietnam. Other Canadian firms involved in Vietnam include Canexo Ltd. (mining), Delta Hotels Ltd., Seagram Co. Ltd., TransCanada Pipelines Ltd., Canadian Occidental Petroleum Ltd., Northern Telecom Ltd., SNC-Lavalin Group Inc., Canadian Oxy (Vietnam) Ltd., Vinatech International (real estate development), and Manulife Financial. The country's state planning committee has indicated a need for over $25 billion in infrastructure improvements over the next five years.

Australia and New Zealand

Job seekers who prefer a Western lifestyle, but are intrigued by emerging career possibilities in the Pacific Rim, should scout out Australia and New Zealand.

Australia sends 60 percent of its exports to the Pacific Rim, competing with Canada to sell minerals, pulp and paper, energy products, and agri-cultural products to this area. For example, it has been actively pursuing projects to exploit the large oil, gas, and mineral reserves found in Vietnam, as well as its agricultural business. (All Australian trade with Vietnam is coordinated through Ernst & Young Australia.)

Eager to exploit its relationship with Pacific Rim countries, Australia is offering incentives for foreign companies to locate their regional head-quarters in Australia. Many large American firms have initiated takeover bids of Australian companies as a means of gaining a foothold in Australasia. With incentives in place to encourage foreign investment, expect to see many job opportunities in agriculture, natural resources, and software as more and more companies set up springboard operations to the Asian countries via Australia. Australia has just begun a 12-year campaign aimed at making 60 percent of its students proficient in Asian languages, particularly Indonesian, Mandarin, and Japanese. Ironically, one of its fastest-growing exports is the setting up of English-speaking schools and universities in Asian countries who prefer to use English as the language of commerce rather than try to master the many languages of the Asian world. Half of Australia's immigrants are Asian in origin, with 60,000 Asian students currently studying in Australia.

Many Canadian companies (Newbridge Networks Corp., FootPrint Software Inc., Eicon Technology, and DBA Telecommunications Products) are taking advantage of the deregulation of Australia's telecommunications market and growing investment in cable, phone, and related services. In 1994, Canadian firms sold $100 million worth of phone, data processing, audio-visual, and broadcast equipment to Australia, which is one of the top users of information technology in the world.

Australia's competitiveness has improved 35 percent since 1981; industrial disputes declined from 2,915 that year to 558 in 1994, and unit labour costs fell 9.3 percent, paving the way for the creation of 2 million jobs. The country still suffers, however, from agriculture protectionist practices in Asia, Europe, and North America. Since fiscal policy had to be tightened in 1996 to rein in inflation, Australia's growth rate was expected to fall to 2.6 percent.

New Zealand has already gone through much of the economic restructuring that Canada is now embarking upon. Indeed, its current economic success is the result of nine years of a restructuring program rivaling that of any of the OECD countries. Businesses are attracted to New Zealand because of its stable economy, flexible immigration and labour laws, functional infrastructure, high productivity rates, and competitive wage structure for skilled workers. Now that the top tax rate has been cut in half to 33 percent, union membership reduced from

41 percent to 24 percent, and the government committed to repaying all foreign debt by 1997, investment funds are pouring in and entrepreneurial ventures are flourishing.

The country has long been famous for meat and forestry exports, but tourism now brings in as much money as either of these industries. Visits by Taiwanese and South Korean tourists have risen by 80 percent annually since 1991, with the overall number of tourists expected to double by the year 2000. As a result, there should be job opportunities in tourist activities such as skiing, birdwatching, and sightseeing, and in preserving New Zealand's environmental beauty.

OTHER ASIAN COUNTRIES
India

With its large domestic market and low wages, India holds many attractions for investors. It has an established stock market and in recent years has welcomed foreign investment and attempted to liberalize trade. Nevertheless, investors have been reluctant because of significant infrastructure problems, high taxes on exports and profits, regulatory restrictions, and difficulties in redeeming dividends and royalties. Moreover, while the country has a well-developed, impartial legal system, it also has such a backlog of court cases that it would take until the end of the next century to hear them all, according to *The Economist.*

Of the foreign investment that has taken place, the bulk is devoted to the manufacturing sector, which includes industrial machinery, transport equipment, electrical equipment, and chemicals. And although misgivings about India's political and currency instability remain, foreign capital is beginning to find its way to India, thanks to a ten-year reform program established in 1991. Public enterprises, which account for 20 percent of India's non-agricultural gross domestic product, will be privatized. The electronics industry has already benefitted from delicensing and reductions in export and import duties, and other industries will eventually share in these reforms. The rupee is now partially convertible and the austerity reforms induced by the International Monetary Fund have led to a trade surplus. Liberalization of trade, however, has hurt the inefficient agricultural industries.

As the reforms are more fully implemented toward the end of the decade, India is expected to enjoy the economic growth rates of the

Asian "dragons." Until then, it should grow at a respectable 4 percent. Foreign institutional investors have responded enthusiastically, buying up $1.6 billion of Indian shares during fiscal 1993–94, mostly in the power and telecommunications areas. However, it is not certain that India's reforms are irreversible. India has 18 official languages, 1,652 dialects, 26 states, and six major religions. If political instability worsens, the budget deficit could rise dramatically as the government tries to buy off lobby groups. Some lobby groups might insist that reforms unfavourable to their industries be reversed, so stay tuned.

Despite India's drawbacks as a place to do business, large multinationals operating there may offer opportunities for Canadians with engineering and technological training. Non-resident Indians are beginning to play a significant role in economic development. Multinationals, eager to placate nationalist sentiments, are looking to hire expatriate or non-resident Indians willing to return and are setting up facilities in India. The scale of opportunity that exists is difficult to fully fathom in a country with 300 million middle-class people; although 577,000 families earn over $55,000 per year, only 21 of India's 3,245 cities and towns have sewer facilities. By 1999, India is expected to spend over $2.5 billion per year on environmental management – four times the amount spent in 1994. The electric industry needs investment of more than $50 billion, roads another $35 billion, and telecommunications an additional $5.5 billion over the next seven years. Foreign investment in India in 1996 should reach $2.5 billion.

Canadian companies taking advantage of these opportunities include the engineering firms H. A. Simons Ltd., Acres International Ltd., and Agra Industries Inc.; the environmental companies Purezone Inc., Winterhawk Development Ltd., Waterworks Technologies Inc., and Alta Terra Ventures Corp. (agri-food and environment); in agriculture, Melville Ridge Hodings Ltd., Farmers Co-operative Dairy Ltd. (Halifax), and Parax Development International Inc.; in communications, Sinclair Technologies Inc., BCE Inc., Willowglen System Inc., Calian Technology Ltd., M&N Publications Ltd., Tele-Direct International Ltd., Bell Canada, and UTV International; and Toronto-Dominion Bank, SLM Software Ltd., ACIC (Canadian) Inc. (pharmaceuticals), Royal Medical Management Inc., InterHealth Canada Ltd., Kryton International Inc. (specialty coatings), Edwards International (fire detection), Northern

Micro Inc. (computer manufacturing), Presson Manufacturing Ltd. (oil), Plitron Manufacturing Inc. (transformers), and MMC Canada Enterprises (management and financial consulting).

India's software industry had sales of $1.2 billion (50 percent exports) in 1995, and this world competitive industry is growing by 40 percent annually as 20,000 computer scientists graduate every year. Foreign investors wary of China have poured in $12 billion since 1991, creating 22.2 million jobs; however, that number could grow to $20 billion per year if more reforms are forthcoming, especially since India has the world's third-largest pool of scientific and technical expertise. Growth of 6 to 7 percent should continue over the medium term.

Pakistan

Political instability and large government deficits have produced a rather grim situation in Pakistan. The country is heavily dependent on foreign credit and external funding for capital spending, making it extremely vulnerable to a withdrawal of needed funds. In short, Pakistan is not a good prospect for career opportunities. In 1995, the IMF suspended its $2 billion lending program to Pakistan, claiming it could no longer continue in the face of yearly high budget deficits resulting from its completely corrupt tax regime. Even Pakistani banks are no longer in a position to lend money to business ventures. More than two-thirds of

BULLETIN BOARD — *INDIA AND THE MIDDLE EAST*

- India presents many business disadvantages – poor infrastructure, a highly litigious and bureaucratic society. However, its large work force, low wages, and a series of business reforms have already lured many foreign investors, creating some opportunities for technical staff with multinational corporations. Pakistan, however, does not offer much in the way of employment opportunities.
- The Middle East has good business potential in natural resources and infrastructure, as well as tourism and some high-tech industry in Israel. However, growth in these industries – as well as your comfort level while living there – is highly dependent on the region's political future.

government funds go to defence and servicing the debt. In this "feudo-democracy," women are jailed for adultery and much use is made of child and bonded labour.

THE MIDDLE EAST

Peace in the Middle East will have a major effect on the economic success of these countries – not to mention the region's desirability as a place to live and work. The road to peace is currently a rather rocky one with bombings and assassinations along the way. Given the opportunity for a confederation between Israel and Jordan and a land-for-peace deal with Syria, there is some hope for cooperation so long as religious fundamentalists do not take control of the political process, since they do not believe in a free market for goods and services any more than they believe in freedom of thought. In response, Persian Gulf regimes are increasing their repression of Islamic opposition groups. If you are considering working in the Middle East, it's important to remember that there is a long history of hostility and political uncertainty in the area which will not be easily or soon resolved. Nonetheless, in 1995, the Middle East was the fastest-growing tourist region, with an 11.8 percent rise in visitors. Recent tensions have slowed this growth somewhat.

Saudi Arabia

Since the 1970s, the Saudi government has spent whatever was required to maintain a modern industrial economy, and Canadian companies have benefitted from that resolve. Saudi Arabia is Canada's largest trading partner in the Middle East, with trade between the two countries amounting to $1 billion. More than 20 Canadian trade delegations were sent to Saudi Arabia in 1993, and there are permanent offices for 18 Canadian-Saudi joint venture companies and over 200 Canadian companies.

Telecommunications and airplane fleet expansion have gained the attention of Bombardier, Northern Telecom, Al Babtain LeBlac Telecommunications Systems Ltd., Bell, and Allied Mechanical Contracting/Twaik Establishment, all of which have offices in Riyadh.

Israel

Israel is typical of many modern industrialized nations, with services accounting for 51 percent of gross domestic product; construction and manufacturing, 44 percent; and agriculture, 5 percent. The electronics and software industries account for 30 percent of the country's exports. Israel's R&D spending level of 3.3 percent of GDP is the highest in the world (versus Canada's 1.3 percent). A poll by *The Economist* in 1993 rated Israel as having a higher overall quality of living than Canada. In recent years, the country has made significant economic and business advances. Its foreign debt declined from 80 percent of its gross domestic product in 1985 to 25 percent in 1993, and although 20 percent of the gross domestic product is accounted for by government-owned companies, privatization plans are beginning to come into effect, with the banks next in line. By law the deficit cannot exceed 3 percent. Reductions in tariff barriers, with the exception of textiles, and liberalization of investment markets are helping the economy. Although the influx of Russian immigrants caused the country's unemployment rate to rise to 11 percent in 1993, it also led to a significant rise in house building. Most of the newcomers are highly skilled: technicians, architects, doctors, nurses, engineers, and scientists.

Peaceful relations with its neighbours, if sustained, should increase tourist trade to Israel as well as to the entire Middle East. Peace would also lead to increased foreign investment and trade with India and China, which have boycotted Israel for political reasons. Multinationals, though, are likely to hold off situating in Israel because of government red tape, trade unions, and the absence of cheap labour. If peace continues, the economy will benefit from the diversion of military expenditures into the market economy.

While Israeli labour may be expensive, it is also highly educated. Fifteen percent of the work force are either engineers or technical specialists, supplying staff for the more than 40 high-tech Israeli companies that are listed on the U.S. stock exchanges. U.S. defence manufacturer Fairchild Industries and Japan's Kyocera have stepped up research and development efforts in Israel. Eastman Kodak, Apple, and Baxter Medical are planning to establish operations in Israel as well. Israel and Canada were planning to sign a free trade agreement in 1996.

Syria

Syria represents a significant opportunity for Canadian companies in the Middle East. The country is expanding its telecommunications network by 930,000 lines, and its international exchange lines will be increasing tenfold. In addition, there are plans to upgrade and expand its power generation and distribution systems. Also in the works is an agriculture modernization program and a conversion of its railway locomotives to Western electric and diesel locomotives. Already, a number of Canadian companies have service contracts worth $65 million in Syria's oil industry in such areas as drilling, oil and gas plant design and construction, pipeline engineering and construction, and the treatment of heavy oil and sour gas. Petroleum accounts for 70 percent of Syria's exports.

Jordan

Jordan is already beginning to reap some of the benefits of a more peaceful Middle East. Jordanian companies have sought Israeli expertise in oil shale development, electric grid linking, overland pipelines for natural gas, and drip irrigation technology. The country now benefits from Israeli tourists visiting Amman and the red rocks of Petra. Pharmaceuticals are Jordan's fourth-biggest export, after potash, phosphates, and cement. Jordan, like Israel, wants to capture a larger share of the medical tourism market.

Egypt

Egypt's conciliatory attitude in Middle East political matters has potential benefits for its economy but has also led to some internal problems. Egypt's tourism, responsible for 50 percent of its gross national product, has declined substantially because of the terrorist activities of Islamic fundamentalists protesting Egypt's position toward Israel. Since tourism is the largest employer in Egypt, the government has executed dozens of extremists and detained thousands of others, causing violence to diminish. Tourism began to pick up in 1995 with heavily discounted rates attracting backpackers from around the world. On the plus side, talks are under way between Egypt and Israel to exploit natural gas deposits found under the Nile Delta and to link up electricity grids. The return of tourism combined with growing ties with Israel should encourage foreign investment. If you're thinking about working in Cairo, bear in mind that it may be the most polluted city in the world at the moment. Its population is growing by 800,000 per year.

AFRICA

While one might imagine that foreign investors would be attracted by
the cheap labour available in Africa, they are, in fact, discouraged by a
number of serious problems on the continent. Many African countries
are experiencing crises because of political, economic, and social instability, disease, and natural disasters. Those countries that are making an
effort to improve circumstances – Ethiopia, Eritrea, Ghana, Namibia, and
Uganda, for example – are surrounded by countries full of political strife
that inevitably spills over their borders. In Zaire, tribal violence is widespread, the main port is no longer functional, and the trains are running
once a week at best.

Throughout much of the continent, business law, including contracts
and private land ownership, is often unenforceable. Often the police
have no gas for their cars and shut down their services at night. Nigeria's
airports are largely unsafe and many people are robbed and murdered
while stuck in traffic jams. According to a World Bank report entitled
"Adjustment in Africa," released in March 1994, "With today's poor policies, it will be 40 years before the region returns to its per capita income
of the mid-70s." The average schooling of Africans is one year. With the
population of 43 African countries expected to double within the next
30 years, many problems will likely become magnified.

The good news for Africa is that the strengthening of demand for
primary commodities could help African economies to grow by
3.8 percent for the rest of the decade, according to the World Bank.
Agricultural exports grew by 4.4 percent per year between 1988 and
1993. Africa's oil and gas reserves are attracting investment, such as a
$200 million offshore power project in Ghana and a $4 billion Nigerian
gas-export facility. Although there has been a significant reduction in
foreign aid to Africa, which will reduce the amount of loan money
available and peacekeeping support, the World Bank established an
$11 billion debt-relief facility in 1996 to soften multilateral debts.

From a strictly business point of view – though certainly not from a
moral one – South Africa has long been the most successful African
country. It is rich in natural resources, with 82 percent of the world's
manganese, 64 percent of the world's platinum, and 44 percent of the
world's diamond reserves. In 1994, the value of trade went up by almost
80 percent, with an additional 54 percent rise in 1995. For instance,

BULLETIN BOARD — *AFRICA*

- The African continent faces major political and social problems. Generally speaking, job seekers should avoid Africa unless they are extremely familiar with the political, economic, and social circumstances surrounding any potential employment area.

Volkswagen sold $280 million worth of cars manufactured in South Africa to China. One of the fastest ways of creating jobs is to attract tourists, which is leading to hotel and shopping mall construction. All told, South Africa needs 300,000 new homes each year. Promising growth areas include financial services, environmental technology, telecommunications, biotechnology, gold mining, energy, and agribusiness.

Although the economy is slated to grow by 2 to 3 percent over the next few years, growth needs to reach at least 6 percent in order to create the number of jobs desired and achieve political and financial stability. Despite these misgivings, the United Kingdom Investment Group rated South Africa's economy number three for investment opportunities in emerging markets, ahead of Mexico, Brazil, Thailand, and China and just behind Chile. Even with population growth of 2.7 percent a year, a high level of illiteracy (only 50 percent of blacks have had a formal education), and a rising government deficit, 29 of the 200 American companies that withdrew in protest between 1985 and 1990 have returned, though almost all are distributors. Canadian firms doing business in South Africa include Acres International Ltd. (consulting engineers, economists, and environmental scientists) and Amarado Resources Ltd. (mining).

EUROPE

While its problems do not approach the level of tragedy found in Africa, Europe is almost as unlikely a place to go job searching in the immediate future, with a few exceptions. The International Monetary Fund predicted that of the 32 million unemployed among the industrialized nations in 1994, 18 million would be in Europe. According to a 1993 unemployment study by the OECD, hardly any new jobs were created outside government over the previous 20 years. During that same period, the U.S. created 38 million new jobs, though it has one-third the population. Roughly 50 percent of those unemployed in Europe have been without a job for over a year. Given this state of affairs, it is no wonder companies have experimented with ideas like job sharing. Unfortunately, these experiments have largely failed: even with wages dropping by 20 percent to accommodate a four-day work week, employers' non-salary costs for benefits have risen and efficiency has fallen.

With the exception of Britain, most of the European industrialized nations have yet to go through the necessary economic restructuring – essentially the dismantling of the welfare state and a reduction of union power and wages. According to a 1994 projection by Salomon Brothers for *Fortune* magazine, by the year 2000, government debt levels for European nations were expected to rise to the highest levels since World War II – 90 percent of gross domestic product in France and 130 percent for Sweden and Italy. With an aging population demanding more in the way of health care and pension payouts, there are serious questions about whether European governments can meet these future obligations. In addition, much of Europe is involved in medium-technology industries that are slow-growing – autos, steel, and heavy machinery, for example. European reluctance to match the U.S. in restructuring these industries has led to higher sustained levels of unemployment. In addition, Europe is way behind in the newer, more promising sectors such as electronics, computer hardware and software, data networking, telecommunications, and multimedia technologies.

Meanwhile, all of Europe and North America is paying the price of Germany's reunification. In order to raise the $100 billion per year that it costs to restore what once lay behind the Berlin Wall, Germany has kept its interest rates high, which in turn has depressed economic activity throughout the continent. And since Europe is the world's largest trader, that has in turn caused a slowdown in worldwide trade. So long as wages remain uncompetitive with workers in the Far East, Europe will continue to have relatively high rates of unemployment. Payroll taxes in Europe now account for 55 to 65 percent of each employee's gross salary (versus less than 20 percent in the U.S.) and are paid by the employer – making employers extremely reluctant to hire anyone.

Because Europe has lost its competitive edge over the U.S. and Japan, protectionist policies will likely emerge, keeping unemployment levels high but increasing trade within Europe. Unfortunately, many of the EEC proposals to allow job seekers to move freely among countries have not lived up to their promise and may be withdrawn as a means of curbing the flow of East European and African refugees and the expansion of the Italian criminal drug trade across borders.

Despite the gloomy news, there is still great economic promise in Europe, especially if the problems of cooperation throughout the EEC are resolved. A united European community, however, is still very much a dream. European negotiations frequently get bogged down in conflicting self-interest, mutual suspicion, and concerns about sovereignty. The notion of a common currency, which would lower interest rates and spur economic growth, is still a receding dream. Even Germany is unable to meet the Maastricht common-currency deficit target of 3 percent of GDP. France is unlikely to meet this goal by 1997 or 1998, and eight out of 15 EU countries now have deficits above 5 percent of GDP. Debt on average was 75 percent of GDP in 1996. This does not bode well for healthy economic growth over the medium term.

Given the current malaise, only highly skilled workers in the knowledge industries will likely find anything more than temporary work in Europe for some time to come. However, since much of the economic activity in Europe will probably come from joint ventures among companies in different countries, there may be job opportunities in coordinating these activities. Anyone who is knowledgeable about international business and speaks more than one European language should consider this possibility.

Germany

Unemployment rates still tell the tale of two countries: western Germany had an unemployment rate of 8.8 percent in January 1994, while eastern Germany suffered a 17 percent unemployment rate. With average hourly wages and benefits of $36, payroll taxes set at 40 percent of basic wage, and severance packages required by law costing as much as $36,000, German workers are in danger of pricing themselves out of the global job market. Indeed, one German worker (whose non-wage costs amount to 80 percent of salary) costs as much as 30 Chinese workers, or two-thirds more than an American. The result? Long-term unemployment has risen

---

BULLETIN BOARD — *EUROPE*

- Although Europe may eventually become a unified trading bloc, it will be besieged, for some time to come, by debt, unemployment, and the need for economic restructuring.
- Since Europe's unemployment levels rival Canada's, it offers few opportunities for Canadians, with the exception of specific industries or multinationals, which are succeeding despite the general malaise.

---

to 46 percent of all people unemployed. Germany now expects to lose 500,000 jobs in the automobile, machine tool, electrical, and chemical industries to downsizing. Volkswagen AG reduced its work force by a third, or 38,000 jobs, in the course of 15 months. Mercedes-Benz and BMW AG are looking to move operations to low-labour-cost countries such as Poland, the Czech Republic, Russia, Portugal, China, Mexico, and even the U.S. Even the Deutsche Bank recently downsized by 20 percent.

Since Germany is only now beginning to restructure its economy, unemployment rates will remain high and relationships between banks, businesses, and unions, once the traditional source of economic strength, will be reassessed and strained during the adjustment period. Indeed, a double-dip recession is a very real possibility, especially since social spending now accounts for a third of Germany's gross domestic product. It's estimated that these reunification and restructuring problems are costing the country $100 billion annually, and the German economy was expected to grow by only 1 percent in 1996 and 2.5 percent in 1997. But the government is hoping the east will grow by 4 to 6 percent; unemployment there is 15 to 30 percent, in contrast to about 10 percent in western Germany.

Germany remains a formidable and highly efficient country whose strength lies in the application of high technology to medium-technology industries. In technological innovation, however, Germany now lags behind the U.S. and Japan. Its future likely lies in the opportunities created by economic reforms in the Eastern European countries. Reunification will create infrastructure opportunities for Canadian companies: rebuilding plans for eastern Germany include a $450 billion

transportation project over the next 18 years, with $200 billion allocated
for 3,220 kilometres of high-speed rail development and 2,415 kilometres
of road improvement. Canada's Teleglobe Inc. is planning on taking
advantage of the fact that at least 20 percent of the public telephone
monopoly was being privatized in 1996 – the second-largest privatization
ever. Forty years of unrestrained pollution by former East Germany now
means abundant opportunities exist for environmental reform. The
number of people employed in the environmental sector is expected
to grow from 680,000 today to 1.1 million in 2000. Canada's Beak
International Inc. is staking out its claim in this market. Renovation
and construction should continue for another five years in the
Berlin/Brandenburg area, which hopes to benefit from the national
government moving there and from the abundant tourist potential
of the area.

France

France will continue to offer poor prospects for job seekers. From
July 1990 to July 1994, unemployment rose from 9 percent of the work
force to 12.5 percent, and public-sector deficits expanded from 2 percent
of GDP to 6 percent. Burdened by one of the highest tax rates in the
world, excessive regulation, and protectionist tendencies, France will
take longer to emerge from the recession and will require a growth rate
of at least 3 percent in order to create jobs; in other words, twice the
growth rate needed by a country with fewer economic constraints.
The 4 percent increase in minimum wage in 1995 gave it the second-
highest minimum wage in Europe (after Holland). Coupled with a social-
security tax contribution equal to 21.6 percent of GDP, a 20.6 percent
value-added tax (sales tax), a social security levy of 20 percent of income
paid by everyone, an additional 58.6 percent top marginal tax rate, plus
other taxes in the works, job prospects are not good and take-home
pay is minimal. Indeed, France's biggest tire manufacturer plans to
cut its work force in half over the next three years while upping its
production. Long-term unemployed now account for 39 percent of
those unemployed.

France is unpromising territory for Canadian job seekers unless you
are approaching a Canadian company expanding in France, such as
Northern Telecom Ltd., Tembec Inc. (forestry), Cascades Inc. (forestry),

Bombardier Inc., McCain Foods Ltd., or Seagram Co. Ltd. Many French firms such as Pechiney SA (aluminum), CSF Thomson SA (electronics), Alcatel Alsthom SA (electronics), Rhône-Poulenc SA (pharmaceuticals), Pneus Michelin SA (tires), Dumez SA (construction), Gaz de France (investment), and Danone SA (yogurt) have invested in Quebec. Those who are interested in the telecommunications industry might approach Alcatel Cable, the world's largest manufacturer of telecommunications, systems, and cable. It specializes in electrical equipment, electrical power plants, high-speed trains, and shipbuilding. Asia, which now accounts for roughly 25 percent of France's market, is buying the country's high-speed rail and power products. The Asian market is serviced through Alcatel's Australian branch.

France was the world's favourite tourist destination in 1995 despite terrorist attacks and nuclear-testing boycotts. Its economy was expected to grow by 1.3 percent in 1996 and 2.6 percent in 1997. Competitively, France dropped from 13th place in 1994 to 17th place in 1995.

Italy

The Italian economy, which continues to be plagued by unemployment, political turmoil, corruption, and a large government debt – 109 percent of its GDP in 1995, compared with Canada's 66.2 percent – was forecast to grow by 1.1 percent in 1994 and 2.5 percent in 1995. Over 200,000 jobs have been lost recently as a result of downsizing. Unless the new Italian government begins to tackle these pressing economic matters, the north, which is eager to take advantage of the European Community, will definitely drift toward separation. As *The Economist* recently stated, "If there is a single, recurrent, almost obsessive theme in the political history of post-war Italy, it is that of the need for reform and of the failure to achieve it." However, perhaps change will finally be forced by the public's anger at corruption, estimated to account for 15 percent of the government's debt.

If you are looking for work in Italy, concentrate on the north, where the standard of living is among the highest in the world and unem ployment rates are significantly lower. Italy's chief industries are steel, machinery, autos, textiles, shoes, machine tools, and chemicals. Best bets for foreign job seekers are likely fashion, textiles, and shoes, since Italy excels in these areas. But get a diploma or degree in fashion or fashion management as well as some Canadian experience before pursuing employment in Italy.

Kraft General Foods Canada Inc. is involved in the Italian food processing industry and may offer some opportunities for Canadians. Since a lot of natural gas underlies much of the Northern Plain and parts of Sicily, Canadians with expertise in gas exploitation may find work in this area. Anyone with expertise in plastics, fertilizers, and synthetic rubber production from natural gas would also stand a reasonable chance of finding a position. And since Italy has always relied on its large and profitable tourist industry to offset its ongoing trade deficit, there will always be jobs in this area.

Britain

Of all the large European countries, Britain has the best long-range job prospects. It has already passed through much of the painful restructuring that other European countries are only now experiencing. In a 1995 World Bank report ranking countries according to natural and human resources and productive assets, Britain placed 22nd. The 1995 World Competitiveness Report saw Britain fall from 14th to 18th position. In the people category, which covers labour force skills, educational system, and work attitudes, Britain fell from 21st place in 1994 to 24th place in 1995. In attitude of work force, it fell to 36th place. With the closed markets of its previous Commonwealth empire all but a fading memory, Britain has failed to make the transition to an internationally competitive economy. The result? A third of British children are reared in poverty and crime has doubled since 1979, giving Britain the highest prison population in Europe.

Aside from the finance industry, which is Britain's competitive claim to fame, the film industry is now flourishing. Its share of the European market rose from 7.7 percent in 1985 to 13.7 percent in 1994. Output increased from 47 movies in 1990 to 70 in 1994, while film production dropped in America and the rest of Europe. Manufacturing was flat during 1995; however, consumer spending was expected to keep the economy afloat in 1996. The economy was expected to grow by 2.2 percent in 1996 and 3.1 percent in 1997. Unemployment in 1996 was expected to stay slightly below Canadian levels, thanks to Britain's lower net national debt level (40 percent of GDP).

Spain

Although Spain has now surpassed Canada as one of the largest industrialized countries, it offers few opportunities to its own citizens, let alone to outsiders. Spanish labour law and practices make it extremely difficult to lay off workers or keep wages in check; consequently, companies are overstaffed and production extremely inefficient. Pensions and health care now constitute 60 percent of the government's budget. Crime rates have risen in major cities since unemployment remains so high. As a result, the black market economy accounts for 20 to 30 percent of gross domestic product. Spain was second in the world as a tourist destination in 1995, with a 4.4 percent increase in visitors. Real GDP increased by 3.3 percent in 1995, versus 2 percent in 1994. The economy was expected to grow by 2.5 percent in 1996 and 2.8 percent in 1997. With its deficit running close to 7 percent per year, Spain will not likely reach the 1999 Maastricht target of 3 percent. Unemployment was 22.8 percent in 1995, the highest in the EU. Since employers must compensate workers 45 days for each year employed, almost everyone is now hired on a contract-renewal basis. One-third of the country's workers are now employed in this manner.

Portugal

Portugal's traditional industries, textiles and clothing, will likely suffer as they are forced to compete with more technologically advanced foreign competitors. However, its modernized car and electrical machinery component sectors should do well, and its political stability and pro-business pragmatism should allow it to survive the transition to greater competitiveness. Portugal's deficit is at 5 percent, but should fall to 3 percent in time to meet the Maastricht target. Economic growth of 4 percent in 1995 helped keep the unemployment rate at about 6 percent. It has the lowest manufacturing labour costs of the major Western industrialized nations, with wages of roughly $6 per hour.

As the poorest country in Western Europe, Portugal is eligible for $240 billion in aid from the European Community over the next several years, along with another $25 billion awarded to Spain, Portugal, Ireland, and Greece as a means of catching up with other European Community nations. As a result, Portugal will be launching a number of competitive changes requiring the help of highly educated consultants and staff.

This, combined with Portugal's economic strengths, is good news for Canadians interested in Portugal, since only 10 percent of Portuguese students go beyond high school, thus creating a shortage of the highly educated workers needed to make these changes.

Greece

The Socialist government in the 1980s was responsible for a quadrupling of the government debt, which reached 120 percent of gross domestic product in 1992. Greece now has the lowest productivity, largest external debt, highest inflation, biggest underground economy, and lowest income per person of all European countries, and the situation is worsening. Although reforms have been instituted, Greece risks complete loss of control over its finances unless it takes serious measures to deal with its Sisyphean debt. The deficit dropped from 9.7 percent of GDP in 1994 to 8.9 percent in 1995. The economy, which has typically grown at half the EU rate (3.2 percent) over the past 15 years, is slowly recovering from negative numbers in 1993, posting a growth rate of 1.5 percent in 1994 and 2 percent in 1995.

Sweden

The measures to trim deficits over the past two years were expected to start paying off in 1996, with an expected growth rate of 2 percent, 2.1 percent in 1997. Nonetheless, labour market rigidities, excessive welfare budgets, and restricted local markets hampered job creation, so unemployment will remain high. In addition, the combination of spending cuts plus tax increases likely reduced consumer spending. In 1994, 33 percent of all workers were employed by the government, up from 21 percent in 1970. With 60 percent of the population directly dependent on the state's spending for income, it is difficult to enact the necessary reforms. Companies prospering in Sweden at the moment include Saab Scania AB, AB Electrolux, AB Astra, L.M. Ericsson Telephone Co. Inc., ABB Asea Brown Boveri Ltd., and Stora.

Finland

Finland, like Sweden, was expected to recapture its 1990 GDP growth rate in 1996. Unemployment in 1995 was 16.8 percent; wages fell each year between 1991 and 1994. However, like Sweden, Finland is cutting deficits and stabilizing debt levels so that it can become a member of the European economic and monetary union. Its deficits are considerably smaller than Sweden's, and it is running a trade surplus. As a sign of economic regional economic integration, Sweden, Norway, and Finland established a common electricity market in 1996. Finland still suffers from serious misjudgments earlier in this decade, such as excessive government spending, an overvalued currency, and poor banking practices (bad loans and property speculation). As a result unemployment hovers around 18 percent. The government's decision to cut government spending by 4 percent of GDP over its four-year term in office will depress consumer spending but boost exports. Finland will likely have its debt level below 60 percent of GDP by 1999 – an EU admission criterion – and will reap the benefit of rising lumber prices. Finland was considered to be more competitive than France in 1995.

Job seekers can contemplate employment opportunities with Nokkia, which controls almost a fifth of the world's cellular phone market share. Consider also entrepreneurial hot spots such as Oulu, Finland, which has over 1,000 startups in software, sensors, optoelectronics, and lasers, accounting for more than $1 billion annually.

Norway

Thanks to the discovery of North Sea petroleum and gas in the late 1960s, Norway manages to enjoy one of the highest standards of living in the world. Petroleum and natural gas exports now account for more than 40 percent of its export market. Meanwhile, Norway's hydroelectric power has become a serious rival to France's nuclear power in supplying the rest of Europe with electricity. It is estimated that by the turn of the century, the export of hydroelectric power could bring in as much revenue as the oil and gas industry.

But Norway's non-oil economy has not grown since 1989, which accounts for the country's high unemployment rate in the early 1990s. So far, oil and gas wealth has allowed Norway to maintain a high level of social support payments. Spending on disability and rehabilitation rose by 80 percent between 1980 and 1990. But unless steps to reform welfare policies are undertaken, most of the rest of the country's economy will continue to languish.

Growing oil and gas exports created a trade surplus of 14 percent of

GDP in 1994, which lowered unemployment to 5.4 percent. Norway has decided not to join the EU, but it is trying to integrate its economy more with other Nordic countries.

Denmark

Denmark's booming exports helped the country's economy grow by 3.5 percent in 1995, which was less than its 4.5 percent growth rate in 1994. Although the economy was expected to grow by only 2.1 percent in 1996 and 2.5 percent in 1997, unemployment seems on a downward slope: 12.2 percent in 1993, 10.1 percent in 1995, and probably 9 percent by 1997. Unemployment will remain structurally high, as will inflationary tendencies during growth periods, owing to Denmark's generous social policies and a public sector that accounts for 31.5 percent of the GDP. Any worker or self-employed person is entitled to an educational leave for up to a year, with the government paying 90 percent of salary up to a $33,000 maximum. Denmark's competitiveness fell from third place in the world in 1993 to ninth place in 1995, but it is still ahead of Canada (12th place). Denmark's main trading partner is Germany, so its economic growth usually mirrors its neighbour's to a large extent.

Denmark's main industries are industrial and construction machinery, textiles, furniture, and electronics. Food processing is also a large part of its export market. Those with electronic engineering and computer backgrounds could contact such well-known multinational industrial manufacturing companies as Unisys, Control Data Systems Ltd., General Dynamics, Amdahl Canada Limited, Raytheon Co., IBM, Hewlett Packard, Motorola, Philips Electronics, and Analog Devices, all of which operate in Denmark. Denmark's North Sea oil drilling has attracted Imperial Oil Limited and Goodyear Canada Inc.

The Netherlands

The Netherlands is also in a good long-range competitive position, ranking seventh, which was just behind Switzerland and Germany but ahead of all other European nations. The Netherlands' strengths lie primarily in finance, its managers, and its domestic economy. Approximately 90 percent of the population can speak English. Its economy was expected to grow by 2 percent in 1996 and 2.6 percent in 1997. The Dutch Central Bank's decade-long habit of shadowing the German mark has kept inflation low, stabilized its currency, and attracted foreign investors. A Price Waterhouse survey puts Holland ahead of Belgium, France, Ireland, the United Kingdom, and Germany with respect to investment and operating conditions, economic conditions, and cost of living. Dutch industries that are prospering and could offer opportunities to Canadians include oil, electronics, and metal and chemical manufacturing. Currently Holland is hoping to attract investment in information technology, biotechnology, medical research, food processing, and distribution. Some of the over 80 Canadian companies in Holland include McCain Foods, Gandalf, Cognos, Aptec Engineering, Concord, Connaught Laboratory, Norboard, and Northern Telecom.

Belgium

The Belgian economy was expected to grow by 1.6 percent in 1996 and 2.3 percent in 1997. Unemployment, which averaged 12.4 percent in 1995, will remain high since Belgium's wages are the second highest in the Western industrialized world, after Germany and Switzerland. Although the country is slowly reducing its deficit, it is projected to fall only to 124 percent of GDP by 1997. Interest on its debt has ended up decreasing R&D to a level far below that of other European nations and to one-third the level of the U.S. Coupled with a huge unfunded liability regarding pensions and health care, its long-range prospects are not good. In 1995, Belgium ranked 19th in overall competitiveness.

Switzerland

Switzerland will continue to be the stable country it has always been. Switzerland is always in contention for top spot as far as quality of life is concerned, and it ranked fifth in the world for competitiveness in 1995. In 1995, Switzerland came out of its worst recession; unemployment rose from 0.5 percent in 1991 to 4.7 percent in 1994, and the economy contracted 0.4 percent between 1991 and 1993. Investment in machinery and equipment grew by 10 percent in 1994, and exports increased, yielding growth rates of 2.1 percent in 1994 and 1.9 percent in 1995. The soaring Swiss franc caused the economy to contract in 1996 and has created a rather bleak short-term outlook; tourism has suffered as well. Unemployment may not drop below 4 percent over the next two years. The best employment opportunities for foreigners will be in the pharmaceutical industry and in Switzerland's famous financial industry, which may benefit from continuing economic and political instability elsewhere in the world.

Austria

The Austrian economy should grow by 1.8 percent in 1996 and 2.3 percent in 1997, and its unemployment rate should stay below 5 percent over the next few years. Austria ranked in 13th spot in competitiveness in 1995, just behind Canada. Because a large part of Austria's economy is controlled by state enterprises, there is some trepidation about joining the European Community. Along with Germany, Austria is well situated to trade and compete with the emerging Eastern European countries. Its domestic economic strength, strong international focus, and highly educated work force (99 percent literacy) will help it make the necessary transitions that all European countries are going through.

The Austrian government is about to devote a considerable amount of money to infrastructure in order to maintain its construction industry, and it will continue to promote tourism to stabilize its currency. Either of these areas could offer opportunities to Canadians.

Russia, the Republics, and Eastern Europe

If you're interested in Russia and the newly emerging republics, bear in mind that social conditions there are still volatile – for instance, the murder rate is over twice as high as in the U.S. And the economy is still in crisis. Crime, corruption, and government instability and interference have created a drag on economic development. In 1995 Russia managed to stem the fall in its GDP to 4 percent and reduced its deficit to roughly 6 percent, an encouraging sign. Inflation, which reached 2,500 percent in 1992, was expected to fall to 60 percent in 1996. In 1996, the economy may have grown for the first time since 1990 – a growth rate of 2 percent was expected. But Russia's economy is still approximately 35 percent to 45 percent smaller than it was in 1989. Canada, with one-fifth as many people, exported three times as much as Russia in 1992. And, as far as standard of living is concerned, the Great Depression of the early 1930s was mild in comparison with the deprivation facing Russia today.

The business news is mixed, however. While production in areas where Russia has no competitive advantage, such as steel, shoes, and

BULLETIN BOARD — *RUSSIA AND EASTERN EUROPE*

- If they can overcome political and social instability and make a successful transition to a market economy, Russia and its former republics and allies offer exciting opportunities for Canadian companies and job seekers.
- In the near future, infrastructure and natural resource development will likely provide the first major job opportunities for foreign workers, since the latter will help pay for the former. Raising capital will also become a major preoccupation, creating opportunities for those who have financial consulting and banking expertise and can speak the appropriate languages. Given the dire state of the environment, there will be opportunities in that field eventually. However, for the moment, pure economic survival industries will take precedence over environmental concerns.

VCRs, has fallen drastically, the production of television sets and refrigerators was up by 10 percent. Oil, which amounts to 5 percent of the country's GDP, accounts for roughly 50 percent of its exports. Should Russian oil producers ever change from bureaucracies into market-oriented companies, they could generate enough wealth to create an economic boom in Russia. Meanwhile, it is impossible to predict what will happen politically. It is possible that Cold War conditions may re-emerge. Already Russia is aligning itself with Iran, Iraq, and the Chinese military and is attempting to assert control over the oil pipeline from Azerbaijan. The retaking of Belarus and Russia's tough stance toward Estonia have caused concern, and the U.S. is worried about a return to a state-controlled economy; it would immediately eliminate all aid should that option be exercised. Already the military accounts for 40 percent of Russia's spending.

Given that two-thirds of the country's GDP now comes from the private sector (over 95 percent of Russia's shops are privately owned) and the state-owned sector is now smaller than Italy's, one can only hope that the current market reforms have built up an irreversible momentum. At the moment there are 200 Western-style supermarkets, 2,500 licensed banks, 600 investment funds, 40 million shareholders, and an invitation for insurance companies to set up shop. Perhaps a healthy sign is the fact that no politician has an approval rating above 10 percent, and 120,000 enterprises have been privatized. By the end of 1996 Russian bonds had received investment-grade ratings from major U.S. rating services, although Canadian banks still refuse to lend money to companies interested in Russia. Foreign investment in Russia should reach $26.9 billion over the next four years now that the economy is under control.

If Russia and the republics can make a successful shift to a market economy, there will be opportunities for Canadian companies that can help exploit the rich natural resources in this region. Another area of opportunity for Canadian companies is environmental and health industries. According to Vladimir Pokorovsky, head of the Russian Academy of Medical Sciences, "We have already doomed ourselves for the next 25 years. The new generation is entering adult life unhealthy. The Soviet economy was developed at the expense of the population's health." The average lifespan of a male in Russia is now 57 – lower than that of males in India. With half the drinking water and a tenth of the food supply contaminated in Russia, and many of its former republics and allies suffering similar problems, there should be work for environmental specialists.

Some Canadian companies have already made the leap into Russia, including Patriot Computer Corp. of Richmond Hill, Ontario, which has sold up to $1 million worth of computers per month to Russia, and Soapberry Shop of Toronto. Other Canadian companies in Russia include Pratt & Whitney Canada Inc., MacDonald's Restaurants of Canada Ltd., PanCanadian Petroleum Ltd., and Canadian Francmaster Ltd. (now the largest foreign oil producer in Russia – it earns half its income there).

The now-independent republics and former Soviet allies offer the same combination of economic potential and political uncertainty. Kazakhstan is rich in oil and gold, Turkmenistan in oil and gas, and Azerbaijan has one of the largest unexploited oil reserves in the world. Many foreign companies have already entered Kazakhstan, which has welcomed privatization. Canadian companies, including Turan Petroleum Cyprus Ltd., Canadian Occidental Petroleum Ltd., Hurricane Hydrocarbons Ltd, and Cameco Corp. (uranium and gold mining), plan to spend over $1.4 billion in Kazakhstan and Kyrgyzstan in the next few years.

Estonia has 4,000 foreign-owned companies, half of which have Finnish partners. The Swedes have invested even more. The country's well-educated work force, inexpensive labour, and stable government are earning it the title "Hong Kong of the Baltic." Many Finnish companies have moved to Estonia because total factory production and management costs are typically a third of Finland's. At the moment, Russia has cut off trade with Estonia and would like to repossess it, much the way China will absorb Hong Kong. The situation is less promising in Ukraine, despite its agricultural resources. In Ukraine, as in Russia, agricultural productivity fell by 4 percent per year between 1970 and 1990. Despite the creation of 350,000 private farms and the early attempts to break up the collective farms, not much has changed since the beginning of the decade.

Among the former allies of the USSR, Hungary is particularly well positioned, since it started its transition to a market economy before the other Eastern European countries and thus avoided the economic shocks its neighbours are now experiencing. For several years Hungary was held back from economic recovery by an extremely slow pace of privatization, but recently this has changed. Hungary sold its state-owned telecommunications industry, its electricity and gas utilities, and a large bank in 1995. The country's main competitive economic strengths are its well educated work force and its strong science and technology focus. Since 75 percent of Hungary's work force has been trained in technical colleges, Ikea, Ford, Philips Electronics, and Suzuki have set up factories there. Hungary attracted $7 billion in foreign investment in 1995 thanks to the many reforms recently instituted – making it by far the most attractive Central European country for investors. Despite its austerity programs and trade deficits, the economy was expected to grow at a 2 percent rate in 1996 as Germany's demand for finished goods increases.

Poland seems to have passed through its transitional period. The Polish economy grew by 7 percent in 1995 and will likely continue to enjoy the fastest growth rate among Central European countries, forecast at 6 percent for 1996. Unemployment was 14.5 percent, inflation 25 percent, and the deficit 61 percent in 1995 – all marked improvements.

There are now 800,000 entrepreneurs in Poland, with the private sector accounting for 60 percent of the economy. With political stability apparently arrived, foreign investment is beginning to pour in at an increasing rate.

The Czech Republic also offers relative political stability and a quick transition to a market economy. Unemployment was high a few years ago, because of privatization, but already Czech exporters are earning 80 percent of their revenues in Western economies, with Germany absorbing 30 percent of these exports. One Canadian company that has given the Czechs a vote of confidence is Bata Industries Limited, which returned to the republic in 1991 and now has a manufacturing plant and 43 stores located there. The company is able to compete in the European import market against other low-priced exports from the Pacific Rim, Portugal, and Italy. Ironically, the current 5 percent unemployment rate, rather than being a good sign, suggests that the country has much economic restructuring ahead of it. Nonetheless the Czech economy is expected to grow by 5 to 6 percent in 1997 and 1998.

Slovakia suffered the most from the collapse in trade among former Communist countries. But it is witnessing a significant rebound now that the after-effects of the breakup are largely behind it. Slovakia's economy should grow by 5 percent per year over the next five years.

THE UNITED STATES

Most Canadians, not willing to go far afield for employment, will look south, to the U.S. While there has been considerable focus on the flaws of the U.S. economy in the past decade, we are now beginning to appreciate some of its strengths. As Canada and Europe struggled with high unemployment, the U.S. rate dropped far more quickly as it eased out of the recession. The key to low unemployment is flexibility: the ability to easily hire workers when needed and to lay them off or reduce their worktime or wages when the economy is performing poorly. In addition, minimum wages must be low enough that employers will continue to hire people instead of automating, but not so low that people will prefer to receive social assistance. Because the U.S. has this kind of hiring and wage flexibility, companies have been able to undergo the necessary restructuring essential to becoming globally competitive. Japan and Europe have rather rigid policies with respect to hiring and wages so that any economic adjustment period is likely to be longer and more painful. For this reason, the U.S. will always be an economic contender even if it must inevitably share its supremacy with the Pacific Rim and Europe.

In general, the U.S. has always had a flexible, innovative approach that has allowed it to get a head start on its competitors. Although the U.S. has many social problems that will challenge its future economic ambitions, it will emerge a strong economic nation so long as it refrains from taxing employers excessively in order to subsidize entitlement programs. Assuming the U.S. does bite the bullet on entitlement programs, politically unpopular though such a move will be, the next question is what are the promising job areas in the U.S. over the long haul.

Over the next decade 730,000 more computer engineers and systems analysts will be needed. There should also be a shortage of engineers and software developers who are familiar with integrated manufacturing, electronics, computer engineering, robotics, and telecommunications systems (such as radio frequency engineers). In other words, look for jobs in the new economy areas, which will hire a greater percentage of qualified applicants because of the large number of medium-sized, large, and multinational companies located in the U.S. America's competitive strengths include its superior productivity in its airlines, retail banking, restaurants, general-merchandise retailing, and telecoms, according to the McKinsey Global Institute. Its service sector is responsible for 80 percent of all jobs and should experience a significant growth in productivity, given the $1 trillion in information technology that now underpins it. Natural disasters such as floods, hurricanes, and earthquakes will continue to fuel building starts and repairs for some time to come.

The Telecommunications Act of 1996 ended many of the government rules that acted as barriers among cable TV, local and long-distance calling, broadcasting, and wireless services. Considerable dealmaking, merger, and acquisition activity will occur as phone companies, Hollywood studios, cable-TV operators, and publishing companies chase after one another's business in what will be a $1 trillion industry by 2000. Cellular calling and other new communications services have increased the total phone industry employment by 54,000 over the past two years, despite downsizings widely reported in the press. The combined convergence of communications, entertainment, and computer industries created 400,000 jobs in 1995, accounting for 20 percent of all new jobs created. As the new infrastructure for the information highway gets built, many suppliers will benefit enormously. For instance, spending on modems, digital switches, and related items rose by 53 percent in 1995, reaching $100 billion – which is double the growth rate of spending on computers and other capital equipment.

Where to find work in the U.S.? The Northeast is suffering from high costs of living and doing business, as is California; however, California's tourist, entertainment, and export industries should keep employment growth above the national average for the next couple of years, although many manufacturers are moving and defence contracts evaporating. The Rocky Mountain states should see double the national average of job creation thanks to the technology sector. Arizona, Colorado, Idaho, New Mexico, Texas, Utah, Washington, and Oregon are involved in semiconductor fabrication, which has attracted billion of dollars in investment. This area may cool eventually, given current worldwide excess capacity. High-tech hiring in Phoenix spurred on job growth by 5 percent and had a similar effect in Albuquerque, New Mexico. Arizona and New Mexico should see job growth of 2 percent in 1996. Other rapidly growing cities are Atlanta and Las Vegas. The Midwest and Southeast states may see a dropoff owing to slower automotive and housing sales; however, the Midwest should benefit from increased machinery and equipment sales. Laggards in 1995 were Mid-Atlantic states such as New York, New Jersey, and Pennsylvania.

The biggest growth industry of the 1990s in the U.S. should be entertainment, which along with recreation created 200,000 new jobs in 1993, representing 12 percent of all new jobs, surpassing the health care industry, which was the biggest job creator in the 1980s. A total of C$450 billion was spent on entertainment in 1993, which represents an after-inflation increase of 13 percent since 1991, or twice the growth rate of consumer spending overall. Over $17 billion is being spent by Blockbuster Entertainment, MCA, and the Walt Disney Company to develop theme parks, casinos, theatres, and ballparks. Once again, the baby boomers, who tend to be the biggest spenders on entertainment, are responsible. Areas of expansion will include both traditional entertainment and new technology. Imax Corp. of Toronto and Iwerks

BULLETIN BOARD — *UNITED STATES*

- Continuing growth as the U.S. economy recovers should provide job opportunities for Canadians, particularly in the entertainment and health care fields.

TIPS

➤ For an outline of the best places in the U.S. to weather an economic downturn, refer to the appendix of *The Great Reckoning* by James Davidson and Lord Rees-Mogg.

Entertainment Inc. of Burbank, California, are in the process of developing entertainment centres with simulator rides, giant screens, and virtual-reality games. Dance clubs with 360 movie screens are a taste of what is in store.

While rising productivity is expected to increase U.S. wages and discretionary spending, rising health care costs could put something of a damper on entertainment spending. But this inevitable rise will constitute another job opportunity area for Canadians. In addition to the same sort of job opportunities found in Canada's health care industries, the U.S. will have more jobs in pharmaceuticals, biotechnology, and medical equipment.

As always, Canadians who want to work in the U.S. will have to convince the government, with the help of their prospective employers, that they offer invaluable skills. But with the demand for knowledge workers increasing as the U.S. economy picks up, this should not be too difficult to do.

Doing Your Homework

While the foregoing discussion should give you a general idea about which areas of the world might be of interest to you in your job search, it is important to do thorough research – especially since conditions are changing constantly. The *Economist* magazine, arguably the best newsmagazine of its type in the world, is an excellent source of information, as are the World Bank's annual editions of *Global Economic Prospects and the Developing Countries* and *The World Competitiveness Report*. World Trade Centres located in each of Canada's major cities are open to inquiries

from individuals wishing to investigate career possibilities in foreign
countries. Very useful is Jean-Marc Hachey's *The Canadian Guide to
Working and Living Overseas for Entry-Level and Seasoned Professionals*, which
contains over 2,400 documented international job resources in its second
edition. The guide includes a complete listing of international study and
internship programs in Canada, plus most Canadian private firms and
public-sector agencies operating abroad. The B.O.S.S. directories also
describe the firms doing business or planning to do business in foreign
countries and the products or services they sell. The following international trade associations are also happy to provide information
to interested job seekers:

☞ ASEAN-Canada Business Council
   The Canadian Chamber of Commerce,
   #1160, 55 Metcalfe St.,
   Ottawa, ON K1P 6N4 Tel. 613-238-4000 Fax: 613-238-7643

☞ Asia Pacific Foundation of Canada
   #666, 999 Canada Pl.,
   Vancouver, BC V6C 3E1 Tel. 604-684-5986 Fax: 604-681-1370

☞ Canadian Exporters Association
   #250, 99 Bank St.,
   Ottawa, ON K1P 6B9 Tel. 613-238-8888 Fax: 613-563-9218

☞ Canadian International Trade Association
   #611, 2 Carlton St.,
   Toronto, ON M5B 1J3 Tel. 416-351-9728 Fax: 416-351-9911

☞ Federation of Export Clubs Canada
   #1402, 67 Yonge St.,
   Toronto, ON M5E 1J8 Tel. 416-364-4112 Fax: 416-364-4074

APPENDIX A: CAREER PROSPECTS

"Career Prospects" is reprinted from *Prospects Canada* (Fall 1996), by permission of Career Information Partnership Canada, a federal government agency. The economic factors discussed in this book should be taken into consideration when analyzing the projections shown here.

Occupations are listed alphabetically. A brief work description is provided for each occupation.
Employment: Refers to the industries where the occupations can be found.
Education and Training: Describes the educational and training requirements of the occupation.
Subjects: Suggested fields of study related to the occupation.

Outlook: The arrows indicate the projected growth between 1995 and the year 2000 for each occupation, according to *Job Futures* (1996): ▲ = getting better; ► = remaining stable; ▼ = getting worse.
Salary: The overall average salary for the occupation, based on 1993 Statistics Canada data, updated to summer 1996.

OCCUPATIONS	WHAT YOU NEED	OUTLOOK & SALARY
BUSINESS, FINANCE AND ADMINISTRATION		
ACCOUNTANTS Work as Chartered Accountants (CAs), Certified General Accountants (CGAs) or Certified Management Accountants (CMAs) in a number of areas, such as auditing, taxation, external reporting, insolvency and reconstruction, management accounting and financial accounting (treasury). **Employment:** Medium- or large-sized firms, government.	**Education and training:** Secondary school graduation (or equivalent) plus mature student status (for CGA candidates); university degree (for CA and CMA candidates); completion of formal studies and practical experience, with periodic examinations; registration, certification or licensing requirements in most provinces and territories; professional accreditation. **Subjects:** business, accounting, law, economics.	▲ $43,900
AUTO PARTS CLERKS Receive and sort incoming stock of automotive parts and supplies, maintain inventory of stocks, sell stock to customers and requisition or order stock as required. **Employment:** Retail stores, wholesalers, repair shops.	**Education and training:** High school completion is usually required; automotive parts apprenticeship (3 to 4 years); or several years experience in auto parts stores plus college parts clerk course; Red Seal certification (interprovincial) is available. **Subjects:** Auto, business.	◄ $30,000
BOOKKEEPERS Maintain complete sets of books or records of financial transactions carried out by businesses or other establishments. May use computer software accounting packages to perform bookkeeping activities. **Employment:**	**Education and training:** High school completion is required plus courses in accounting or bookkeeping; or several years experience in financial, bookkeeping or accounting work; or college program in accounting or related	▲ $24,700

Banks, insurance companies, wholesalers.

CLAIMS ADJUSTERS/INVESTIGATORS
Investigate insurance claims for damage or loss. Determine the amount of damage or loss and whether the policyholder is covered. **Employment:** Insurance firms.

Education and training: Secondary school completion is required; a bachelor's degree, college diploma or some post-secondary education or several years of experience is required. **Subjects:** Business, law.

↑ $35,500

DESKTOP PUBLISHING OPERATORS OR SPECIALISTS
Operate electronic publishing and word-processing equipment to design, lay out and produce camera-ready copy for brochures, manuals, bulletins, books, newsletters, in-house and other publications. Use computer graphics software to provide illustrations for publications. **Employment:** Typesetting firms, newspapers.

Education and training: High school completion is required; college graphic arts program; or training in computer typesetting or desktop publishing or typography is usually required. **Subjects:** Art, English, graphics, visual arts.

← $29,500

GENERAL OFFICE CLERKS
Record and process information. Type and file correspondence, reports and other materials. Answer telephones and attend to counter inquiries. Operate photocopiers and perform other clerical activities. **Employment:** Public and private sectors.

Education and training: High school completion is preferred; business or high school commercial courses may be required; typing or word-processing skills may be required. **Subjects:** Business, English.

↑ $27,700

HOSPITAL ADMINISTRATORS
Are responsible for the general administration, including financial controls, of a hospital or other health care institution. Develop policies to set the direction and goals of the hospital/health care institution and usually report to a board of directors. **Employment:** Hospitals, health care institutions.

Education and training: University degree or college diploma in business or hospital administration or related discipline is usually required; extensive experience (10 to 15 years) in subordinate positions in hospital/health administration is usually required. **Subjects:** Business, English, family studies.

↑ $42,600

HUMAN RESOURCES/PERSONNEL MANAGERS
Develop and put into place programs for hiring and training employees. Classify jobs and install pay and benefits procedures. Organize and may conduct employee information sessions and develop management training programs. Also attend to many other personnel problems and details. **Employment:** Medium- or large-sized firms, government.

Education and training: University degree in business administration, industrial relations or a related field; or professional development program in personnel administration plus extensive experience as a personnel officer. **Subjects:** Social studies.

↑ $42,200

LOAN OFFICERS

Interview persons who want loans or credit, and evaluate their financial and credit status and their ability to repay the loans. Can authorize loans or credit up to an amount set by the institution or recommend approval of larger amounts to a loan manager. **Employment:** Bank, trust companies, credit unions.

Education and training: High school completion plus several years general banking experience; or university degree or college diploma related to commerce or economics; internal loan or credit training program (6 to 12 months) is usually provided. **Subjects:** Business, mathematics.

▲ $30,400

MEDICAL RECORDS TECHNICIANS

Process, code, store and retrieve medical records and statistics of medical patients. Usually operate computerized record-keeping systems. **Employment:** Hospitals, health care institutions.

Education and training: High school completion is required; college medical records technician course (1 to 2 years); or Canadian Hospital Association correspondence course plus work experience in medical or other record keeping. **Subjects:** Mathematics, keyboarding, business, health care.

▲ $27,700

PURCHASING OFFICERS

Purchase the goods, materials, supplies and services needed to operate a business. Determine requirements, negotiate prices and delivery. **Employment:** Retail stores, government offices.

Education and training: A bachelor's degree or college diploma in business administration, commerce or economics is usually required. **Subjects:** Business, marketing, retailing.

▼ $47,000

RECEPTIONISTS

Greet people entering offices or reception areas and direct them to appropriate persons or services. Answer telephones, take messages and schedule appointments. May type data. Perform other clerical duties. **Employment:** Public and private sectors.

Education and training: Some high school, but high school completion is preferred; specific typing speed or word-processing experience may be required. **Subjects:** Office procedures, word processing.

▲ $27,700

SECRETARIES

Type correspondence, reports and other data. Arrange and schedule appointments, meetings and business travel. Operate word processors, typewriters, microcomputers and other electronic office equipment. May take dictation using shorthand. Perform many other clerical and administrative duties. **MEDICAL AND LEGAL SECRETARIES** usually have specialized training, and **EXECUTIVE SECRETARIES** usually have considerable secretarial experience. **Employment:** Public and private sectors.

Education and training: High school completion is usually required; college secretarial program (1 to 2 years); or previous clerical experience including typing or word processing; college legal or medical secretarial program (1 to 2 years) is usually required for these specializations. **Subjects:** English, office procedures, word processing.

▼ $26,800

Occupation	Education and training	Salary
SHIPPERS AND RECEIVERS Record and ship parts, supplies, equipment and other materials from manufacturing plants, wholesale and retail warehouses and other storage facilities. Inspect and record goods received. May pack, unpack, load or unload goods, move goods into storage or route goods to storage areas. May also operate computerized inventory systems. **Employment:** Retailers, wholesalers, manufacturing companies.	**Education and training:** High school completion and some warehouse experience are usually required. **Subjects:** Business.	◄ $30,000
STOCKBROKERS Advise clients on investment opportunities, and buy and sell mutual funds, bonds, stocks, commodity futures and other securities on clients' behalf. May work for individual investors or institutions. **Employment:** Investment and stockbrokerage firms.	**Education and training:** University degree in economics, business administration or a related discipline; or high school completion plus extensive experience; Canadian Securities Commission examination; licensing. **Subjects:** Business, mathematics.	► $38,700
TELLERS Serve customers at banks or other financial institutions. Process customers' cheques or cash deposits, withdrawals, credit card payments and other banking transactions. Calculate foreign exchange currency. Perform related clerical duties such as balancing cash and preparing and filing statements. **Employment:** Banks, credit unions, trust companies.	**Education and training:** High school completion is required; on-the-job training is provided. **Subjects:** Accounting, keyboarding.	► $22,700
WORD PROCESSOR OPERATORS Type correspondence, reports, financial statements, charts and other data. Operate word processors, typewriters and microcomputers. Also usually perform some clerical duties such as photocopying and filing. **Employment:** Public and private sectors.	**Education and training:** Some high school, but high school completion is preferred; word processing course certificate may be required; specific typing speed is usually required. **Subjects:** Word processing, business, English, graphics.	▲ $27,700
NATURAL AND APPLIED SCIENCES		
AIR PILOTS Operate airplanes to transport passengers and cargo to and from scheduled destinations and to provide services such as aerial surveying, spraying and crop dusting, and search and rescue. Also operate helicopters. **Employment:** Crop spraying companies, flying schools, airlines.	**Education and training:** High school completion; flying school certification; or aviation school completion; commercial pilot's licence; Canadian restricted telephone certificate (Department of Transport Canada); Department of Transport Canada special ratings or endorsements for flying different types of aircraft. **Subjects:** Mathematics, sciences, geography.	▲ $51,300

AIR TRAFFIC CONTROLLERS

Direct air traffic within a particular airspace to ensure safe landings and takeoffs of aircraft and to control the activities of all moving aircraft and service vehicles on airport tarmacs. Observe aircraft from airport towers. Watch radar and other monitors. Operate radio and other communications and electronic equipment. **Employment:** Federal government, airlines.

Education and training: High school completion; Department of Transport Canada's air traffic controller's training program completion; telephone operator's licence; air traffic controller's licence. **Subjects:** Mathematics, sciences.

▲ $44,900

ARCHITECTS

Design buildings and develop plans regarding design specifications, materials, cost and construction time. May specialize in designing residential, industrial, commercial, institutional or public buildings (for example, fire stations, airports, museums, galleries). **Employment:** Architectural firms, government, construction.

Education and training: University degree in architecture; or 8 years on-the-job training with registered architect plus syllabus of studies from the Royal Architectural Institute of Canada; provincial/territorial examinations; internship (2 years). **Subjects:** Mathematics, sciences, art, graphics.

▲ $44,500

BIOLOGICAL TECHNOLOGISTS AND TECHNICIANS

Conduct laboratory tests and analyses, field surveys, and perform other technical activities for scientists and engineers. Work in areas such as agriculture, resource management, plant and animal biology, microbiology, cell and molecular biology; health science, and in fish hatcheries and greenhouse and livestock production programs. (Technologists perform their duties under general supervision, often independently; while technicians usually work under the direct supervision of professionals or technological staff.) **Employment:** Laboratories, chemical companies.

Education and training: College technologist's diploma (2 to 3 years) or technician's (1 to 2 years) in a field related to agriculture, biology, microbiology, wildlife or resource management. **Subjects:** Biology, chemistry, mathematics.

▼ $37,200

BIOLOGISTS

Conduct studies to extend knowledge of living organisms, their characteristics and behaviours. May specialize in a particular field such as zoology, botany, virology, microbiology or entomology. Often work in laboratories or in field settings. **Employment:** Universities, hospitals, government.

Education and training: University degree in biology, biochemistry or a related natural science; master's or doctorate degree is usually required for research scientists. **Subjects:** Mathematics, chemistry, biology, physics.

▼ $41,200

BIOMEDICAL TECHNOLOGISTS

Install, calibrate, test, modify and repair electrical, electronic and electro-mechanical medical equipment in hospitals and other health care institutions. Usually instruct nursing and other staff in the use of monitoring or

Education and training: College electronics or electrical engineering technologist's diploma (2 to 3 years) plus experience in hospital biomedical department or courses in biomedical engineering technology. **Subjects:**

◄ $40,100

◄	$40,100
◄	$43,000
▲	$46,700
▲	$45,800

other patient care equipment. **Employment:** Communications, electrical and electronics industries.

CHEMICAL TECHNOLOGISTS AND TECHNICIANS
Perform various technical functions for scientists or other professionals involved in areas such as chemical and biochemical research and analysis, industrial chemistry, chemical engineering and environmental monitoring. (Technologists perform their duties under general supervision, often independently, while technicians usually work under the direct supervision of professionals or technological staff.) **Employment:** Hospitals, government, food processing companies.

Education and training: College technologist's program (2 to 3 years) or technician's program (1 to 2 years) in chemical, biochemical, chemical engineering or related discipline is usually required; university degree in chemistry or biochemistry may be required for chemical technologists. **Subjects:** Mathematics, chemistry.

CHEMISTS
Conduct basic research into the chemical properties, composition and structure of substances, and conduct applied research to develop new or improved materials, compounds and substances for industrial, commercial or other purposes. Carry out quality control programs in manufacturing plants, investigate chemical aspects of drug action and perform other research and development activities. May specialize in areas such as biochemistry and analytical or physical chemistry. **Employment:** Scientific firms, mining companies, hospitals.

Education and training: University degree in chemistry, biochemistry or a related discipline; master's or doctorate degree is usually required for research chemists; licensing may be required. **Subjects:** Mathematics, chemistry, physics.

CIVIL ENGINEERS
Plan, design, develop and manage projects for the construction or repair of structures such as bridges, dams, ports, water and waste management systems, pipelines, roads and buildings. Also conduct feasibility, traffic pattern, environmental impact and other studies for construction proposals, and make recommendations. **Employment:** Railways, construction, electrical utilities.

Education and training: University degree in civil engineering or a related engineering discipline; registration as a professional engineer is often required. **Subjects:** Mathematics, sciences.

COMPUTER ENGINEERS
Plan, design, develop and test computers and related equipment for applications in process and machine control, robotics, instrumentation, environmental monitoring, remote sensing and related engineering and scientific applications. Also design and develop computer software. **Employment:** Banks, insurance firms, software companies.

Education and training: Bachelor's degree in computer or electrical or electronics engineering or engineering physics, computer science or mathematics or a related discipline; registration as a professional engineer may be required. **Subjects:** Mathematics, computer science, business.

Occupation	Education and training	Salary	Trend
COMPUTER PROGRAMMERS Write detailed step-by-step instructions or programs that tell a computer what it must do to solve a problem. May work as application programmers and write programs or software for specific jobs such as accounting and inventory control, or as systems programmers who write programs for software that controls the operation of an entire computer system. **Employment:** Banks, software companies, government.	**Education and training:** Bachelor's degree in computer science or related discipline such as mathematics or commerce; or college computer science diploma; post-secondary study or experience in science, engineering or other technical areas is usually required for application programmers in those fields. **Subjects:** Mathematics, computer science, business.	$40,700	◄
COMPUTER SYSTEMS ANALYSTS Analyze business, scientific, engineering or other technical requirements or problems, and design computer systems to meet clients' needs. Write specifications for computer programmers to implement and follow. Plan and implement computer security systems. Develop computer languages or software packages. **Employment:** Insurance and software companies, government.	**Education and training:** Bachelor's degree in computer science, mathematics, commerce, business administration or engineering; or college computer science diploma plus extensive experience in computer programming; post-secondary study or experience in science, engineering or other specialized technical areas may be required. **Subjects:** Mathematics, computer science, business.	$40,700	◄
DRAFTSPERSONS Prepare accurate working or detailed drawings for construction, engineering, manufacturing, mapping, machinery installations and other purposes. Work from notes, sketches, calculations, specification sheets and other data. Usually operate computer-aided drafting and design systems (CAD/CAM). **Employment:** Construction, manufacturing, engineering.	**Education and training:** High school completion is usually required; college drafting diploma; or apprenticeship (4 years) in drafting or several years related experience plus college or industry drafting courses. **Subjects:** Mathematics, sciences, industrial drafting and design.	$38,700	▲
ELECTRICAL AND ELECTRONICS ENGINEERING TECHNOLOGISTS Develop and test power equipment and systems; industrial process control systems; telecommunications, broadcasting and recording systems; computer systems and networks; and computer software. Conduct or supervise the installation and operation of electrical and electronic equipment and systems, and perform many other technical functions. Work under the general direction of engineers or other professional staff. **Employment:** Airlines, government, radio and TV networks.	**Education and training:** College electrical or electronics engineering technologist's diploma (2 to 3 years). **Subjects:** Mathematics, physics, electronics.	$38,000	◄

ELECTRICAL AND ELECTRONICS ENGINEERS

Design, plan and evaluate electrical and electronics equipment and systems, and direct or supervise installations, testing, inspection and maintenance activities. Specialize in many areas such as electrical power generation and transmission, communication systems, instrumentation and control systems, computer applications and software design. **Employment:** Communications, engineering, electrical utilities.

Education and training: University degree in electrical or electronics engineering or an appropriate related engineering discipline; registration as a professional engineer is usually required. **Subjects:** Mathematics, physics, electronics.

↑ $47,500

FOREST TECHNOLOGISTS AND TECHNICIANS

Conduct and supervise forest inventories and surveys. Assist in the preparation of forest management and harvesting plans. Monitor activities of logging companies. Supervise and participate in tree seeding, planting and nursery operations and other forest preservation activities. **Employment:** Forest industry, government, consulting firms.

Education and training: College forestry technology course (1 to 3 years) is usually required. **Subjects:** Agriculture (resources), biology.

↓ $37,200

GEOLOGISTS

Conduct exploration and research programs to extend knowledge of the structure, composition and processes of the earth and surface and subsurface waters; to locate oil, natural gas and mineral deposits; and to plan the extraction or exploitation of those resources. Also advise in areas such as waste management and selection of sites for construction purposes. **Employment:** Mining companies, government.

Education and training: University degree in geology or a related discipline. **Subjects:** Mathematics, sciences, geography.

← $43,000

HOME ENTERTAINMENT EQUIPMENT TECHNICIANS

Diagnose problems and repair radios, TVs, VCRs, tape decks and compact disc players. **Employment:** Retailers, wholesalers, engineering.

Education and training: Completion of a college program (2 to 3 years) in electronics or completion of a 4-year apprenticeship program in electronics servicing and repair. **Subjects:** Mathematics, physics, business, electronics.

← $30,600

INDUSTRIAL DESIGNERS

Develop designs and prepare specifications for a wide variety of products to be manufactured (such as furniture, electronics, keyboards, mechanical products). **Employment:** Manufacturing, design firms.

Education and training: University degree in industrial design, architecture or engineering; or college industrial design diploma plus work experience in industrial design; portfolio. **Subjects:** Physics, art, graphics.

↑ $38,700

INDUSTRIAL ENGINEERS

Determine the most effective and efficient ways for an organization to use the basic elements of production — people, machines, materials, informa-

Education and training: A bachelor's degree in industrial engineering or in a related engineering discipline is required; registration as a professional

↑ $45,800

Occupation	Salary	Trend

tion and energy. **Employment:** Manufacturing, transportation, engineering.

LANDSCAPE ARCHITECTS — ↓ $37,200
Plan and design the landscaping of parks and other public areas, subdivisions, buildings and building grounds, private residences and other areas. Plans include features such as trees, shrubs, gardens, walkways, patios, lighting and fences. **Employment:** Architectural and landscaping firms, development agencies.
Education and training: University degree in landscape architecture is usually required; extensive (minimum 7 years) landscaping experience plus college landscape architecture diploma may be accepted; licensing may be required. **Subjects:** Mathematics, sciences, art, construction, agriculture.
engineer by a provincial or territorial association is often required. **Subjects:** Mathematics, sciences.

MARINE ENGINEER OFFICERS — ↑ $45,800
Operate the main engines of ships and other water transport vessels, as well as the machinery and auxiliary equipment such as boilers, steering and deck machinery, motors, pumps and generators. Also supervise the engine room crew. **Employment:** Marine transportation, government, Canadian Forces.
Education and training: High school completion is required; marine engineering cadet program (3 years); or 30 months engine room sea service plus 6 months approved formal training in marine engineering institute; or 30 months experience as a mechanic plus minimum 6 months sea service. **Subjects:** Physics, technical studies.

MECHANICAL ENGINEERS — ↑ $47,300
Research and design machinery and systems for heating, ventilating and air conditioning, power generation, transportation vehicles, processing and manufacturing and other activities. Also perform functions related to the installation, operation and maintenance of machinery and systems. **Employment:** Engineering, manufacturing, mining companies.
Education and training: University degree in mechanical engineering or in a related engineering discipline; registration as a professional engineer is usually required. **Subjects:** Mathematics, sciences.

METEOROLOGISTS — ↓ $43,000
Analyze and interpret information received from meteorological stations, satellite imagery and computer models to forecast the weather. Research weather patterns and climates, and the transportation of pollutants by the atmosphere. **Employment:** Broadcasting, universities, research laboratories.
Education and training: Bachelor or Master of Science degree in meteorology or a closely related field; doctoral degree is usually required for research scientists in meteorology; formal training is provided by the Atmospheric Environment Service (up to 6 months). **Subjects:** Mathematics, physics, geography.

PHARMACOLOGISTS — ↑ $40,100
Study the actions and effects of drugs and other substances on human and animal cells, tissues, organs and life processes. Test drugs for medicinal use dosages. **Employment:** Government, pharmacies, health clinics.
Education and training: Master's or doctorate degree in pharmacology or a related biological science is usually required. **Subjects:** Biology, chemistry, mathematics.

PHYSICISTS

Conduct research to extend knowledge of natural phenomena and to develop innovations in fields such as electronics, communications, power generation and distribution, aerodynamics, optics and lasers, remote sensing, and medicine and health. **Employment:** Research centres, universities.

Education and training: Master's or doctorate degree in physics, engineering physics or a closely related field. **Subjects:** Mathematics, physics.

◄ $43,000

SURVEYORS

Conduct surveys of land and establish the legal boundaries and ownership of land. Prepare and maintain the associated records and drawings or maps. Operate electronic and non-electric survey equipment to measure distances, angles and land elevations. **Employment:** Private sector land surveying, government.

Education and training: University degree in survey science or civil engineering; or college survey technology diploma; articling period; licensing. **Subjects:** Mathematics, physics.

▲ $44,500

URBAN AND LAND USE PLANNERS

Prepare plans for zoning, transportation, public utilities, community facilities, parks, housing and related services for cities, towns and rural areas. Also prepare and recommend plans for the provision of wildlife preserves, national and provincial parks, protection of watersheds and the prevention of soil erosion. **Employment:** Government, land developing, engineering.

Education and training: University degree in urban design, planning, geography, engineering or a related discipline; graduate degree in regional and urban planning, design and environmental planning, architectural engineering or a related discipline is usually required; association membership is usually required (Canadian Institute of Planners). **Subjects:** Geography, social studies.

▲ $44,500

HEALTH

AUDIOLOGISTS

Diagnose hearing problems using specialized audiometric equipment and plan and implement rehabilitative programs for patients, including the selection and fitting of hearing aids or devices. **Employment:** Hospitals, schools, rehabilitation centres.

Education and training: University degree in audiology; certification with Canadian Audiology and Speech Language Pathology Association is mandatory. **Subjects:** Social sciences, sciences.

▲ $34,000

CHIROPRACTORS

Diagnose patients' conditions. Adjust and manipulate the spinal column and other parts of the body. Employ massage, heat, electrical and other therapies to treat patients' disorders. **Employment:** Private practice.

Education and training: 4-year program at an accredited chiropractic college after 2 year undergraduate studies in science; examination; licensing. **Subjects:** Sciences, social sciences.

▼ $58,100

Occupation	Education and training	Salary
COMMUNITY AND HOSPITAL PHARMACISTS Prepare and dispense pharmaceuticals according to doctors' prescriptions. INDUSTRIAL PHARMACISTS formulate and test newly developed drug products. **Employment:** Drugstores, hospitals, large supermarkets.	**Education and training:** A Bachelor of Science in pharmacy; supervised practical training for community and hospital pharmacists; licensing for community and hospital pharmacists. **Subjects:** Chemistry, mathematics.	↑ $34,700
DENTAL ASSISTANTS Assist dentists during the examination and treatment of patients. Sterilize and maintain instruments and equipment. Take X-rays and perform routine laboratory procedures and other duties as directed. **Employment:** Dental clinics.	**Education and training:** High school completion is preferred; college program (3 months to 1 year); or on-the-job training; certification required for intra-oral duties. **Subjects:** Dental assisting, office procedures.	↑ $32,400
DENTISTS Diagnose and treat diseases, injuries, malformations and other disorders of the teeth, gums and surrounding tissues, and prescribe and administer preventive procedures. May specialize in areas such as orthodontics, periodontics, endodontics and dental surgery. **Employment:** Private practice.	**Education and training:** Dentistry degree; licensing (general practice); licensing (dental specialization). **Subjects:** Mathematics, chemistry, physics.	↓ $74,600
DIETITIANS Plan, administer and supervise food preparation and service programs in commercial establishments, hospitals, schools and other educational institutions. Act as consultants to private companies, government and individuals in the areas of nutrition, diet and food selection. Also plan special therapeutic diets and menus for hospital patients and others. **Employment:** Hospitals, personal care homes, government.	**Education and training:** Bachelor's degree in dietetics, nutrition or a related science such as food and nutritional science or biochemistry; 1 to 2 years supervised practical training; certification (Canadian Dietetic Association). **Subjects:** Chemistry, home economics.	↑ $34,700
EMERGENCY MEDICAL TECHNICIANS (PARAMEDICS) Provide emergency medical care to sick or injured persons until and while they are transported to hospitals or other medical facilities. Administer cardio-pulmonary resuscitation (CPR) and oxygen. Connect equipment for persons with ventilation or circulation complications. Provide other life-support care. Apply bandages and splints. Also care for patients during air ambulance flights. **Employment:** Hospitals, government, manufacturing.	**Education and training:** High school completion is preferred; college, hospital-based or other recognized emergency medical technology program (up to 24 months); or courses in emergency health care plus supervised practical training; certification; emergency vehicle licence. **Subjects:** Health care, sciences.	↑ $33,500

379

MEDICAL LABORATORY TECHNOLOGISTS

Conduct laboratory experiments. Test and analyze human blood, tissue or other samples to assist in the diagnosis, treatment and prevention of disease. **Employment:** Hospitals, clinics, laboratories.

Education and training: Bachelor of Science degree or equivalent; or college medical laboratory technologists program (2 to 3 years) plus supervised practical training; certification (Canadian Society of Laboratory Technologists) is usually required. **Subjects:** Mathematics, chemistry, biology.

▲ $35,400

NURSES (RNs)

Provide nursing care to patients in hospitals, clinics and other health care agencies, in doctors' offices and in private homes. Also provide nursing services to students in schools and to employees in government offices, industrial plants and other establishments. May specialize in hospital units such as cardiology, surgery or obstetrics; in public, occupational or industrial health; or as consultants or researchers. **Employment:** Hospitals, schools, health clinics.

Education and training: College nursing program completion; or Bachelor of Science degree in nursing; or regional hospital or independent school of nursing diploma; registered nurse certification; additional education, nursing courses or training are required for specializations. **Subjects:** Mathematics, chemistry, English, biology, health care.

▲ $32,700

NURSES AIDES AND ORDERLIES

Assist with the care of patients in hospitals, nursing homes and other health care facilities. Perform activities such as feeding patients, transporting them in wheelchairs or on stretchers, lifting them, bathing and dressing them, and taking and recording their temperatures. **Employment:** Hospitals, nursing homes.

Education and training: Some high school, but high school completion is preferred; college or institution nurse aide, health care or long-term aide program (3 to 5 months); or college nursing orderly program (10 to 12 months); or on-the-job training. **Subjects:** Mathematics, sciences, English, health care.

▲ $32,400

OCCUPATIONAL THERAPISTS

Plan and carry out specially designed activities for patients with physical or mental health problems to enhance or help patients regain their ability to care for themselves and to engage in work and recreational pursuits. Advise on health risks in the workplace or other environments, and on the modification or addition of equipment to assist persons with disabilities. **Employment:** Hospitals, rehabilitation services, nursing homes.

Education and training: Bachelor of Science degree in occupational therapy or rehabilitation; period of field work; national certification examination; licensing or registration. **Subjects:** Chemistry, physics, English.

▲ $31,400

OPTICIANS

Fit clients with prescription glasses or contact lenses. Help clients select frames and order the lenses. May grind, polish, cut, edge or otherwise finish lenses and fit lenses into frames. Instruct clients on the use of contact lenses. **Employment:** Optical retail outlets, optical dispensing firms.

Education and training: College program (2 to 3 years) and apprenticeship; or night school program (2 to 3 years) plus supervised practical experience; or 2-year correspondence course plus supervised practical experience; licensing is usually required. **Subjects:** Physics.

▲ $33,500

Occupation	Education and training	Salary
PHYSICIANS AND SURGEONS Conduct physical examinations of patients. Prescribe laboratory and other tests. Make diagnoses. Prescribe medicines and treatments for diseases, disorders and injuries. Perform surgery. Advise patients on preventive medicine techniques. May specialize in a particular type of medicine such as family practice, cardiology, orthopaedics, neurology or obstetrics. **Employment:** Hospitals, clinics, government.	**Education and training:** Bachelor of Science degree plus medical degree; internship or residency program is required for family or general practitioners; internship plus residency plus lengthy training (up to 7 years) including subspecialty training are required for specialists. **Subjects:** Sciences, mathematics, English, health care.	▼ $74,600
PHYSIOTHERAPISTS Plan and carry out physical treatments to maintain, improve or restore the physical functioning of patients with muscle, bone, nerve or joint problems. Use equipment such as ultrasonic and microwave machines, infrared and ultraviolet lamps, laser and other electrotherapeutic equipment, as well as massage and therapeutic exercises. **Employment:** Hospitals, physiotherapy clinics.	**Education and training:** Bachelor's degree in physiotherapy; supervised clinical practice; registration. **Subjects:** Chemistry, physics, biology, physical education.	▲ $34,000
RADIOTHERAPY TECHNOLOGISTS Administer radiation treatments to cancer patients as prescribed by physicians called **RADIATION ONCOLOGISTS**. Operate and monitor specialized radiotherapy equipment. May also help prepare sealed radioactive substances to apply to the patient's body. **Employment:** Hospitals, X-ray clinics.	**Education and training:** High school completion; college, hospital school or other approved program (2 years) in radiation therapy plus supervised practical training. **Subjects:** Mathematics, physics, chemistry, biology.	▲ $39,200
REGISTERED NURSING ASSISTANTS (RNAs) Assist registered nurses in providing nursing care to patients. RNAs with operating room technician's training set out surgical instruments and perform other activities to assist surgical teams. RNAs who obtain a specialized certificate may assist in dispensing drugs and medications to patients. Are sometimes called certified or licensed nursing assistants or licensed practical nurses. **Employment:** Hospitals, nursing homes, clinics.	**Education and training:** College- or hospital-based RNA diploma; additional academic training on operating room techniques or on-the-job training is required for operating room technicians; licensing is usually required. **Subjects:** Mathematics, chemistry, biology, health care.	▲ $29,800
RESPIRATORY THERAPISTS Operate and monitor specialized medical equipment to treat patients with breathing difficulties caused by disorders such as asthma, emphysema, bronchitis, pneumonia and heart disorders, or to treat heart attack victims or patients experiencing complications after surgery or other medical	**Education and training:** High school completion; college or hospital respiratory therapy (2 to 3 years) including clinical training; licensing may be required. **Subjects:** Mathematics, chemistry, biology.	▲ $35,400

↑ $35,400

↓ $74,600

↑ $29,100

↓ $40,800

↓ $43,200

problems. Also provide home care. **Employment:** Hospitals, health care institutions.

ULTRASOUND TECHNOLOGISTS (MEDICAL SONOGRAPHERS)

Operate and monitor specialized equipment that produces and records images of the body's internal parts. Record the imaging on film, tape or computer. Report the results to physicians to assist them in diagnosing patients' conditions. **Employment:** Hospitals, clinics.

Education and training: Completion of an approved allied training program such as diagnostic radiology, nuclear medicine or nursing plus college- or hospital-based program (1 year) in diagnostic medical sonography and supervised practical training; certification and registration are usually required. **Subjects:** Technical studies.

VETERINARIANS

Diagnose and treat diseases and disorders in animals. Inoculate animals, set bones and perform surgery on animals. Advise owners of animals on feeding, hygiene, preventive measures against disease and general health care of animals. **Employment:** Veterinary clinics, private practice.

Education and training: Preveterinary university undergraduate studies (2 to 4 years) or CEGEP health science program diploma in veterinary medicine; national certification examination; licensing. **Subjects:** Chemistry, mathematics, physics.

SOCIAL SCIENCE, EDUCATION AND GOVERNMENT SERVICE

EARLY CHILDHOOD EDUCATORS/PRESCHOOL TEACHERS

Plan, organize and lead children in activities, such as indoor and outdoor games, crafts, singing and music sessions and story times, to help the children develop intellectually, physically and emotionally. **Employment:** Day-care centres.

Education and training: Bachelor's degree or college diploma in early childhood education; or Bachelor of Education degree. **Subjects:** Child care, family studies, social studies.

ECONOMISTS

Research and analyse economic data and prepare estimates, forecasts and reports on the basis of past and current economic trends. This information is used by governments, educators, businesses, industries and others to help them in planning their future activities and projects. **Employment:** Government, banks, investment companies.

Education and training: Bachelor of Economics degree (minimum); graduate degree in economics is usually required. **Subjects:** Mathematics, economics, political studies, computer science, history.

ELEMENTARY SCHOOL TEACHERS

Plan lessons that are appropriate for the particular grade or grades being taught according to approved curricula. Teach subjects such as reading, writing, arithmetic, social studies, natural science and computer operation. In senior elementary grades, may specialize in particular subjects such as

Education and training: Bachelor of Education degree; undergraduate degree; provincial/territorial teaching certificate. **Subjects:** Mathematics, sciences, English.

music, physical education, mathematics or science. **Employment:** Elementary schools.	
ESL/FSL TEACHERS (TEACHERS OF ENGLISH OR FRENCH AS A SECOND LANGUAGE) Teach English or French to civil servants or teach immigrants and others who wish to learn either of Canada's official languages. (To teach in educational institutions, ESL and FSL teachers require the same qualifications as other teachers.) **Employment:** Government, specialized schools. **Education and training:** Bachelor's degree with a specialization in education, linguistics or a related area is usually required; ESL or FSL certification is usually required; teaching experience is usually required. **Subjects:** English/French, family studies.	➡ $40,700
HIGH SCHOOL TEACHERS Prepare lessons according to approved curricula and teach academic subjects such as mathematics, music, science, history and literature; technical and vocational subjects such as auto mechanics, machine shop, drafting and hairdressing; or business subjects such as typing and accounting. Pupils include high school students and adults. **Employment:** Junior and senior high schools. **Education and training:** Academic teachers – undergraduate degree plus Bachelor of Education degree (1 year course) or a Bachelor of Education degree (3 to 4 years). Technical/vocational/business teachers – Bachelor of Education degree; high school completion or college diploma plus specific number of years experience in subject(s) taught; provincial/territorial teaching certificate. **Subjects:** Mathematics, sciences, English, family studies, social studies.	➡ $43,200
HOME ECONOMISTS (HUMAN ECOLOGISTS) Provide information and advice to individuals, groups and the general public on subjects such as food and nutrition, family relations and studies, housing and interior design, clothing and textiles, and other consumer products. Teach in schools and also work in many different areas such as food or consumer products testing, journalism, marketing and product development, and food service. **Employment:** Government, consulting firms, schools. **Education and training:** Degree in home economics/human ecology. **Subjects:** Family studies, social studies, home economics.	⬆ $34,700
LAWYERS Interpret the law and advise clients on legal matters. Plead cases and conduct prosecutions in law courts. Draw up legal documents such as contracts and wills. Represent clients at courts or other assemblies. Lawyers may specialize in areas of law such as criminal, corporate, commercial, real estate, family, estate and labour law. **Employment:** Law firms, government. **Education and training:** Bachelor's degree in law; articling period; bar admission course; bar exam; licensing. **Subjects:** Law, English, social studies.	➡ $65,800

	Education and training
MARKET RESEARCH ANALYSTS Conduct research on market conditions in local, regional or national areas to determine the sales levels for particular products or services and to assess potential markets and future trends. **Employment:** Government, marketing firms, business associations.	**Education and training:** University degree in economics, commerce or a related discipline is usually required. **Subjects:** Business, social studies, mathematics.	➜ $41,400
PARALEGALS Research records and court files and prepare legal documents, court and other reports and affidavits. Interview clients. Perform other activities to assist lawyers in law firms or in legal departments of companies or governments. **Employment:** Law firms, government.	**Education and training:** University degree in law; or college legal assistant or law clerk program; or paralegal in-house training in a law firm or other legal establishment. **Subjects:** English, mathematics, keyboarding, law.	➜ $38,300
PROBATION AND PAROLE OFFICERS Provide general supervision of criminal offenders serving probationary terms or serving the remainder of sentences after being released into the community on parole. **Employment:** Government, community centres, correctional centres.	**Education and training:** Bachelor's degree in social work, criminology, psychology or other related social science is required. (Note: For parole officers, experience plus passing a university equivalency test may substitute for formal education requirements.) **Subjects:** Social studies, law, family studies.	➜ $35,900
PSYCHOLOGISTS Study or diagnose behavioural, mental and emotional disorders. May work in clinical practices and provide counselling and therapy to clients to help them overcome or adjust to personal, marital, social, vocational or other problems. **Employment:** Schools, hospitals, community health facilities.	**Education and training:** Doctoral degree in psychology is preferred; master's degree in psychology may be acceptable; licence to practise is usually required. **Subjects:** English, social studies, family studies.	➜ $35,900
RECREATION AND SPORTS PROGRAM DIRECTORS/SUPERVISORS Plan, organize and supervise various sports programs (such as swimming, aerobics and fitness, gymnastics, tennis and team sports) or recreational activities (such as arts and crafts, drama, teen clubs, camping and outings) for senior citizens and persons with disabilities. Recruit and train full-time staff, volunteers and part-time leaders and instructors. May instruct or lead groups themselves. **Employment:** Municipalities, community or professional athletic organizations.	**Education and training:** University degree in physical education, recreology, sports administration or related disciplines; or college diploma in recreation plus experience in recreation and sport activities. **Subjects:** Languages, business, social studies, physical education.	➜ $35,800

REHABILITATION TEACHERS
Teach blind or sight-impaired students to read and write braille. Instruct deaf or hearing-impaired students in lip reading, finger spelling and sign language and help them develop the ability to speak. Teach physically disabled students to use aids that lessen the effects of their disabilities. Teach in elementary and high schools and may also teach school curricula. Are often called special education teachers. **Employment:** High schools, elementary schools.

Education and training: Bachelor of Education degree; teaching certification; certificates/diplomas in special education programs. **Subjects:** Social studies, family studies, physical education.

➡ $42,900

SCHOOL AND GUIDANCE COUNSELLORS
Advise students on course selection and career planning. Counsel students regarding personal and social issues such as family problems, self-esteem, drug and alcohol abuse and depression. **Employment:** Schools, counselling centres, government.

Education and training: Bachelor's degree in education; graduate courses in counselling usually required; teacher's certificate is required; some teaching experience is usually required. **Subjects:** Family studies, community services, social studies.

➡ $43,200

SOCIAL WORKERS
Help people who have personal, financial, medical, housing, marital or other problems. Provide counselling to individuals and groups, and may refer them to other professionals or social services for assistance. May specialize in a particular age group or area such as adults, youth, geriatrics or clinical social work. **Employment:** Community services, hospitals, correctional facilities.

Education and training: Undergraduate degree in social work; graduate degree is preferred. **Subjects:** Family and community services, languages, social studies.

➡ $35,900

SOCIOLOGISTS
Study the origins, development and activities of human society. Also study the family, community, education, industrial relations, crime, politics, poverty and other social issues. Conduct surveys, analyze data and present their findings, which are often of interest to the general public. **Employment:** Government and private sector.

Education and training: Master's or doctoral degree in sociology is usually required. **Subjects:** Family studies, social studies, history.

⬆ $42,800

ART AND CULTURE

ANNOUNCERS AND BROADCASTERS
Introduce programs, interview guests and read the news, weather and traffic conditions, commercials and other announcements for radio and television. May specialize in broadcasting sports activities, weather reports,

Education and training: High school completion; college radio or television arts program is usually required; auditions are required. **Subjects:** Dramatic arts, English.

⬆ $33,600

film reviews or other subject matter. **Employment:** Radio and TV stations, advertising firms.

Occupation	Salary
AUDIO AND VIDEO RECORDING TECHNICIANS Operate specialized electronic equipment to record stage productions, live programs or events, and studio recordings. Edit and reproduce tapes for compact discs, records and cassettes, for radio and television broadcasting and for motion picture productions. **Employment:** Film, video and concert production, sound recording firms. **Education and training:** High school completion is usually required; college or other program in recording engineering or audio-visual production; or experience in a recording studio as an assistant. **Subjects:** Music, electronics.	↑ $32,700
COMMERCIAL ARTISTS / GRAPHIC DESIGNERS Create graphics, illustrations and other artwork for magazines, advertisements, films, posters, signs and various publications. May also create logos for companies, organizations or individuals. **Employment:** Printers, publishers, graphic design firms. **Education and training:** University degree or college diploma in visual arts with a specialization in commercial or graphic arts or photography; or high school completion plus on-the-job training in commercial or graphic arts; portfolio. **Subjects:** Art, commercial art, graphics.	↑ $31,800
CONSERVATION AND RESTORATION TECHNICIANS Clean dirt, paint, varnish and other substances from museum or gallery exhibits. Make minor repairs to paintings or other works of art. Apply preservatives and perform other tasks to conserve or restore exhibits. Work under the direct supervision of a conservator who may specialize in a particular field. **Employment:** Museums, art galleries. **Education and training:** High school completion; college museum or conservation technology program completion; or extensive technical training with a conservator. **Subjects:** Technical studies.	→ $31,700
EDITORS AND WRITERS Review, evaluate and revise or edit books, magazines, journals, manuals, press dispatches, scripts, newsletters, pamphlets and other material. Work in many different settings such as newspaper offices, publishing houses, radio and TV stations or may work freelance. **Employment:** Newspapers, magazines, publishing houses. **Education and training:** University degree in journalism, literature, history or a related field is usually required (i.e., science degree for editors of scientific publications). **Subjects:** English, journalism, word processing.	← $38,300
FILM AND VIDEO CAMERA OPERATORS Use cameras and related equipment to record scenes for motion pictures, TV and video productions or to film news events, field assignments or other programs. **Employment:** TV networks, video production companies. **Education and training:** High school completion is usually required; college program in film and video or a related field such as broadcasting is usually required; some on-the-job training; motion picture camera operators require considerable experience. **Subjects:** Art, graphics, technical studies.	↑ $32,700

Occupation	Education and training	Avg. salary
INTERIOR DESIGNERS Develop plans for the use of interior space in offices, public buildings, homes and other establishments. Prepare detailed sketches and three-dimensional models showing the arrangement of walls, lighting and other fixtures, and estimate costs and amounts of materials needed. **Employment:** Architectural firms, interior design firms, retail stores.	**Education and training:** University degree in interior or architectural design; or college interior or architectural design diploma plus work experience in interior design; provincial/territorial association registration may be required; portfolio. **Subjects:** Art, graphics, visual arts.	▲ $28,700
JOURNALISTS AND REPORTERS Conduct research, interview people and visit particular locations to collect background material about newsworthy events or topics of interest. Prepare stories for newspapers, other print media, radio, TV or film. May report the material on TV or in other media. Journalists and reports may also travel to other countries as foreign correspondents to report on political unrest, wars or other news stories. **Employment:** Radio and TV networks, newspapers, magazines.	**Education and training:** University degree or college diploma in journalism is usually required. **Subjects:** English, social studies, history.	◀ $38,300
LIBRARIANS Develop, organize and maintain library collections of materials such as books, magazines, films, videos and reference publications and assist library users in locating and using these materials. Develop and operate computerized information systems to organize library collections and to locate or borrow requested items from other libraries. **Employment:** Libraries, universities, schools.	**Education and training:** Master's degree in library science; librarian accreditation/certification is usually required. **Subjects:** English, social studies, keyboarding.	▶ $36,500
LIBRARY TECHNICIANS Assist librarians in cataloguing new library books, manuscripts and other materials and in conducting reference searches. Assist library users in locating books, articles or other materials. Also operate computerized library systems and perform other library duties. **Employment:** Libraries, archives, schools.	**Education and training:** High school completion is required; college library technician (1 to 2 years), or CEGEP certificate is usually required. **Subjects:** English, social studies, keyboarding.	▶ $31,700
PHOTOGRAPHERS Operate still cameras to take pictures of people, events, scenes, products and many other subjects. May specialize in portraits; in commercial, industrial, medical or scientific photography; or in police work or photojournalism. **Employment:** Photography studios, magazines, newspapers.	**Education and training:** Bachelor's degree in visual arts (specialization in photography); or college photography program; or extensive experience plus on-the-job training in photography; portfolio demonstrating creative and technical ability. **Subjects:** Art, graphics, visual arts, technical studies.	▲ $32,700

387

PUBLIC RELATIONS CONSULTANTS Organize and implement publicity or information campaigns designed to promote products, clients and services. Often represent clients in dealings with radio, TV and other media. **Employment:** Government, business associations.	**Education and training:** University degree or college diploma in public relations; communications, journalism or a related discipline is usually required. **Subjects:** English, social studies.	◄	$38,300

TRANSLATORS
Translate written documents from one language into another. May specialize in translating scientific, medical, legal or other technical documents. **INTERPRETERS** translate speeches, proceedings and individual conversations as they take place. Some interpret for people with hearing impairments, translating speech into sign language and vice versa. **Employment:** Translation and interpretation agencies, government, media.

Education and training: Bachelor's degree in translation with specialization at the graduate level is usually required for translators; college diploma in interpreting is the minimum requirement for interpreters; certified translator diploma may be required (Canadian Translators and Interpreters Council); knowledge of three languages may be required for translators and interpreters; knowledge of sign language may be required. **Subjects:** Languages, English.

◄ $38,300

SALES AND SERVICE

ADVERTISING MANAGERS
Direct and manage the activities of advertising departments or agencies which develop advertising and promotional programs to promote productions or services. **Employment:** Marketing and public relations companies, government.

Education and training: University degree or college diploma in public relations, communications or a related discipline plus several years experience in advertising or a related field such as public relations, are usually required. **Subjects:** Business, English, visual arts.

▲ $41,900

AIRLINE PASSENGER AND TICKET AGENTS
Issue tickets and assign or reserve seats. Check passengers' baggage. Prepare boarding passes. Announce flight information. Tend boarding gates and assist passengers who are preboarding. May look after baggage and cargo shipments and other duties at small airports. **Employment:** Airline companies.

Education and training: High school completion is usually required; formal on-the-job training is provided. **Subjects:** Keyboarding, languages, hospitality.

▼ $27,300

BAKERS
Prepare and bake bread, rolls, muffins, pies, cakes and other baked goods. **Employment:** Bakeries, grocery stores, hotels.

Education and training: Some high school, but high school completion is preferred; apprenticeship; or on-the-job training; trade certification may be required. **Subjects:** Baking, cooking.

◄ $28,100

Job	Description	Education and training	Salary
BARBERS AND HAIRDRESSERS	Cut and style customers' hair. May wave or colour hair, shave beards, shampoo hair and apply scalp treatments. **Employment:** Hairdressing salons, barber shops.	**Education and training:** Some secondary school education is required; completion of an apprenticeship (2 or 3 years) or completion of a college program in hairstyling combined with on-the-job training is required. **Subjects:** Cosmetology.	↑ $18,200
BARTENDERS	Mix and serve alcoholic and non-alcoholic beverages to customers or prepare beverages for serving staff. **Employment:** Hotels, restaurants, clubs.	**Education and training:** Some high school, but high school completion is preferred; college bartending course; or mixology course; or on-the-job training. **Subjects:** Hotel/hospitality, business.	← $21,000
BUYERS	Select and buy merchandise to be sold in retail and wholesale stores. Study market reports and sales promotion materials, attend trade shows, visit factories and showrooms, and negotiate prices, shipping arrangements and other details to meet the stores' merchandise requirements. **Employment:** Wholesalers, retail stores.	**Education and training:** High school completion is usually required; university degree or college diploma in business, marketing or a related area is usually required; sales experience is required. **Subjects:** Business, family studies, marketing, retailing.	↑ $36,800
CHEFS	Plan menus and estimate food requirements. May supervise other chefs and cooks. May also prepare and cook food. Executive chefs in large hotels, restaurants, hospitals and similar establishments spend most of their time in administration and supervision activities and may cook only for special guests or occasions. **Employment:** Hotels, restaurants, clubs.	**Education and training:** Some high school, but high school completion is preferred; apprenticeship; or other formal training; 3 to 6 years commercial food preparation experience (additional cooking and supervisory experience are required for executive chefs); trade certification may be required. **Subjects:** Cooking, food services, home economics.	← $21,200
COOKS	Prepare and cook food in many different settings and have varying levels of responsibility. May cook complete meals or short-orders, or prepare special dishes or ethnic foods. May prepare menus, estimate food costs and order supplies or work under the direction of a specialist chef in a large hotel or restaurant. **Employment:** Airlines, hotels, restaurants, clubs.	**Education and training:** Some high school, but high school completion is preferred; apprenticeship; or 2 to 4 years commercial cooking experience; or on-the-job training; trade certification may be required; Red Seal certification (interprovincial) is available. **Subjects:** Cooking, food services, home economics.	← $21,200
CORRECTIONAL SERVICES OFFICERS	Guard prison inmates and detainees, and maintain order in penitentiaries, jails and other correctional institutions. **Employment:** Government, correctional facilities, juvenile institutions.	**Education and training:** High school completion is required; college program for correctional workers may be required. **Subjects:** Family and community services.	→ $39,000

Occupation	Duties and Employment	Education and Training	Salary
FIREFIGHTERS	Control and extinguish fires, conduct fire prevention programs and assist in other emergencies. **Employment:** Government, large industrial establishments.	**Education and training:** High school completion is required; firefighters training course is provided; specific physical requirements. **Subjects:** Technical studies, physical education.	↓ $39,900
FLIGHT ATTENDANTS	Explain safety procedures to passengers and make announcements. Serve food and beverages. Attend to passengers' needs during flights. **Employment:** Airline companies.	**Education and training:** High school completion is required; Department of Transport Canada training program. **Subjects:** English, languages, hospitality, social studies.	↓ $27,300
FOOD SERVICE SUPERVISORS	Direct, supervise and co-ordinate the activities of workers preparing and serving food in food service business. **Employment:** Cafeterias, catering companies, hospitals.	**Education and training:** High school completion is usually required; college food service administration or hotel and restaurant management or a related program; or several years experience in food preparation and service including some supervisory functions. **Subjects:** Home economics, food services, business.	◄ $35,800
HOTEL FRONT DESK CLERKS	Register guests, assign rooms and issue room keys. Answer inquiries about hotel services. Compile and present bills to departing guests. Accept payments and prepare related records. May make reservations. Usually operate computerized hotel registration and accounting systems. **Employment:** Hotels, motels, resorts.	**Education and training:** High school completion is required; college front desk operations or hotel management program may be required. **Subjects:** English, languages, hospitality, keyboarding, social studies.	↓ $27,300
HOTEL MANAGERS	Plan, direct and control the operations of hotels, motels, resorts or other lodging facilities. **Employment:** Hotels, motels, resorts.	**Education and training:** University degree or college diploma in hotel management or a related discipline; or several years experience working in various hotel positions including administrative and supervisory functions. **Subjects:** English, languages, family studies, food and hospitality, business.	◄ $35,800
INSURANCE AGENTS	Sell life, fire, accident, automobile, endowment, marine and other types of insurance to clients. Calculate rates or premiums from charts and other predetermined data and arrange for payment schedules. Also attend to clients regarding insurance coverage after car accidents, fires or other calamities. **Employment:** Insurance companies.	**Education and training:** High school completion; industry-sponsored insurance training course is required; provincial/territorial licensing. **Subjects:** Marketing, business, social studies.	↑ $36,800

Occupation	Education and training	Salary
INTERNATIONAL MARKETING SPECIALISTS Conduct research on international markets and prepare marketing plans and strategies. Attend world and other fairs to market Canadian products and services. Travel to other countries to negotiate sales of products and services. **Employment:** Public and private sectors.	**Education and training:** Undergraduate degree in business administration, economics, commerce, marketing or a related discipline; specialization in international marketing may be required; MBA may be required; knowledge of a particular foreign language or languages may be required; foreign travel experience is an asset. **Subjects:** Business, social studies, geography, marketing.	➡ $41,400
JANITORS, CARETAKERS AND BUILDING SUPERINTENDENTS Clean and maintain offices, apartment houses, shopping malls, schools and similar establishments. Make minor repairs to plumbing, heating and electrical systems, and perform other maintenance activities such as painting, cutting grass and shovelling snow. May also advertise and show apartments, collect rents and supervise other workers. **Employment:** School boards, hospitals, shopping malls.	**Education and training:** Some high school, but high school completion is preferred; previous cleaning and maintenance experience may be required.	↗ $23,400
MANUFACTURERS' AGENTS AND SALES REPRESENTATIVES Sell products in an allotted region to stores, wholesalers, professionals or manufacturers. Find new customers, quote prices, arrange delivery and keep up with new products. **Employment:** Wholesalers, manufacturers.	**Education and training:** Completion of secondary school is required; a university degree or completion of a college or other program may be required; experience in sales or in an occupation related to the product is usually required. **Subjects:** Retailing, marketing, business.	⬅ $31,200
MEAT CUTTERS Cut meat carcasses into large portions for processing or packaging, and cut meat portions into steaks, chops, roasts and other specific cuts to be shipped to institutional, commercial or wholesale customers. **RETAIL BUTCHERS** prepare cuts of meat, poultry, fish and shellfish for sale in grocery stores, butcher shops and supermarkets, and often serve customers and cut meat to order. **Employment:** Meat packing plants, grocery stores, meat markets.	**Education and training:** High school completion may be required for retail butchers, college program in industrial meat cutting or retail meat cutting may be required; on-the-job training is usually provided for retail butchers.	⬅ $28,100
POLICE OFFICERS Detect and investigate crimes and arrest criminal suspects. Provide testimony in law courts and information on crime prevention and safety. Perform other activities to maintain law and order. Also patrol assigned areas on foot, motorcycle, horseback, bicycle, cruiser car or other vehicle. **Employment:** Government, Canadian Forces.	**Education and training:** High school completion is required; police training program is provided; specific physical requirements; college program or university degree in law and security is an advantage. **Subjects:** Languages, social studies, family studies, community services.	➡ $39,900

REAL ESTATE AGENTS

Buy and sell houses, apartments, commercial and industrial buildings, land and other properties on behalf of clients. Estimate selling prices. Advertise and list properties. Arrange for clients to see properties. Advise clients on market conditions, mortgages and related matters. Draw up sales agreements. **Employment:** Real estate agencies, housing developers.

Education and training: High school completion is usually required; real estate training course is required; provincial/territorial licensing. **Subjects:** Retailing, marketing, business.

↑ $36,800

RESTAURANT AND FOOD SERVICE MANAGERS

Plan, direct and manage the operations of establishments serving food and beverages to ensure that good service is provided and that budgets are maintained. **Employment:** Hotels, restaurants, self-employment.

Education and training: High school completion; college restaurant management program; or several years experience in the food service sector including administrative and supervisory functions. **Subjects:** English, food and hospitality, home economics, business.

◄ $35,800

SALES CLERKS

Help customers select products and either receive payments of direct customers to cashiers. May need to be knowledgeable about the product if selling products such as fine china, yard goods, cameras, computers, hardware and building supplies, automobiles and motorcycles. **Employment:** Retail stores, wholesalers, other industries.

Education and training: High school completion is preferred; demonstrated sales ability and product knowledge are usually required for selling certain products. **Subjects:** Business, retailing.

◄ $28,900

SALES MANAGERS

Direct and manage sales departments or groups of salespersons directly or through subordinates. Approve or establish sales territories, sales quotas and objectives. Confirm or assign salespersons to territories. May determine prices, advertising and promotional activities. **Employment:** Retail stores, wholesalers, other industries.

Education and training: University or college program in business administration with a specialization in sales or marketing plus extensive sales experience is usually required. **Subjects:** Business, retailing, marketing.

↑ $41,900

SECURITY GUARDS

Watch entrances to plants or other buildings and issue passes. Perform security checks of passengers and luggage at airports. Patrol buildings and outside properties to guard against theft, vandalism, illegal entry and fire. May work as armoured car guards and pick up and deliver money and other valuables to stores, banks and other establishments, and must carry firearms to protect themselves and their cargo. **Employment:** Retail stores, wholesalers, other industries.

Education and training: Some high school, but high school completion is preferred; training is usually provided; firearms licence may be required.

► $39,000

TECHNICAL SALES SPECIALISTS Sell technical goods and services such as scientific and industrial products, electricity, telecommunications and computer services. May specialize in selling a particular line of goods or services. **Employment:** Manufacturers, pharmaceutical companies, computer service firms.	**Education and training:** High school completion is required; university degree or college diploma in a program related to the product or service is usually required; previous sales experience or experience in a related technical occupation is usually required. **Subjects:** Technical studies, business, marketing.	◄ $31,400
TRAVEL COUNSELLORS Provide information to clients on trip costs and schedules. Plan itineraries and reserve hotel rooms or other accommodation. Prepare air, train or other tickets. Receive payments and attend to other travel details for clients. **Employment:** Travel agencies.	**Education and training:** High school completion; college travel and tourism program may be required. **Subjects:** Geography, keyboarding.	▼ $24,300
VISITING HOMEMAKERS Look after individuals and families during times of illness, convalescence or some other family disruption. May look after infants and children or persons who are chair- or bedridden. Perform routine housekeeping duties and prepare meals. **Employment:** Government, home care agencies, self-employment.	**Education and training:** Some high school, but high school completion is preferred; certification may be required. **Subjects:** Family studies, health care, home economics.	▲ $26,000
WAITERS/WAITRESSES Take orders from customers and serve food and beverages to them. May also prepare and serve flambés and other specialty foods at customers' tables and recommend wines. **Employment:** Restaurants, hotels, clubs.	**Education and training:** Some high school, but high school completion is preferred; minimum of 6 months to 1 year experience is usually required for formal/French service. **Subjects:** Food services, hotel/hospitality, business.	◄ $21,000
TRADES, TRANSPORT AND EQUIPMENT OPERATION		
AIRCRAFT MECHANICS Maintain, repair and overhaul, modify and install aircraft mechanical systems. **AIRCRAFT INSPECTORS** certify aircraft for airworthiness when the mechanical systems have met established standards for safety and performance. Some inspectors work as mechanics as well as being responsible for inspections. Aircraft inspectors are usually called aircraft maintenance engineers. **Employment:** Air transport firms, aerospace manufacturers.	**Education and training:** High school completion; college/CEGEP aircraft maintenance course (1 to 3 years) may be required; training of several years provided; licence (aircraft maintenance engineer) plus endorsements for specific aircraft and systems from the Department of Transport Canada are required for aircraft inspectors. **Subjects:** Mathematics, sciences, mechanics, electronics.	◄ $33,500

AIR TRANSPORT RAMP ATTENDANTS Drive and operate vehicles and equipment such as food service trucks, aircraft-towing tractors, de-icer sprayers and lavatory service trucks at airports. Handle baggage, load and unload freight and perform other ground support duties. **Employment:** Airlines and air services, federal government.	**Education and training:** High school completion is usually required; driver's licence is usually required. **Subjects:** Technical studies. ◄ $36,800
APPLIANCE SERVICERS/TECHNICIANS Repair household electrical appliances such as refrigerators, stoves, washers, dryers and window air conditioners. May repair the appliances in customers' homes, in repair shops or in repair and service departments of companies. **Employment:** Repair shops, retail stores, wholesalers.	**Education and training:** High school completion is preferred; apprenticeship (3 years); or college program in appliance repair; trade certification may be required. **Subjects:** Technical studies, electrical, business. ◄ $31,100
AUTO BODY REPAIRERS Replace and repair damaged fenders, hoods, bumpers, doors, glass and other exterior parts of motor vehicles. Straighten bent frames and remove dents. Sand and paint motor vehicle bodies. Also repair and replace seat frame assemblies, upholsteries, floor coverings and other interior furnishings. **Employment:** Auto body repair shops, auto dealerships.	**Education and training:** Some high school, but high school completion is preferred; apprenticeship (4 years); or college automotive body repair technology program plus several years experience in auto body repair; trade certification may be required; Red Seal certification (interprovincial) is available. **Subjects:** Mathematics, auto body repair. ▲ $35,000
AUTO MECHANICS/ TECHNICIANS Repair and service the mechanical, electrical and electronic systems and components of cars, trucks and buses. May take extra training to specialize in a particular area of repair or to obtain special knowledge of cars from a particular manufacturer to repair and service them properly. **Employment:** Auto dealerships, service stations, truck transportation.	**Education and training:** High school completion is preferred; apprenticeship (4 years); or college automotive technology program (2 years) plus 2 years experience in automotive repair; trade certification is usually required; Red Seal certification (interprovincial) is available. **Subjects:** Mathematics, sciences, mechanics, electronics. ▲ $35,400
BRICKLAYERS Lay concrete blocks, bricks, precut stone and similar materials to construct or repair walls, foundations, fireplaces, chimneys, smokestacks and other structures. Line or reline furnaces, kilns and similar installations. Some bricklayers specialize in stonework and are called stonemasons. **Employment:** Construction contractors, self-employment.	**Education and training:** High school completion is preferred; apprenticeship (3 to 4 years); or 4 years experience in the trade plus college or industry courses in bricklaying; trade certification is usually required; Red Seal certification (interprovincial) is available. **Subjects:** Building construction, technical studies. ◄ $32,100

Occupation	Description	Education and training	Salary
BUS DRIVERS	Operate buses and receive money, tickets or passes. **TRANSIT OPERATORS** operate subway trains and light rail transit vehicles to transport passengers over established routes. **Employment:** Urban transit systems, school divisions.	**Education and training:** Some high school, but high school completion is preferred; on-the-job training including formal instruction is provided; driver's abstract/record; age requirements; minimum 1 year driving experience is required; experience as a public transit bus driver is usually required for subway/transit operators.	↑ $32,200
CABINETMAKERS	Construct and repair cabinets, furniture, fixtures and similar products using mainly wood and wood-veneer materials. May construct built-ins or other special cabinets for custom orders. **Employment:** Furniture manufacturers, construction.	**Education and training:** High school completion is preferred; apprenticeship (3 to 4 years); or 4 years experience in the trade plus college courses in cabinetmaking; trade certification is usually required; Red Seal certification (interprovincial) is available. **Subjects:** Carpentry, technical studies, woodworking.	← $27,800
CARPENTERS	Construct, erect, install, renovate and repair buildings and other structures made of wood, wood substitutes and other materials. May specialize in residential, commercial/institutional, industrial, maintenance or restoration and renovation carpentry. **Employment:** Construction, wood products manufacturers.	**Education and training:** High school completion is preferred; apprenticeship (3 to 4 years); or 4 years experience in the trade plus college or industry courses in carpentry; trade certification is usually required; Red Seal certification (interprovincial) is available. **Subjects:** Building construction, carpentry, technical studies, woodworking.	← $31,300
COMMERCIAL DIVERS	Search for drowned persons, submerged watercraft, automobiles and other articles. Perform underwater construction activities such as welding, drilling and placing explosives. Perform many other activities using cameras, sonar and related equipment and cutting torches. **Employment:** Commercial diving, shipping and marine construction.	**Education and training:** Some high school, but high school completion is preferred; scuba certification; commercial diver's licence is usually required; provincial blaster's licence is usually required for setting and detonating explosives; medical certificate. **Subjects:** Technical studies, physical education.	← $34,300
CONSTRUCTION MANAGERS	Plan and supervise construction of roads and bridges, hydro-electric dams and buildings. Prepare cost estimates and timetables, arrange loans and co-ordinate work of construction trades. **Employment:** General contractors.	**Education and training:** A university degree in civil engineering or a college diploma in construction technology is usually required; several years experience in the construction industry, including experience as a construction supervisor or field superintendent, is usually required. **Subjects:** Construction, business, technical studies.	↑ $38,500

	Education and training	
CONSTRUCTION MILLWRIGHTS Engage in the initial installation of machinery and mechanical equipment in industrial plants. **INDUSTRIAL MECHANICS** maintain and repair machinery and mechanical equipment, and usually operate machining tools to make replacement or other parts. **Employment:** Construction, industrial plants.	**Education and training:** High school completion is preferred; apprenticeship (3 to 4 years); or over 5 years experience in the trade plus high school, college or industry courses in millwrighting or industrial machinery repair; trade certification is usually required; Red Seal certification (interprovincial) is available for industrial mechanics (millwrights). **Subjects:** Industrial mechanics, technical studies, mathematics.	◄ $35,800
CRANE OPERATORS Operate cranes to lift, move, position or place machinery, equipment and other large objects at construction or industrial sites, ports, railway yards, offshore drilling rigs and other locations. Operate cranes equipped with dredging attachments to dredge waterways and other areas. **Employment:** Construction, industrial cargo handling companies.	**Education and training:** Some high school, but high school completion is preferred; apprenticeship (1 to 3 years); or college or industry courses in crane operating; or on-the-job training; trade or company certification is usually required; Red Seal certification (interprovincial) is available for mobile crane operators. **Subjects:** Construction.	◄ $33,800
DELIVERY DRIVERS Drive light trucks, vans or other motor vehicles to pick up and deliver various products such as newspapers, dairy products, drugstore items, dry cleaning, pizzas and groceries. **Employment:** Dairies, drugstores, newspapers.	**Education and training:** Some high school, but high school completion is preferred; 1 year driving experience is usually required; licence for type for vehicle driven.	▲ $32,300
DIESEL ENGINE MECHANICS Repair and maintain diesel engines in industrial, farm, construction and transportation equipment. **Employment:** Major trucking firms, railways.	**Education and training:** Some secondary school education is required; apprenticeship (4 years) or a combination of over 4 years of work experience in the trade and some high school, college or industry courses in heavy equipment repair is usually required to be eligible for trade certification. **Subjects:** Mathematics, mechanics, electrical.	▲ $35,000
DRYWALL INSTALLERS AND FINISHERS Measure, cut and install drywall sheets to form walls and ceilings in buildings and other structures. Install acoustic and other special ceilings. Apply careful finishing techniques to the seams so the seams won't show after they are painted. **Employment:** Construction contractors, self-employment.	**Education and training:** Some high school, but high school completion is preferred; apprenticeship (3 to 4 years); or over 3 years experience in the trade plus college or industry courses in drywall installing and finishing; trade certification may be required. **Subjects:** Construction.	◄ $32,100

Occupation	Education and training	Average salary
ELECTRICAL POWER LINE AND CABLE WORKERS Erect and maintain poles and towers. Install overhead and underground power lines, cables, insulators, conductors, switches, transformers and other associated equipment. Work at heights from ladders or hydraulic lifts, or in confined spaces such as trenches and tunnels. May also work in isolated areas and rough terrain. **Employment:** Electrical utilities, construction.	**Education and training:** High school completion is required; government-regulated or internal company apprenticeship (4 years) is required; or college or CEGEP electrical technology/electricity courses plus 4 years experience in the trade; Red Seal certification (interprovincial) is available. **Subjects:** Mathematics, electrical.	◄ $40,300
ELECTRICIANS Install, test, troubleshoot and repair electrical wiring, fixtures, control devices and related equipment in houses and other buildings and structures. Often called construction electricians. **Employment:** Construction, industry.	**Education and training:** High school completion is usually required; apprenticeship (4 to 5 years); trade certification is usually required; **Red** Seal certification (interprovincial) is available. **Subjects:** Construction, mathematics, electrical.	◄ $35,400
ELECTRONICS EQUIPMENT SERVICE TECHNICIANS Install, service and repair home and office equipment such as stereos, TVs, VCRs, computers, printers and photocopiers. Work either at the customer's premises or remove the equipment to shops for testing and further repair. **Employment:** Public and private sectors.	**Education and training:** High school completion is usually required; apprenticeship (4 years); or college program in electronics (2 to 3 years); or college or technical school training in electronics servicing and repair plus on-the-job training. **Subjects:** Technical studies, electrical/electronics.	◄ $38,000
FLOOR COVERING INSTALLERS Install carpeting, wood flooring, linoleum, vinyl and other resilient floor coverings in residential, commercial, industrial and institutional buildings. **Employment:** Construction, floor-covering and carpet outlets.	**Education and training:** Some high school, but high school completion is preferred; apprenticeship (1 to 3 years); or over 3 years experience in the trade; trade certification is required. **Subjects:** Construction.	◄ $31,500
FORKLIFT OPERATORS Drive industrial trucks equipped with various attachments to move materials to and from storage areas and to place materials in designated locations. **Employment:** Retail stores, wholesalers, warehouses.	**Education and training:** Some high school, but high school completion is preferred.	◄ $27,900
GAS FITTERS Install, test and repair gas lines, meters, regulators, heating units and appliances in residential, commercial, institutional and industrial establishments. **Employment:** Gas utilities, gas servicing companies.	**Education and training:** High school completion is preferred; apprenticeship (3 years); or 2 to 3 years experience in the pipe fitting trade plus college or industry gas fitter program; trade certification is usually required; gas fitter licence is usually required. **Subjects:** Construction.	◄ $32,400

GLAZIERS
Prepare, install and replace glass in residential, commercial and industrial buildings; on exterior walls of buildings and other structures; and in vehicles, furniture and other products. **Employment:** Construction, glass installation, retail services.

Education and training: High school completion is preferred; apprenticeship (4 years); or over 4 years experience in the trade plus college or industry courses for glaziers; trade certification is usually required; Red Seal certification (interprovincial) is available. **Subjects:** Construction.

↞ $31,500

HEAVY-DUTY EQUIPMENT MECHANICS
Repair, overhaul and maintain heavy mobile equipment used in construction (such as bulldozers, cranes, graders and backhoes) as well as heavy mobile mining, forestry, material-handling, land-clearing, farming and similar heavy equipment. **Employment:** Heavy construction, construction equipment dealerships.

Education and training: High school completion preferred; apprenticeship (4 years); or over 4 years experience in the trade plus high school, college or industry heavy equipment repair courses; trade certification is usually required; farm equipment repair certification; mine equipment repair certification. **Subjects:** Mathematics, mechanics, auto.

↞ $32,800

HEAVY EQUIPMENT OPERATORS
Operate backhoes, bulldozers, graders, dredgers, pavers, compactors, power shovels, side-booms and similar equipment used in the construction and maintenance of roads, bridges, airports and gas and oil pipelines; in the construction of buildings and other structures; in mining and quarrying activities; and in material-handling work. **Employment:** Construction, public works, pipeline industry.

Education and training: Some high school, but high school completion is preferred; apprenticeship (1 to 2 years); or college or industry courses in heavy equipment operation; or on-the-job training; trade certification may be required. **Subjects:** Construction, auto.

↟ $34,700

INDUSTRIAL PAINTERS
Operate spray-painting, dip-painting or flow-painting equipment or systems, and painting machines, or use brushes or hand-held spray guns to apply various paints, lacquers and coatings to surfaces of equipment, parts and other items in manufacturing and industrial plants and other establishments. **Employment:** Construction, painting, building maintenance.

Education and training: High school completion is usually required; college or other training in automated painting systems may be required. **Subjects:** Construction, visual arts.

↞ $28,100

IRONWORKERS
Assemble, join and erect structural ironwork, precast and reinforced concrete components, curtain walls and other metalwork used in the construction of buildings, bridges, tanks and other structures. Make, install and repair ornamental and other structures such as metal stairways, railings and power doors. May work at great heights. **Employment:** Construction, ironwork contractors.

Education and training: High school completion is preferred; apprenticeship (2 to 3 years); or over 3 years experience in the trade; trade certification is usually required; Red Seal certification (interprovincial) is available. **Subjects:** Construction, technical studies.

↞ $33,900

Occupation	Education and training	Salary
JEWELLERS Make and repair jewellery. Design special jewellery mountings or settings for custom orders. Use fine precision instruments. **Employment:** Jewellery, clock and watch manufacturers.	**Education and training:** High school completion is usually required; apprenticeship (3 to 4 years); or several years on-the-job training plus college jeweller's program; trade certification may be required. **Subjects:** Art, visual arts.	◄ $22,000
MACHINISTS Set up and operate various machine tools, including computerized numerically controlled tools to shape metal parts or products of precise dimensions. The machine tools are used for milling, boring, planing, drilling, precision grinding and other operations. **Employment:** Metal fabricators, machinery manufacturers.	**Education and training:** High school completion is preferred; apprenticeship (4 years), or 4 years experience in the trade plus college or industry courses in machining; trade certification is usually required; Red Seal certification (interprovincial) is available. **Subjects:** Mathematics, industrial drafting and design.	◄ $35,400
MATERIAL HANDLERS Load and unload products and materials to and from warehouses, railway cars, trucks and other transportation vehicles, containers and areas. Move loads by hand or using equipment such as hand trucks, dollies, forklift trucks, winches, tractors and loaders. Also operate equipment for handling liquid and bulk materials. **LONGSHORE WORKERS** work at ship- and docksides and may operate cranes to handle the cargoes. **Employment:** Transportation, storage and moving companies.	**Education and training:** Some high school, but high school completion is preferred.	◄ $27,900
PAINTERS AND DECORATORS Apply paint and other finishes to interior and exterior surfaces of buildings and other structures. Apply wallpaper and other coverings to interior surfaces of buildings. **Employment:** Construction contractors, self-employment.	**Education and training:** High school completion is preferred; apprenticeship (2 to 3 years); or over 3 years experience in the trade; trade certification is usually required; Red Seal certification (interprovincial) is available. **Subjects:** Construction, visual arts.	◄ $31,500
PLUMBERS Install and repair piping and fittings for water distribution and waste disposal in homes and commercial, institutional and industrial establishments. Install domestic fixtures such as sinks, toilets, bathtubs and specialized industrial and commercial fixtures. **Employment:** Construction contractors, self-employment.	**Education and training:** High school completion is preferred; apprenticeship (4 to 5 years); or over 5 years experience in the trade plus high school, college or industry courses in plumbing; trade certification is usually required; Red Seal certification (interprovincial) is available. **Subjects:** Construction, technical studies.	◄ $32,400

PRINTING PRESS OPERATORS
Set up and operate sheet web-fed and offset presses to print on paper, plastic, sheet metal and other materials. **Employment:** Printing and publishing firms.

Education and training: Completion of secondary school is usually required; completion of a college program in printing technology, an apprenticeship in printing (4 years) or on-the-job training is usually required. **Subjects:** Mathematics, graphic arts, production arts.

↓ $31,400

PUBLIC WORKS EQUIPMENT OPERATORS
Drive heavy street-cleaning and snow removal equipment, garbage trucks, salting and sanding trucks and other vehicles to clean and maintain streets and highways. **Employment:** Public works, private sectors.

Education and training: Some high school, but high school completion is preferred; driver's licence (appropriate for vehicles driven); on-the-job training is provided.

↑ $34,700

REFRIGERATION AND AIR CONDITIONING MECHANICS
Install, maintain, repair and overhaul central air conditioning systems in private homes, commercial and industrial refrigeration and air conditioning systems and combined heating and cooling systems. **Employment:** Air conditioning and refrigeration equipment dealers.

Education and training: High school completion is preferred; apprenticeship (4 years); or 5 years work experience in the trade plus college or industry courses in refrigeration and air conditioning; trade certification is usually required; Red Seal certification (interprovincial) is available. **Subjects:** Mathematics, electrical/electronics, technical studies.

← $34,200

ROOFERS
Install and repair all types of non-metal roofs. Replace coverings such as hot asphalt-saturated felt or waterproof sheet materials on flat roofs, and asphalt and wood shingles or shakes (roofing tiles) on steep roofs. **Employment:** Roofing contractors, self-employment.

Education and training: High school completion is preferred; apprenticeship (2 to 3 years); or several years experience in the roofer trade; trade certification may be required; Red Seal certification (interprovincial) is available. **Subjects:** Construction.

← $31,300

SHEET METAL WORKERS
Make, install and repair sheet metal products such as ventilation shafts, eavestroughs, air and heat ducts and sheet metal buildings. Also specialize in installing and repairing metal roofs. Operate various types of machines and equipment to perform cutting, drilling, shaping and other functions to make sheet metal products. **Employment:** Construction and aircraft manufacturers, railways.

Education training: High school completion is preferred; apprenticeship (3 to 4 years); or over 4 years experience in the trade plus high school, college or industry courses in sheet metal working; trade certification may be required; Red Seal certification (interprovincial) is available. **Subjects:** Mathematics, machine shop, industrial drafting and design, construction.

← $32,900

SHOE REPAIRERS
Replace heel lifts, soles and other parts of shoes, boots and other footwear. Stitch or otherwise repair the upper parts of footwear. Repair purses and

Education and training: Some high school, but high school completion is preferred; apprenticeship (2 to 3 years); trade certification may be

← $22,000

required. **Subjects:** Technical studies.

other leather products. May make custom or orthopedic footwear if they are very experienced or have extra training. **Employment:** Shoe repair shops, custom shoemaking establishments.

SMALL ENGINE MECHANICS — $34,700

Test, repair and service gasoline- and diesel-powered small engine equipment such as outboard motors, air-cooled engines, lawn mowers and similar equipment. **Employment:** Dealership service shops.

Education and training: Some high school, but high school completion is preferred; apprenticeship (3 to 4 years); or several years small engine repair experience plus college courses in small engine equipment repair; trade certification may be required. **Subjects:** Auto, technical studies.

STATIONARY ENGINEERS (POWER ENGINEERS) — $41,400

Operate, monitor and maintain stationary engines and auxiliary equipment such as boilers, turbines, generators, compressors and other equipment to provide heat, ventilation, refrigeration, light and power for buildings, industrial plants and other sites. **Employment:** Industrial and manufacturing plants, hospitals.

Education and training: High school completion is preferred; apprenticeship; or on-the-job training plus correspondence or college program in stationary engineering; trade certification (1st, 2nd, 3rd and 4th class) is usually required. **Subjects:** technical studies.

STEAM FITTERS AND PIPE FITTERS — $32,400

Install, repair and service high- and low-pressure piping systems carrying steam, water, oil and other liquids and gases used in heating, cooling, and lubricating systems. **SPRINKLER SYSTEM INSTALLERS** install, test and maintain piping and fixtures used in automatic sprinkler systems for fire protection in buildings. **Employment:** Maintenance departments of factories, pipe-fitting and sprinkler system contractors.

Education and training: High school completion is preferred; apprenticeship (4 to 5 years); or over 5 years experience in the trade plus high school, college or industry courses in steam fitting, pipe fitting or sprinkler system installation; trade certification as steam fitter/pipe fitter or sprinkler system installer is usually required; Red Seal certification (interprovincial) is available for both trades. **Subjects:** Technical studies.

TILE SETTERS — $32,100

Apply ceramic, marble, quarry, mosaic and terrazzo tiles on interior and exterior walls, floors and ceilings of buildings and on other surfaces to provide a protective finish and a decorative appearance. **Employment:** Construction companies, masonry contractors.

Education and training: Some high school, but high school completion is preferred; apprenticeship (3 to 4 years); or 3 to 4 years experience in the trade plus college or industry courses in tile setting. **Subjects:** Construction.

TOOL AND DIE MAKERS — $39,800

Set up and operate machine tools to make, repair and modify custom-made tools, jigs, fixtures and gauges. Compute dimensions and tolerances from specifications. **Employment:** Aircraft manufacturers, metal fabricators.

Education and training: High school completion is preferred; apprenticeship (4 years); or over 5 years experience in the trade plus college or industry courses in tool and die making; trade certification is usually required. **Subjects:** Mathematics, machine shop, industrial drafting and design.

TRACTOR-TRAILER DRIVERS
Operate tractor-trailer combinations to transport goods and materials within or between cities, towns, and rural areas, between provinces and over international boundaries. Operate two-way radios or other communication systems to maintain contact with dispatchers, or may operate on-board computers. May carry hazardous or dangerous goods. **Employment:** Truck transport companies, wholesalers, retail stores.

Education and training: Some high school, but high school completion is preferred; tractor-trailer driver's licence and permit; driver's abstract/record is usually required; certificate for transportation of dangerous goods may be required. **Subjects:** Technical studies.

▲ $34,600

WELDERS
Operate welding equipment to fuse metal parts together. May specialize in particular types of welding such as aerospace precision welding, pressure vessel welding, pipeline construction welding or custom welding. May require experience welding certain types of metals such as stainless steel, titanium and zirconium. **Employment:** Metal fabricators, machinery manufacturers, transport companies.

Education and training: High school completion is preferred; apprenticeship (3 to 4 years); or over 3 years experience in the trade plus college welding courses; trade certification is usually required; Red Seal certification (interprovincial) is available. **Subjects:** Mathematics, welding, machine shop.

◄ $35,500

PRIMARY INDUSTRY

AQUACULTURE WORKERS
Assist in the operation of fish hatcheries and fish or aquaculture farms. Perform activities such as feeding stock, culling unsatisfactory stock and marking or banding stock. Also maintain and clean aquaculture enclosures, pumps, filters and other equipment. **Employment:** Public or private fish hatcheries.

Education and training: Some high school, but high school completion is preferred. **Subjects:** Biology, technical studies.

▲ $25,600

FARM WORKERS
Plant, cultivate and harvest crops, and raise livestock and poultry. Operate equipment such as tractors and trucks; seeding, cultivating and harvesting equipment; haying and foraging equipment; and automated feeding, watering, egg-gathering, milking, manure and storage-handling systems. Perform many other activities that involve physical labour. May also maintain and repair farm equipment and buildings. **Employment:** Crop, livestock and specialty farms.

Education and training: Some high school, but high school completion is preferred; farm experience is preferred; driver's licence may be required. **Subjects:** Technical studies.

▲ $25,600

Occupation	Education and training	Salary
LANDSCAPE WORKERS Plant trees, flowers, shrubs and hedges. Sod lawns, install walkways, patios and decks. May perform related maintenance work. **Employment:** Landscaping and lawn care companies, cemeteries.	**Education and training:** Some high school, but high school completion an asset; licence required if applying chemical herbicides and pesticides. **Subjects:** Botany, technical studies.	▲ $25,600
MINERS Work in underground and surface (or open pit) mines. Work in either soft rock mining (coal, potash, salt) or hard rock mining (iron ore, nickel). Operate various machines such as diamond, long hole and rotary drilling machines, haulage equipment and front-end loaders. Handle explosives and must be very safety-conscious. **Employment:** Mining companies.	**Education and training:** Some high school, but high school completion is preferred; safety and other training is usually required; blaster's licence is usually required; miner certification may be required; mine hoist operators require a hoist operator's licence. **Subjects:** Technical studies.	▲ $25,600
OIL WELL DRILLING CREWS Assist in drilling for oil or natural gas and work under the general direction of supervisors called tool pushers. Operate stationary engines and oil drilling machinery; guide drills into place and perform various other activities. Drill wells of different depths on land and offshore from semi-submersible platforms, barges or other sea drilling rigs. **Employment:** Petroleum companies, drilling and well services.	**Education and training:** Some high school, but high school completion is preferred; training is provided; various certificates (blowout prevention, safety, first aid, etc.) are usually required. **Subjects:** Technical studies.	▲ $25,600

PROCESSING, MANUFACTURING AND UTILITIES

Occupation	Education and training	Salary
AIRCRAFT ASSEMBLERS AND AUTO ASSEMBLERS Assemble, fit and install aircraft skins, frames and other structural parts on aircraft in addition to mechanical systems such as flight controls, rigging and hydraulics. Work at benches or directly on aircraft and use hand and power tools. **AUTO ASSEMBLERS** assemble and install engines, transmissions, door and instrument panels and other parts. Operate hand and power tools, robotic and other automated assembling equipment, hoists and other specialized equipment. **Employment:** Aircraft manufacturers, auto manufacturers.	**Education and training:** High school completion; college or CEGEP aircraft manufacturing course (1 to 3 years) may be required for aircraft assemblers; on-the-job training plus formal classroom training is usually provided for aircraft assemblers; on-the-job training is provided for auto assemblers. **Subjects:** Technical studies, auto, mechanics.	◄ $34,900
ELECTRONICS ASSEMBLERS Assemble by hand various electronic components such as resistors, transistors, capacitors and other parts and solder them to printed circuit boards, or operate automatic and semi-automatic machines to position and solder	**Education and training:** Some high school, but high school completion is preferred. **Subjects:** Technical studies, electrical/electronics.	◄ $27,500

the parts to circuit boards. May also assemble microcircuits requiring the use of microscopes and fine-hand assembly. **Employment:** Electronics manufacturers.

FURNITURE ASSEMBLERS

Operate hand and power tools to assemble furniture and fixtures made of wood, metal, cane, plastic and other materials. **Employment:** Furniture manufacturing companies.

◄ $28,100

Education and training: Some high school, but high school completion is preferred. **Subjects:** Technical studies, woodworking.

PHOTOGRAPHIC FILM PROCESSORS

Operate automatic equipment to develop negatives and slides; to print black and white and colour photographs; and to develop motion picture film. Retouch photographic negatives or original prints to correct defects. Workers in retail photo-finishing outlets operate automatic equipment that develops colour negatives, prints and slides. **Employment:** Film processing laboratories, retail photo-finishing.

► $31,400

Education and training: High school completion is usually required; college or CEGEP program (2 years) is required for photographic and film laboratory processors; or extensive experience; usually no previous experience is required for workers in retail photo-finishing outlets. **Subjects:** Graphics, visual arts, technical studies.

WOODWORKING MACHINE OPERATORS

Set up and operate saws, routers, planers, drills, sanders and other woodworking machines to make or repair wooden parts for furniture. **Employment:** Furniture, fixture and wood products manufacturers.

◄ $33,500

Education and training: Some high school, but high school completion is preferred. **Subjects:** Construction, woodworking.

APPENDIX B: EMPLOYABILITY SKILLS PROFILE

WHAT ARE EMPLOYERS LOOKING FOR?

Employability skills are the generic skills, attitudes and behaviours that employers look for in new recruits and that they develop through training programs for current employees. In the workplace, as in school, the skills are integrated and used in varying combinations, depending on the nature of the particular job activities.

EMPLOYABILITY SKILLS PROFILE: THE CRITICAL SKILLS REQUIRED OF THE CANADIAN WORKFORCE

Academic Skills	Personal Management Skills	Teamwork Skills
Those skills which provide the basic foundation to get, keep and progress on a job to achieve the best results. Canadian employers need a person who can:	The combination of skills, attitudes and behaviours required to get, keep and progress on a job and to achieve the best results. Canadian employers need a person who can demonstrate:	Those skills needed to work with others on a job and achieve the best results. Canadian employers need a person who can:

Communicate
- Understand and speak the languages in which business is conducted
- Listen to understand and learn
- Read, comprehend and use written materials, including graphs, charts and displays
- Write effectively in the languages in which business is conducted

Think
- Think critically and act logically to evaluate situations, solve problems and make decisions
- Understand and solve problems involving mathematics and use the result
- Use technology, instruments, tools and information systems effectively
- Access and apply specialized knowledge from various fields (e.g., skilled trades, technology, physical sciences, arts and social sciences)

Learn
- Continue to learn for life

Positive Attitudes and Behaviours
- Self-esteem and confidence
- Honesty, integrity and personal ethics
- A positive attitude toward learning, growth and personal health
- Initiative, energy and persistence to get the job done

Responsibility
- The ability to set goals and priorities in work and personal life
- The ability to plan and manage time, money and other resources to achieve goals
- Accountability for actions taken

Adaptability
- A positive attitude toward change
- Recognition of and respect for people's diversity and individual differences
- The ability to identify and suggest new ideas to get the job done – creativity

Work with Others
- Understand and contribute to the organization's goals
- Understand and work within the culture of the group
- Plan and make decisions with others and support the outcomes
- Respect the thoughts and opinions of others in the group
- Exercise "give and take" to achieve group results
- Seek a team approach as appropriate
- Lead when appropriate, mobilizing the group for high performance

Employability Skills Profile: What Are Employers Looking For?, Brochure 1992 E (Ottawa: The Conference Board of Canada, 1992). Reprinted with Permission

SELECT
BIBLIOGRAPHY

BUSINESS:
Ambry, Margaret, and Cheryl Russell. *The Official Guide to the American Marketplace.*
Ithaca: New Strategist, 1992.
Boyett, Joseph, and Henry Conn. *Workplace 2000: The Revolution Reshaping American
Business.* New York: Plume, 1991.
Clemmer, Jim. *Firing On All Cylinders: The Service/Quality System for High-Powered Corporate
Performance*, 2nd ed. Toronto: Macmillan Canada, 1992.
Hammer, Michael, and James Champy. *Reengineering the Corporation.* New York:
HarperCollins, 1993.
Senge, Peter. *The Fifth Discipline: The Art and Practice of the Learning Organization.*
New York: Doubleday, 1990.
Sharwood, Gordon. *At the Threshold: Canada's Medium-Sized Businesses Prepare for the
Global Marketplace of the 90s.* Toronto: Sharwood and Company, 1989.

CANADA'S ECONOMIC FUTURE:
Beck, Nuala. *Shifting Gears: Thriving in the New Economy.* Toronto: HarperCollins, 1992.
Highly recommended as an introduction to the changing economy.
Canada. Employment and Immigration Canada. *Success in the Works: A Profile of Canada's
Emerging Workforce.* Ottawa, 1989.
_____. *Job Futures: Occupational Outlooks, Vol. 1.* Ottawa, 1996.
_____. *Software and National Competitiveness: Human Resource Issues and Opportunities.*
Ottawa, 1992.
C.D. Howe Institute. *Canada at Risk? Canadian Public Policy in the 1990s.* Toronto, 1991.
Cohen, Dian, and Guy Stanley. *No Small Change: Succeeding in Canada's New Economy.*
Toronto: Macmillan Canada, 1993.
Crane, David. *The Next Canadian Century: Building a Competitive Economy.* Toronto:
Stoddart Publishing, 1992.
Ernst & Young. *Canada's Technology Industries in the 1990s: How to Win in a World of
Change.* Toronto, 1990.
Lipsey, Richard. *Economic Growth: Science and Technology and Institutional Change in the
Global Economy.* Toronto: Canadian Institute for Advanced Research, 1991.
Luciani, Patrick. *What Canadians Believe, But Shouldn't About Their Economy.* Toronto:
Addison-Wesley, 1993.
Mansell, Jacquie. *Workplace Innovation in Canada.* Ottawa: Economic Council of Canada,
1987.
Porter, Michael. *Canada at the Crossroads: The Reality of a New Competitive Environment.*
Ottawa: Monitor Co., 1991.
Slater, David. *The Contribution of Investment and Savings to Productivity and Economic
Growth in Canada.* Ottawa: Investment Canada, 1992.

CAREERS:
Adams Job Almanac. Holbrook: Bob Adams Inc., 1997.
Angle, Susan, and Alex Hiam. *Adventure Careers.* Hawthorne: Career Press, 1992.

Basta, Nicholas. *Top Professions: The 100 Most Popular, Dynamic, and Profitable Careers in America Today.* Princeton, NJ: Peterson's Guides, 1989.

_____. *Environmental Career Guide.* New York: Wiley, 1991.

Beck, Nuala. *Excelerate: Growing in the New Economy.* Toronto: HarperCollins, 1995. Relies too heavily on out-of-date Statistics Canada information in predicting job growth areas, so some of the star ratings are way off.

Bolles, Richard. *The Three Boxes of Life.* Berkeley, CA: Ten Speed Press, 1981.

_____. *What Color Is Your Parachute?* Berkeley, CA: Ten Speed Press, 1997.

Canada. Employment and Immigration. *Software and National Competitiveness: Human Resource Issues and Opportunities.* Ottawa, 1992.

Career Associates. *Career Choices: Art, Business, Communications and Journalism, Computer Science, Economics, English, History, Law, Mathematics, MBA, Political Science and Government, Psychology.* New York: Walker and Co., 1990.

_____. *Encyclopedia of Career Choices for the 1990s.* New York: Putnam, 1993.

The Career Directory. Toronto: Edcore Publishing Co., 1993.

"Careers in ..." series: *Accounting, Advertising, Business, Communications, Computers, Education, Engineering, Health Care, High-Tech, Law, Marketing, Medicine, Science.* Lincolnwood: National Textbook Co., 1990-93.

Centron, Marvin, and Owen Davies. *The Great Job Shake-Out: How to Find a Career After the Crash.* New York: Simon & Schuster, 1988.

Cornish, Edward, ed. *Careers Tomorrow: The Outlook for Work in a Changing World.* Bethesda: World Future Society, 1988.

Damp, Dennis. *Health Career Job Explosion.* Coraopolis: Damp Publications, 1993.

Didsbury, Howard, Jr., ed. *The World of Work: Careers and the Future.* Bethesda: World Future Society, 1983.

Drozdyk, Charlie. *Hot Jobs: The No-Holds-Barred Tell-It-Like-It-Is Guide to Getting the Jobs Everyone Wants.* New York: HarperCollins, 1994.

Farr, J. Michael, and Kathleen Martin, eds. *America's Fastest Growing Jobs: An Authoritative Information Source.* Indianapolis: JIST Works, 1991.

Feather, Frank. *Canada's Best Careers Guide.* Toronto: Warwick Publishing, 1996.

_____. *Tomorrow's Best Canadian Careers.* Thornhill: Global Management Bureau, 1987.

Feingold, Norman, and Maxine Atwater. *New Emerging Careers: Today, Tomorrow, and in the 21st Century.* Garrett Park: Garrett Park Press, 1989.

Field, Shelly. *100 Best Careers for the Year 2000.* New York: Prentice Hall/Arco, 1992.

Fischgrund, Tom, ed. *The Insider's Guide to the Top 20 Careers in Business & Management: What It's Really Like to Work in Advertising, Computers, Banking, Management, and More.* Toronto: McGraw-Hill, 1994.

Frank, Tema. *Canada's Best Employers for Women: A Guide for Job Hunters, Employees and Employers.* Toronto: Frank Communications, 1994.

Gale, Barry, and Linda Gale. *Discover What You're Best At.* New York: Simon & Schuster, 1990.

Glenn, Reed. *The Ten Best Opportunities for Starting a Home Business Today.* Boulder: Live Oak Press, 1993.

Harkavy, Michael. *101 Careers: A Guide to the Fastest Growing Opportunities.* New York: Wiley & Sons, 1990.

Innes, Eva, et al. *The 100 Best Companies to Work for in Canada.* Toronto: HarperCollins, 1990-91.

Job Opportunities for Business and Liberal Arts Graduates. Princeton, NJ: Peterson's Guides, 1993.

Job Opportunities for Engineering, Science, and Computer Graduates. Princeton, NJ: Peterson's Guides, 1993.

Job Seeker's Guide to Private and Public Companies. Detroit: Gale Research, 1992.

Kavanagh, Robert. *New Scientists and Engineers from Canadian Universities.* Ottawa: Natural Sciences and Engineering Research Council, 1991.

Kleinman, Carol. *The 100 Best Jobs for the 1990s and Beyond.* Chicago: Dearborn Financial
    Publishing, 1992.
Krannich, Ronald L., and Caryl Rae Krannich. *The Educator's Guide to Alternative Jobs and
    Careers.* Manassas Park: Impact Publications, 1991.
_____. *The Best Jobs for the 1990s and into the 21st Century.* Manassas Park: Impact
    Publications, 1993.
_____. *Careering and Re-Careering for the 1990s.* Manassas Park: Impact Publications, 1993.
Krantz, Les. *The Jobs Rated Almanac.* New York: Pharos Books, 1992.
Lewis, Adele, and Doris Kuller. *Fast-Track Careers for the 90s.* Glenview: Professional
    Books Group, 1990.
Mast, Jennifer. *The Job Seeker's Guide to 1000 Top Employers.* Detroit: Visible Ink Press,
    1993.
Morgan, Bradley, ed. *The Career Advisory Series: Advertising, Book Publishing, Business and
    Finance, Health Care, Magazine Publishing, Marketing and Sales, Newspaper Publishing,
    Public Relations, Radio and Television, Travel and Hospitality.* Detroit: Visible Ink
    Press, 1992-93.
Norback, Craig. *Careers Encyclopedia.* Lincolnwood: National Textbook, 1992.
"Opportunities in..." series, 1984-1993. Over 160 titles. Lincolnwood: National
    Textbook Co.
Orpwood, Graham. *The Chemical Professions of Canada: Employment and Education for
    the Future.* Ottawa: Chemical Institute of Canada, 1991.
Petras, Kathyrn, and Ross Petras. *Jobs '97.* New York: Simon & Schuster, 1997.
Rubin, K. *Flying High in Travel.* New York: Wiley, 1992.
Satterfield, Alan. *Where the Jobs Are: The Hottest Careers for the '90s.* Hawthorne:
    Career Press, 1992.
Shenk, Ellen. *Outdoor Careers.* Harrisburg: Stackpole Books, 1992.
Smith, Carter. *America's Fast Growing Employers.* Holbrook: Bob Adams, Inc., 1992.
Snelling, Robert, and Anne Snelling. *Jobs! What They Are, Where They Are, What They Pay!*
    New York: Simon & Schuster, 1992.
Stienstra, Tom. *Careers in the Outdoors.* San Francisco: Foghorn Press, 1992.
Student Employment Network. *The 1996 Ontario Student Employment Guide: A Job Seekers
    Guide to Ontario's Top Employers.* Toronto: Student Employment Network, 1996.
U.S. Department of Labor. *Occupational Outlook Handbook.* Washington, 1993.
Wegman, Robert, et al., eds. *Work in the New Economy: Careers and Job Seeking into the
    21st Century.* Indianapolis: JIST Works, 1989.
Wright, John. *American Almanac of Jobs and Salaries.* New York: Avon, 1990.

DEMOGRAPHICS:

Barna, George. *The Invisible Generation: Baby Busters.* Barna Research Group, 1992.
Dychtwald, Ken, and Joe Flower. *Age Wave: The Challenge and Opportunities of an Aging
    America.* New York: Bantam, 1989.
Foot, David. *Boom, Bust & Echo.* Toronto: Macfarlane Walter & Ross, 1996.
Gollub, James. *The Decade Matrix.* Toronto: Addison-Wesley, 1991.

EDUCATION:

Centron, Marvin, and Owen Davies. *American Renaissance: Our Life at the Turn of the
    21st Century.* New York: St. Martin's Press, 1989.
Economic Council of Canada. *A Lot to Learn: Education and Training in Canada.* Ottawa,
    1992.
National Center on Education and Economy. *America's Choice: High Skills or Low Wages.*
    Rochester, 1990.
Perelman, Lewis. *The Learning Enterprise.* Council of State Planning Agencies, 1985.
_____. *School's Out: Hyperlearning, the New Technology, and the End of Education.* New York:
    William Morrow & Co., 1993.

FUTURE TRENDS:

Abrams, Malcolm, and Harriet Bernstein. *More Future Stuff: Over 250 Inventions That Will Change Your Life by 2001*. New York: Penguin Books, 1991.

Barker, Joel. *Paradigms: The Business of Discovering the Future*. New York: Harper, 1992.

Celente, Gerald, and Tom Milton. *Trend Tracking: The System to Profit From Today's Trends*. Toronto: John Wiley & Sons, 1990.

Coates, Joseph, and Jennifer Jarratt. *What Futurists Believe*. Bethesda: World Future Society, 1989.

Coates, Joseph, et al. *Future Work: Seven Critical Forces in North America*. New York: Josey-Bass, 1990.

Cornish, Edward, ed. *The 1990s and Beyond*. Bethesda: World Future Society, 1990.

Didsbury, Howard, Jr., ed. *The Future: Opportunity Not Destiny*. Bethesda: World Future Society, 1989.

_____. *The Years Ahead: Perils, Problems and Promises*. Bethesda: World Future Society, 1993.

Feather, Frank. *G-Forces Reinventing the World: The 35 Global Forces Restructuring Our Future*. Toronto: Summerhill Press, 1989.

Future Vision: The 189 Most Important Trends of the 1990s by the editors of Research Alert. Trabuco Canyon: Sourcebooks, 1991.

Kennedy, Paul. *Preparing for the 21st Century*. Toronto: HarperCollins, 1993.

Makridakis, Spyros. *Forecasting, Planning, and Strategy for the 21st Century*. New York: The Free Press/Macmillan, 1990.

Minkin, Barry. *Future In Sight: 100 of the Most Important Trends, Implications and Predictions for the New Millennium*. New York: Macmillan, 1995.

Modis, Theodore. *Predictions: Society's Telltale Signature Reveals the Past and Forecasts the Future*. New York: Simon & Schuster, 1992.

Naisbitt, John. *Megatrends Asia: Eight Asian Megatrends That Are Reshaping Our World*. New York: Simon & Schuster, 1996.

Naisbitt, John, and Patricia Aburdene. *Megatrends 2000: Ten New Directions for the 1990's*. New York: Avon Books, 1990.

Ogden, Frank. *The Last Book You'll Ever Read*. Toronto: Macfarlane Walter & Ross, 1993.

_____. *Navigating in Cyberspace: A Guide to the Next Millennium*. Toronto: Macfarlane, Walter & Ross, 1995.

Popcorn, Faith. *The Popcorn Report on the Future of Your Company, Your World, Your Life*. Toronto: HarperCollins, 1991.

Saaty, Thoma, and Larry Boone. *Embracing the Future: Meeting the Challenge of Our Changing World*. Westport: Praeger, 1990.

Toffler, Alvin. *Powershift: Knowledge, Wealth and Violence at the Edge of the 21st Century*. New York: Bantam Books, 1991.

Watt, Kenneth. *Taming the Future: A Revolutionary Breakthrough in Scientific Forecasting*. Davis: Contextured Web Press, 1992.

Worzel, Richard. *Facing the Future: The Seven Forces Revolutionizing Our Lives*. Toronto: Stoddart, 1994.

TECHNOLOGIES TRANSFORMING THE WORKPLACE:

Burrus, Daniel, with Roger Gittines. *Technotrends: 24 Technologies That Will Revolutionize Our Lives*. New York: HarperCollins, 1993.

Caudill, Maureen. *In Our Image: Building an Artificial Person*. New York: Oxford University Press, 1992.

Conway, McKinley. *A Glimpse of the Future: Technology Forecasts for Global Strategists*. New York: Conway Data, 1992.

Economic Council of Canada. *Making Technology Work: Innovation and Jobs in Canada*. Ottawa, 1987.

Ernst & Young. *Canada's Technology Industries in the 1990s: How to Win in a World of Change*. Toronto, 1990.

Keen, Peter. *Shaping the Future: Business Design Through Information Technology.* Cambridge: Harvard Business School Press,1991.

Kennedy, Paul. *Preparing for the 21st Century.* Toronto: HarperCollins, 1993.

Kroelsch, Frank. *The Infomedia Revolution: How It Is Changing Our World and Your Life.* Toronto: McGraw-Hill Ryerson, 1995.

Lipsey, Richard. *Economic Growth: Science and Technology and Institutional Change in the Global Economy.* Toronto: Canadian Institute for Advanced Research, 1991.

Martino, Joseph. *Technological Forecasting for Decision Making.* New York: McGraw-Hill, 1993.

Organization for Economic Co-operation and Development. *Technology in a Changing World: The Technology/Economy Program.* Paris, 1991.

Tapscott, Don. *The Digital Economy: Promise and Peril in the Age of Networked Intelligence.* New York: McGraw-Hill Ryerson, 1996.

____. *Paradigm Shift: The New Promise of Information Technology.* Toronto: McGraw-Hill, 1993.

Winslow, Charles, and William Bramer. *Future Work: Putting Knowledge to Work in the Knowledge Economy.* Toronto: Maxwell Macmillan Canada, 1994.

UNDERSTANDING THE NEW GLOBAL ECONOMY:

Bridges, William. *JobShift: How to Prosper in a Workplace Without Jobs.* Reading, MA: Addison-Wesley, 1994.

Burrows, Brian, et al. *Into the 21st Century: A Handbook for a Sustainable Future.* New York: Adamantine Press, 1991.

Carnevale, Anthony. *America and the New Economy: How New Competitive Standards Are Radically Changing American Workplaces.* San Francisco: Jossey-Bass, 1991.

Davidson, James, and Lord William Rees-Mogg. *The Great Reckoning: Protect Yourself in the Coming Depression.* New York: Simon & Schuster, 1993.

Dent, Harry. *The Great Boom Ahead: Your Comprehensive Guide to Personal and Business Profit in the New Era of Prosperity.* New York: Hyperion, 1993.

____. *Job Shock: The Four Principles Transforming Our Work And Business.* New York: St. Martin's Press, 1995.

Didsbury, Howard, Jr., ed. *The Global Economy: Today, Tomorrow, and the Transition.* Bethesda: World Future Society, 1985.

Drache, Daniel, and Meric Gertler, eds. *The New Era of Global Competition: State Policy and Market Power.* Kingston, ON: McGill- Queen's University Press, 1991.

Drucker, Peter. *Post-Capitalist Society.* New York: HarperCollins, 1993.

Figgie, Harry, Jr., *Bankruptcy 1995: The Coming Collapse of America and How to Stop It.* New York: Little, Brown & Co., 1992.

Henderson, Hazel. *Paradigms in Progress: Life Beyond Economics.* New York: Knowledge Systems Inc., 1991.

Hoover, Gary, et al. *Hoover's Handbook of American Business* and *Hoover's Handbook of World Business.* Austin: The Reference Press, 1993.

Kester, Carl. *Japanese Takeovers: The Global Contest for Corporate Control.* Boston: Harvard Business School Press, 1991.

Kotter, John. *The New Rules: How to Succeed in Today's Post-Corporate World.* Toronto: Maxwell Macmillan Canada, 1994.

____. *Success: The New Rules.* Toronto: Maxwell Macmillan Canada, 1995.

Malabre, Alfred, Jr. *Understanding the New Economy.* Homewood: Dow-Jones Irwin, 1993.

Porter, Michael. *The Competitive Advantage of Nations.* New York: The Free Press, 1990.

Reich, Robert. *The Work of Nations: Preparing Ourselves for 21st Century Capitalism.* New York: A.A. Knopf, 1991.

Thurow, Lester. *The Future of Capitalism: How Today's Economic Forces Shape Tomorrow's World.* New York: William Morrow, 1996.

____. *Head to Head: The Coming Battle Among Japan, Europe, and America.* New York: Warner Brothers, 1993.

The World Competitiveness Report 1995. Geneva: World Economic Forum, 1995.

Yoffie, David, ed. *Beyond Free Trade: Firms, Governments, and Global Competition.* Boston: Harvard Business School Press, 1993.

WORKING ABROAD:

Beckmann, David, et al. *The Overseas List.* Minneapolis: Augsburg Publishing, 1986.

Franz, Del, and Laxaro Hernandez, eds. *Work, Study, Travel Abroad: The Whole World Handbook,* 11th ed., 1992-1993. New York: St. Martin's Press, 1992.

Hachey, Jean-Marc. *The Canadian Guide to Working and Living Overseas: For Entry-Level and Seasoned Professionals,* 2nd ed. Ottawa: Intercultural Systems, 1995.

Kocher, Eric. *International Jobs.* Reading: Addison-Wesley, 1989.

Krannich, Ronald L., and Caryl Rae Krannich. *Jobs for People Who Love Travel.* Manassas Park: Impact Publications, 1990.

____. *The Almanac of International Jobs and Careers.* Manassas Park: Impact Publications, 1991.

____. *The Complete Guide to International Jobs and Careers.* Manassas Park: Impact Publications, 1992.

A Practical Guide to Living and Working in Japan. Ottawa: Transglobal Publications.

Sanborn, Robert. *How to Get a Job in Europe.* Chicago: Surrey Books, 1990.

____. *How to Get a Job in the Pacific Rim.* Chicago: Surrey Books, 1992.

INTERNET JOB HUNTING:

Dixon, Pam, and Sylvia Tiersten. *Be Your Own Headhunter Online.* New York: Random House, 1995.

Glossbrenner, Alfred, and Emily Glossbrenner. *Finding a Job on the Internet.* New York: McGraw-Hill, 1995.

Gonyea, James. *The On-Line Jobs Search Companion.* New York: McGraw-Hill, 1995.

Kennedy, Joyce Lain. *Hook Up, Get Hired!: The Internet Job Search Revolution.* New York: John Wiley & Sons, 1995.

MAGAZINES AND NEWSLETTERS:

- *Asia Inc., Far Eastern Economic Review,* and *Asiaweek* provide information on Pacific Rim developments.
- *Canadian Business* provides a good overview of various Canadian business developments.
- *The Economist* is a must-read magazine which covers current topics in-depth including discussions of global developments affecting finance, politics, science, and economic prosperity.
- *Forbes* and *Fortune* are the stalwart U.S. business publications along with *Businessweek.*
- *The Harvard Business Review* provides in-depth discussion of current business issues.
- *Mergers & Acquisitions* helps you keep up with the activities of larger corporations and industry consolidation in general.
- *Newsletter on Newsletters,* 44 West Market St., Rhinebeck, NY 12572, helps you find newsletters on any desired topic.
- *World Press Review* acts as a monthly digest of articles in newspapers and magazines from a worldwide perspective.
- *Information Week* monitors computer-related trends.
- *The Futurist, Fast Company,* and *Wired* provide leading-edge business and technology trend information.

NEWSPAPERS:

- *The Globe & Mail Report on Business* is a dependable source of relevant daily information and industry analysis.
- *The Financial Post* provides in-depth analysis of Canadian business and stock market activities.

- *The Toronto Star*'s business section covers many industry-related developments affecting careers.
- *USA TODAY* is full of trend-related information.
- *The Wall Street Journal* and *Barron's* provide highly accurate in-depth reports of important business matters.

ELECTRONIC INFORMATION SOURCES:

Besides using the information resources of reference and university libraries, which have considerable information access through Internet, you may wish to use the following resources to acquire information on particular careers, job markets, and trends.

BOOKS:

Directory of On-Line Data Bases (Cuadra Associates)
Encyclopedia of Information Systems and Services (Gale Research Co.)

TELEPHONE INFORMATION SERVICES:

AT&T Information Services: 800-567-4672
Business Information Exchange International: 800-263-5925
Compuserve Information Services: 800-544-4079
Globe Information Services: 416-585-5280
Infomart Online (news and business): 416-445-6641
Mead Data Central International Inc. (business and legal): 416-361-6323
SkillsLink (government training resources, products, and services): 800-387-1234

USENET JOB-RELATED SITES:

ab.jobs, bc.jobs, can.jobs, kw.job, nb.jobs, nf.jobs, ns.jobs, ont.jobs, ott.jobs, qc.jobs, sk.jobs, tor.jobs

CANADA EMPLOYMENT CENTRES:

http://www.ffa.ucalgary.ca/hrdc
http://www.island.net/~cec (Nanaimo, B.C.)
http://www.the-wire.com/hrdc/hrdc.html (Toronto)
http://www.ein.ccia.st-thomas.on.ca/agencies/cec
http://www.islandnet.com/~cec5916 (Victoria, B.C. area)
http://www.sunshine.net/www/200/sn0253 (B.C.'s Sunshine Coast)

OTHER RESOURCES:

http://www.careerworld.com
http://www.homeshoppingunlimited.com
http://canworknet.ingenia.com//canworknet
http://www.careermosaic.com/cm
http://www.wpi.edu/Admin/Depts/CDC/
http://www.gov.mb.ca/manitoba/educate/cg-home.html
http://www.ein.ccia.st-thomas.on.ca/agencies/cec/jobs/jobbank.html (National Job Bank)
http://www.ccn.cs.dal.ca/Government/HRD-NS/hrd.html
http://www.occ.com/occ
http://www.monster.com
http://www.netjobs.com:8001
http://qb.islan.net/~careers
http://www.cfn.cs.dal.ca/Commerce/PSI/psi_ind.html
http://www.umanitoba.ca/counselling/cnews.html
http://www.adm.uwaterloo.ca/infocecs/CRC/Career_Resource_Centre.html
http://www.hrdc-drhc.gc.ca/hrdc/corp/stratpol/jobs/english/index.html
http://www.theglobeandmail.com/careerconnect

http://www.jcitech.com/jobmatch
http://www.irus.rri.uwo.ca/%7Ejlaw/job_can.html
http://www.jobtrak.com/jobguide/
http://www.utoronto.ca/careers/
http://careerexplorer.com/
http://www.interactive.line.com/cyber/jobs.html
http://www.vjf.com/
http://www.careerkey.com/
http://www.science.uwaterloo.ca:80/earth/geoscience/careers.html
http://www.ualberta.ca:80/~slis/guides/direct/career.htm
http://www.cacee.com/workweb
http://qsilver.queensu.ca/business/cdc/
http://www.jobweb.com/
http://www.enviroindustry.com/employment/
http://www.unn.ac.uk/~ecu1/links.html
http://www.overseasjobs.com/netjobor.html

INDEX

italic indicates boxed text

Colin Campbell and Carole Hood are the founders of **Human Resource Strategies Inc.**, a Toronto company that specializes in the design and development of learning organization resource centres, job search programs, career and professional development programs, employment opportunity agencies, and entrepreneurship umbrella organizations that bring together entrepreneurs with complementary skills or businesses. The company offers a month-long self-marketing job search program to clients who have received unemployment insurance within the past three years (contact Carole Hood for more information). In addition, Human Resource Strategies Inc. is involved in employment prescreening and helps assess and prepare employees for overseas assignments. A related enterprise is New Economy Network Inc., a non-profit company that takes an innovative, cooperative approach to finding employment or promoting home-based services.

Human Resource Strategies Inc. has two Internet sites, careerworld.com and homeshoppingunlimited.com. Résumés and jobs may be posted on these sites at no charge to either employers or prospective employees. The sites provide information on company services, recent employment trend information, a job search discussion group, business and personal networking opportunities, and notice of upcoming events.

For more information or to arrange for speakers or workshops, contact:
Human Resource Strategies Inc./Career World
2032 Gerrard St. East
Toronto, Ontario M4E 2B1
Tel: 416-690-1972
Fax: 416-690-9329
E-mail: career@netcom.ca or admin@careerworld.com

Colin Campbell is president of Career World and CEO of Human Resource Strategies Inc. He holds master's degrees in business administration and applied psychology and is much in demand as a keynote speaker and consultant. Mr. Campbell won the 1996 NATCON award for making the biggest contribution to career and vocational counselling in Canada in 1995. His second book, *Jobscape*, was published in 1997.

Carole Hood, managing partner of Human Resource Strategies Inc., is a former college professor with extensive experience in the human resource field as a consultant to international firms. She holds master's degrees in administration and divinity. Ms. Hood will be donating 10 percent of her royalties to schizophrenia research at the Clarke Institute of Psychiatry in Toronto.

This book was designed and set into type by James Ireland Design Inc., Toronto.

The text face is ITC New Baskerville, a digital issue of the popular and highly readable English typeface designed by John Baskerville in the 1750s. All headings are set in Franklin Gothic and Franklin Gothic Extra Condensed, designed by American Morris Benton in 1903.